This helpful classroom presentation tool features:

- Lecture PowerPoint slides

- *New* Supplementary Image Bank with additional images for each chapter, beyond those found in the text

- Art PowerPoints featuring photographs and drawn figures from the text

...and to help students learn

STUDYSPACE WEB SITE ·································>

wwnorton.com/studyspace

StudySpace tells students what they know, shows them what they still need to review, and then gives them an organized study plan to master the material.

Students rely on effective and well-designed online resources to help them succeed in their courses—StudySpace is unmatched in providing a one-stop solution that's closely aligned with the textbook. This free and easy-to-navigate Web site offers students an impressive range of exercises, interactive learning tools, assessment, and review materials, including:

- *NEW* Video Exercises ask students to apply core IR concepts to current events
- IR Simulations put students in the place of key actors in international relations
- International Relations in the News RSS feed highlights important news stories from the *New York Times* and BBC News
- Study plan
- Chapter outlines
- Critical thinking questions
- Vocabulary flashcards
- Diagnostic quizzes

NORTON GRADEBOOK

With the free, easy-to-use Norton gradebook, instructors can easily access StudySpace student quiz results and avoid email inbox clutter. No course setup required. For more information and an audio tour of the gradebook, visit wwnorton.com/college/nrl/gradebook.

EBOOK

An affordable and convenient alternative, Norton ebooks retain the content and design of the print book and allow students to highlight and take notes with ease, print chapters as needed, and search the text. Norton ebooks are available online and as downloadable PDFs. They can be purchased directly from our Web site, or with a registration folder that can be sold in the bookstore.

Assign the accompanying reader and save your students money

***Essential Readings in World Politics*, edited by Karen Mingst and Jack Snyder,** introduces students to key literature on international relations—from classics in the field to the contemporary issues that are debated by scholars today. With readings that correspond to each chapter in *Essentials of International Relations*, it is the perfect supplement for the course.

50% off when packaged with the text. Add *Essential Readings in World Politics* to your order for *Essential Readings in International Relations*, and your students will save 50% off the already low price of the reader. Contact your Norton representative for a special package ISBN in order to receive the discount.

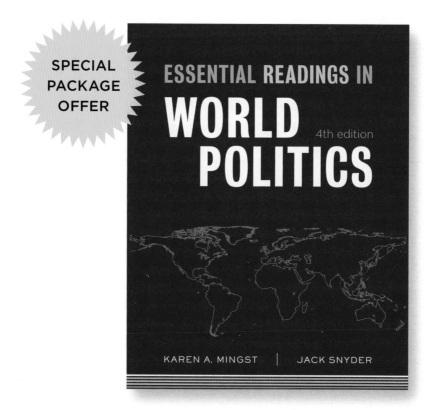

COMBINED BOOK AND READER TABLE OF CONTENTS

Essentials of International Relations

fifth edition

Essentials of International Relations

fifth edition

Karen A. Mingst

UNIVERSITY OF KENTUCKY

Ivan M. Arreguín-Toft

BOSTON UNIVERSITY

W. W. NORTON & COMPANY
NEW YORK · LONDON

Copyright © 2011, 2008, 2004, 2002, 1999 by W. W. Norton & Company, Inc.
Printed in the United States of America

Editor: Ann Shin
Editorial Assistant: Jake Schindel
Project Editor: Kathleen Feighery
Production Manager: Benjamin Reynolds
Photo Editor: Stephanie Romeo
E-Media Editor: Lorraine Klimowich
Book Design: Hope Miller Goodell
Composition: Innodata Isogen

Library of Congress Cataloging-in-Publication Data
Mingst, Karen A., 1947–
    Essentials of international relations / Karen A. Mingst, Ivan M. Arreguín-Toft. — 5th ed.
        p. cm.
    Includes bibliographical references and index.
ISBN 978-0-393-93529-5 (pbk.)
1. International relations.   I. Arreguín-Toft, Ivan M.   II. Title.
    JZ1305.M56 2011
    327—dc22
                          2010028022

W.W. NORTON & COMPANY has been independent since its founding in 1923, when William Warder Norton and Mary D. Herter Norton first published lectures delivered at the People's Institute, the adult education division of New York City's Cooper Union. The firm soon expanded its program beyond the Institute, publishing books by celebrated academics from America and abroad. By midcentury, the two major pillars of Norton's publishing program—trade books and college texts—were firmly established. In the 1950s, the Norton family transferred control of the company to its employees, and today—with a staff of four hundred and a comparable number of trade, college, and professional titles published each year—W.W. Norton & Company stands as the largest and oldest publishing house owned wholly by its employees.

CONTENTS

Contending Perspectives: How to Think about International Relations Theoretically

The International System

05   The State

08 War and Strife

PREFACE

Brief textbooks are now commonplace in International Relations. This textbook was originally written to be not only smart and brief, but also, in the words of Roby Harrington of W. W. Norton, to include "a clear sense of what's essential and what's not." We are pleased that this book's treatment of the essential concepts and information has stood the test of time.

This fifth edition of *Essentials of International Relations*, published more than a decade after the first, preserves the overall structure of earlier editions. Students need a brief history of international relations to understand why we study the subject and how current scholarship is informed by what has preceded it. This background is provided in Chapters 1 and 2. Theories provide interpretative frameworks for understanding what is happening in the world, and levels of analysis—the international system, the state, and the individual—help us further organize and conceptualize the material. In Chapters 3–7, competing theories are presented and used to illustrate how each level of analysis can be applied and how international organizations, nongovernmental organizations, and international law are viewed. Then the major issues of the twenty-first century—security, economics, and transnational issues—are presented and analyzed in Chapters 8–10.

This fully revised Fifth Edition has been made possible by the addition of a co-author, Ivan Arreguín-Toft of Boston University. A security expert whose teaching reflects a firm grounding in history, Professor Arreguín-Toft brought his insights as a scholar and experience as an instructor to Chapters 2, 3, 8, and 10 in particular. Recognizing the major changes in international political economy, Chapter 9 on the international political economy has been completely reorganized, with attention to not only development, but international finance, as well as the global economic crisis of 2008–09. Case studies and more extended examples are offered in almost every chapter, answering the suggestions of a number of very capable reviewers.

The constructivist perspectives have also been more systematically introduced and enhanced.

The rich pedagogical program of previous editions has been expanded based on suggestions from adopters and reviewers:

- **Newly expanded Global Perspectives units** encourage students to consider a specific issue from the vantage point of a particular state. These popular features have been expanded to two pages each.

- **New end-of-chapter review materials** have been added at the request of instructors. These include Discussion Questions and a list of key terms from the chapter, as well as information about the review materials available on the free StudySpace website (wwnorton.com/studyspace).

- **Theory in Brief boxes, In Focus boxes, Essential Debates,** and **numerous maps, figures, and tables** appear throughout the text.

- **A new design** offers a visually appealing text with illustrative photos.

Many of these changes have been made at the suggestion of expert reviewers; primarily faculty who have taught the book in the classroom. While it is impossible to act on every suggestion (not all the critics themselves agree), we have carefully studied the various recommendations and thank the reviewers for taking time to offer critiques. We thank the following reviewers for their input on this new edition: Emily Acevedo, California State University, Los Angeles; William Newmann, Virginia Commonwealth University; Robert Ostergard, University of Nevada-Reno; Anthony Posey, United States Military Academy; Alexander Thompson, Ohio State University; Carlos Yordan, Drew University; Alison McCartney, Towson University; Ellen Pirro, Iowa State University; and Matthew Hoffman, University of Toronto.

In this edition, Karen Mingst owes special thanks to her colleagues Dr. Horace Bartilow and Dr. Evan Hillebrand, both experts in international political economy. A number of students in the Patterson School of Diplomacy and International Commerce at the University of Kentucky were instrumental in making suggestions on expanding the "Global Perspectives" boxes and drafting examples. Those students include Laura Stevens, Patrick Smith, P.J. Lonneman, Julia Dzingailo, and Blake Stabler. My daughter Ginger Stauffer collated the various critiques, spurring me on to tackle all the changes. My son Brett Stauffer, too, came to the rescue during a difficult summer. My husband Robert Stauffer has always provided both space and encouragement, as well as holding up more than one-half of the marriage bargain.

Ivan Arreguín-Toft owes thanks to a number of people; including Roby Harrington, Karen Mingst, and Monica, Sam, and Ingrid Toft. I thank Roby Harrington for bringing me into what turned out to be both a fascinating and challenging project. I also thank Karen Mingst; especially for her patience, wisdom, and guidance; and for her willingness to share creative control over a decade's intellectual and pedagogical achievement: a comprehensive, interesting, and yet brief international relations textbook. Finally, I owe a special thanks to my wife Monica Toft, and my children Sam and Ingrid.

Ann Shin, editor of the last three editions, knows this book as well as its authors. She has been a constant fountain of ideas and enthusiasm, keeping her authors in line and on task, understanding that we all balance a range of both professional and personal obligations. We owe her more thanks than we know how to express. Thanks also to Jake Schindel, who provided constant support as the book wound its way through the lengthy editorial process.

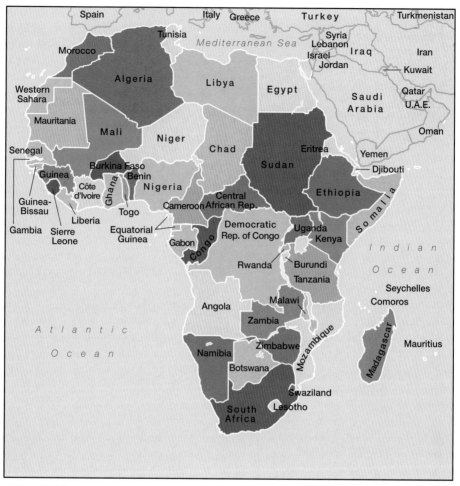

Africa, 2010

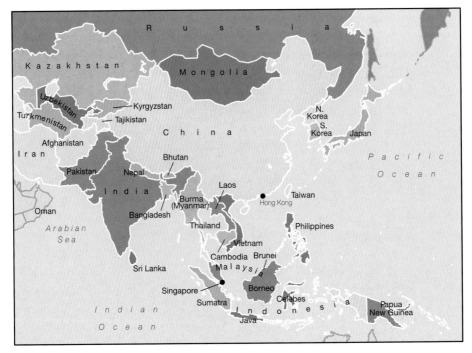

Asia, 2010

Europe, 2010

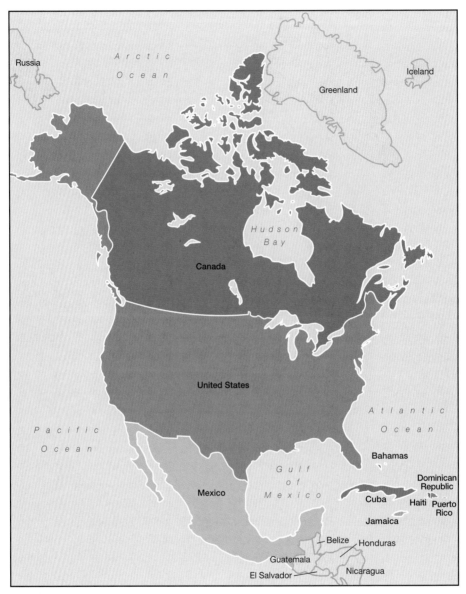

North America, 2010

Latin America, 2010

The World, 2010

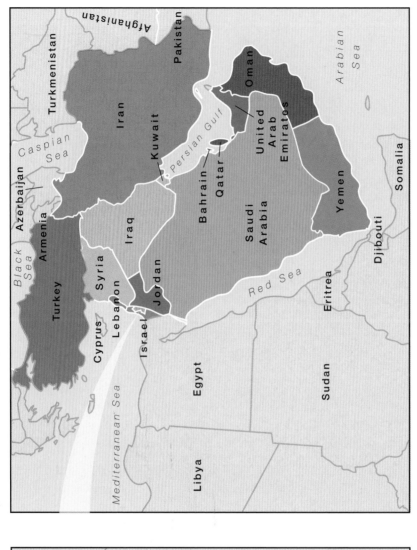

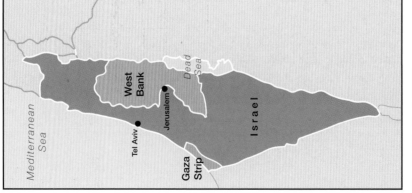

The Middle East, 2010

01

Approaches to
International Relations

- How does international relations affect you in your daily life?
- Why do we study international relations theory?
- How have history and philosophy been used to study international relations?
- What is the contribution of behavioralism?
- What alternative approaches have challenged traditional approaches? Why?

International Relations in Daily Life

OPEN THE DOOR TO your closet and examine your clothing labels. Workers in India, Vietnam, China, El Salvador, and Turkey sewed your clothing. Visit the produce and meat or fish counters at the supermarket. Our food is grown in Mexico and the Philippines, slaughtered in New Zealand, and fish-farmed in Thailand and China. Your classmates include people born in Europe, Asia, Latin America, and Africa. Your fellow students have studied abroad in these same regions. People in your town or city have marched in support of free elections in Iran, voiced support for Israel, and marched in silence to protest oppression in Myanmar and Zimbabwe. And that is before you read the newspaper or visit the Web. In both places, you may read about the wars in Iraq, Afghanistan, and the Democratic

1

World events affect our daily lives in countless ways. When a devastating earthquake struck Haiti in 2010, people around the world contributed to the relief effort. The UN sent troops, as did the U.S. and other countries.

Republic of Congo, piracy off the Somali coast, the worldwide economic crisis, or reports of deforestation and global warming. Places and events once regarded as far away now influence our lives every day.

Historically, international activities were overwhelmingly the results of decisions taken by central governments and heads of state, not by ordinary citizens. Increasingly, however, these activities involve different actors, some of whom *you* directly influence. You may be a member of a nongovernmental organization—Amnesty International, the Red Cross, or Greenpeace—with a local chapter in your community or at your college. With your fellow members around the globe, you may try to influence the local, as well as the national and international, agenda. Your city or state may be actively courting foreign private investment, competing against both neighboring municipalities and other countries. These activities can directly affect the job situation in your community, creating new employment possibilities or taking away jobs to areas with cheaper wages. As a businessperson, you may be liberated or constrained by business regulations—internationally mandated standards established by the World Trade Organization to facilitate the movement of goods and commerce across national borders.

Thus the variety of actors in international relations includes not just the 194 states recognized in the world today, and their leaders and government bureaucracies, but also municipalities, for-profit and not-for-profit private organizations, international organizations, and you. **International relations** is the study of the interactions among the various actors that participate in international politics, including states, international organizations, nongovernmental organiza-

In Focus ◉

FOUNDATIONAL QUESTIONS OF INTERNATIONAL RELATIONS

- How can human nature be characterized?
- What is the relationship between the individual and society?
- What are the characteristics and role of the state?
- How is the international system organized?

tions, subnational entities such as bureaucracies and local governments, and individuals. It is the study of the behaviors of these actors as they participate individually and together in international political processes.

How, then, can we begin to study this multifaceted phenomenon called international relations? How can we begin to think theoretically about events and trends in international relations? How can we make sense of the seemingly disconnected events that we read about or hear about on the news? How can we begin to answer the foundational questions of international relations: What are the characteristics of human nature and the state? How is the international system organized?

Thinking Theoretically

Political scientists develop theories or frameworks both to understand the causes of events that occur in international relations every day and to answer the foundational questions in the field. Although there are many contending theories, four of the more prominent theories are developed in this book: liberalism and neoliberal institutionalism, realism and neorealism, radical perspectives whose origins lie in Marxism, and constructivism.

In brief, realism posits that states exist in an anarchic international system. Each state bases its policies on an interpretation of national interest defined in terms of power. The structure of the international system is determined by the distribution of power among states. In contrast, liberalism is historically rooted in several philosophical traditions that posit that human nature is basically good. Individuals form groups and, later, states. States generally cooperate and follow international norms and procedures that they have agreed on. Radical theory is rooted in economics. Actions of individuals are largely determined by economic class; the state is an agent of international capitalism; and the international system is highly stratified, dominated by an international capitalist system. And international relations constructivists, in contrast to both realists and liberals, argue that the key structures in the state system are not material but instead are intersubjective and social. The interest of states is not fixed but is malleable and ever changing. All four of these theories are subject to different interpretations, and theorists differ among themselves.

These different theoretical approaches help us see international relations from different viewpoints. As the political scientist Stephen Walt explains, "No single approach can capture all the complexity of contemporary world politics. Therefore we are better off with a diverse array of competing ideas rather than a single theoretical orthodoxy. Competition between theories helps reveal their strengths and weaknesses and spurs subsequent refinements, while revealing flaws in conventional wisdom."[1] We will explore these competing ideas, and their strengths and weaknesses, in the remainder of the book.

Developing the Answers

How do political scientists find the answers to the questions posed? How do they find information to assess the accuracy, relevancy, and potency of their theories? The tools they use to answer the foundational questions include history, philosophy, and the scientific method.

History

Answers have often been discovered in history. Without any historical background, many of today's key issues are incomprehensible. History tells us that the bombings in Israel are part of a dispute over territory between Arabs and Jews, a dispute with its origins in biblical times and with its modern roots in the establishment of the state of Israel in 1948. Sudan's twenty-year-old civil war between the north and south, and the Darfur crisis beginning in 2003, are both products of long-standing neglect by the central government of marginalized areas. The civil war was exacerbated by religious differences (the north is Muslim; the south is Christian and animist); the second was magnified by natural disasters. History also provides a guide to understanding the major changes in the People's Republic of China in the twentieth century, from the civil war won by Mao's revolutionaries to its isolation during the turbulent years of the Cultural Revolution, to its current status as a global economic power.

Thus, history provides a crucial background for the study of international relations. History has been so fundamental to the study of international relations that there was no separate international relations subdiscipline until the early twentieth century. Before that time, especially in both Europe and the United States,

Some scholars draw on history to help understand world politics. When the U.S. invaded Iraq first in the 1991 Gulf War and then in the 2003 Iraq War, many observers raised comparisons to the Vietnam War. However, there were significant differences between these situations.

international relations was studied under the umbrella of diplomatic history in most academic institutions.

History invites its students to acquire detailed knowledge of specific events, but it also can be used to test generalizations. Having deciphered patterns from the past, students of history can begin to explain the relationships among various events. For example, having historically documented the cases when wars occur and described the patterns leading up to war, the diplomatic historian can search for explanations for, or causes of, war. The ancient Greek historian Thucydides (c. 460–401 B.C.E.), in *History of the Peloponnesian War*, used this approach. Distinguishing between the underlying and the immediate causes of wars, Thucydides found that what made that war inevitable was the growth of Athenian power. As that city-state's power increased, Sparta, Athens's greatest rival, feared losing its own power. Thus, the changing distribution of power was the underlying cause of the Peloponnesian War.[2]

Many scholars following in Thucydides' footsteps use history in similar ways. But those using history must be wary. History may be a bad guide; the "lessons" of Munich and Allied appeasement of Germany before World War II or the "lessons" of the war in Vietnam or of the 1991 Gulf War are neither clear cut nor agreed on.

Nor are the analogies made between the 2003 Iraq War and the U.S. war against Vietnam unambiguous. In both cases, the United States fought a lengthy war against a little understood, often unidentifiable enemy. In both, the United States adopted the strategy of supporting state building so that the central government could continue the fight, a policy labeled Vietnamization and Iraqization in the respective conflicts. The policy led to a quagmire in both places when American domestic support waned. Yet the differences are also evident. Vietnam has a long history and a strong sense of national identity, forged by wars against both the Chinese and French. Iraq, in contrast, is a relatively new state with significant ethnic and religious divisions, whose various groups seek a variety of different objectives. In Vietnam, the goal was defense of the U.S. ally South Vietnam against the communist north, backed by the Soviet Union. In Iraq, the goal was first to oust Saddam Hussein, who was suspected of building weapons of mass destruction, and of creating a democratic Iraq, which would eventually lead the region to greater stability.[3] Thus, although we cannot ignore history, neither can we draw simple "lessons" from other historic experiences.

Philosophy

We can also deduce answers to international relations questions from classical and modern philosophy. Much classical philosophizing focuses on the state and its leaders—the basic building blocks of international relations—as well as on methods of analysis. For example, the ancient Greek philosopher Plato (c. 427–347 B.C.E.), in *The Republic*, concluded that in the "perfect state" the people who should govern are those who are superior in the ways of philosophy and war. Plato called these ideal rulers "philosopher-kings."[4] Though not directly discussing international relations, Plato introduced two ideas seminal to the discipline: class analysis and dialectical reasoning, both of which were bases for later Marxist analysts. Radicals, like Marxists, see economic class as the major divider in domestic and international politics; this viewpoint will be explored in depth in Chapters 3 and 9. Marxists also acknowledge the importance of dialectical reasoning—that is, reasoning from a dialogue or conversation that leads to the discovery of contradictions in the original assertions and in political reality. In contemporary Marxist terms, such an analysis reveals the contradiction between global and local policies, whereby, for example, local-level textile workers lose their jobs to foreign competition and are replaced by high-technology industries.

Just as Plato's contributions to contemporary thinking were both substantive and methodological, the contributions of his student, the philosopher Aristotle (384–322 B.C.E.), lay both in substance (the search for an ideal domestic political system) and in method (the comparative method). Analyzing 168 constitutions,

Aristotle looked at the similarities and differences among states, becoming the first writer to use the comparative method of analysis. He came to the conclusion that states rise and fall largely because of internal factors—a conclusion still debated in the twenty-first century.[5]

After the classical era, many of the philosophers of relevance to international relations focused on those foundational questions. The English philosopher Thomas Hobbes (1588–1679), in *Leviathan*, imagined a state of nature, a world without governmental authority or civil order, where men rule by passions, living with the constant uncertainty of their own security. To Hobbes, the life of man is solitary, selfish, and even brutish. Extrapolating to the international level, in the absence of international authority, society is in a "state of nature," or **anarchy**. States in this anarchic condition act as man does in the state of nature. For Hobbes the solution to the dilemma is a unitary state—a leviathan—where power is centrally and absolutely controlled.[6]

The French philosopher Jean-Jacques Rousseau (1712–78) addressed the same set of questions but, having been influenced by the Enlightenment, saw a different solution. In "Discourse on the Origin and Foundations of Inequality among Men," Rousseau described the state of nature as an egocentric world, with man's primary concern being self-preservation—not unlike Hobbes's description of the state of nature. Rousseau posed the dilemma in terms of the story of the stag and the hare. In a hunting society, each individual must keep to his assigned task in order to find and trap the stag for food for the whole group. However, if a hare happens to pass nearby, an individual might well follow the hare, hoping to get his next meal quickly and caring little for how his actions will affect the group. Rousseau drew an analogy between these hunters and states. Do states follow short-term self-interest, like the hunter who follows the hare? Or do they recognize the benefits of a common interest?[7]

Rousseau's solution to the dilemma posed by the stag and the hare was different from Hobbes's leviathan. Rousseau's preference was for the creation of smaller communities in which the "general will" could be attained. Indeed, according to Rousseau, it is "only the general will," not a leviathan, that can "direct the forces of the state according to the purpose for which it was instituted, which is the common good."[8] In Rousseau's vision, "each of us places his person and all his power in common under the supreme direction of the general will; and as one we receive each member as an indivisible part of the whole."[9]

Still another philosophical view of the characteristics of international society was set forth by the German philosopher Immanuel Kant (1724–1804), in both *Idea for a Universal History* and *Perpetual Peace*. Kant envisioned a federation of states as a means to achieve peace, a world order in which man is able to live without fear of war. Sovereignties would remain intact, but the new federal order would be both

TABLE 1.1

Contributions of Philosophers to International Relations Theory

PLATO (427–347 B.C.E.)	Greek political philosopher who argued that the life force in man is intelligent. Only a few people can have insight into what is good; society should submit to the authority of these philosopher-kings. Many of these ideas are developed in *The Republic*.
ARISTOTLE (384–322 B.C.E.)	Greek political philosopher who addressed the problem of order in the individual Greek city-state. The first to use the comparative method of research, observing multiple points in time and suggesting explanations for the patterns found.
THOMAS HOBBES (1588–1679)	English political philosopher who in *Leviathan* described life in a state of nature as solitary, selfish, and brutish. Individuals and society can escape from the state of nature through a unitary state, a Leviathan.
JEAN-JACQUES ROUSSEAU (1712–78)	French political philosopher whose seminal ideas were tested by the French Revolution. In "Discourse on the Origin and Foundations of Inequality among Men," described the state of nature in both national and international society. Argued that the solution to the state of nature is the social contract, whereby individuals gather in small communities where the "general will" is realized.
IMMANUEL KANT (1724–1804)	German political philosopher key to the idealist or utopian school of thought. In *Idea for a Universal History* and *Perpetual Peace*, advocated a world federation of republics bound by the rule of law.

preferable to a "super-leviathan" and more effective and realistic than Rousseau's small communities. Kant's analysis was based on a vision of human beings that was different from that of either Rousseau or Hobbes. In his view, though admittedly selfish, man can learn new ways of cosmopolitanism and universalism.[10]

The tradition laid down by these philosophers has contributed to the development of international relations by calling attention to fundamental relationships: those between the individual and society, between individuals *in* society, and between societies. These philosophers had varied, often competing visions of what these relationships are and what they ought to be. Some of their more important contributions are summarized in Table 1.1. The early philosophers have led contemporary international relations scholars to the examination of the characteristics of leaders, to the recognition of the importance of the internal dimensions of the state, to the analogy of the state and nature, and to descriptions of an international community.

History and philosophy permit us to delve into the foundational questions—the nature of man and the broad characteristics of the state and of international society.

They allow us to speculate on the **normative** (or moral) element in political life: What *should be* the role of the state? What *ought to be* the norms in international society? How *might* international society be structured to achieve order? When is war just? Should economic resources be redistributed? Both history and philosophy are key tools for international relations scholars.

The Scientific Method: Behavioralism

In the 1950s, some scholars became dissatisfied with utilizing the traditional tools of history and philosophy. They found the scientific method a more useful tool; they could provide empirical answers to the foundational questions. Is individual behavior more predictable than the largely contextual descriptions of the historian or the assumptions of the philosopher? Are there recurrent patterns to how states behave? Are there subtle patterns to diplomatic history? Are states as power hungry as the philosophers who compare the anarchic international system with the state of nature would have us believe? How can we explain empirical findings? Can we use those findings to predict the future?

Scholars seeking answers to these new questions were poised to contribute to the behavioral revolution in U.S. social sciences during the 1950s and 1960s. **Behavioralism** proposes that individuals, both alone and in groups, act in patterned ways. The task of the behavioral scientist is to suggest plausible hypotheses regarding those patterned actions and to systematically and empirically test those hypotheses. Using the tools of the scientific method to describe and explain human behavior, these scholars hope ultimately to predict future behavior. Many will be satisfied, however, with being able to explain patterns, because prediction in the social sciences remains an uncertain enterprise.

The Correlates of War project, research based at the University of Michigan, permits us to see the application of behavioralism. Beginning in 1963, the political scientist J. David Singer and his historian colleague Melvin Small attacked one of the fundamental questions in international relations: Why is there war?[11] As Singer himself later acknowledged, he was motivated by the normative philosophical concern—how can there be peace? The two scholars chose a different methodological approach than did their historian colleagues. Rather than focusing on one war, one of the "big ones" that change the tide of history, as Thucydides did in his study of the Peloponnesian War, they sought to find patterns among a number of different wars. Believing that there are generalizable patterns to be found across all wars, Singer and Small turned to statistical data to discover the patterns.

The initial task of the Correlates of War project was to collect data on international wars (not civil wars) between 1865 and 1965 in which one thousand or more deaths had been reported. For each of the ninety-three wars that fitted these criteria, the researchers found data on the magnitude, severity, and intensity of wars, as well as the frequency of war over time. This data-collection process proved a much larger task than Singer and Small had anticipated, employing a bevy of researchers and graduate students.

Once the wars were codified, the second task was to generate specific, testable hypotheses that might explain the outbreak of war. Is there a relationship between the number of alliance commitments in the international system and the number of wars that are fought? Is there a relationship between the number of great powers in the international system and the number of wars? Is there a relationship between the number of wars over time and the severity of the conflicts? In the Correlates of War studies and in subsequent studies using the same data, hundreds of such relationships have been verified, although the relative importance of some of these findings is questionable.

The ultimate goal of the project is to connect all the relationships that are found into a coherent theory of why wars occur. Which groups of factors are *most* correlated over time with the outbreak of war? And how are these factors related to each other? Although answering these questions will never *prove* that a particular group of factors is the cause of war, it could suggest some high-level correlations that merit theoretical explanation. Are characteristics of specific warring states most correlated with the outbreak of war? What is the correlation between international system–level factors—such as the existence of international organizations—and the outbreak of war? If the Correlates of War project finds consistently high correlations between alliances and war or between international organizations and war, then it can explain why wars break out, and perhaps policy makers may be able to predict the characteristics of the actors and the location for future wars. That is the goal of the research project. Yet methodological problems abound. The Correlates of War database looks at all international wars, irrespective of the different political, military, social, and technological contexts. So although the generalizations gleaned may be provocative, richer description is needed to really explain the different patterns between wars of the late 1800s and wars of the early 2000s.

Although the methods of behavioralism, as illustrated in the Correlates of War project, have never been an end in themselves, only a means to improve explanation, during the 1980s and 1990s scholars seriously questioned the behavioral approach. Their disillusionment has taken several forms. To some, many of the foundational questions—the nature of humanity and society—are neglected by behavioralists because they are not easily testable by empirical methods. These critics suggest returning to the philosophical roots of international relations. To others, the questions behavioralists pose are the salient ones, but their attention to methods has overwhelmed the substance of their research. Few would doubt the importance of J. David Singer and Melvin Small's initial excursion into the causes of war, but even the researchers themselves admitted losing sight of the important questions in their quest to compile data and hone research methods. Some scholars, still within the behavioralist orientation, suggest simplifying esoteric methods in order to refocus on the substantive questions. Others remain firmly committed to behavioralism and the scientific method, pointing to the lack of funding and time as an explanation for their meager results.

Alternative Approaches

Some international relations scholars are dissatisfied with using history, philosophy, or behavioral tools. The postmodernists, for example, seek to deconstruct the basic concepts of the field, such as the state, the nation, rationality, and realism, by searching the texts (or sources) for hidden meanings underneath the surface, in the subtext. Once those hidden meanings are revealed, the postmodernists seek to replace the once-orderly picture with disorder, to replace the dichotomies with multiple portraits.

Researchers have begun to deconstruct core concepts and replace them with multiple meanings. The political scientist Cynthia Weber, for example, argues that sovereignty (the independence of a state) is neither well defined nor consistently grounded. Digging below the surface of sovereignty, going beyond evaluations of the traditional philosophers, she has discovered that conceptualizations of sovereignty are constantly shifting, depending on the exigencies of the moment and sanctioned by different communities. The multiple meanings of sovereignty are conditioned by time, place, and historical circumstances.[12] This analysis has profound implications for the theory and practice of international relations, which are rooted in state sovereignty and accepted practices that reinforce sovereignty. It challenges conventional understandings.

Postmodernists also seek to find the voices of "the others," those individuals who have been disenfranchised and marginalized in international relations. The feminist Christine Sylvester illustrates her approach with a discussion of the Greenham Common Peace Camp, a group of mostly women who in the early 1980s left their homes and neighborhoods in Wales and walked more than a hundred miles to a British air force base to protest against plans to deploy missiles at the base. Although the marchers were ignored by the media—and thus were "voiceless"—they maintained a politics of resistance, recruiting other political action groups near the camp and engaging members of the military stationed at the base. The women learned how to maintain a peace camp, forcing down the barriers between the militarized and demilitarized and between women and men. In 1988, when the Intermediate Range Nuclear Force Treaty was signed, dismantling the missiles, the women moved on to another protest site, drawing public attention to the role of Britain in the nuclear era.[13]

Alternative approaches to understanding international relations may place more emphasis on individuals whose perspectives are often overlooked. Initially ignored by the media, the women of the Greenham Common Peace Camp drew attention to the cause of nuclear disarmament through their long-term protest.

Others, such as the constructivists, have turned to discourse analysis to answer the questions posed. To trace how ideas shape identities, they analyze culture, norms, procedures, and social practices. They probe how identities are shaped and change over time. They use texts, interviews, and archival material, as well as research local practices by riding public transportation and standing in lines. By using multiple sets of data, they create thick description. The case studies found in Peter Katzenstein's edited volume *The Culture of National Security* utilize this approach. Drawing on analyses of Soviet foreign policy at the end of the Cold War, German and Japanese security policy from militarism to antimilitarism, and Arab national identity, the authors search for security interests defined by actors who are responding to changing cultural factors. These studies show how social and cultural factors shape national security policy in ways that contradict realist or liberal expectations.[14]

No important question of international relations today can be answered with exclusive reliance on any one method. History, whether in the form of an extended case study (Peloponnesian War) or a study of multiple wars (Correlates of War), provides useful answers. Philosophical traditions offer both cogent reasoning and the framework for the major discussions of the day. But behavioral methods still dominate. And the newer methods of deconstructionism and thick description and discourse analysis provide an even richer base from which the international relations scholar can draw.

TABLE 1.2

Tools for Studying International Relations

TOOL	METHOD
HISTORY	Examines individual or multiple cases.
PHILOSOPHY	Develops rationales from core texts and analytical thinking.
BEHAVIORALISM	Finds patterns in human behavior and state behavior using empirical methods, grounded in scientific method.
ALTERNATIVES	Deconstructs major concepts and uses discourse analysis to build thick description. Finds voices of "others."

In Sum: Making Sense of International Relations

How can we, as students, begin to make sense of international political events in our daily lives? How have scholars of international relations helped us make sense of the world around us? In this chapter, major theories of international relations have been introduced, including the realist, liberal, radical, and constructivist frameworks. These theories provide frameworks for asking and answering core foundational questions. To answer these questions, international relations scholars turn to many other disciplines, including history, philosophy, behavioral psychology, and critical studies (see Table 1.2). International relations is a pluralistic and eclectic discipline.

Where Do We Go from Here?

To understand the development of international relations theory, we need to examine general historical trends for developments in the state and the international system, particularly events in Europe during the nineteenth and twentieth centuries. This "stuff" of diplomatic history is the subject of Chapter 2. Chapter 3 is designed to help us think about the development of international relations theoretically through several frameworks—liberalism, realism, radicalism, and constructivism. Chapters 4, 5, and 6 examine the levels of analysis in international relations. Each of these chapters is organized around the theoretical frameworks. Thus, in Chapter 4 the international system is examined; in Chapter 5, the state; and in Chapter 6, the individual. In each of these chapters the focus is on comparing liberal, realist, and radical descriptions and explanations, augmented, when appropriate, with constructivism. Chapter 7 explores and analyzes the roles of international organizations, nongovernmental actors, and international law. In the last three chapters, the major issues of international relations are studied: in Chapter 8, war and strife; in Chapter 9, international political economy; and in Chapter 10, the transnational issues of the twenty-first century.

DISCUSSION QUESTIONS

1. Your father picked up this book and saw the word *theory* in the first chapter. He is skeptical about the value of theory. Explain to him the utility of developing a theoretical perspective.

2. Philosophy is your passion, but you find international relations moderately interesting. How can you integrate your passion with this pragmatic interest? What questions can you explore?

3. You are a history major skilled in researching the historical archives. Suggest two research projects that you might undertake to further your understanding of international relations.

4. How can the study of international relations be made more scientific? What are the problems with doing so?

KEY TERMS

anarchy, p. 7   international relations, p. 3
behavioralism, p. 9   normative, p. 9

 Find chapter outlines, practice quizzes, flashcards, and other study and review materials for this chapter at wwnorton.com/studyspace.

02

The Historical Context of Contemporary International Relations

- Which historical periods have most influenced the development of international relations?
- What are the historical origins of the state?
- Why do international relations scholars use the Treaties of Westphalia as a benchmark?
- What are the historical origins of the European balance-of-power system?
- How could the Cold War be both a series of confrontations between the United States and the Soviet Union and a "long peace"?
- What key events have shaped the post–Cold War world?

STUDENTS OF INTERNATIONAL RELATIONS need to understand the events and trends of the past. Theorists recognize that core concepts in the field—concepts such as the state, the nation, sovereignty, power, balance of power—were developed and shaped by historical circumstances. Policy makers search the past for patterns and precedents to guide contemporary decisions. Theorists often ask the questions they do as a result of unexpected or unexplained real-world events. In large part, the major antecedents to the contemporary international system are found in Europe-centered Western civilization.

Great civilizations thrived in other parts of the world too, of course: India and China, among others, had extensive, vibrant civilizations long before the historical events covered below. But the European emphasis is justified because for better or worse, in both theory and practice contemporary international relations is rooted in the European experience. In this chapter, we will first examine the pre-Westphalian world before looking at Europe in the period immediately preceding and following the Thirty Years War (1648, a seminal year for students of international relations), then Europe's relationship with the rest of the world during the nineteenth century, and finally the major transitions during the twentieth century.

The purpose of this historical overview is to trace important trends over time: the emergence of the state and the notion of sovereignty, the development of the international state system, the causes and continuing consequences of colonialism and two world wars, and changes in the distribution of power among key states. These trends have a direct impact on international relations theory and practice today.

The Pre-Westphalian World

Most international relations theorists date the contemporary system from 1648, the year the Treaties of Westphalia ended the Thirty Years War. These treaties marked the end of rule by religious authority in Europe and the emergence of secular authorities. With secular authority came the principle that has provided the foundation for international relations ever since: the notion of the territorial integrity of states—legally equal and sovereign participants in an international system. Yet key developments preceded and shaped the Westphalian order, especially changes in centralization and decentralization during the Middle Ages.

The Middle Ages: Centralization and Decentralization

When the Roman Empire disintegrated in the fifth century, power and authority became decentralized in Europe, but other forms of interaction flourished—travel, commerce, and communication, not just among the elites but also among merchant groups and ordinary citizens. By the year 1000, three civilizations had emerged from the rubble of Rome. First among them was the Arabic civilization, which had the largest geographic expanse, stretching from the Middle East and Persia through North Africa to the Iberian Peninsula. United under the religious and political domination of the Islamic caliphate, the Arabic language, and advanced mathematical and technical accomplishments, the Arabic civilization was a potent force. Second was the Byzantine Empire, located nearer the core of the old Roman Empire in Constantinople and united by Christianity. Third was the rest of Europe, where with the demise of the Roman Empire central authority was absent, languages and cultures proliferated, and the networks of communication and transportation developed by the Romans were beginning to disintegrate.

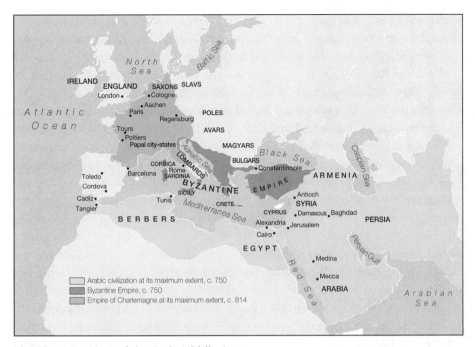

The Three Empires of the Early Middle Ages

Much of western Europe reverted to feudal principalities, controlled by lords and tied to fiefdoms that had the authority to raise taxes and exert legal authority. Lords exercised control over vassals, who worked for the lords in return for the right to manage the land and enjoy the lords' protection. Feudalism, which placed authority in private hands, was the response to the prevailing disorder. Power and authority were located at different overlapping levels.

The preeminent institution in the medieval period in Europe was the church; virtually all other institutions were local in origin and practice. Thus, authority was centered either in the pope in Rome (and in his agents, the bishops, dispersed throughout medieval Europe) or in the local fiefdom. Yet even the bishops seized considerable independent authority despite their overarching allegiance to the church. Economic life was also intensely local.

In the late eighth century, the church's monopoly on power was challenged by Carolus Magnus, or Charlemagne (742–814), the leader of the Franks in what is today France. Charlemagne was granted authority to unite western Europe in the name of Roman Catholicism against the Orthodox Christian Byzantine Empire in the East; the pope made him emperor of the Holy Roman Empire. In return, Charlemagne offered the pope protection. The struggle between religious and secular authority and the debate over which should rule would continue for hundreds of years, with writers periodically offering their views on the subject. One such writer was Dante Alighieri (1265–1321), who argued in *De monarchia* that there should be a strict separation of the church from political life.[1] This question was not resolved until three hundred years later by the Treaties of Westphalia.

The Holy Roman Empire itself was a weak secular institution; as one famous saying goes, it was not very holy, very Roman, or much of an empire. Yet Charlemagne's successors did provide a limited secular alternative to the church. The contradictions remained, however in the desire of the church for universalism versus the medieval reality of small, fragmented, diverse authorities. These small units, largely unconnected to each other and with dispersed populations, all prevented the establishment of centralized governmental authority.

Similar trends of centralization and decentralization, political integration and disintegration, were also occurring in other geographic areas. In Africa, for example, the ancient kingdom of Ghana (not to be confused with the contemporary state) centralized power between the fifth and thirteenth centuries. During the thirteenth and fourteenth centuries, the kingdom of Mali prevailed. Each was a powerful political and economic entity. Each had a sophisticated system of tax collection and was an important center of commerce with the Muslims in North Africa, trading gold and salt with their Arab neighbors. Each was an empire with a standing army but with traditional rulers left in place in the outlying districts. On the opposite side of the globe, in what is now Latin America, independent civilizations flourished—the Maya from 100 to 900 c.e. and the Aztecs and Incas from 1200.

Japan was another country where centralization followed a period of warfare and decentralized authority. Whereas the fifteenth and sixteenth centuries were largely characterized by turmoil, a period of over two hundred years of more centralized control followed. During the Tokugawa period from 1603 to 1868, Japan was ruled by a shogun. This was a period of strict class hierarchy, led by the warrior caste of samurai, followed by farmers, artisans, and traders. Although the disparate economic conditions led to unrest and violent confrontations occurred, none of these events posed a direct threat to the established feudal system. Yet in Japan as in other regions, it was intervention by Europeans in later centuries that challenged this order.

The Late Middle Ages: Developing Transnational Networks in Europe and Beyond

Although the intellectual debate was not yet resolved, after the year 1000 secular trends began to undermine both the decentralization of feudalism and the universality of Christianity in Europe. Commercial activity expanded into larger geographic areas, as merchants traded along increasingly safer transportation routes. All forms of communication improved. New technology, such as water mills and windmills, not only made daily life easier but also provided the first elementary infrastructure to support agrarian economies. Municipalities such as the reinvigorated city-states of the northern Italian peninsula—Genoa, Venice, Milan, and Florence— established trading relationships, setting up meeting places at key locations, arranging for the shipment of commercial materials, and even agreeing to follow certain diplomatic practices to facilitate commercial activities. These diplomatic practices—establishing embassies with permanent staff, dispatching special consuls to handle commercial disputes, and sending diplomatic messages through specially protected channels—were the immediate precursors of contemporary diplomatic practice.

These economic and technological changes led to fundamental changes in social relations. First, a new group of individuals emerged—a transnational business community—whose interests and livelihoods extended beyond its immediate locale. This group acquired cosmopolitan experiences outside the realm of the church and its teachings, which had so thoroughly dominated education up to this point. Individual members developed new interests in art, philosophy, and

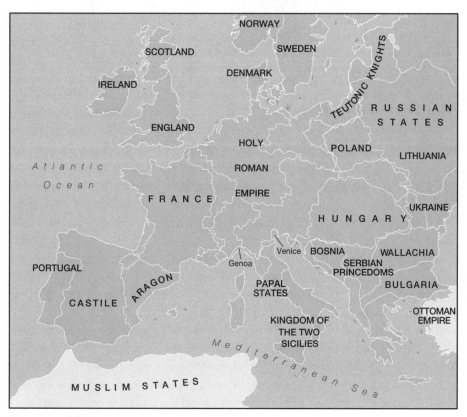

Europe, c. 1360

Niccolò Machiavelli's famous treatise *The Prince* reflected the shift away from religious authority and toward secular government in the Late Middle Ages. Written in 1513, *The Prince* was not published until 1532, after Machiavelli's death.

history, acquiring considerable wealth along the way. They believed in themselves, becoming the individualists and humanists of the Renaissance. Second, writers and scholars rediscovered ancient classical literature and history, finding intellectual sustenance and revelation in Greek and Roman thought.

More than any other writer, the Italian philosopher Niccolò Machiavelli (1469–1527) reflects the changes taking place and the ensuing gulf between the medieval world of the church and newer, secular institutions. In *The Prince* Machiavelli elucidated the qualities that a leader needs to maintain the strength and security of the state. Realizing that the dream of unity in Christianity was unattainable (and probably undesirable), Machiavelli called on leaders to articulate their own political interests. He argued that having no universal morality to guide them, leaders must act in the state's interest, answerable to no moral rules. The cleavage between the religiosity of medieval times and the humanism of the later Renaissance was thus starkly drawn.[2]

The desire to expand economic intercourse even further, coupled with the technological inventions that made ocean exploration safer, fueled a period of European territorial expansion. Spaniards and Italians were among the earliest of these adventurers. Christopher Columbus sailed to the New World in 1492, Hernán Cortés to Mexico in 1519, and Francisco Pizarro to the Andes in 1533, all disrupting the existing indigenous orders. During this age of exploration, European civilization spread to distant shores. For some theorists, it is these events—the gradual incorporation of the less-developed peripheral areas into the world capitalist economy and the international capitalist system—that mark the beginning of history relevant for contemporary international relations.

During the 1500s and 1600s, as explorers and even settlers moved into the New World, the old Europe remained in flux. In some key locales such as France, England, and Aragon and Castile in Spain, feudalism was being replaced by an increasingly centralized monarchy. The move toward centralization did not go uncontested; the masses, angered by taxes imposed by newly emerging states, rebelled and rioted. New monarchs needed the tax revenue to build armies; they used their armies to consolidate their power internally and to conquer more territory. Other parts of Europe were mired in the secular-versus-religious controversy, and western Christianity itself was torn by the Catholic and Protestant split. In 1648, that controversy inched its way toward resolution.

In Focus ◎

KEY DEVELOPMENTS BEFORE 1648

- The sovereign Greek city-states reach the height of their power in 400 B.C.E., they carry out cooperative functions through diplomacy and classic power politics.

- The Roman Empire (50 B.C.E.-C.E. 400) originates imperialism, developing the practice of expanding territorial reach. The empire is united through law and language, while allowing some local identity.

- The Middle Ages (400–1000) witness the centralization of religious authority in the church, with decentralization in political and economic life.

- The Late Middle Ages (1000–1500) foster the development of transnational networks during the age of exploration.

The Emergence of the Westphalian System

The formulation of **sovereignty**—a core concept in contemporary international relations—was one of the most important intellectual developments leading to the Westphalian revolution. Much of the development of the notion is found in the writings of the French philosopher Jean Bodin (1530–96). To Bodin, sovereignty was the "absolute and perpetual power vested in a commonwealth."[3] It resides not in an individual but in a state; thus it is perpetual. Sovereignty is "the distinguishing mark of the sovereign that he cannot in any way be subject to the commands of another, for it is he who makes law for the subject, abrogates law already made, and amends obsolete law."[4]

Although sovereignty is absolute, according to Bodin, it is not without limits. Leaders are limited by divine law or natural law: "All the princes on earth are subject to the laws of God and of nature." They are also limited by the type of regime—"the constitutional laws of the realm"—be it a monarchy, an aristocracy, or a democracy. And last, leaders are limited by covenants, contracts with promises to the people within the commonwealth, and treaties with other states, though there is no supreme arbiter in relations among states.[5] Thus, Bodin provided the conceptual glue of sovereignty that would emerge with the Westphalian agreement.

The Thirty Years War (1618–48) devastated Europe. The war, which had begun as a religious dispute between Catholics and Protestants, ended as a result of mutual exhaustion, bankruptcy, and the virtual depopulation of Europe. Princes and mercenary armies ravaged the central European landscape, fought frequent battles and savage sieges, and could be supplied in the field only by plundering the civilian population. But the treaty that ended the conflict had a profound impact on the practice of international relations. First, the **Treaties of Westphalia** embraced the notion of sovereignty. With one stroke, virtually all the small states in central Europe attained sovereignty. The Holy Roman Empire was dead. Monarchs in the West gained the authority to decide which version of Christianity was appropriate for their people. This meant that each monarch, and not a supranational church, had religious authority over his or her population. With the pope and the emperor stripped of power, the notion of the territorial state came into focus and was increasingly accepted as normal. The treaties not only legitimized territoriality and the right of *states*—as the sovereign, territorially contiguous principalities increasingly came to be known—to choose their own religion, but it also established that states could determine their own domestic policies, free from external pressure and with full jurisdiction in their own geographic space. They also introduced the right of noninterference in the affairs of other states.

Second, the leaders of Europe's most powerful countries had seen the devastation caused by mercenaries in war. Thus, after the Treaties of Westphalia, these countries sought to establish their own permanent national militaries. The growth of such forces led to increasingly centralized control, since the state had to collect taxes to pay for these militaries and leaders assumed absolute control over the troops. The state with a national army emerged, its sovereignty acknowledged and its secular base firmly established. And that state became increasingly powerful. Larger territorial units gained an advantage as armaments became more standardized and more lethal.

Third, the Treaties of Westphalia established a core group of states that dominated the world until the beginning of the nineteenth century: Austria, Russia, Prussia, England, France, and the United Provinces (the area now comprising the Netherlands and Belgium). Those in the west—England, France, and the United Provinces—underwent an economic revival under the aegis of capitalism, whereas those in the east—Prussia and Russia—reverted to feudal practices. In the west,

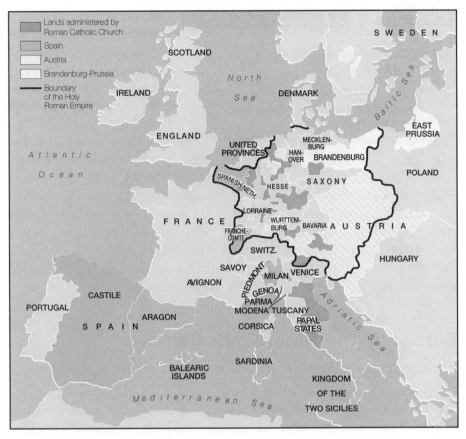

Europe, c. 1648

private enterprise was encouraged. States improved their infrastructure to facilitate commerce, and great trading companies and banks emerged. In contrast, in the east, serfs remained on the land, and economic change was stifled. Yet in both regions, absolutist states dominated, with Louis XIV (1638–1715) ruling in France, Peter the Great (1672–1725) in Russia, and Frederick II (1712–86) in Prussia. Until the end of the eighteenth century, European politics was dominated by multiple rivalries and shifting alliances. These rivalries were also played out in regions beyond Europe, where contending European states vied for power, most notably Great Britain and France in North America.

The most important social theorist of the time was the Scottish economist Adam Smith (1723–90). In *An Inquiry into the Nature and Causes of the Wealth of Nations*, Smith argued that the notion of a market should apply to all social orders. Individuals—laborers, owners, investors, consumers—should be permitted to pursue their own interests, unfettered by state regulation. According to Smith, each individual acts rationally to maximize his or her own interests. With groups of

In Focus ◉ █████████████

- Notion and practice of sovereignty develops.
- Centralized control of institutions under military grows.
- Capitalist economic system emerges.

individuals pursuing their self-interests, economic efficiency is enhanced, and more goods and services are produced and consumed. At the aggregate level, the wealth of the state and that of the international system are similarly enhanced. What makes the system work is the so-called invisible hand of the market; when individuals pursue their rational self-interests, the system (the market) operates effortlessly.[6] Smith's explication of how competing units enable capitalism to ensure economic vitality has had a profound effect on states' economic policies and political choices, which we shall explore in Chapter 9. But other ideas of the period would also dramatically alter governance in the nineteenth, twentieth, and twenty-first centuries.

Europe in the Nineteenth Century

Two revolutions ushered in the nineteenth century—the American Revolution (1776) against British rule and the French Revolution (1789) against absolutist rule. Each revolution was the product of Enlightenment thinking as well as social contract theory. Enlightenment thinkers saw individuals as rational, capable of understanding the laws governing them, and of working to improve their condition in society.

The Aftermath of Revolution: Core Principles

Two core principles emerged in the aftermath of the American and French revolutions. The first was that absolutist rule is subject to limits imposed by man. In *Two Treatises of Government,* the English philosopher John Locke (1632–1704) attacked absolute power and the notion of the divine right of kings. Locke argued that the state is a beneficial institution created by rational men in order to protect both their natural rights (life, liberty, and property) and their self-interests. Men freely enter into this political arrangement, agreeing to establish government to ensure natural rights for all. The crux of Locke's argument is that political power ultimately rests with the people, rather than with a leader or monarch. The monarch derives **legitimacy** from the consent of the governed.[7]

The second core principle that emerged at this time was **nationalism,** wherein a people comes to identify with a common past, language, customs, and practices.

Individuals who share such characteristics are motivated to participate actively in the political process as a **nation**. For example, during the French Revolution, a patriotic appeal was made to the masses to defend the French *nation* and its new ideals. This appeal forged an emotional link between the people and the state, regardless of social class. These two principles—legitimacy and nationalism—arose out of the American and French revolutions to provide the foundation for politics in the nineteenth and twentieth centuries.

John Locke's *Two Treatises of Government*, first published in 1689, influenced ideas about the legitimacy of the state.

The Napoleonic Wars

The political impact of these twin principles was far from benign in Europe. As a result, the nineteenth century opened with war in Europe on an unprecedented scale. Modest changes in technology—in particular more efficient cultivation of the potato—made possible the advent of a *magazine* system, whereby supplies for war could be stored in prepositioned locations along likely campaign routes for retrieval by troops on the move without the need to stop and forage for food. This, in combination with nationalism, made it possible for the French—who had been weakened by years of internal fighting following the French Revolution—to field larger, more mobile, and more reliable armies that could make use of innovative tactics unavailable to the smaller, professional armies of France's rivals, such as the highly regarded Prussian army.

France's apparent weakness and its status as a revolutionary power in Europe made it ripe for intervention aimed at stamping out the contagious idea of government by popular consent. As a result, following its revolution, France became embroiled in an escalating series of wars with Austria, Britain, and Prussia, which culminated in the rise of a "low-born" Corsican artillery officer named Napoleon

The defeat of Napoleon and the French military in 1815 marked the beginning of a new, relatively peaceful, period in international relations, at least in Europe.

Bonaparte to leader of the French military and, eventually, to the rank of emperor of France.

Bonaparte, with help from other talented officers, set about reorganizing and regularizing the French military. Making skillful use of French national zeal, Bonaparte was able to field large, well-armed, and passionately motivated armies. Through a series of famous battles, including those at Jena and Aurstedt (1806), in which his armies shattered those of Prussia, Napoleon was able to conquer nearly the whole of Europe in a few short years.

Yet the same nationalist fervor that brought about much of Napoleon's success also led to his downfall. In Spain and Russia, Napoleon's armies met nationalists who fought a different sort of war. Rather than facing French forces in direct confrontations, Spanish *guerrillas* made use of intimate local knowledge to mount hit-and-run attacks on French occupying forces. The Spanish guerrillas also enjoyed the support of Britain, which due to its unrivaled mastery of the seas was able to lend supplies and occasional expeditionary forces. When local French forces attempted to punish the Spanish into submission by barbarism (including looting, torture, rape, and execution of prisoners and suspected insurgents without trial), resistance to French occupation became even more intense and more deadly. The cost to France was high, draining away talented soldiers and cash and damaging French morale far beyond Spain. In Russia, which Napoleon invaded in 1812 with an army numbering a staggering 422,000, the Russians also refused to give direct battle. Instead, they retreated toward their areas of supply, burning all available food and shelter as they went in a policy now called "scorched earth." The advancing French began to suffer from severe malnutrition, the entire army slowly starving to death as it advanced to Moscow.

By the time the French reached the Russian capital, the government had already evacuated. The French army that occupied Moscow had dwindled to a mere 110,000. Napoleon waited in vain for the tsar to surrender to France. After realizing the magnitude of his vulnerability, Napoleon attempted to return in good order to France before Russia's harsh winter set in. But it was already too late.

As the French abandoned Moscow, leaving it in flames (no one is certain how the fire started), the first snowflakes had already fallen. Now instead of avoiding battle, fast-moving Russian light cavalry, the Cossacks, harassed the French on their retreat to France and safety. The French sought desperately to choose a route home that offered a chance to find food and shelter, but Cossack attacks forced them to retreat along the same desolate route by which they had come. With the temperature dropping rapidly, the retreat soon became a rout. Entire French units deserted; others, decimated by exposure and starvation, simply vanished. By the time French troops crossed the original line of departure at the Nieman River, Napoleon's Grande Armeé had been reduced to a mere 10,000. The proud emperor's final defeat by English and Prussian forces at The Battle of Waterloo (in present-day Belgium) three years later was assured.

Peace at the Core of the European System

Following the defeat of Napoleon in 1815 and the establishment of peace by the Congress of Vienna, the five powers of Europe—Austria, Britain, France, Prussia, and Russia—ushered in a period of relative peace in the international political system, the so-called Concert of Europe. These great powers fought no major wars after the defeat of Napoleon until the Crimean War in 1854, and in that war both Austria and Prussia remained neutral. Other local wars of brief duration were fought, in which some of the five major powers also remained neutral. Held together by agreements reached at a series of ad hoc conferences over the course of the nineteenth century, all five powers were never involved in conflict with each other. Meeting over thirty times before World War I, the group became a club of like-minded leaders. Through these meetings they legitimized both

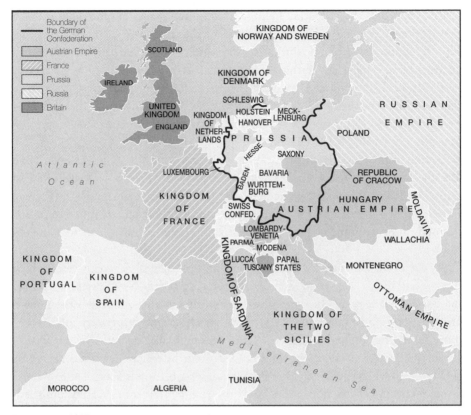

Europe, c. 1815

the independence of new European states and the division of Africa among the colonial powers.

The fact that peace among great powers prevailed during this time seems surprising, since major economic, technological, and political changes were radically altering the landscape.

Industrialization, a critical development at the time, was a double-edged sword. During the second half of the nineteenth century, all attention was focused on the processes of industrialization. Great Britain was the leader, outstripping all rivals in its output of coal, iron, and steel and the export of manufactured goods. In addition, Britain became the source of finance capital, the banker for the Continent and, in the twentieth century, for the world. Industrialization spread through virtually all areas of western Europe as the masses flocked to the cities and entrepreneurs and middlemen scrambled for economic advantage. In addition, more than any other factor, industrialization led to the capture of political power by the middle classes that were its vanguard, at the expense of the aristocratic classes. As machine power became more and more indispensable to the survival and prosperity of states, so land power began to yield to it and to the industrial, inventive, and entrepreneurial middle classes that mastered it.

The population soared, and commerce surged as transportation corridors were strengthened. Political changes were dramatic: Italy was unified in 1870; Germany was formed out of thirty-nine different fragments in 1871; Holland was divided into the Netherlands and Belgium in the 1830s; and the Ottoman Empire gradually disintegrated, leading to independence for Greece in 1829 and for Moldavia and Wallachia (Romania) in 1856. With such dramatic changes under way, what explains the absence of major war? At least three factors were involved.

First, Europe's political elites were united in their fear of revolution among the masses. In fact, at the Congress of Vienna, the Austrian diplomat Count Klemens von Metternich (1773–1859), architect of the Concert of Europe, believed that Europe could best be managed by returning it to the age of absolutism. Elites envisioned grand alliances that would bring European leaders together to fight revolution from below. During the first half of the century, these alliances were not altogether successful. In the 1830s, Britain and France sided together against the three eastern powers (Prussia, Russia, and Austria). In 1848, all five powers were confronted by the masses with demands for reform. But during the second half of the century, European leaders acted in concert, ensuring that mass revolutions did not spread from state to state. In 1870, in the turmoil following France's defeat in the Franco-Prussian War, the leader Napoleon III was isolated quickly for fear of a revolution that never occurred. Fear of revolt from below thus united European leaders, making interstate war less likely.

Second, two of the major conflicts of interest confronting the core European states were internal ones: the unifications of Germany and Italy. Both German and Italian unification had powerful proponents and opponents among the European powers. For example, Britain supported Italian unification, making possible Italy's annexation of Naples and Sicily. Austria, on the other hand, was preoccupied with the increasing strength of Prussia and thus did not actively oppose what may well have been against its national interest—the creation of two sizable neighbors out of myriad independent units. German unification was acceptable to Russia as long as Russian interests in Poland were respected. German unification also got support from Britain's dominant middle class, which viewed a stronger Germany as a potential counterbalance to France. Thus, although the unifications of Germany and Italy were finally solidified through small local wars, a general war was averted since both were preoccupied with territorial unification.

The third factor in supporting peace in Europe was the complex and crucial phenomenon of imperialism/colonialism.

Imperialism and Colonialism in the European System before 1870

The discovery of the "new" world by Europeans in 1492 led to rapidly expanding communication between the Americas and Europe. The same technology also made contact with Asia less costly and more frequent. The first to arrive were explorers seeking discovery, riches, and personal glory; merchants seeking raw materials and trade relations; and clerics seeking to convert "savages" to Christianity (Catholicism initially). But the staggering wealth that was revealed, and the relative ease with which it could be acquired, led to increasing competition among European powers for territories in far-distant lands. Most of the European powers became empires and, once established, claimed the lands sparsely occupied by indigenous peoples as sovereign components. This is the origin of the term **imperialism**, the annexation of distant territory (most often by force) and its inhabitants to an empire. **Colonialism**, which often followed or accompanied imperialism, refers to the settling of people from the home country (say, European Spain) among indigenous peoples of a distant territory (say, Mexico). The two terms are thus subtly different, because most but not all imperial powers settled their own citizens among the peoples whose territories they annexed, and some colonies were established by states which did not identify themselves as empires. Still, most scholars use the two terms interchangeably.

This process of annexation by conquest or treaty continued for four hundred years. As the technology of travel and communications shifted from sail to steam, and as Europeans developed vaccines and cures for tropical diseases, the costs to European powers of imposing their will on indigenous people continued to drop. Europeans were welcomed in some places but were resisted in most. In most cases that resistance was overcome with very little cost or risk. Spears were met with machine guns, and horses with heavy artillery. By the close of the nineteenth century, almost the whole of the globe was "ruled" by European states. Great Britain was the largest and most successful of the imperial powers, but even small states such as Portugal and the Netherlands maintained important colonies abroad.

The process also led to the establishment of a "European" identity. European states enjoyed a solidarity among themselves, based on their being European, Christian, "civilized," and white. These traits differentiated "us"—white Christian Europeans—from the "other"—the rest of the world. With the rise of mass literacy and increasing contact with the colonial world brought about by industrialization, Europeans more than ever saw their commonalities, the uniqueness of being "European." This was, in part, a return to the unity in the Roman Empire and in Roman law, a secular form of medieval Christendom, and a larger Europe as envisioned by Kant and Rousseau. The Congress of Vienna and the Concert of Europe gave more concrete form to these beliefs. The flip side of these beliefs was the ongoing exploration, conquest, and exploitation of the non-European world and the subsequent establishment of colonies.

The Industrial Revolution provided the European states with the military and economic capacity to engage in territorial expansion. Some imperial states were motivated by economic gains, seeking new external markets for manufactured goods and obtaining, in turn, raw materials to fuel their industrial growth. For others, the motivation was cultural and religious—to spread the Christian faith and the ways of white "civilization" to the "dark"

In the nineteenth century, explorers often paved the way for the colonization of African, Asian, and Latin American lands by European powers. Here, a French expedition seeks to stake a claim in Central Africa.

continents and beyond. For still others, the motivation was political. Since the European balance of power prevented direct confrontation in Europe, European state rivalries were played out in Africa and Asia.

To mollify Germany's ambitions, for example, during the Congress of Berlin in 1885 the major powers divided up Africa, giving Germany a sphere of influence in East Africa (Tanganyika), West Africa (Cameroon and Togo), and Southern Africa (Southwest Africa). European imperialism provided a convenient outlet for Germany's aspirations as a unified power without endangering the delicate balance of power within Europe itself. By the end of the nineteenth century, 85 percent of Africa was under the control of European states.

In Asia, only Japan and Siam (Thailand) were not under direct European or U.S. influence. China is an excellent example of external domination. Under the Qing dynasty, which began in the seventeenth century, China had slowly been losing political, economic, and military power for several hundred years. During the nineteenth century, British merchants began to trade with China for tea, silk, and porcelain, often paying for them with smuggled opium. In 1842, the British defeated China in the Opium War, forcing China to cede various political and territorial rights to foreigners through a series of unequal treaties. European states and Japan were able to occupy large portions of Chinese territory, claiming to have exclusive trading rights in particular regions. Foreign powers exercised separate "spheres of influence" in China. By 1914, Europeans controlled four-fifths of the world.

The United States eventually became an imperial power as well. Having won the 1898 Spanish-American War, pushing the Spanish out of the Philippines, Puerto Rico, Cuba, and other small islands, the United States acquired its own colonies.

The struggle for economic power led to heedless exploitation of the colonial areas, particularly in Africa and Asia. One striking aspect of the contest between the Europeans and the peoples they encountered in Africa and Asia is that European weapons and communications technology proved very difficult for indigenous peoples to resist. European states and their militaries became accustomed to winning battles against vastly more numerous adversaries, and often attributed their ability to do so to their military technology. As one famous apologist for colonialism put it: "Thank God that we have got/the Maxim gun, and they have not."[8]

But as the nineteenth century drew to a close, the assumption that vast stretches of distant territory containing large numbers of aggrieved or oppressed people could be controlled cheaply with a few colonial officers and administrators was being challenged with increasing frequency. For Great Britain, the world's most successful colonial power, the future of colonialism was clearly signaled by Britain's "victory" in the Second Anglo-Boer War (1899–1900, also known as the South African War). In this war, which pitted British soldiers against Boer commandoes (descendants of Dutch immigrants to South Africa in the 1820s), Britain was forced to fight a lengthy and bitter counterinsurgency war that claimed the lives, through British negligence, of over 20,000 Boer women and children. The war, which Britain expected to last no longer than three months and cost no more than 10 million pounds sterling, ended up costing 230 million pounds and lasting two years and eight months. It proved the most expensive war, by an order of magnitude, in British colonial history. The war was largely unpopular in Europe and led to increased tensions between Britain and Germany, because the Boer had purchased advanced infantry rifles from Germany and sought German diplomatic and military intervention during the war. The five European powers had still not fought major wars directly against each other.

In sum, much of the competition, rivalry, and tension traditionally marking relations among Europe's states could be acted out far beyond Europe itself. Europeans raced to acquire colonies in order to acquire increased status, wealth, and power vis-à-vis their rivals. Europeans could imagine themselves as bringing the light of civilization to the "dark" regions of the world, while at the same time acquiring the material resources (mineral wealth and "native levies") they might need in the event of a future war in Europe. Each colonial power understood it might take years to accumulate sufficient resources to gain an advantage in a major European war. Therefore each state maintained an interest in managing crises so as not to escalate a conflict of interest to all-out war. Thus the "safety valve" of colonialism both reinforced European unity and identity and prevented the buildup of tension in Europe. By the end of the nineteenth century, however, the toll of political rivalry and economic competition had become destabilizing. Germany's unification, rapid industrialization, and population growth led to an escalation of tension that could not be assuaged in time to prevent war. In 1870 France and Germany fought a war in which France was defeated. In what for France became a humiliating peace treaty, it was forced to surrender the long-contested provinces of Alsace and Lorraine, which became part of the new Germany. The war and the simmering resentments to which it gave birth were mere harbingers of conflicts to come.

Balance of Power

An important theoretical way to describe and explain how the interaction of the common interests of conservative European elites, distraction over unifications of German and Italian principalities, and colonialism combined to support a long peace is the concept of **balance of power**. During the nineteenth century, a balance of power emerged because the independent European states, each with relatively equal power, feared the emergence of any predominant state (**hegemon**) among them. Thus, they formed alliances to counteract any potentially more powerful faction, thus creating a balance of power. The idea behind a balance of power is simple. States will hesitate to start a war with an adversary whose power to fight and win wars is relatively balanced (symmetrical), because the risk of defeat is high. When one state or coalition of states is much more powerful than its adversaries (asymmetrical balance), war is relatively more likely. The treaties signed after 1815 were designed not only to quell revolution from below but to prevent the emergence of a hegemon, such as France under Napoleon had become. Britain or Russia, at least later in the century, could have assumed a dominant leadership position—Britain because of its economic capability and naval prowess, and Russia because of its relative geographic isolation and extraordinary manpower. However, neither sought to exert hegemonic power because each one's respective capacity to effect a balance of power in Europe was declining, and because the status quo was acceptable to both states.

Britain and Russia did play different roles in the balance of power. Britain most often played the role of balancer, for example, by intervening on behalf of the Greeks in their struggle for independence from the Turks in the late 1820s, on behalf of the Belgians during their war of independence against Holland in 1830, on behalf of Turkey against Russia in the Crimean War in 1854–56 and again in the Russo-Turkish War in 1877–78. Thus Britain ensured that other states did not interfere in these conflicts and that power in Europe remained balanced. Russia's

Europe, c. 1878

role was as a builder of alliances. The Holy Alliance of 1815 kept Austria, Prussia, and Russia united against revolutionary France, and Russia used its claim on Poland to build a bond with Prussia. Russian interests in the Dardanelles, the strategic waterway linking the Mediterranean Sea and the Black Sea, and in Constantinople (today's Istanbul) overlapped with those of Britain. Thus, these two states, located at the margins of Europe, played key roles in making the balance-of-power system work.

During the last three decades of the nineteenth century, the Concert of Europe frayed, beginning with the Franco-Prussian War (1870) and the Russian invasion of Turkey (Russo-Turkish War, 1877–78). Alliances began to solidify as the balance-of-power system began to weaken. The advent of the railroad gave Continental powers such as Germany and Austria-Hungary an enhanced level of strategic mobility equal to that of maritime powers such as Britain. This reduced Britain's ability to balance power on the Continent. Russia, for its part, began to fall markedly behind in the industrialization race, and its relatively few railroads meant that its massive advantage in manpower would be less and less able to reach a battlefield in time to affect an outcome. So its power began to wane compared with that of France, Germany, and Austria-Hungary. Outside the core European region, conflict escalated. All the Central and South American states had won their independence from Spain and Portugal by 1830, and the United States and Great Britain prevented further European competition in South America.

In Focus ◎

KEY DEVELOPMENTS IN NINETEENTH-CENTURY EUROPE

- From revolutions emerge two concepts: absolutist rule subject to limitations, and nationalism.
- A system managed by the balance of power brings relative peace to Europe. Elites are united in fear of the masses, and domestic concerns are more important than foreign policy.
- European imperialism in Asia and Africa helps to maintain the European balance of power.
- The balance of power breaks down due to solidification of alliances, resulting in World War I.

The Breakdown: Solidification of Alliances

By the waning years of the nineteenth century, that balance-of-power system had weakened. Whereas previously alliances had been fluid, flexible, and changeable, now alliances had solidified. Two camps emerged: the Triple Alliance (Germany, Austria-Hungary, and Italy) in 1882 and the Dual Alliance (France and Russia) in 1893. In 1902, Britain broke from the "balancer" role, joining in a naval alliance with Japan to prevent a Russo-Japanese rapprochement in China. This alliance marked a significant turn: for the first time, a European state (Great Britain) turned to an Asian one (Japan) in order to thwart a European Power (Russia). And in 1904, Britain joined with France in the Entente Cordiale.

In that same year, Russia and Japan went to war (the Russo-Japanese War) in a contest widely expected, in Europe, to result in a Japanese defeat. After all, the Japanese had come late to industrialization, and although their naval forces looked impressive on paper, their opponents would be white Europeans. But this is where Russia's industrial backwardness was to affect it severely. The lack of railroads made it difficult for Russia to support its forces in the Far East by rail and forced Russia to attempt to relieve its besieged Port Arthur with naval forces. These forces, in turn, had to sail all the way from Russia's Baltic ports, around Cape Hope, past India, and from there into Asian waters. Russia had been a continental power with some maritime power ambitions, but in its fight with tiny Japan, its weaknesses at sea were magnified. Port Arthur was captured while the Russian relief fleet was still on its eighteen-thousand-mile journey

Europe, 1914

from its Baltic home ports. In May of 1905, the Russian and Japanese fleets met in Tsushima Bay, and the result was perhaps the greatest naval defeat in history: Russia lost eight battleships and over five thousand sailors. The Japanese, under the command of Admiral Togo, lost three torpedo boats and 116 sailors. After that, Russia was forced to sue for peace, but the importance of the Japanese victory would be far greater than the mere defeat of Russia in the Far East. The war contained important insights about killing technology (modern artillery and automatic weapons in particular) that were widely ignored by European observers. More important, the defeat of a white colonial power by an Asian power seriously compromised one of the core ideological foundations of colonialism—that "whites" were inherently superior to "nonwhites." The Russian defeat spurred Japanese expansion and caused Germany to discount Russia's ability to interfere with German ambitions in Europe. Above all, Russia's defeat severely compromised the legitimacy of the tsar, setting in motion a revolution that, after 1917, was to topple the Russian empire and replace it with the Union of Soviet Socialist Republics (USSR).

The final collapse of the balance-of-power system came with World War I. The two sides were enmeshed in a struggle made all the more dangerous by the rise of German power. Germany had not been satisfied with the solutions meted out at the Congress of Berlin after the Franco-Prussian War. By 1912 it had exceeded France and Britain in both heavy industrial output and population growth. Germany feared Russian efforts to modernize its relatively sparse railroad network. Being "latecomers" to the core of European power, many Germans felt that their nation had not received the diplomatic recognition and status it deserved. Thus, with the assassination of Archduke Franz Ferdinand, the heir to the throne of the Austro-Hungarian empire, in 1914 in Sarajevo, Germany encouraged Austria to crush Serbia. After all, Germany did not want to see its major ally disintegrate.

Under the system of alliances, once the fateful shot was fired, states honored their commitments to their allies, sinking the whole Continent in warfare. Through their support of Serbia, the unlikely allies Russia, France, and Great Britain became involved; through its support of Austria-Hungary, Germany entered the fray. In a twist of fate, the Ottoman Empire entered the war on the side of Germany and Austria-Hungary. Both sides anticipated a short, decisive war, but it was neither. Between 1914 and 1918, soldiers from more than a dozen countries endured the persistent degradation of trench warfare and the horrors of poison gas. The "Great War" saw the introduction of strategic bombing and unrestricted submarine warfare as well. Britain's naval blockade of Germany caused widespread suffering and privation for German civilians. More than 8.5 million soldiers and 1.5 million civilians lost their lives. The defeat and subsequent dismemberment of the Ottoman Empire by France and Britain—which created new states subject to control and manipulation by each—continues to affect interstate peace in the Middle East to this day.

The nineteenth century had come to a symbolic close: the century of relative peacefulness ended in a bitter colonial counterinsurgency war.

The Interwar Years and World War II

The end of World War I saw critical changes in international relations. First, three European empires were strained and finally broke up during or near the end of World War I. With those empires went the conservative social order of Europe; in its place emerged a proliferation of nationalisms. Russia exited the war in 1917, as revolution raged within its territory. The tsar was overthrown and eventually replaced by not only a new leader (Vladimir Ilyich Lenin) but a new ideology that would have profound implications for the remainder of the twentieth century. The Austro-Hungarian and Ottoman Empires also broke apart. Austria-Hungary was replaced by Austria, Hungary, Czechoslovakia, part of Yugoslavia, and part of Romania. The Ottoman Empire was also reconfigured. Having gradually lost power throughout the nineteenth century, its defeat resulted in the final overthrow of the Ottomans. Arabia rose against Turkish rule, and British forces occupied Jerusalem and Baghdad. A diminished Turkey was the successor state.

The end of the empires accelerated and intensified nationalisms. In fact, one of President Woodrow Wilson's Fourteen Points in the treaty ending World War I called for self-determination, the right of national groups to self-rule. The nationalism of these various groups (Austrians, Hungarians) had been stimulated by technological innovations in the printing industry and by a mass audience, now literate. Now it was easy and cheap to publish material in the multitude of different European languages and so offer differing interpretations of history and national life. Yet in reality, many of these newly created entities had neither shared histories nor compatible political histories, nor were they economically viable.

Second, Germany emerged out of World War I an even more dissatisfied power. Germany had been defeated on the battlefield, but German forces ended the war in occupation of enemy territory, and its leaders had not been honest with the German people. Since many German newspapers had been predicting a major breakthrough and victory right up until the armistice of November 11, the myth grew that the German military had been "stabbed in the back" by "liberals" in Berlin. Even more devastating was the fact that the Treaty of Versailles, which formally ended the war, made the subsequent generation of Germans pay the economic cost of the war through reparations—$32 billion for wartime damages. As Germany printed more money to pay its reparations, Germans suffered from hyperinflation, causing widespread impoverishment of the middle classes. Finally, Germany was no longer allowed to have a standing military, and its most productive industrialized region, the Ruhr Valley, was occupied by French and British troops. Bitterness over these excessively harsh penalties provided the climate for the emergence of Adolf Hitler, who publicly dedicated himself to righting the "wrongs" that had been imposed on the German people.

Third, enforcement of the Treaty of Versailles was given to the ultimately unsuccessful **League of Nations,** the intergovernmental organization designed to prevent all future wars. But the organization itself did not have the political weight, the legal instruments, or the legitimacy to carry out the task. The political weight of the League was weakened by the fact that the United States, whose president, Woodrow Wilson, had been the principal architect of the League, itself refused to join, retreating instead to an isolationist foreign policy. Nor did Russia join, nor were any of the vanquished of the war permitted to participate. The League's legal authority was weak, and the instruments it had for enforcing the peace proved ineffective.

Fourth, a vision of the post–World War I order had clearly been expounded, but it was a vision stillborn. That vision was spelled out in Wilson's Fourteen Points. He called for open diplomacy—"open covenants of peace, openly arrived at, after which there shall be no private international understandings of any kind but diplomacy shall proceed always frankly and in public view."[9] Point three was a reaffirmation of economic liberalism, the removal of economic barriers among all the nations consenting to the peace. And of course, the League, as a "general association of nations," was designed to ensure that war would never occur again. But that vision was not to

In Focus ◉

KEY DEVELOPMENTS IN THE INTERWAR YEARS

- Three empires collapse: Russia by revolution, the Austro-Hungarian Empire by dismemberment, and the Ottoman Empire by external wars and internal turmoil. This leads to a resurgence of nationalisms.

- German dissatisfaction with the World War I settlement leads to facism. Germany finds allies in Italy and Japan.

- A weak League of Nations is unable to respond to Japanese, Italian, and German aggression. Nor does it respond to widespread economic unrest.

be: In the words of the historian E. H. Carr, "The characteristic feature of the twenty years between 1919 and 1939 was the abrupt descent from the visionary hopes of the first decade to the grim despair of the second, from a utopia which took little account of reality to a reality from which every element of utopia was rigorously excluded."[10] Liberalism and its utopian and idealist elements were replaced by realism as the dominant international relations theory—a fundamentally divergent theoretical perspective. (Both realism and liberalism are developed in Chapter 3.)

The world from which these realists emerged was a turbulent one. The world economy collapsed; the German economy imploded; the U.S. stock market plummeted; Japan marched into Manchuria in 1931 and into the rest of China in 1937; Italy overran Ethiopia in 1935; fascism, liberalism, and communism clashed. These were the symptoms of the interwar period.

World War II

In the view of most Europeans and many in the United States, World War II was started by Germany, and in particular by Adolf Hitler. But Japan and Italy also played major roles in the breakdown of interstate order in the 1930s. In 1931, Japan staged the Mukden incident as a pretext for assaulting China and annexing Manchuria. The Japanese invasion of China was marked by horrifying barbarity against the Chinese people (including the rape, murder, and torture of Chinese civilians) and by the increasing inability of Japan's civilian government to restrain its generals in China. Japan's record in Korea was equally brutal. Japan's reputation for savagery against noncombatants in China reached its peak in the Rape of Nanking, as most historians name the six-week period following the capture of the city by Japanese forces in December 1937. At that time, Nanking was the capital of China, and the Japanese were determined to capture it. In the weeks that followed, hundreds of thousands of noncombatants were murdered by Japanese forces under unspeakable conditions. Japanese historians acknowledge the killing of 100,000 to 200,000 Chinese, but dispute the charges of murder and rape. Chinese historians have estimated the death toll at 300,000, close to the 260,000 estimated by the War Crimes Tribunal following World War II. The atrocities were made known to the rest of the world as foreign business delegations and members of religious organizations witnessed the brutality firsthand and reported it. When news of the massacres and rapes reached the United States—itself already embroiled in a dispute with Japan over its previous conduct in China—a diplomatic crisis ensued that was not resolved until the Japanese attacked the U.S. Seventh Fleet at Pearl Harbor, Hawaii four years later, and the United States declared war on Japan.

In 1935, Italy invaded Ethiopia with armored vehicles, aircraft, heavy artillery, and yperite (a form of mustard gas outlawed by the Geneva Protocol of 1925, to which Italy had been a signatory). The Ethiopians fielded elite warriors, but had very few rifles and no vehicles, and most fought barefoot. Although the Italians expected a rapid victory, the Ethiopians fought so bravely and tenaciously that they threatened to surround and cut off the invading Italian and allied Eritrean forces. But once the Italians resorted to spraying yperite on the Ethiopian soldiers from the air, their defeat was inevitable. Even so, it took Italy a full year to conquer Ethiopia and force its emperor, Haile Selassie, to flee into exile.

But Nazi Germany proved to be the greatest challenge. Rearmed under Hitler in the 1930s, buoyed by helping the Spanish fascists during the Spanish Civil War, and successful in reuniting ethnic Germans from far-flung territories, Germany was ready to right the wrongs imposed by the Treaty of Versailles. Many of these wrongs were real: Germany had been forced to accept exclusive responsibility for World War I and to pay a heavy indemnity in gold. (The reparations led to hyperinflation and the impoverishment of Germany's middle class.) It had lost Alsace, Lorraine, and East Prussia; its industrial heartland was occupied by French troops; and the armed forces it could have for its defense were severely restricted. The excessive harshness of the Versailles treaty, as well as the Great Depression and the rise of national self-determination as a powerful new norm of interstate politics enabled Germany's charismatic leader, Adolf Hitler, to rise to power and to persuade Britain (though not France) that his diplomatic aggression was aimed merely at uniting ethnic Germans into a single state. For these and other reasons (both Britain and France had been severely damaged economically by World War I), Britain and France acquiesced to Germany's resurgence. German fascism uniquely mobilized the masses in support of the state. It drew on the belief that war and conflict were noble activities from which ultimately superior civilizations would be

Europe, 1939

formed. It drew strength from the belief that certain racial groups were superior and others inferior and mobilized the disenchanted and the economically weak on behalf of its cause. In 1938, Britain agreed to let Germany occupy Czechoslovakia, in the hope of averting more general war. But this was a false hope. In September 1939, after having signed a peace treaty with the Soviet Union that divided Poland between them, German forces stormed into Poland from the west while Soviet forces assaulted from the east. Poland was quickly overcome, but because Britain and France had guaranteed Polish security, the invasion prompted a declaration of war, and World War II had begun.

The power of fascism—in German, Italian, and Japanese versions—led to an uneasy alliance between the communist Soviet Union and the liberal United States, Great Britain, and France, among others (the Allies). That alliance was intended to check the Axis powers (Germany, Italy, and Japan), by force if necessary. Thus, when World War II broke out, those fighting against the Axis powers acted in unison, regardless of their ideological disagreements.

At the end of the war, the Allies prevailed. Both the German Reich and impe-
rial Japan lay in ruins. In Europe, the Soviet Union paid the highest price for
Germany's aggression, and with some justification considered itself the victor in
Europe, with help from the United States and Britain. In the Pacific, the
United States, China, and Korea paid the highest price for Japan's aggression.
With some justification, the United States considered itself the victor in the Pacific.
Two other features of World War II demand attention as well.

First, the German military invasion of Poland, the Baltic states, and the Soviet
Union was followed by organized killing teams whose sole aim was the mass
murder of human beings, regardless of their support for or resistance to the German
state. Jews in particular were singled out, but Nazi policy extended to gypsies,
communists, and even ethnic Germans with genetic defects such as cleft palate or
club feet. In Germany, Poland, the Baltic states, Yugoslavia, and the Soviet Union,
persons on target lists were forced to abandon their homes. They were made to work
in forced-labor camps or killing pits under cruel conditions, and then either slowly
or rapidly murdered by their captors. In East Asia, Japanese forces acted with
similar cruelty against Chinese, Vietnamese, and Korean noncombatants. Victims
were often tortured or forced to become subjects in gruesome experiments before
being murdered. In many places, women were forced into army-run brothels, or
"comfort stations," as Japanese rhetoric of the day described them. The nearly
unprecedented brutality of the Axis powers against noncombatants in areas of
occupation during the war led to war crimes tribunals and, ultimately, to a major
new feature of international politics following the war: the Geneva Conventions of
1948 and 1949. These conventions—which today have the force of international
law—criminalized the many abuses (e.g., torture, murder, food deprivation)
heaped on noncombatants in areas of German and Japanese occupation during
Word War II. The conventions are collectively known as international humanitarian law (IHL); their effectiveness has often been called into question.

But German and Japanese forces were not the only forces for whom race
was a factor in Word War II. As documented by John Dower in his book
War Without Mercy, U.S. and British forces fighting in the Pacific tended to
view the Japanese as "apes" or "monkey men." As a result they were less likely
to take prisoners and more comfortable in undertaking massive strategic air
assaults on Japanese cities. In the United States, citizens of Japanese descent
were summarily interned for the duration of the war. In the Pacific theater,
in other words, racism affected the conduct and strategies of armed forces on
both sides.

Second, although Germany surrendered unconditionally in May 1945, the war
did not end until the Japanese surrender in August of that year. By this point in
the war, Japan had no hope of winning and waited only for one final effort in

defense of its homeland from an expected invasion by U.S. and possibly Soviet forces. Japan had made it clear as early as January that it might be willing to surrender, so long as the emperor Hirohito was not tried or imprisoned by Allied forces. But the Allies had already agreed they would accept no less than unconditional surrender, so Japan prepared for invasion, hoping that the threat of massive Allied casualties might yet win it a chance to preserve the emperor from trial and punishment. Instead, on August 6, the United States dropped an atomic bomb on Hiroshima and three days later a second bomb on Nagasaki. The casualties were no greater than some of those experienced in firebombings of major Japanese cities earlier that year. But the new weapon, combined with a Soviet declaration of war on Japan the same day as the Nagasaki bombing (and Japanese determination that the emperor might be spared) led to Japan's surrender on August 15, 1945.

All three Axis powers had suffered from overextension as well. In Germany and Japan, the widespread belief in the inherent racial superiority of Germans and Japanese (respectively) led both to a persistent underestimation of their adversaries and to a level of cruelty and genocide that backfired. In the steppes of western Russia and across the mountains of Yugoslavia and China, guerrilla armies—partisans and Mao Zedong's Red Army—proved an increasing drain on resources and on operations, setting the stage for a major shift in the pattern of conflicts that would soon follow.

The end of World War II resulted in a major redistribution of power. The victorious United States would now be pitted against the equally victorious Soviet Union. The war also changed political boundaries. The Soviet Union absorbed the Baltic states and portions of Finland, Czechoslovakia, Poland, and Romania; Germany and Korea were divided; and Japan was ousted from much of Asia. Each of these changes contributed to the new international conflict: the **Cold War**.

The Cold War

The leaders of the victors of World War II—Britain's prime minister Winston Churchill, the United States' president Franklin Roosevelt, and the Soviet Union's premier Joseph Stalin—planned during the war for a postwar order. Indeed, the Atlantic Charter of August 14, 1941, called for collaboration on economic issues and prepared for a permanent system of security. These plans were consolidated in 1943 and 1944 and came to fruition in the United Nations in 1945. Yet several other outcomes of World War II provided the foundation for the Cold War that followed.

Origins of the Cold War

The most important outcome of World War II was the emergence of two **superpowers**—the United States and the Soviet Union—as the primary actors in the international system and the attendant decline of Europe as the epicenter of international politics. The United States had been reluctant to fight, entering the war only after a direct attack on its territory at Pearl Harbor. For its part, the Soviet Union had had much more aggressive ambitions. In 1939 it fought two offensive wars—one against tiny Finland and one in alliance with Germany to dismember Poland. Hitler's assault on the Soviet Union in 1941 had come as a severe shock, first in its timing (too early), and second in its success (over 5 million Soviet soldiers were killed or captured between June and December 1941). But both the United States and the Soviet Union survived and rallied. By the end of the war, each had become a military superpower.

The second outcome of the war was the recognition of fundamental incompatibilities between these two superpowers in both national interests and ideology. Differences surfaced immediately over geopolitical national interests. Having been invaded from the west on several occasions, including during World War II, the USSR used its newfound power to solidify its sphere of influence in the buffer states of Eastern Europe—Poland, Czechoslovakia, Hungary, Bulgaria, and Romania. The Soviet leadership believed that ensuring friendly neighbors on its western borders was vital to the country's national interests. As for the United States, as early as 1947, policy makers argued that U.S. interests lay in containing the Soviet Union. The diplomat and historian George Kennan published in *Foreign Affairs* the famous "X" article, in which he argued that because the Soviet Union would always feel military insecurity, it would conduct an aggressive foreign policy. Containing the Soviets, Kennan wrote, should therefore become the cornerstone of the United States' postwar foreign policy.[11]

The United States put the notion of **containment** into action in the Truman Doctrine of 1947. Justifying material support in Greece against the communists, President Harry Truman asserted, "I believe that it must be the policy of the United States to support free peoples who are resisting attempted subjugation by armed minorities or by outside pressures. I believe that we must assist free peoples to work out their own destinies in their own way."[12] But almost immediately, the United States retreated from containment, drastically reducing the size of its armed forces in hopes of returning to a more peaceful world. In 1948, when the Soviets blocked western transportation corridors to Berlin, the German capital—which had been divided into sectors by the Potsdam Conference of 1945—the United States realized that its interests were broader. Thus, containment, based on U.S. geostrategic interests, became the fundamental doctrine of U.S. foreign policy during the Cold War.

The United States and the Soviet Union also had major ideological differences. These differences pitted two contrasting visions of society and of the international order against one another. The United States' democratic liberalism was based on a social system that accepted the worth and value of the individual; a political system that depended on the participation of individuals in the electoral process; and an economic system, **capitalism,** that provided opportunities to individuals to pursue what was economically rational with little or no government interference. At the international level, this logically translated into support for other democratic liberal regimes and support of capitalist institutions and processes, including, most critically, free trade.

Soviet communist ideology also influenced that country's conception of the international system and state practices. The Soviet state embraced Marxist ideology, which holds that under capitalism one class (the bourgeoisie) controls the ownership of the means of production and uses the institutions and authority of the state to maintain that control and exploit the workers, or proletariat. The solution to the problem of class rule, according to Marxism, is revolution, whereby the exploited proletariat takes control from the bourgeoisie by using the state to seize the means of production. Thus, capitalism is replaced by **socialism.** The leaders of the Soviet Union saw themselves in an interim period—after the demise of the capitalist state and before the victory of socialism. This ideology had critical international elements as well: capitalism will try to extend itself through imperialism in order to generate more capital, larger markets, and greater control over raw materials. Soviet leaders thus felt themselves surrounded by a hostile capitalist camp and argued that the Soviet Union "must not weaken but must in every way strengthen its state, the state organs, the organs of the intelligence service, the army, if that country does not want to be smashed by the capitalist environment."[13] Soviet leaders believed they must support other international movements, exporting the revolution in order to undermine world capitalism and promote the new social order in other countries.

Differences between the two superpowers were exacerbated by mutual misperceptions. Kennan cited powerful examples of misperceptions by each superpower:

The Marshall Plan, the preparations for the setting up of a West German government, and the first moves toward the establishment of NATO [the North Atlantic Treaty Organization] were taken in Moscow as the beginnings of a campaign to deprive the Soviet Union of the fruits of its victory over Germany. The Soviet crackdown on Czechoslovakia [1948] and the mounting of the Berlin blockade, both essentially defensive . . . reactions to these Western moves, were then similarly misread on the Western side. Shortly thereafter there came the crisis of the Korean War, where the Soviet attempt to employ a satellite military force in civil combat to its own advantage, by way of reaction to the American

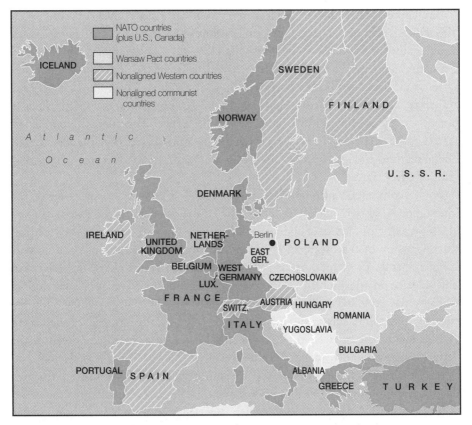

Europe during the Cold War

decision to establish a permanent military presence in Japan, was read in Washington as the beginning of the final Soviet push for world conquest; whereas the active American military response, provoked by this move, appeared in Moscow . . . as a threat to the Soviet position in both Manchuria and in eastern Siberia.[14]

Although such misperceptions did not cause the Cold War, they certainly added fuel to the confrontation.

The third outcome of the end of World War II was the collapse of the colonial system, a development few foresaw. The defeat of Japan and Germany meant the immediate end of their respective imperial empires. The other colonial powers were spurred by the UN Charter's endorsement of the principle of national self-determination, faced with the reality of their economically and politically weakened position, and confronted with newly powerful indigenous movements for independence. These movements were equipped with leftover small arms from

World War II, led by talented commanders employing indirect defense strategies such as "revolutionary" guerrilla warfare, and inspired to great self-sacrifice by the ideals of nationalism. The victorious powers granted independence to their former colonies, beginning with Britain's giving India independence in 1947. It took the military defeat of France in Indochina in the early 1950s to bring decolonization to that part of the world. African states, too, became independent between 1957 and 1963. Although the process of decolonization occurred over an extended time period, it was a relatively peaceful transition. The Europeans, together with their U.S. ally, were more interested in fighting communism than in retaining control of their colonial territories.

The fourth outcome was the realization that the differences between the two emergent superpowers would be played out indirectly, on third-party stages, rather than through direct confrontation. Both the rivals came to believe the risks of a direct military confrontation were too great. The "loss" of any potential ally, no matter how poor or distant, might begin a cumulative process leading to a significant shift in the balance of power. As the number of decolonized, newly independent states proliferated in the postwar world, the superpowers wooed these new states in order to project power to areas outside their traditional spheres of influence. Thus, the Cold War resulted in the globalization of conflict to all continents. International relations became truly global.

Other parts of the world did not merely react to Cold War imperatives. They developed new ideologies or recast the dominant discourse of Europe in ways that addressed their own experience. Nowhere was this truer than in Asia. Both Ho Chi Minh of Vietnam and Zhou Enlai of China lived in Europe for a time, where they joined communist parties. Returning home, they imported communist ideology, reinterpreting it in ways compatible with their national circumstances. For example, in China, the beginning of the communist revolution predated World War II. Taking to the countryside to build a revolution of agrarian peasants, Zhou and his colleague Mao Zedong insisted that China was a semifeudal society in which the proletariat was the rural peasantry. The Chinese Communist party became the vanguard of this group and the People's Army its instrument for guerrilla

In Focus ◎

KEY DEVELOPMENTS IN THE COLD WAR

- Two superpowers emerge—the United States and the Soviet Union. They are divided by national interests, ideologies, and mutual misperceptions. These divisions are projected into different geographic areas.

- A series of crises occurs—Berlin blockade (1948–49), Korean War (1950–53), Cuban missile crisis (1962), Vietnam War (1965–73), Soviet invasion of Afghanistan (1979).

- A long peace is sustained by mutual deterrence.

action. Mao's revolution was successful: the communists took control of mainland China in 1949 and established the People's Republic of China.

The globalization of post–World War II politics thus meant the rise of new contenders for power. Although the United States and the Soviet Union retained their dominant positions, new alternative ideologies acted as powerful magnets for populations in the independent and developing states of Africa, Asia, and Latin America. Later in the 1970s, these states advanced a new economic ideology, summarized in the program of the New International Economic Order (See Chapter 9).

The Cold War as a Series of Confrontations

The Cold War itself (1945–89) can be characterized as forty-five years of overall high-level tension and competition between the superpowers but with no direct military conflict. The advent of nuclear weapons created a deterrence stalemate, in which each side acted cautiously, only once coming close to the precipice of direct war. As nuclear technology advanced it become increasingly obvious to both sides that in a nuclear war each would be destroyed beyond hope of recovery. This state

For the United States, Vietnam became a symbol of the Cold War rivalries in Asia. In the Vietnam War, the United States supported the South Vietnamese forces against the communist regime in the North. Here, a female Vietcong guerrilla prepares to fire an anti-tank rifle during the Tet offensive of 1968.

of affairs was called "mutual assured destruction"—aptly underlined by its acronym: MAD. Each state backed down from particular confrontations, either because its national interest was not sufficiently strong to risk a nuclear confrontation or because its ideological resolve wavered in light of military realities.

The Cold War, then, was a series of events that directly or indirectly pitted the superpowers against each other. Some of those events were confrontations just short of war, whereas others were confrontations between proxies (North Korea versus South Korea, North Vietnam versus South Vietnam, Ethiopia versus Somalia) that, in all likelihood, neither the United States nor the Soviet Union had intended to escalate as they did. Still other confrontations were fought over words; these usually ended in treaties and agreements. Some of these confrontations involved only the United States and the Soviet Union, but more often than not, the allies of each became involved. Thus, the Cold War comprised not only superpower confrontations but confrontations between two blocs of states: the United States, with Canada, Australia, and much of Western Europe (allied in the **North Atlantic Treaty Organization,** or **NATO**); and the Soviet Union, with its **Warsaw Pact** allies in Eastern Europe. Over the life of the Cold War, these blocs loosened, and states sometimes took positions different from that of the dominant power. But for much of this time, bloc politics was operative. Table 2.1 shows a time line of major events related to the Cold War.

One of those high-level, direct confrontations between the superpowers took place in Germany. Germany had been divided immediately after World War II into zones of occupation. The United States, France, and Great Britain administered the western portion; the Soviet Union, the eastern. Berlin, Germany's capital, was similarly divided but lay within Soviet-controlled East Germany. In 1948, the Soviet Union blocked land access to Berlin, prompting the United States and Britain to airlift supplies for thirteen months. In 1949, the separate states of West and East Germany were declared. In 1961, East Germany erected the Berlin Wall around the West German portion of the city in order to stem the tide of East Germans trying to leave the troubled state. The U.S. president John F. Kennedy responded by visiting the city and declaring, "Ich bin ein Berliner" ("I am a Berliner"), committing the United States to the security of the Federal Republic of Germany at any cost. Not surprisingly, it was the dismantling of that same wall in November 1989 that symbolized the end of the Cold War.

The Cold War in Asia and Latin America

China, Indochina, and especially Korea became the symbols of the Cold War in Asia. In 1946, after years of bitter and heroic fighting against the Japanese occupation, communists throughout Asia rose to take control of their respective states following Japan's surrender. In China, the wartime alliance between the

TABLE 2.1

Important Events of the Cold War

YEAR	EVENT
1945–48	Soviet Union establishes communist regimes in Eastern Europe.
1947	Announcement of Truman Doctrine; United States proposes Marshall Plan for the rebuilding of Europe.
1948	Marshal Tito separates Yugoslavia from the Soviet bloc.
1948–49	Soviets blockade Berlin; United States and allies carry out airlift.
1949	Soviets test atomic bomb, ending U.S. nuclear monopoly; Chinese communists under Mao win civil war, establish People's Republic of China; United States and Allies establish NATO.
1950–53	Korean War
1953	Death of Stalin leads to internal Soviet succession crisis.
1956	Soviets invade Hungary; Nasser of Egypt nationalizes the Suez Canal, leading to confrontation with Great Britain, France, and Israel.
1957	Soviets launch *Sputnik*, symbolizing superpower scientific competition.
1960–63	Congo crisis and UN action to fill power vacuum.
1960	United States' U-2 spy plane shot down over Soviet territory, leading to the breakup of the Paris summit meeting.
1961	Bay of Pigs invasion of Cuba, sponsored by the United States, fails; Berlin Wall constructed.
1962	United States and Soviet Union brought to the brink of nuclear war following the discovery of Soviet missiles in Cuba; eventually leads to thaw in superpower relations.
1965	United States begins large-scale intervention in Vietnam.
1967	Israel defeats Egypt, Syria, and Jordan in the Six-Day War; Glassboro summit signals détente, loosening of tensions between the superpowers.
1968	Czech government liberalization halted by Soviet invasion; Nuclear Non-proliferation Treaty (NPT) signed.
1972	Nixon visits China and Soviet Union; United States and Soviet Union sign SALT I arms limitation treaty.
1973	Arab-Israeli War leads to energy crisis.

TABLE 2.1

Important Events of the Cold War (Continued)

YEAR	EVENT
1975	Proxy and anticolonial wars fought in Angola, Mozambique, Ethiopia, and Somalia. U.S. ends official military involvement in Vietnam.
1979	Shah of Iran, a U.S. ally, overthrown by Islamic revolution; United States and Soviet Union sign SALT II; Soviet Union invades Afghanistan; U.S. Senate fails to ratify SALT II.
1981–89	Reagan Doctrine provides basis for U.S. support of "anticommunist" forces in Nicaragua and Afghanistan.
1983	United States invades Grenada.
1985	Gorbachev starts economic and political reforms in Soviet Union.
1989	Peaceful revolutions in Eastern Europe replace communist governments; Berlin Wall is dismantled, Soviet Union withdraws from Afghanistan.
1990	Germany reunified.
1991	Resignation of Gorbachev; Soviet Union collapses.
1992–93	Russia and other former Soviet republics become independent states.

Kuomintang and Mao Zedong's Red Army dissolved into renewed civil war, in which the United States attempted to support the Kuomintang with large shipments of arms and military equipment. By 1949, however, the Kuomintang had been defeated, and its leaders fled to the island of Formosa (now Taiwan).

In what was then French Indochina (an amalgamation of the contemporary states of Cambodia, Laos, and Vietnam), Ho Chi Minh raised the communist flag over Hanoi, declaring Vietnam to be an independent state. The French quickly returned to take Indochina back, but though French forces fought bravely and with skill, they proved unable to uproot the communists (known as the Viet Minh). In 1954, after having laid a trap for the Viet Minh in a fortified town called Dien Bien Phu, the French were themselves trapped: sixteen thousand French legionnaires were surrounded by fifty thousand Viet Minh combat forces, aided by an additional fifty thousand support personnel. Although in broader strategic terms, the French might have absorbed the defeat at Dien Bien Phu, in France itself the loss proved the proverbial straw that broke the camel's back. France abandoned Indochina, which was then divided by a peace treaty in Paris of that same year into four political entities: Laos, Cambodia, North Vietnam, and South Vietnam.

In 1950, after North Korean leader Kim Il-Sung spent years seeking support from the USSR to unify the Korean peninsula under communist rule, Joseph Stalin finally agreed to his request for tanks, heavy artillery, and combat support aircraft to facilitate North Korea's planned assault on noncommunist South Korea. On June 25 of that year, communist North Korean troops, led by heavy tanks supplied by the USSR, sliced into a weak South Korea. The North Korean offensive quickly captured Seoul, South Korea's capital, and then forced the retreat of the few surviving South Korean and American armed forces all the way to the outskirts of the port city of Pusan. In one of the most dramatic military reversals in history, U.S. forces—now fighting for the first time under the auspices of the United Nations (which had declared North Korea's invasion an "unprovoked aggression" and a violation of international law)—landed a surprise force at Inchon. Within days they cut off and then routed the North Korean forces. By mid-October, UN forces had captured North Korea's capital, Pyongyang, and by the end of the month, the destruction of North Korea's forces was nearly complete. Yet the war did not end. Against the wishes of the U.S. president Harry Truman, General Douglas MacArthur ordered his victorious troops—now spread somewhat thin—to finish off the defeated North Koreans, who by this time were encamped very close to the border with communist China. The Chinese had warned they would intervene if their territory was approached too closely, and in November they did. The relatively poorly equipped but highly motivated Chinese soldiers attacked the UN forces, causing the longest retreat of U.S. armed forces in American history. The two sides became mired in a three-year stalemate. The fighting finally ended in an armistice in 1953. But as with the Berlin crisis, the armistice was followed over the years by numerous diplomatic skirmishes—over the basing of U.S. troops in South Korea, the use of the demilitarized zone between the north and the south, and North Korean attempts to become a nuclear power even after the end of the Cold War, the last still a source of conflict today.

The 1962 Cuban missile crisis was a high-profile direct confrontation between the superpowers in another area of the world. The United States viewed the Soviet Union's installation of missiles in Cuba as a direct threat to its territory: no weapons of a powerful enemy had ever been located so close to U.S. shores. The way in which the crisis was resolved suggests unequivocally that neither party sought a direct confrontation. The United States chose to blockade Cuba to prevent further Soviet shipments of missiles; in an important step, it rejected as first options more coercive military alternatives—land invasion or air strikes—although those options were never entirely foreclosed. Through behind-the-scenes, unofficial contacts in Washington and direct communication between President Kennedy and the Soviet premier Nikita Khrushchev, the crisis was defused and war was averted.

Vietnam provided a test of a different kind. The Cold War was played out there not in one dramatic crisis but in an extended civil war. Communist North Vietnam and its Chinese and Soviet allies were pitted against the "free world"— South Vietnam, allied with France, the United States, and assorted supporters including South Korea, the Philippines, and Thailand. To most U.S. policy makers in the late 1950s and early 1960s, Vietnam was yet another test of the containment doctrine: communist influence must be stopped, they argued, before it spread like a chain of falling dominos through the rest of Southeast Asia and beyond (hence the term **domino effect**). Thus, the United States supported the South Vietnamese dictators Ngo Dinh Diem and Nguyen Van Thieu against the rival communist regime of Ho Chi Minh in the north, which was underwritten by both the People's Republic of China and the Soviet Union. But as the South Vietnamese government and military faltered on their own, the United States stepped up its military support, increasing the number of its troops on the ground and escalating the air war over the north.

In the early stages the United States was fairly confident of victory; after all, a superpower with all its military hardware and technically skilled labor force could surely beat a poorly trained Vietcong guerrilla force. American policy makers were quickly disillusioned, however, as communist forces proved adept at avoiding the massive technical firepower of U.S. forces, and the corrupt leadership of South Vietnam siphoned away many of the crucial resources needed to win its more vital struggle for popular legitimacy. As U.S. casualties mounted, with no prospects for victory in sight, the public grew disenchanted. Should the United States use all of its conventional military capability to prevent the "fall" of South Vietnam and stave off the domino effect? Should the United States fight until victory was guaranteed for liberalism and capitalism? Or should it extricate itself from this unpopular quagmire? Should the United States capitulate to the forces of ideological communism? These questions, posed in both geostrategic and ideological terms, defined the middle years of the Cold War, from the Vietnam War's slow beginning in the late 1950s until the dramatic departure of U.S. officials from the South Vietnamese capital, Saigon, in 1975, symbolized by U.S. helicopters leaving the U.S. embassy roof while hundreds of desperate Vietnamese tried to grab on to the boarding ladders and escape with them.

The U.S. effort to avert a communist takeover in South Vietnam failed, yet contrary to expectations, the domino effect did not occur. Cold War alliances were shaken on both sides: the friendship between the Soviet Union and China had long before degenerated into a geostrategic fight and a struggle over the proper form of communism, especially in Third World countries. But the Soviet bloc was left relatively unscathed by the Vietnam War. The U.S.-led Western alliance was seriously jeopardized, as several allies (including Canada) strongly opposed U.S. policy toward Vietnam. The bipolar structure of the Cold War–era international system was coming apart. Confidence in military alternatives was shaken in the United States, undermining for over a decade the United States' ability to commit itself militarily. The power of the United States was supposed to be righteous power, but in Vietnam it was neither victorious in its outcome nor righteous in its effects.

The "Cold" in "Cold War"

It was not always the case that when one of the superpowers acted, the other side responded. In some cases, the other side chose not to act, or at least not to respond in kind, even though it might have escalated the conflict. Usually this was out of concern for escalating a conflict to a major war. For example, the Soviet Union invaded Hungary in 1956 and Czechoslovakia in 1968, both sovereign states and allies in the Warsaw Pact. The United States verbally condemned these aggressive actions by the Soviets. Under other circumstances it might have responded with counterforce, but the actions themselves went unchecked. In 1956, the United States, preoccupied with the Suez Canal crisis, kept quiet, aware that it was ill prepared to respond militarily. In 1968, the United States was mired in Vietnam and beset by domestic turmoil and a presidential election. The United States was relatively complacent, although angry, when the Soviets invaded Afghanistan in 1979. The Soviets likewise kept quiet when the United States took aggressive action within its sphere of influence, invading Grenada in 1983 and Panama in 1989. Thus, during the Cold War, even blatantly aggressive actions by one of the superpowers did not always lead to a response by the other.

Many of the events of the Cold War involved the United States and the Soviet Union only indirectly; proxies often fought in their place. Nowhere was this so true as in the Middle East. For both the United States and the Soviet Union, the Middle East was a region of vital importance, because of its natural resources (including an estimated one-third of the world's oil and more than one-half of the world's oil reserves), its strategic position as a transportation hub between Asia and Europe, and its cultural significance as the cradle of three of the world's major religions. Not surprisingly, following the establishment of Israel in 1948 and its recognition diplomatically first by the United States, the region was the scene of a superpower confrontation by proxy between the U.S.-supported Israel and the Soviet-backed Arab states Syria, Iraq, and Egypt. During the Six-Day War in 1967, Israel crushed the Soviet-equipped Arabs in six short days, seizing the strategic territories of the Golan Heights, Gaza, and the West Bank. During the Yom Kippur War of 1973, which the Egyptians had planned as a limited war, the Israeli victory was not so overwhelming, because the United States and the Soviets negotiated a cease-fire before more damage could be done. But throughout the Cold War, these "hot" wars were followed by guerrilla actions supported by all parties. As long as the basic balance of power was maintained between Israel (and the United States) on one side and the Arabs (and the Soviets) on the other, the region was left alone; when that balance was threatened, the superpowers acted through proxies to maintain the balance. Other controversies plagued the region, as evidenced by events after the end of the Cold War.

In parts of the world that were of less strategic importance, confrontation through proxies was even more the modus operandi during the Cold War. Africa presents numerous examples of such events. When the colonialist Belgians abruptly left the Congo in 1960, a power vacuum arose. Civil war broke out, as various contending factions sought to take power and bring order out of the chaos. One of the contenders, the Congolese premier Patrice Lumumba (1925–61), appealed to the Soviets for help in fighting the Western-backed insurgents and received both diplomatic support and military supplies. However, Lumumba was dismissed by the Congolese president, Joseph Kasavubu, an ally of the United States. Still others, such as Moise Tshombe, leader of the copper-rich Katanga province, who was also closely identified with Western interests, fought for control. The three-year civil war could have become another protracted proxy war between the United States and the Soviet Union for influence in this emerging continent. However, the United Nations averted a proxy confrontation by sending in peacekeepers, whose primary purpose was to fill the vacuum and prevent the superpowers from making the Congo yet another arena of the Cold War.

In both Angola and the Horn of Africa (Ethiopia and Somalia), however, participants in civil wars were able to transform their struggles into Cold War confrontations by proxy, thereby gaining military equipment and technical expertise from one or other of the superpowers. Such proxy warfare served the interests of the superpowers, permitting them to project power and support geostrategic interests (oil in Angola, transportation routes around the Horn) and ideologies without directly confronting one another.

The Cold War was also fought and moderated in words, at **summits** (meetings between leaders) and in treaties. Some Cold War summits were relatively successful: the 1967 Glassboro summit (between U.S. and Soviet leaders) began the loosening of tensions known as **détente**, but the meeting between President Dwight Eisenhower and Premier Nikita Khrushchev in Vienna in 1960 ended abruptly when the Soviets shot down a U.S. U-2 spy plane over Soviet territory. Treaties between the two parties placed self-imposed limitations on nuclear arms. For example, the first Strategic Arms Limitations Treaty (SALT I), in 1972, placed an absolute ceiling on the numbers of intercontinental ballistic missiles (ICBMs), deployed nuclear warheads, and multiple independently targetable reentry vehicles (MIRVs); and limited the number of antiballistic missile sites maintained by each superpower. So the superpowers did enjoy periods of accommodation, when they could agree on principles and policies.

The Cold War as a Long Peace

It is important to note that the term *Cold War* is itself largely an artifact of a European bias. World War III—a war widely anticipated to be as destructive in comparison to World War II as World War II had been in comparison to World War I—did not happen; or at least not in Europe. But as many as 40 million human beings lost their lives in the proxy and other wars that were fought in Asia, Africa, and Latin America from 1945 to 1991. So how "cold" the Cold War truly was is largely a matter of perspective.

That said, if the Cold War is largely remembered as a series of crises and some direct and indirect confrontations, what explains the "cold" in Cold War or, as the diplomatic historian John Lewis Gaddis prefers, the "long peace"? The term itself was meant to dramatize the remarkable and unexpected absence of major wars among great powers during the Cold War. Just as major interstate war was averted in nineteenth-century Europe, so too has it been avoided since World War II. Why?

Gaddis attributes the long peace to five factors, no single explanation being sufficient. Probably the most widely accepted explanation revolves around the role of nuclear **deterrence**. Once both the United States and the Soviet Union had acquired nuclear weapons, neither was willing to use them, because their very deployment jeopardized both states' existence. This argument will be elaborated further in Chapter 8. Another explanation attributes the long peace to the roughly equal division of power between the United States and the Soviet Union. Such a parity of power led to stability in the international system, as will be explained in Chapter 4. However, because the advent of nuclear weapons occurred simultaneously with the emergence of the bipolar system, it is impossible to disentangle one explanation from the other.

A third explanation for the long peace is the stability imposed by the hegemonic economic power of the United States. Being in a superior economic position for much of the Cold War, the United States willingly paid the price of maintaining stability. It provided military security for Japan and much of northern Europe, and its currency was the foundation of the international monetary system. Yet although this argument explains why the United States acted to enhance postwar economic stability, it does not explain Soviet actions.

A fourth explanation gives credit for maintaining the peace not to either of the superpowers but to economic liberalism. During the Cold War, the liberal economic order solidified and became a dominant factor in international relations. Politics became **transnational** under liberalism—based on interests and coalitions across traditional state boundaries—and thus great powers became increasingly obsolete. Cold War peace can therefore be attributed to the dominance of economic liberalism.

Finally, Gaddis explores the possibility that the long peace of the Cold War was predetermined, as simply one phase in a long historical cycle of peace and war. He argues that every one hundred to one hundred fifty years, war occurs on a global scale; these cycles are driven by uneven economic growth. This explanation suggests that the Cold War is but one event in a long cycle, and specific events or conditions occurring during the Cold War have no explanatory power.[15]

Whatever the "right" combination of explanations, the international relations theorist Kenneth N. Waltz has noted the irony of the long peace: both the United States and the Soviet Union, "two states, isolationist by tradition, untutored in the ways of international politics, and famed for impulsive behavior, soon showed themselves—not always and everywhere, but always in crucial cases—to be wary, alert, cautious, flexible, and forbearing."[16] The United States and the Soviet Union, wary and cautious of one another, also became predictable and familiar to one another. Common interests in economic growth and system stability overcame their long-adversarial relationship.

The Post–Cold War Era

The fall of the Berlin Wall in 1989 symbolized the end of the Cold War, but actually its end was gradual. The Soviet premier at the time, Mikhail Gorbachev, and other Soviet reformers had set in motion two domestic processes—*glasnost* (political openness) and *perestroika* (economic restructuring)—as early as the mid-1980s. *Glasnost*, combined with a new technology—the videocassette player—made it possible for the first time since the October Revolution for average Soviet citizens to compare their living standards with those of their Western counterparts. The comparison proved dramatically unfavorable. It also opened the door to criticism of the political system, culminating in the emergence of a multiparty system and the massive reorientation of the once-monopolistic Communist party. *Perestroika* undermined the foundation of the planned economy, an essential part of the communist system. At the outset, Gorbachev and his reformers sought to save the system, but once initiated, these reforms led to the dissolution of the Warsaw Pact, Gorbachev's resignation in December 1991, and the disintegration of the Soviet Union itself in 1992–93.

Gorbachev's domestic reforms also led to changes in the orientation of Soviet foreign policy. Needing to extricate the country from the political quagmire and economic drain of the war in Afghanistan while seeking to save face, Gorbachev suggested that the permanent members of the UN Security Council "could become guarantors of regional security."[17] Afghanistan was a test case, where a small group of UN observers monitored and verified the withdrawal of more than one hundred thousand Soviet troops in 1988 and 1989—an action that would have

Explaining the End of the Cold War: A View from the Former Soviet Union

Many scholars of American diplomatic history attribute the end of the Cold War to policies initiated by the United States: the build-up of a formidable military capable of winning either a nuclear or a conventional war against the Soviet Union; the development of the strongest, most diversified economy the world has ever known. However, within the Soviet Union, the events leading to the end of the Cold War were perceived differently.

The predominant viewpoint in the former Soviet Union is that the explanation for the end of the Cold War can be found in a very long and complex chain of *internal*, domestic developments in the Soviet Union itself. Those political, economic, and demographic factors led to what seemed to be an abrupt disintegration of the Soviet Union and hence the end of the Cold War. International relations theorists did not predict it; perhaps they were not looking at domestic factors within the Soviet state itself and did not have a sufficiently long historical perspective.

The political dominance and authority of the Communist Party, the main ideological pillar of the Soviet Union, had significantly eroded by the late 1980s. The revelation of Joseph Stalin's horrific crimes against the Soviet people, especially ethnic minorities, intensified animosity in the far-flung parts of the Soviet empire. Many of the smaller republics and subnational regions bore a grudge against the central government for forced Russification, the resettlement of certain minorities from the 1930s to the 1950s, and other atrocities such as induced famines in Russia and Ukraine in the early 1930s. Increasingly open discussion of such events undermined the ideological fervor of the common population and shook their trust in the "people's government."

During the 1960s, some Soviet leaders saw stagnation in the spheres of economy, technology, and agriculture. Internal critics of the regime blamed the top-level political leadership, which had become ossified. The policy of lifelong appointments to leading posts, which remained in effect until the mid-1980s, meant that political appointees stayed in their posts for twenty or more years, regardless of their performance. There were few efforts to reform and modernize the system, and younger people had little opportunity to exercise political leadership. These failures in leadership, exemplified in the poor economy, led to widespread discontent and resentment in all layers of the society.

Moreover, the Soviet Union was a very ethnically diverse state, consisting of fifteen major republics, some of which also contained the "autonomous" republics and regions, inhabited by hundreds of ethnicities. Although the Soviet Union had benefitted economically from extracting resources found in the far reaches of its territories, the costs of keeping the empire together were high. Subsidies flowed to the outer regions at the expense of the Soviet state. With growing economic discontent and the erosion of the ideology promoted by the Communist Party, local nationalist movements started to fill the ideological vacuum by the late 1980s.

Before the mid-1980s, the inherent distortions and inefficiencies of the Soviet planned economy were partially offset by the profits from the energy sector based on oil and gas exports. However, the Soviet industrial and agricultural

The rapid dissolution of the Eastern bloc led to a dramatic shift in the balance of power in the international system. Rising nationalist movements and local liberal forces gained momentum and won significant representation in the local parliaments after the first competitive elections in the former Socialist republics. Eventually, Russia became one of the first to declare independence and affirm sovereignty, with the rest of the republics following suit in the "sovereignty parade" in 1991. The de facto dissolution of the Soviet Union marked an important (final?) chapter in the history of the Cold War.

sectors lagged behind, inefficient and uncompetitive. Technological development stagnated, too. The sharp decline in world oil prices in the 1980s compounded the problems. The resulting rationing of basic food products and the poor quality of domestically manufactured products totally discredited the socialist economic model and added to the general discontent. The declining state budget could no longer bear the burden of the arms race with the United States, finance an expensive war in Afghanistan, and keep the increasingly fractured empire within its orbit.

The interplay of all these factors came to a climax when Mikhail Gorbachev (pictured above) took power in 1985. Acknowledging the urgent need for change, he launched ambitious domestic reforms collectively referred to as *perestroika,* literally, "restructuring" of economic relations, including stepping back from central planning and curbing government subsidies. *Glasnost* was the political component, an "opening" that relaxed censorship and encouraged democratization. In foreign policy, "New Thinking" meant improving relations with the United States and the possibility of the coexistence of the capitalist and socialist systems through shared human values. The underlying reasons for most of these domestic changes were economic. Reducing military expenditures and gaining access to Western loans became critical for the survival of the troubled state.

For Critical Analysis

Answer these questions on wwnorton.com/studyspace

1. *How would a realist refute the Soviet view of why the Cold War ended?*

2. *Radicals are economic determinists. To what extent is the Soviet explanation of the end of the Cold War a confirmation of radical theories?*

3. *Constructivists explain the end of the Cold War by referring to changes in ideas. How did the ideas held by the Soviet elite change?*

been impossible during the height of the Cold War. Similarly, the Soviets agreed to and supported the 1988 withdrawal of Cuban troops from Angola. The Soviet Union had retreated from international commitments near its borders, as well as others farther abroad. Most important, the Soviets agreed to cooperate in multilateral activities to preserve regional security.

These changes in Soviet policy and the eventual demise of the empire itself mark the beginning of the post–Cold War era and are the subject of much study in international relations today. What explains these remarkable changes? Did the West's preparations for war or its strong alliance system force the Soviet Union into submission? Were Western power and policy responsible for the USSR's demise and thus the end of the Cold War? Did Western military strength convince the Soviets to become less bellicose and less threatening? Or did events within the Soviet Union itself lead to its end? Was it the fault of communism, an impractical economic structure? Was it due to the resistance of those who opposed communism in Soviet domestic politics? Was it the fact that communism not only failed to deliver on its promises but actually resulted in more poverty and more political repression? Or was it the failure of the Soviet bureaucratic system that led to the country's ultimate disintegration? Did the United States, too, exhaust its capacity to carry on global confrontation, as Russian realist theorists contend? No single answer suffices; elements of each played a role.

The first post–Cold War test of the so-called new world order came in response to Iraq's invasion and annexation of Kuwait in August 1990. Despite its long-standing relationship with Iraq, the Soviet Union (and later Russia), along with the four other permanent members of the UN Security Council, agreed first to take economic sanctions against Iraq. Then they agreed in a Security

In Focus ◎

KEY DEVELOPMENTS IN THE POST-COLD WAR ERA

- Changes are made in Soviet/Russian foreign policy, with the withdrawals from Afghanistan and Angola in the late 1980s, monitored by the United Nations.

- Iraqi invasion of Kuwait in 1990 and the multilateral response unite the former Cold War adversaries.

- *Glasnost* and *perestroika* continue in Russia, as reorganized in 1992-93.

- The former Yugoslavia disintegrates into independent states; civil war ensues in Bosnia and Kosovo, leading to UN and NATO action.

- Widespread ethnic conflict arises in central and western Africa, Central Asia, and the Indian subcontinent.

- Al Qaeda terrorist network commits terrorist acts against the homeland of the United States and U.S. interests abroad; U.S. and coalition forces respond militarily in Afghanistan and Iraq.

- Terrorist attacks occur in Saudi Arabia, Spain, and Great Britain.

Council resolution to support the means to restore the status quo—to oust Iraq from Kuwait with a multinational military force. Finally, they supported sending the UN Iraq-Kuwait Observer Mission to monitor the zone and permitted the UN to undertake humanitarian intervention and create safe havens for the Kurdish and Shiite populations of Iraq. Although forging a consensus on each of these actions (or in the case of China, convincing it to abstain) was difficult, the coalition held, a unity unthinkable during the Cold War.

The end of the Cold War denotes a major change in international relations, the end of one historical era and the beginning of another, which a few scholars have labeled the age of globalization. The overwhelming military power of the United States, combined with its economic power, appeared to many to usher in an era of U.S. primacy in international affairs to a degree not matched even by the Romans or Alexander the Great. The United States seemed able to impose its will on other states even against the strong objections of its allies. Yet this moment of primacy appears doubtful today; it proved insufficient to deter or prevent ethnic conflict, civil wars, and human rights abuses from occurring.

The 1990s were marked by the struggle of former allies and enemies to find new identities (and attached interests) in a world bereft of the certainties and simplicities of the Cold War. As the threat of World War III vanished, what was the purpose of an organization such as NATO? What was the purpose or focus of state foreign policy to be if not the deterrence of aggression by other states? The United States and Israel, for example, were unparalleled in their capacity to fight and win interstate wars. But who might these other states be? What role might armed forces specialized to win interstate wars play in substate violence? Yugoslavia's violent disintegration played itself out over the entire decade despite Western attempts to resolve the conflict peacefully. At the same time, the world witnessed ethnic tension and violence in the Great Lakes region of central Africa. Genocide in Rwanda and Burundi was effectively ignored by the international community. And despite U.S. military primacy, Russia maintains enough military power and political influence to prevent U.S. intervention in ethnic hostilities in the Transcaucasus region.

These dual realities converged and diverged throughout the 1990s and continue to do so today. The disintegration of Yugoslavia culminated in an American-led war against Serbia to halt attacks on the ethnic Albanian population in Kosovo. Despite European hesitancy to engage militarily and the inability to obtain a UN resolution supporting military action, the United States drove NATO to intervene. The seventy-eight-day air war against Serb forces in Kosovo ended with the capitulation of the Serbs and the turning over of the province of Kosovo to UN administration. The war also severely challenged core principles of international law: technically, the action of NATO in Kosovo was a violation of Serbian sovereignty. Yet NATO's leaders cited Serb rapes, lootings, and murders constituted a greater harm, arguing that the harm of violating the principle of sovereignty was less than the harm of allowing Serbia to murder and torture Kosovar Albanians. The repercussions of the Kosovo precedent continue to affect interstate politics to this day.

But the biggest change in interstate politics following the end of the Cold War was the elevation of terrorism—once a relatively minor threat—from a law-enforcement problem to a vital national security interest (and therefore a military problem). On September 11, 2001, the world witnessed deadly, psychologically devastating, and economically disruptive terrorist attacks organized and funded by Al Qaeda against New York and Washington, D.C. These attacks, directed by Osama bin Laden, set into motion a U.S.-led global "war on terrorism." Buoyed by an outpouring of support from around the world and by the first-ever invocation of Article V of the NATO Charter, which declares an attack on one NATO member to be an attack on all, the United States undertook to lead an ad hoc coalition to combat terrorist organizations with global reach. This new **war on terrorism** combines many elements into multiple campaigns with different foci in different countries. Many countries have arrested known terrorists and their supporters and frozen their monetary assets. The United States fought a war in Afghanistan to oust the Taliban regime, which was providing safe haven to Osama bin Laden's Al Qaeda organization and a base from which it freely planned, organized, and trained operatives to carry out a global terror campaign against the United States and its allies.

Following an initially successful campaign in Afghanistan in 2001 and 2002 that specifically targeted terrorists and their supporters and paved the way for popular elections in that country, the United States broke from its allies. Convinced that Iraq maintained a clandestine **weapons of mass destruction (WMD)** program and posed a continued threat through backing terrorist organizations, the United States attempted to build support in the United Nations for authorization to remove Saddam Hussein forcibly from power and find the hidden WMD. When the United Nations refused to back this request, the United States built its own coalition along with Great Britain, destroyed the Iraqi military, and overthrew Iraq's government. No weapons of mass destruction were found, but additional justifications included promoting democracy for Iraq's three main component peoples—Kurds, Sunni Arabs, and Shia Arabs—within a single state. The fight in Iraq continues today, although Hussein himself was executed in 2006 and U.S. troops have begun a gradual withdrawal.

Even after the economic downturn following the September 11 terrorist attacks and the financial crisis that developed in 2008, the U.S. military and economy remain the strongest in the world. Yet despite this strength, the United States does not feel secure from attack. The global war against terrorism is far from over and appears no nearer to victory. The issue of whether U.S.

power will be balanced by an emerging power (or coalition of powers) is also far from resolved. The war in Afghanistan has once again become a major source of concern, threatening to replace the Iraq War as a major expenditure of both cash and casualties.

For all states in the post–Cold War world, the major issue moving forward is, *Toward what ends should we devote our national energies, military, economic, cultural, diplomatic, and political*? In the case of the United States, the original "destiny" of taming the great frontier was finished by 1900. Soon after, the United States found a new national purpose as a successor to Britain in its role as guardian of freedom of the seas, maritime commerce, and offshore balances. This reluctant engagement abroad led ultimately to intervention in World War II. Following the war, the U.S. national purpose shifted to the rather dismal aim of "containment" of communism. Now what? Will containing or rooting out terrorism become the new national aim of states? Will it be preventing global environmental catastrophe? Other states like China, India, and those in the European Union are also struggling with the task of finding a new purpose; and as the twenty-first century advances, the nature of these purposes are far from clear.

In Sum: Learning from History

Will the post–Cold War world be characterized by increasing cooperation among the great powers, or will the era be one of conflict among states and over new ideas? Does the post–Cold War era signal a return to the **multipolar** system of the nineteenth century? Or is the entire concept of polarity an anachronism? How can we begin to predict how the current era will best be characterized or what the future will bring? How will changing state identities affect the interests and capabilities of states moving forward?

We have taken the first step toward answering these questions by looking to the past. Our examination of the development of contemporary international relations has focused on how core concepts of international relations have emerged and evolved over time, most notably the state, sovereignty, the nation, and the international system. These concepts, developed within a specific historical context, provide the building blocks for contemporary international relations. The state is well established, but its sovereignty may be eroding from without (Chapters 7, 9, 10) and from within (Chapter 5). The principal characteristics of the contemporary international system are in the process of changing with the end of the **bipolarity** of the Cold War (Chapter 4).

To help us understand the trends of the past and how those trends influence contemporary thinking and to predict future developments, we turn to theory.

Theory gives order to analysis; it provides generalized explanations for specific events. In Chapter 3 we will look at competing theories of international relations. These theories view the past from quite different perspectives.

DISCUSSION QUESTIONS

1. The Treaties of Westphalia are often viewed as the beginning of modern international relations. Why are they a useful benchmark? What factors does this benchmark ignore?

2. Colonization by the great powers of Europe has officially ended. However, the effects of the colonial era linger. Explain with specific examples.

3. The Cold War has ended. Discuss two current events where Cold War politics persists.

4. The developments of international relations as a discipline has been closely identified with the history of Western Europe and the United States. With this civilizational bias, what might we be missing?

KEY TERMS

balance of power, p. 33
bipolarity, p. 63
capitalism, p. 45
Cold War, p. 43
colonialism, p. 30
containment, p. 44
détente, p. 55
deterrence, p. 56
domino effect, p. 53
hegemon, p. 33
imperialism, p. 30
League of Nations, p. 38
legitimacy, p. 24
multipolar, p. 63

nation, p. 25
nationalism, p. 24
North Atlantic Treaty Organization
   (NATO), p. 49
socialism, p. 45
sovereignty, p. 21
summits, p. 55
superpowers, 44
transnational, p. 56
Treaties of Westphalia, p. 22
war on terrorism, p. 62
Warsaw Pact, p. 49
weapons of mass destruction
   (WMD), p. 62

 Find chapter outlines, practice quizzes, flashcards, and other study and review material for this chapter at wwnorton.com/studyspace.

03

Contending Perspectives

HOW TO THINK ABOUT INTERNATIONAL RELATIONS THEORETICALLY

- What is the value of studying international relations from a theoretical perspective?
- Why do scholars pay attention to the levels-of-analysis problem?
- What are the major theoretical underpinnings of realism and neorealism? Of liberalism and neoliberal institutionalism? Of radicalism? Of constructivism?
- Can you analyze a contemporary event by using theoretical perspectives?

Thinking Theoretically

HOW CAN THEORY HELP us make sense of international relations? In this chapter we will use the example of the 2003 Iraq War to explore major international relations theories and their explanations for political events. Why did the United States and its coalition partners invade Iraq? Why did Iraq continue to refuse to comply with the demands of the international community? We need to begin by examining the historical record. That provides the key context for understanding the actions of the United States.

The international community was concerned about Saddam Hussein's behavior, Iraq's weapons, and the possibility that Saddam was supporting international

The destruction of a statue of Saddam Hussein in Baghdad became a symbol of his regime's defeat in 2003 by a U.S.-led coalition. Theory can help us understand why Saddam risked war with a more powerful country, and why the U.S. chose to invade Iraq.

terrorist activities, especially after his ouster of UN weapons inspectors from Iraq in 1998. Following the September 11, 2001, attacks on U.S. territory, that concern became urgent. In his 2002 State of the Union address, President George W. Bush included Iraq in what he described as an "axis of evil." The administration subsequently lobbied for UN resolutions during the fall of 2002 to have Iraq declared in material breach of prior UN resolutions. Although successful in convincing the UN Security Council to declare a material breach, the United States was unable to muster support for a UN-authorized military action against Iraq. In March 2003, the United States went ahead without such authorization and launched a military attack against Iraq. Three weeks later, the Iraqi regime fell, and the United States imposed temporary rule over Iraq. Table 3.1 lists the major events of the crisis and the war.

This examination of history shows that the United States was motivated by several factors: regret at not having ousted Saddam in the 1991 Gulf War; the possibility that the regime possessed weapons of mass destruction; concern that Saddam's regime was involved in both domestic and international terrorism; the need for stability in the oil-rich state; and the hope that a democratic Iraq could be the centerpiece of a new liberal democratic order in the Middle East. Similarly, to

TABLE 3.1

Major Events Leading Up to and of the 2003 Iraq War

DATE	EVENT
SEPTEMBER 11, 2001	Terrorist attacks against the World Trade Center and the Pentagon are answered by an immediate commitment by the U.S. government to fight global terrorism and punish those responsible.
OCTOBER 7, 2001	United States strikes targets in Afghanistan in order to oust the Taliban, whose government harbors Al Qaeda terrorists.
NOVEMBER 14, 2001	United States announces ouster of Taliban from power in Afghanistan.
JANUARY 29, 2002	President George W. Bush labels Iraq, Iran, and North Korea members of an "axis of evil" threatening world peace.
OCTOBER 2, 2002	U.S. Congress authorizes the president to use U.S. armed forces against Iraq.
OCTOBER 8, 2002	UN resolution holds Iraq in material breach of previous resolutions.
MARCH 2003	United States stops trying to fashion a UN resolution authorizing use of military force, acknowledging failure to get approval of five permanent members of the Security Council.
MARCH 17, 2003	United States issues a forty eight-hour ultimatum for the Baathist regime and its leader, Saddam Hussein, to leave Iraq.
MARCH 19, 2003	Decapitation attack is launched against Saddam. U.S. Special Operations forces enter Iraq, followed by the movement of coalition ground forces into Iraq.
APRIL 9, 2003	Iraqi regime falls.
APRIL 2003–PRESENT	Efforts continue to establish security amid resistance to U.S. presence and sectarian violence.

understand Iraq's refusal to comply with international demands, we must understand the roots of its strong nationalism, its history of being controlled by Western colonialists, and a Saddam Hussein who augmented his power and legitimacy by standing up to the West. Theories will help explain more generally why these events occurred. Yet the stronger the theory, the more seemingly unrelated or unique cases it can explain.

A **theory** is a set of propositions and concepts that seeks to explain phenomena by specifying the relationships among the concepts; theory's ultimate purpose is to predict phenomena. Good theory generates groups of testable **hypotheses**: specific statements positing a particular relationship among two or more variables. By testing groups of interrelated hypotheses, theory is supported and refined, and new relationships are found that demand subsequent testing.

Moving from description to explanation to theory and from theory to testable hypotheses is not a unilinear process. Although theory depends on a logical deduction of hypotheses from assumptions and a testing of the hypotheses as more and more data are collected in the empirical world, theories have to be revised or adjusted. This is, in part, a creative exercise, in which we must be tolerant of ambiguity, concerned about probabilities, and distrustful of absolutes.

International relations theories come in a variety of forms. In this chapter, we introduce four general theories, or theoretical perspectives, in the study of international relations: realism (and neorealism); liberalism (and its newest variant, neoliberal institutionalism), and radical theory (in this case, Marxism). We also introduce constructivism as one of the newest theoretical perspectives in international relations. Before we examine these theories more closely, we should consider the various levels at which we can analyze events and trends.

Theory and the Levels of Analysis

Why did the United States and its coalition partners invade Iraq in 2003? The list of possible explanations can be organized according to three **levels of analysis** (see Figure 3.1). There are good reasons to pay attention to levels of analysis. They help orient our questions and suggest the appropriate type of evidence to explore. Paying attention to levels of analysis helps us make logical deductions and enables us to explore all categories of explanation.

In a categorization first used by Kenneth Waltz and amplified by J. David Singer, three different sources of explanations are offered. If the *individual level* is the focus, then the personality, perceptions, choices, and activities of individual decision makers (Saddam Hussein and George W. Bush) and individual participants (Defense Secretary Donald Rumsfeld, Saddam's sons) provide the explanation. If the *state level*, or domestic factors, are the focus, then the explanation is derived from characteristics of the state: the type of government (democracy or authoritarianism), the type of economic system (capitalist or socialist), interest groups within the country, or even the national interest. If the *international system level* is the focus, then the explanation rests with the anarchic characteristics of that system or with international and regional organizations and their strengths and weaknesses.[1]

Box 3.1 categorizes possible explanations of the conflict according to these three levels of analysis. Of course, explanations from all three levels probably contributed to the United States' decision to invade Iraq in 2003. The purpose of theory is to

FIGURE 3.1 | **Levels of Analysis in International Relations**

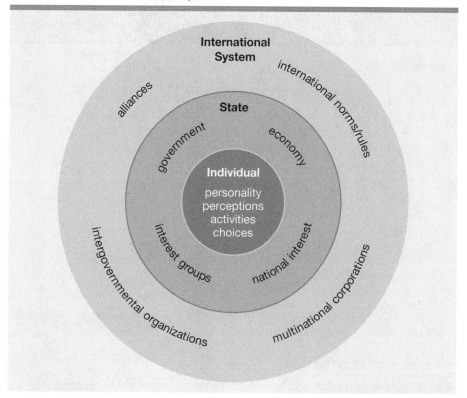

guide us toward an understanding of which of these various explanations are the necessary and sufficient explanations for the invasion.

Although all scholars acknowledge the utility of paying attention to levels of analysis, they differ on how many levels are useful in explaining events. Most political scientists apply between three and six levels. Although adding more layers may provide more descriptive context, it makes explanation and prediction more problematic. The most important differentiation in theory must be made between the international level and the domestic level. In this book we will use the three levels explained above: individual, state, and international system.

Good theory, then, should be able to explain phenomena at a particular level of analysis; better theory should also offer explanations across different levels of analysis. The general theories outlined in the rest of this chapter are all comprehensive, meaning they incorporate all three levels of analysis. Yet each of the theories is not so simple or so unified as presented. Many authors have introduced variations, modifications, and problematics, and have even changed positions over time. Thus, the theories are discussed only in terms of their essential characteristics.

BOX 3.1

Possible Explanations for the United States' Invasion of Iraq in 2003 by Level of Analysis

INDIVIDUAL LEVEL

1. Saddam Hussein was an evil leader who committed atrocities against his own people and defied the West.
2. Saddam Hussein was irrational, otherwise he would have capitulated to the superior capability of the U.S. and British coalition.
3. George W. Bush and his advisers targeted Saddam Hussein and Iraq in 2001.

STATE LEVEL

4. The United States must protect its national security, and Iraq's weapons of mass destruction threatened U.S. security.
5. Ousting the Taliban from Afghanistan was only the first step in the war on terrorism; Iraq, a known supporter of terrorism, was the second.
6. The United States must be assured of a stable oil supply, and Iraq has the world's second largest reserves.
7. The United States must not permit states that support terrorism or terrorist groups access to destructive weapons.
8. It is in the U.S. national interest to build a progressive Arab regime in the region.

INTERNATIONAL SYSTEM LEVEL

9. UN resolutions condemning Iraq had to be enforced in order to maintain the legitimacy of the United Nations.
10. A unipolar international system is uniquely capable of responding to perceived threats to the stability of the system, and the U.S. invasion was one manifestation of this capability.
11. There is an international moral imperative for humanitarian intervention—to oust evil leaders and install democratic regimes.

Realism and Neorealism

Realism is the product of a long historical and philosophical tradition, even though its direct application to international affairs is of more recent vintage. Realism is based on a view of the individual as primarily fearful, selfish and power seeking. Individuals are organized in states, each of which acts in a unitary way in pursuit of its own **national interest,** defined in terms of power. "Power," in turn, is primarily thought of in terms of the material resources necessary to physically harm or coerce other states: to fight and win wars. These states exist in an anarchic international system, a characterization in which the term anarchy is meant to highlight the absence of an authoritative hierarchy. Under this condition of anarchy, states in the international system can rely only on themselves. Their most important concern, then, is to manage their insecurity, which arises out of the anarchic system. They rely primarily on balancing the power of other states and on deterrence to keep the international system intact and as nonthreatening as possible.

At least four of the essential assumptions of realism are found in Thucydides' *History of the Peloponnesian War.*[2] First, for Thucydides, the state (Athens or Sparta) is the *principal actor* in war and in politics in general, just as latter-day realists posit. Although other actors, such as international institutions, may participate, their impact on the system is marginal.

Second, the state is assumed to be a **unitary actor.** Although Thucydides includes fascinating debates among different officials from the same state, he argues that once a decision is made to go to war or capitulate, the state speaks and acts with one voice. There are no subnational actors trying to overturn the decision of the government or subvert the interests of the state.

Third, decision makers acting in the name of the state are assumed to be **rational actors.** Like most educated Greeks, Thucydides believed that individuals are essentially rational beings and that they make decisions by weighing the strengths and weaknesses of various options against the goal to be achieved. Thucydides admitted that there are potential impediments to rational decision making, including wishful thinking on the part of leaders, confusing intentions and national interests, and misperceptions about the characteristics of the counterpart decision maker. But the core notion—that rational decision making leads to the pursuit of the national interest—remains. Likewise for modern realists, rational decisions advance the national interest—the interests of the state—however ambiguously that national interest is formulated.

Fourth, Thucydides, like contemporary realists, was concerned with security issues—the state's need to protect itself from enemies both foreign and domestic. A state augments its security by increasing its domestic capacities, building up its economic prowess, and forming alliances with other states based on similar interests. In fact, Thucydides found that before and during the Peloponnesian War, it was fear of a rival that motivated states to join alliances, a rational decision on the part of the leader. In the Melian dialogue, perhaps the most famous section of *History of the Peloponnesian War,* Thucydides posed the classic dilemma between realist and liberal thinking: "[T]he strong do what they can and the weak suffer what they must." More generally, do states have rights based on the conception of an international ethical or moral order, as liberals suggest? Or is a state's power, in the absence of an international authority, the deciding factor?

Thucydides did not identify all the tenets of what we think of as realism today. Indeed, the tenets and rationale of realism have unfolded over centuries, and not all realists agree on what they are. For example, six centuries after Thucydides lived, the Christian bishop and philosopher Saint Augustine (354–430) added a fundamental assumption of realism, arguing that humanity is flawed, egoistic, and selfish, although not predetermined to be so. Augustine blames war on this basic characteristic of humanity.[3] Although subsequent realists dispute Augustine's biblical explanation for humanity's flawed, selfish nature, few realists dispute the fact that humans are basically power seeking and self-absorbed.

The implications of humanity's flawed nature for the state are developed further in the writings of the Italian political philosopher Niccolò Machiavelli (1469–1527). In *The Prince*, Machiavelli elucidated the qualities that a leader needs to maintain the strength and security of the state. He argued that a leader needs to be ever mindful of threats to his personal security and the security of the state. Machiavelli promoted the use of alliances and various offensive and defensive strategies to protect the state.[4]

The central tenet accepted by virtually all realist theorists is that the chief constraint on "better" state behavior—especially enduring peace—is that states exist in an anarchic international system. This tenet was forcefully articulated by Thomas Hobbes (see Chapter 1). Hobbes, who lived and wrote during one of history's greatest periods of turmoil (the Thirty Years War, 1618–48) and the English Civil Wars (1641–51), maintained that just as individuals in the state of nature have the responsibility and the right to preserve themselves, so too does each state in the international system. In his most famous treatise, Hobbes argued that the only cure for perpetual war within a state was the emergence of a single powerful prince who could overawe all others: a leviathan. Applying his arguments to relations among sovereigns, Hobbes depicted a state of international anarchy where the norm for states is "having their weapons pointing, and their eyes fixed on one another."[5] In the absence of international authority, there are few rules or norms that restrain states. War, in other words, would be perpetual.

In the aftermath of World War II, the international relations theorist Hans Morgenthau (1904–80) wrote the seminal synthesis of realism in international politics and offered a methodological approach for testing this theory. For Morgenthau, just as for Thucydides, Augustine, and Hobbes, international politics is best characterized as a struggle for power. That struggle can be explained at the three levels of analysis: (1) the flawed individual in the state of nature struggles for self-preservation; (2) the autonomous and unitary state is constantly involved in power struggles, balancing power with power and reacting to preserve what is in the national interest; and (3) because the international system is anarchic—there is no higher power to put an end to the competition —the struggle is continuous. Because of the imperative to ensure a state's survival, leaders are driven by a morality quite different from that of ordinary individuals. Morality, for realists, is to be judged by the political consequences of a policy.[6]

Morgenthau's textbook *Politics among Nations* became the realist bible for the years following World War II. Policy implications flowed naturally from the theory: the most effective technique for managing power is balance of power. Both George Kennan (1904–2005), a writer and chair of the State Department's Policy Planning Staff in the late 1940s and later the U.S. ambassador to the Soviet Union, and Henry Kissinger (b. 1923), a scholar and foreign policy adviser and the secretary of state to presidents Richard Nixon and Gerald Ford, are known to have based their policy recommendations on realist theory.

As we saw in Chapter 2, Kennan was one of the architects of the U.S. Cold War policy of containment, an interpretation of the balance of power. The goal of containment was to prevent Soviet power from extending into regions beyond that country's immediate, existing sphere of influence (Eastern Europe). Containment was achieved by balancing U.S. power against Soviet power. During the 1970s, Kissinger encouraged the classic realist balance of power by supporting weaker powers such as China and Pakistan to exert leverage over the Soviet Union and to offset India's growing power, respectively. (At the time, India was an ally of the Soviets.)

Whereas realism appears to offer clear policy prescriptions, not all realists agree on what an ideal realist foreign policy might look like. Defensive realists observe that few if any major wars in the last century ended up benefitting the state or states that started them. When threatened, states tend to balance against aggressors, eventually overwhelming and reversing whatever initial gains were made. Conquest, in other words, does not pay. As a result, defensive realists argue that states in the international system should pursue policies of restraint, whether through military, diplomatic, or economic channels. Such defensive moderate postures can be pursued without leading to dangerous levels of mistrust among states.

Offensive realists, on the other hand, note that periodically demonstrating a willingness to engage in war, though perhaps costly in the short run, may pay huge dividends by way of reputation enhancement later. They argue that under conditions of international anarchy, states cannot be 100 percent certain of others' intentions. They posit that all states should seek opportunities to improve their relative positions and that states should strive for power even if their goal is merely to preserve their own independence. Conquest, in other words, pays. States may thus pursue expansionist politics, building up their relative power positions and intimidating potential rivals into cooperation.

Defensive and offensive realists have significant differences of view about the appropriate course of action.[7] In fact, realism encompasses a family of related arguments, sharing common assumptions and premises. It is not a single, unified theory. Among the various reinterpretations of realism, the most powerful is **neorealism** (or structural realism), as delineated in Kenneth Waltz's *Theory of International Politics*.[8] Waltz undertook this reinterpretation of classical realism in order to make political realism a more rigorous theory of international politics. Neorealists are so bold as to propose general laws to explain events: they therefore attempt to simplify explanations of behavior in anticipation of being better able to explain and predict general trends.

Neorealists give precedence in their analyses to the structure of the international system as an explanatory factor over states, which are emphasized by traditional realists, and over the innate characteristics of human beings. According to Waltz, the most important object of study is the structure of the international system. Attempting to understand the international system by reference to states is analogous, in Waltz's view, to attempting to understand a market by reference to individual firms: unproductive at best. Neorealism thus advances two arguments. The first is that we need theory in order to understand international politics (and that prior to the publication of Waltz's book we had none); and the second is that his theory, neorealism, explains international politics from 1648 (the date cited by most international relations scholars for the advent of the states system, as explained in Chapter 2) to the present. Critics of classical realism had noted that if the human desire for power, inscribed on states, was driving the recurrence of interstate war, how can we explain long periods of peace? How, in other words, can a constant explain a variable? Waltz responded by substituting structure as a variable in place of the constant of human nature. He argued that the structure of a particular system is determined by its ordering principle, namely, the presence or absence of overarching authority, and the distribution of capabilities among states. Those capabilities define a state's position in the system. (Bigger is better.) The distribution of capabilities in an anarchic system can also be described in structural terms as having one of two values: bipolarity (fairly equal rivals, such as Athens and Sparta at the start of the Peloponnesian Wars or the United States and Soviet Union during the height of the Cold War); or multipolarity (three or more great powers, as in Europe in 1914). According to neorealists, the structure of the system, rather than the characteristics of individual

THEORY IN BRIEF

Realism / Neorealism

KEY ACTORS	International system, states
VIEW OF THE INDIVIDUAL	Power seeking; selfish; antagonistic
VIEW OF THE STATE	Power seeking; unitary actor; following its national interest
VIEW OF THE INTERNATIONAL SYSTEM	Anarchic; reaches relative stability in a balance-of-power system
BELIEFS ABOUT CHANGE	Low change potential; slow structural change
MAJOR THEORISTS	Thucydides, Saint Augustine, Machiavelli, Hobbes, Morgenthau, Waltz, Gilpin, Mearsheimer

states, determines outcomes; this is why the closer the overall distribution of power approaches the ideal of unipolarity, the greater, in the neorealist view, is the likelihood (but never the certainty) of peace.[9] Note that logically, unipolarity (the emergence of a leviathan) would suspend the condition of anarchy and overturn all the causes of war that are said to inevitably follow from that condition.

This observation leads to another key question, the answers to which lie at the root of the disagreement between liberals and realists. Why, we might ask, haven't two or more great powers ever cooperated to become a single leviathan, thus ending war? Neorealists posit two answers: first, cooperation is difficult under conditions of anarchy, due to concerns over relative gains; and second, states in an anarchic system must be on constant guard against cheating. In an anarchic system, the possibilities for international cooperation are logically slim:

> When faced with the possibility of cooperating for mutual gain, states that feel insecure must ask how the gain will be divided. They are compelled to ask not "Will both of us gain?" but "Who will gain more?" If an expected gain is to be divided, say, in the ratio of two to one, one state may use its disproportionate gain to implement a policy intended to damage or destroy the other. Even the prospect of large absolute gains for both parties does not elicit their cooperation so long as each fears how the other will use its increased capabilities.[10]

The importance of relative power means that states hesitate to engage in cooperation if the benefits to be gained might be distributed unevenly among participating states. Even if cooperation could produce absolute gains for any one state, these gains will be discounted by that state should cooperation produce greater gains for other states. In a neorealist's balance-of-power world, a state's survival depends on its having more power than other states. Thus all power (and gains in power) are viewed in relative terms.[11]

Neorealists are also concerned with cheating. States may be tempted to cheat on agreements in order to gain a relative advantage over other states. Fear that other states will renege on existing cooperative agreements is especially potent in the military realm, in which changes in weaponry can result in a major shift in the balance of power. Self-interest provides a powerful incentive for one state to take advantage of another. The awareness that such incentives exist, combined with states' rational desire to protect their own interests, tends to preclude cooperation among states.

Scholars have developed other interpretations of realism as well. Although neorealism simplifies the classical realist theory and focuses on a few core concepts (system structure and balance of power), other reinterpretations add increased complexity to realism. In *War and Change in World Politics*, Robert Gilpin of Princeton University offers one such reinterpretation. Accepting the realist assumptions that states are the principal actors, decision makers are basically rational, and the international system structure plays a key role in determining power, Gilpin examines twenty-four hundred years of history, finding that "the distribution of power among states constitutes the principal form of control in every international system."[12] What Gilpin adds is the notion of dynamism, of history as a series of cycles—cycles of the birth, expansion, and demise of dominant powers. Whereas classical realism offers no satisfactory rationale for the decline of powers, Gilpin does, on the basis of the importance of economic power. Hegemons decline because of three processes: the increasingly marginal returns of controlling an empire, a state-level phenomenon; the tendency for economic hegemons to consume more over time and invest less, also a state-level phenomenon; and the diffusion of technology, a system-level phenomenon through which new powers challenge the hegemon. As Gilpin explains, "disequilibrium replaces equilibrium, and the world moves toward a new round of hegemonic conflict."[13]

Whereas Gilpin adds dynamism to a largely static theory of realism, the feminist political scientist Ann Tickner and her colleagues add gender, and hence more complexity, to realism. According to Tickner, classical realism is based on a very limited—indeed, *masculine*—notion of both human nature and power. She argues that human nature is not fixed and unalterable; it is multidimensional and contextual. Power cannot be equated exclusively with control and domination. Tickner thinks that realism must be reoriented toward a more inclusive notion of power, in which power is the ability to act in concert (not just in conflict) or to engage in a symbiotic relationship (instead of outright competition). In other words, power can also be a concept of connection rather than one only of autonomy.[14]

In short, there is no single tradition of political realism; there are "realisms." Although each is predicated on a key group of assumptions, each attaches different importance to the various core propositions. Yet what unites proponents of realist theory—their emphasis on the unitary, autonomous state in an international anarchic system—distinguishes them clearly from both the liberals and the radicals.

Liberalism and Neoliberal Institutionalism

Liberalism (sometimes referred to as idealism) holds that human nature is basically good and that people can improve their moral and material conditions, making societal progress possible. Bad or evil human behavior, such as injustice and war, is the product of inadequate or corrupt social institutions and of misunderstandings among leaders. Thus, liberals believe that injustice, war, and aggression are not inevitable but can be moderated or even eliminated through institutional reform or collective action. According to liberal thinking, the expansion of human freedom is best achieved in democracies and through market capitalism.

The origins of liberal theory are found in eighteenth-century Enlightenment optimism, nineteenth-century political and economic liberalism, and twentieth-century Wilsonian idealism. The contribution of the Enlightenment to liberalism rests on the Greek idea that individuals are rational human beings, able to understand the universally applicable laws governing both nature and human society. Understanding such laws means that people have the capacity to improve their condition by creating a just society. If a just society is not attained, then the fault rests with inadequate institutions, the result of a corrupt environment.

The writings of the French philosopher Charles-Louis de Secondat, Baron de La Brède et de Montesquieu, (1689–1755) reflect Enlightenment thinking. He argued that it is not human nature that is defective, but that problems arise as humanity enters civil society and forms separate nations. War is a product of society, not an attribute inherent in individuals. To overcome defects in society, education is imperative; it prepares one for civil life. Groups of states are united according to the law of nations, which regulates conduct even during war. Montesquieu optimistically stated that "different nations ought in time of peace to do one another all the good they can, and in time of war as little harm as possible, without prejudicing their real interests."[15]

Likewise, the writings of Immanuel Kant (1724–1804) form the core of Enlightenment beliefs. According to Kant, international anarchy can be overcome through some kind of collective action—a federation of states in which sovereignties would be left intact. Kant offered hope that humans would learn ways to avoid war through cosmopolitanism and universalism—though, as he admitted, the task will not be easy.[16]

Nineteenth-century liberalism took the rationalism of the Enlightenment and reformulated it by adding a preference for democracy over aristocracy and for free trade over national economic self-sufficiency. Sharing the Enlightenment's optimistic view of human nature, nineteenth-century liberalism saw humanity as capable of satisfying its natural needs and wants in rational ways. These needs and wants could be met most efficiently by each individual's pursuing his or her own freedom and autonomy in a democratic state, unfettered by excessive governmental restrictions. Likewise, political freedoms are most easily achieved in capitalist states, where rational and acquisitive human beings can improve their own conditions, maximizing both individual and collective economic growth and economic welfare. Free markets must be allowed to flourish, and governments must permit the free flow of trade and commerce. Liberal theorists believe that free trade and commerce create interdependencies among states, thus raising the cost of war.

Twentieth-century idealism also contributed to liberalism, finding its greatest adherent in the U.S. president Woodrow Wilson. Wilson authored the covenant of the League of Nations—hence the term *Wilsonian idealism*. The basic proposition of this idealism is that war is preventable; more than half of the League covenant's twenty-six provisions focused on preventing war. The covenant even included a provision legitimizing the notion of **collective security,** whereby aggression by one state would be countered by collective action, embodied in a "league of nations."

Thus, the League of Nations illustrated the importance that liberals place on international institutions to deal with war and the opportunity for collective problem solving in a multilateral forum. Liberals also place faith in international law and legal instruments such as mediation, arbitration, and international courts. Still other liberals think that all war can be eliminated through disarmament. Whatever the specific prescriptive solution, the basis of liberalism remains firmly embedded in the belief in the rationality of human beings and in the unbridled optimism that through learning and education, humans can develop institutions to bring out their best characteristics.

During the interwar period, when the League of Nations proved incapable of maintaining collective security, and during World War II, when atrocities made many question the basic goodness of humanity, liberalism came under intense scrutiny. Was humankind inherently good? How could an institution fashioned under the best assumptions have failed so miserably? Liberalism as a theoretical perspective fell out of favor, replaced by realism and its solution, the balance of power.

Since the 1970s, liberalism has been revived under the rubric of **neoliberal institutionalism.** Neoliberal institutionalists such as the political scientists Robert Axelrod and Robert O. Keohane ask *why* states choose to cooperate most of the time, even under the anarchic conditions of the international system. One answer is found in the simple but profound story of the prisoner's dilemma.[17]

The **prisoner's dilemma** is the story of two prisoners, each being interrogated separately for an alleged crime. The interrogator tells each prisoner that if one of them confesses and the other does not, the one who confessed will go free, but the one who kept silent will get a long prison term. If both confess, both will get somewhat reduced prison terms. If neither confesses, both will receive short prison terms based on lack of evidence. Let's say that both prisoners confess, and thus each serves a longer sentence than if they had cooperated and kept silent. Why did cooperation fail to occur? Each prisoner is faced with a one-time choice. Neither prisoner knows how the other will respond; the cost of not confessing if the other confesses is extraordinarily high. So both will confess, leading to a less-than-optimal outcome for both.

But if the situation is repeated, the possibility of reciprocity makes it rational to cooperate. Had the two prisoners cooperated with one another by both remaining silent, then the outcome would have been much better for both. It was actually in the self-interest of each to cooperate! Similarly, states are not faced with a one-time situation; they confront each other over and over again on specific issues. Unlike classical liberals, neoliberal institutionalists do not believe that individuals naturally cooperate out of an innate characteristic of humanity. The prisoner's dilemma provides neoliberal institutionalists with a rationale for mutual cooperation in an environment where there is no international authority mandating such cooperation.

Neoliberal institutionalists arrive at the same prediction as liberals do— cooperation—but their explanation for why cooperation occurs is different. For classical liberals, cooperation emerges from humanity's establishing and reforming institutions that permit cooperative interactions and prohibit coercive actions. For neoliberal institutionalists, cooperation emerges because when actors have continuous interactions with each other, it is in the self-interest of each to cooperate. Institutions help prevent cheating in another way: they reduce transaction and opportunity costs for those who seek gains from cooperation within them, thus further increasing the benefits of cooperation over unregulated exchange. Thus for neoliberals, institutions are essential; they facilitate cooperation by building on common interests, hence maximizing the gains for all parties. Institutions help shape state preferences, solidifying cooperative relationship.

For neoliberal institutionalists, security is essential, and institutions help to make security possible. Institutions provide a guaranteed framework of interactions; they suggest that there will be an expectation of future interactions. These interactions will occur not only on security issues but on a whole suite of international issues, including human rights (a classic liberal concern), the environment, immigration, and economics.[18] Thus, for neoliberals, institutions are critical; they facilitate cooperation by building on common interests, thus maximizing the gains for all parties. Institutions help shape state preferences, solidifying cooperative relationships.

With the end of the Cold War in the 1990s, liberalism as a general theoretical perspective has achieved new credibility. Two particular areas stand out. First, researchers of the so-called democratic peace (discussed in more detail in Chapter 5) are trying to determine *why* democracies do not fight each other.

THEORY IN BRIEF	
Liberalism / Neoliberal Institutionalism	
KEY ACTORS	States, nongovernmental groups, international organizations
VIEW OF THE INDIVIDUAL	Basically good; capable of cooperating
VIEW OF THE STATE	Not an autonomous actor; having many interests
VIEW OF THE INTERNATIONAL SYSTEM	Interdependence among actors; international society; anarchy
BELIEFS ABOUT CHANGE	Probable; a desirable process
MAJOR THEORISTS	Montesquieu, Kant, Wilson, Keohane, Mueller

Realist theorists have difficulty explaining the continued cooperation between states like France and Germany—once bitter enemies—following the end of World War II. Here, French president Nicolas Sarkozy meets with German prime minister Angela Merkel in 2010.

A variety of liberal explanations provide the answer. One argument is that shared democratic norms and culture inhibit aggression; leaders in democracies hear from a multiplicity of voices that tend to restrain decision makers and therefore lessen the chance of war. Another argument is that transnational and international institutions that bind democracies together through dense networks act to constrain behavior. These explanations are based on liberal theorizing.

Second, post–Cold War theorists such as the scholar and former policy analyst Francis Fukuyama see not just a revival but a victory for international liberalism, in the absence of any viable theoretical alternatives. He admits that some groups, such as Palestinians and Israelis, Sinhalese and Tamils, or Armenians and Azeris, will continue to have grievances against one another. But large-scale conflict has been less frequent than in earlier eras. For the first time, Fukuyama argues, the possibility exists for the "universalization of Western liberal democracy as the final form of human governance."[19] Indeed, the political scientist John Mueller makes the liberal argument even more strongly. Just as dueling and slavery, once acceptable practices, have become morally unacceptable, nations of the developed world increasingly see war as immoral and repugnant. The terrifying moments of World Wars I and II have led to the obsolescence of war, says Mueller (see Chapter 8).[20]

Liberalism, then, has provided the major counterpoint to realism. Although these two theories differ in many respects, they are both rationally based and both conceptualize power in materialist terms.

The Radical Perspective

Radicalism offers the third overarching theoretical perspective on international relations. Whereas agreement is widespread concerning the appropriate assignment of the liberal and realist labels, there is no such agreement about the label *radicalism*.

The writings of Karl Marx (1818–83) are fundamental to all radical thought, even though he did not directly address all the issues of today. Marx based his theory of the evolution of capitalism on economic change and class conflict: the capitalism of nineteenth-century Europe emerged out of the earlier feudal system. According to Marx, in the capitalist system, private interests control labor and market exchanges, creating bondages from which certain classes try to free themselves. A clash inevitably arises between the controlling, capitalist bourgeois class and the controlled workers, called the proletariat. It is from this violent clash that a new socialist order is born.[21]

A group of core beliefs unites those espousing a radical, largely Marxist, perspective. The first set of radical beliefs is found in historical analysis. Whereas for most realists and liberals, history provides various data points from which to glean appropriate generalizations, radicals see historical analysis as fundamental. Of special relevance is the history of the production process. During the evolution of the production process from feudalism to capitalism, new patterns of social relations were developed. Radicals are concerned most with explaining the relationships among the means of production, social relations, and power.

Basing their analyses of history on the importance of the production process, most radical theorists also assume the primacy of economics for explaining virtually all other phenomena. This clearly differentiates radicalism from either realism or liberalism. For liberals, economic interdependence is one possible explanation for international cooperation, but only one among many factors. For realists and neorealists, economic factors are one of the ingredients of power, one component of the international structure. In neither theory, though, is economics the determining factor. In radicalism, on the other hand, economic factors assume primary importance. For example, radical feminists based in the Marxist tradition suggest that the roots of oppression against women are found in the exploitative capitalist system.

A third group of radical beliefs centers on the structure of the global system. That structure, in Marxist thinking, is hierarchical and is largely the by-product of imperialism, or the expansion of certain economic forms into other areas of the world. The British economist John A. Hobson (1858–1940) theorized that expansion occurs because of three conditions: overproduction of goods and services in the more developed countries, underconsumption by workers and the lower classes in developed nations because of low wages, and oversavings by the upper classes and the bourgeoisie in the dominant developed countries. In order to solve these three economic problems, developed states historically have expanded abroad, and radicals argue that developed countries still see expansion as a solution. Goods find new markets in underdeveloped regions, workers' wages are kept low because of foreign competition, and savings are profitably invested in new markets rather than in improving the lot of the workers. Imperialism leads to rivalry among the developed countries, evoking, in the realist interpretation, a "scramble" to balance power.[22]

For radicals, imperialism produces the hierarchical international system, which offers opportunities to some states, organizations, and individuals but imposes significant constraints on behavior for others. Developed countries can expand, enabling them to sell goods and export surplus wealth that they cannot use at home. Simultaneously, the developing countries are increasingly constrained by and dependent on the actions of the developed world. Hobson, who condemned imperialism as irrational, risky, and potentially conflictual, did not see it as necessarily inevitable. But most radicals drawing on Marx's analysis critique capitalism as inevitably leading to crises. Whereas free-market capitalists maintain that equilibrium would be found through the market, radicals predict a series of deep crises.

Radical theorists emphasize the techniques of domination and suppression that arise from the uneven economic development inherent in the capitalist system. Uneven development empowers

THEORY IN BRIEF

Radicalism / Dependency Theory

KEY ACTORS	Social classes, transnational elites, multinational corporations
VIEW OF THE INDIVIDUAL	Actions determined by economic class
VIEW OF THE STATE	An agent of the structure of international capitalism and the executing agent of the bourgeoisie
VIEW OF THE INTER-NATIONAL SYSTEM	Highly stratified; dominated by international capitalist system
BELIEFS ABOUT CHANGE	Radical change desired
MAJOR THEORISTS	Marx, Hobson, Lenin, Prebisch

and enables the dominant states to exploit the underdogs; the dynamics of capitalism and economic expansion make such exploitation necessary if the top dogs are to maintain their position and the capitalist structure is to survive. Whereas realists see balancing the power of other states and diplomacy as the mechanisms for gaining and maintaining power, Marxists and radicals view the economic techniques of domination and suppression as the means of power in the world; the choices for the underdog are few and ineffective.

One latter-day school of radicalism recognizes that capitalists can apply additional, more sophisticated techniques of control to developing markets. Contemporary radicals such as **dependency theorists** attribute primary importance to the role of **multinational corporations (MNCs)** and international banks based in developed countries in exerting fundamental controls over the developing countries. These organizations are seen as key players in establishing and maintaining dependency relationships; they are agents of penetration, not benign actors, as liberals would characterize them, or marginal actors, as realists would. These organizations are able to forge transnational relationships with elites in the developing countries, so that domestic elites in both exploiter and exploited countries are tightly linked in a symbiotic relationship.

Dependency theorists, particularly those from Latin America (Raul Prebisch, Enzo Faletto, Fernando Henrique Cardoso), believe that options for states on the periphery are few. Since the basic terms of trade are unequal, these states have few external options. Nor do they have many internal options, because their internal constraints are just as real: land tenure and social and class structures.[23] Thus, like the realists, dependency theorists are rather pessimistic about the possibility of change.

Finally, virtually all radical theorists, regardless of their specific emphases, are uniformly normative in their orientation. They evaluate the hierarchical capitalist structure as "bad," its methods exploitative. They have clear normative and activist positions about what should be done to ameliorate inequalities among both individuals and states—ranging from forming radical organizations supported by Leninists to more incremental changes suggested by dependency theorists.

In some quarters, radicalism has been discredited as an international relations theory. Radicalism cannot explain why cooperation was emerging between capitalist and socialist states even before the end of the Cold War. And it cannot explain the divisiveness among noncapitalist states. Neither can radicalism explain why and how some of the developing countries such as India have been able to adopt a capitalist approach and escape from economic and political dependency. Radicalism could not have predicted such developments. And radicalism, just like liberalism and realism, did not foresee or predict the demise of the Soviet Union, arguably one of the most significant changes in the twentieth century. Each theory, despite claims of comprehensiveness, has significant shortcomings.

In other circles, radicalism has survived as a theory of economic determinism and as a force advocating major change in the structure of the international system. Radicalism helps us understand the role of economic forces both within and between states and to explain the dynamics of late-twentieth-century economic globalization and the 2008 economic crisis, as discussed in Chapter 9.

Constructivism

A late-twentieth-century addition to international relations, **constructivism** has returned international relations scholars to foundational questions, including the nature of the state and the concepts of sovereignty, identity, and citizenship. In addition, constructivism has opened new substantive areas to inquiry, such as the roles of gender and ethnicity, which have been largely absent from other international relations theories. Yet like liberalism, realism, and radicalism before it, constructivism is not a uniform theory. Indeed, some scholars question whether it is a substantive theory at all. Most constructivists share a number of ideas.

The major theoretical proposition to which all constructivists subscribe is that neither individual, state, nor international community interests are predetermined or fixed, but are socially constructed through constant interaction. State behavior is shaped by elite beliefs, identities, and social norms. Individuals in collectivities forge, shape, and change culture through ideas and practices. State and national interests are the result of the social identities of these actors. Thus, the object of study is the norms and practices of individuals and the collectivity.[24] Ted Hopf offers a simple analogy:

> The scenario is a fire in a theater where all run for the exits. But absent knowledge of social practices of constitutive norms, structure, even in this seemingly overdetermined circumstance, is still indeterminate. Even in a theater with just one door, while all run for that exit, who goes first? Are they the strongest or the disabled, the women or the children, the aged or the infirm, or is it just a mad dash? Determining the outcome will require knowing more about the situation than about the distribution of material power or the structure of authority. One will need to know about the culture, norms, institutions, procedures, rules, and social practices that constitute the actors and the structure alike.[25]

Constructivists eschew the idea that material structures have a necessary, fixed, or inherent meaning. Instead, they argue that people bring meaning to material structures. Alexander Wendt, one of the best-known constructivists, argues that on its own, a political structure—whether one of anarchy or a particular distribution of material capabilities—explains nothing. It tells us little about state behavior: "It does not predict whether two states will be friends or foes, will recognize each other's sovereignty, will have dynastic ties, will have revisionist or status quo powers, and so on."[26] Many constructivists emphasize normative structures. What we need to know is identity, and identities change as a result of cooperative behavior and learning. Whether the system is anarchic depends on the distribution of identities, not the distribution of military capabilities, as the realists would have us believe. If a state identifies only with itself, then the system may be anarchic. If a state identifies with other states, then there is no anarchy. In short, "anarchy is what states make of it."[27]

Like the realists and neoliberal institutionalists, constructivists see power as important. But whereas the former see power only in material terms (military, economic, political), constructivists also see power in discursive terms—the power of ideas, culture, and language. Thus, to constructivists, power includes such ideas as legitimacy; states may alter their actions in order to be viewed as legitimate by other members of the international community. Power exists in every exchange among actors, and the goal of constructivists is to find the sources of that power. Their unique contribution may well be in elucidating the sources of power in ideas and in showing how ideas shape and change identity. An example of constructivist contributions can be seen in the discussion of sovereignty. Constructivists see sovereignty not as an absolute but as a contested concept. They point out that states have never had exclusive control over territory. State sovereignty has always been challenged and is being challenged continuously by new institutional forms and new national needs.

Constructivist theory offers different explanations of change. Change can occur through diffusion of ideas or the internationalization of norms, as well as through socialization, adopting the identities of peer groups. These explanations help us understand that ideas are spread both within a national setting and crossnationally. This is how democracy is diffused; how ideas about human rights protection have been internationalized: and how such states as the new members of the European Union become socialized into the community's norms and practices.

Constructivists utilize multiple methods to make contingent generalizations. They generally rely on interpretative techniques and ethnography to uncover the meanings that actors give to their practices. Most often those meanings are found in culture. But some constructivists have adopted other methods.

For all the renewed intellectual vigor that constructivism has fostered, this approach has been criticized. If, as constructivists claim, there is no objective reality, if "the world is in the eye of the beholder," then there can be no right or wrong answers, only individual perspectives. With no authoritative texts, all texts are equally valid—both the musings of the elites and the practices of everyday men and women. Throughout this textbook, selected examples from constructivist scholarship will allow you to see this approach in use so that you can begin to develop a feel for this theoretical perspective.

Theory in Action: Analyzing the 2003 Iraq War

The contending theoretical perspectives discussed in the preceding sections see the world and even specific events quite differently. What theorists and policy makers choose to see, what they each seek to explain, and what implications they draw—all these elements of analysis can vary, even though the facts of the event are the same. Analyzing the 2003 Iraq War by applying these different theories allows us to compare and contrast them in action.

Realist interpretations of the 2003 Iraq War would focus on state-level and international-level factors. Realists see the international system as anarchic, with no international authority and few states other than the United States able and willing to act to rid the world of the Iraq threat. Iraq posed a security threat to the United States with its supposed stockpiles of weapons of mass destruction, and the United States therefore saw a need to eliminate those weapons and at the same time to ensure a stable oil supply to the West. The only way to achieve these objectives was to oust the Baathist regime from power in Iraq. Having escalated its threats and amassed its troops on Iraq's borders to coerce the regime to give up power, the United States had no choice but to act militarily when that coercion failed.

Yet not all realists agree that the policy the United States pursued was the correct one. Realists are carrying on an interesting discussion about whether or not the U.S. operation was necessary. John Mearsheimer, an offensive realist, and Stephen Walt, a defensive realist, have jointly argued that the war was not necessary. Before the war began, they wrote that any threat posed by Saddam, even his possible attainment of nuclear weapons, could be effectively deterred by U.S. military power. They further argued that even if the war went well and had positive long-term consequences, it would be unnecessary and could engender long-term animosity toward the United States both in the Middle East and around the world. The policy of deterrence employed by the United States had worked previously and could have continued to work.[28]

But many realist theorists, and George W. Bush, believed that Saddam was not being effectively deterred. Bush argued that Saddam's use of chemical weapons against the Kurds in the past meant that it was probable he would use these weapons to threaten the United States. This perceived threat influenced the Bush administration's decision to invade. In addition, some realists in the Bush administration argued that a forceful response to Saddam's flouting of his obligations to the international community (his government was in violation of agreements it signed as part of the settlement that ended the first Gulf War in 1991) would put other enemies of the United States and its allies on notice. Perhaps force would also curtail what the administration referred to as state-sponsored terrorism. Realists clearly can draw different policy prescriptions from theory.

THEORY IN BRIEF

Contending Theoretical Perspectives

	LIBERALISM / NEOLIBERAL INSTITUTIONALISM	REALISM / NEOREALISM	RADICALISM / DEPENDENCY THEORY	CONSTRUCTIVISM
KEY ACTORS	States, nongovernmental groups, international organizations	International system, states first	Social classes, transnational elites, multinational corporations	Individuals, collective identities
VIEW OF THE INDIVIDUAL	Basically good; capable of cooperating	Power seeking; selfish; antagonistic	Actions determined by economic class	Major unit, especially elites
VIEW OF THE STATE	Not an autonomous actor; having many interests	Power seeking; unitary actor; following its national interest	Agent of the structure of international capitalism; executing agent of the bourgeoisie	State behavior shaped by elite beliefs, collective norms, and social identity
VIEW OF THE INTERNATIONAL SYSTEM	Interdependence among actors; international society; anarchic	Anarchic; reaches stability in balance-of-power system	Highly stratified; dominated by international capitalist system	Nothing explained by international material structures alone
BELIEFS ABOUT CHANGE	Inevitable, but slow	Lasting peace impossible; only greater or lesser stability	Revolutionary change inevitable	Belief in possibility of evolutionary change

A liberal view of the 2003 Iraq War would utilize all three levels of analysis. With respect to the individual level, Saddam was clearly an abusive leader whose atrocities against his own population were made evident in the aftermath of the war, with the discovery of mass graves. He was aggressive not only against domestic opponents of his regime but also against other peoples within the region, and even supported terrorist activities against enemies in the West. With respect to the state level, liberals would emphasize the characteristics of the Iraqi regime—mainly its authoritarian nature—and the notion that replacement by a democracy would decrease the coercive threat of the Iraqi state and would enhance stability in the Middle East. A democratic Iraq would be a beacon for other nascent democracies

Canadian Views of the War in Afghanistan

Policies made by states are rooted in one theoretical perspective. Skeptics or dissenters often have a different theoretical perspective. Their justifications and the evidence they provide reflect different international relations theories.

On October 7, 2001, just hours after U.S. and British planes began bombing Afghan cities, Prime Minister Jean Chrétien announced that Canada would join the U.S. war in Afghanistan. In January–February 2002, regular military troops arrived in the country. Now part of the International Security Assistance Force (ISAF), between 2,500 and 2,800 Canadian troops are engaged in action in several parts of the country, including Kabul and Kandahar. In 2006, the Canadian Forces came under NATO command. One key part of Canadian participation is the 330-person Kandahar Provincial Reconstruction Team (PRT), deployed to support reconstruction efforts in the region. One hundred forty-two Canadian troops have died in the cause, the third highest absolute number of deaths of any foreign participating state.

In 2001, the Canadian defense minister provided unequivocal support for Canadian involvement in Afghanistan: "We're in all the way when it comes to dealing with the problem of terrorism."[a] The discovery of the 2006 plot to carry out terrorism in Ottawa and Toronto reaffirmed the salience of the global terrorist threat to Canadian territory. In 2006 Prime Minister Stephen Harper framed Afghanistan policy clearly in a realist perspective. Canada's participation in Afghanistan is a projection of Canadian power in the national interest, which is to protect itself and support its closest ally. After all, Canada has congruent interests with the United States, exemplified in Canada's membership in the G8 and its participation in NATO operations in Kosovo and other U.S.-led coalitions

(Korea and the 1991 Gulf War). These policies reaffirm that Canada's security, borders, and economy are interdependent with those of the United States. The former Prime Minister Pierre Trudeau once remarked that for Canada, living on the northern border of the United States is "like sleeping with an elephant. No matter how friendly and even tempered the beast . . . . one is affected by every twitch and grunt."[b] But this was no "grunt." All of North America was threatened. Canadian troops under NATO contribute to the task of rooting out the terrorists and establishing a government in Afghanistan capable of resisting Taliban influences.

But liberals might ask, Should this fight against terrorism be waged under one dominant power or even under NATO? Canada has historically been a strong supporter of the United Nations, where it has shouldered special responsibilities. Canada sent UN-based peacekeepers to every Cold War operation, reflecting its strong support for multilateral institutions. In this post-Cold War era, Canada trains peacekeepers from developing countries and provides communications and humanitarian assistance. Canada opposed the 2003 Iraq operation because it was not approved by the UN. How was Afghanistan different? Canada prefers that policies be legitimized by the UN, which differentiates its policy from that of its neighbor.

Liberals in Canada initially supported Canada's involvement in Afghanistan for reasons beyond the terrorist threat. Is not the establishment of democratic institutions a worthy goal? Doesn't Canada's diplomacy support improving the lives of individuals? Doesn't Canada stand for human rights for women? Clearly, economic development and respect for human rights were severely compromised under the Taliban. Liberals might point to Canadian involvement in projects that serve this agenda. In 2003 under Operation Athena, for example, Canadian troops helped improve civilian infrastructure by digging wells and repairing buildings. And Canada has provided funds for Afghan elections, education, and health programs.

But liberals may be disappointed with the rate of progress. Representatives from the New Democratic Party, in particular, believe the reconstruction of Afghanistan is being undermined by the counterinsurgency operations themselves. Women's groups point to few improvements in the emancipation of women—girls are still being attacked and sometimes maimed for attending school, and women are still afraid to speak out. As York University's Afghanistan Canada Research Group found, few development projects of any importance have been finished by the Canadian Forces or the Canadian International Development Agency. Liberals think that the money would be better spent on social programs at home.

Radical dissatisfaction with Canadian policy would focus on two arguments. Canadian involvement in what is viewed as America's war is a sad illustration of the reluctance and unwillingness of the Canadian government to distance itself from the United States, although the case of Iraq shows some independence from the hegemon. In addition, Canadian and international businesses are profiting from the war. After all, Canada is the sixth-largest arms supplier in the world. And any reconstruction will need to involve expansion of Afghanistan's potentially rich mining sector. The Canadian mining industry is the world's leader in exploration and development. Canadian business would benefit economically from the country's involvement, much as radicals would predict.

Constructivists could point to the power of Canadian identity to explain the country's policies in Afghanistan. That identity revolves around Canada's global citizenship and its support of peacekeeping, multilateralism, NGOs, and human security issues. Yet critics suggest that this identity is but a myth, perpetuated by an elite that for much of the post–World War II era has served the interests of both Canada and the United States. So policies in Afghanistan can be seen as either a manifestation of Canada's identity, or a continuation of an identity myth.

For Critical Analysis

Answer these questions on wwnorton.com/studyspace

1. *To what extent does Canada's relationship with the United States influence its foreign policy strategies?*

2. *Canada supports U.S. policy in Afghanistan, but not American policy in Iraq. Which theory best explains the difference in the Canadian positions?*

3. *Domestic factors help to explain Canada's position. How?*

4. *Which explanation of Canada's position do you find most convincing? Why?*

---

[a] Quote by Defence Minister Art Eggleton in Lee Parsons, "Canada joins war on Afghanistan," 16 October 2001, World Socialist Web Site, www.wsws.org/articles/2001/oct2001/can-o16.shtml (accessed 12/28/09).

[b] Pierre Elliott Trudeau, "On Relations with the United States," address to the National Press Club, Washington, D.C. March 26, 1969.

nearby. The fact that many liberals believed that Saddam's regime had or was very close to acquiring weapons of mass destruction (WMD) only added to the urgency of regime change. With respect to the international level, liberals would emphasize that Iraq was not conforming to its obligations under various UN Security Council resolutions. Thus, the international community had an obligation to support sanctions and continue inspections and, failing that, undertake collective action, fighting a war to punish Saddam's regime and allow an alternative government to take root.

Why did the international community not respond as some liberals would have predicted? The inability of the United States to win the endorsement of the UN Security Council for collective action can be attributed to the fact that some members of the council, including France and Russia, and some other powerful states, including Germany, believed that containment of the Iraqi regime was effective, that there was insufficient evidence of weapons of mass destruction, and that there was no need to take immediate action in light of the higher priority given to fighting Al Qaeda in Afghanistan.

A radical interpretation would tend to focus mainly on the international system structure. That system structure, for radicals, is embedded in the historical colonial system and its contemporary legacies. Radicals hold that political colonialism spawned an imperialist system in which the economic needs of the capitalist states were paramount. In the Middle East, that meant imperialist action by the West to secure oil resources. In the nineteenth-century colonial era, imperialism was state organized; today imperialism is practiced by multinational corporations. In this view, the instability of the oil supply coming from Iraq explains the U.S. invasion of Iraq in 2003. Many radicals (and many in the Arab world) believe that the United States wants to control Iraq's oil. They point to the fact that one of the United States' first military objectives was the seizure of the Rumaila oil field in southern Iraq. Oil fields all over the country were protected by U.S. troops even when civil disorder and looting of precious cultural monuments went unchecked. Restarting the oil pipelines was given priority over providing for the basic needs of the Iraqi people.

Radicals, especially dependency theorists, would not be at all surprised that the core states of the capitalist system—the United States and its allies—responded with force when Iraq threatened their critical interests in oil. Nor would they expect the end of the Cold War to make any difference in the structure of the system. The major changes in international power relationships that radicals seek—and predict—have not yet come.

A constructivist view of the 2003 Iraq War would focus on several factors. These theorists would emphasize the social construction of threat; how U.S. policy makers constructed Saddam Hussein and the purported weapons of mass destruction as threats to the United States, even though UN inspectors claimed that the weapons program had been dismantled. The rhetoric of the threat accelerated as Saddam was portrayed as an evil tyrant, having power beyond materialist considerations. Constructivists would also point to the importance of legitimacy. The United States recognized the need for legitimacy for its actions, being socialized into those norms. That explains the considerable effort the United States expended in trying to obtain UN Security Council approval for the invasion, though in the long run, those efforts failed. In constructivist thinking, international organizations such as the UN play a powerful legitimizing and socializing role in international relations.

In Sum: Seeing The World Through Theoretical Lenses

How each of us sees international relations depends on his or her own theoretical lens. Do you see things through a realist framework? Are you inclined toward a liberal interpretation? Or do you adhere to a radical or constructivist view of the world? These theoretical perspectives differ not only in whom they identify as key actors, but also in their views about the individual, the state, and the international system—the three levels of analysis. Equally important, these perspectives support different views about the possibility and desirability of change in the international system.

In the next four chapters, we examine in more detail how each of these four perspectives sees the international system, the state, the individual, and international organizations. First we will examine the most general level of analysis—the international system.

DISCUSSION QUESTIONS

1. Choose a current event. Describe and explain that event using the three levels of analysis.

2. President Barack Obama: is he a realist, a liberal, or a radical? Provide evidence to support your position.

3. A realist and a liberal are discussing the role of domestic politics. Recreate that conversation, highlighting the differing perspectives.

4. Constructivists assert that the power of norms and ideas is continuously shaping and reshaping state behavior. Select a political idea—equality, democracy, or human rights. How has that idea been changed over time? How has state behavior changed?

KEY TERMS

collective security, p. 78

constructivism, p. 84

dependency theorists, p. 83

hypotheses, p. 67

levels of analysis, p. 68

liberalism, p. 76

multinational corporations
    (MNCs), p. 83

national interest, p. 70

neoliberal institutionalism, p. 78

neorealism, p. 73

prisoner's dilemma, p. 78

radicalism, p. 81

rational actor, p. 71

realism, p. 70

theory, p. 67

unitary actor, p. 71

 Find chapter outlines, practice quizzes, flashcards, and other study and review materials for this chapter at wwnorton.com/studyspace.

The International System

- Why is the concept of a system a powerful descriptive and explanatory device?
- What concepts do realists employ to analyze the international system?
- How would a liberal theorist view the international system?
- How do radicals view the international system? Constructivists?
- How does each of the contending theoretical perspectives explain change in the international system?
- What are the problems and/or weaknesses with the notion of the international system?

The Notion of a System

EACH OF THE CONTENDING theoretical perspectives examined in Chapter 3 described an international system. For realists and radicals, the concept of an international system is vital to their analyses, whereas for liberals, the international system is less precise as an explanatory mechanism and less consequential. For constructivists, the concept of an international system is tied to notions of change.

To understand the international system, the notion of a system itself must be clarified. Broadly defined, a **system** is an assemblage of units, objects, or parts united by some form of regular interaction. The concept of systems is essential to the physical and biological sciences; systems are composed of different interacting units, whether at the micro (cell, plant, animal) or the macro (natural ecosystem or global climate) level. Because these units interact, a change in one unit causes changes in all the others. With their interacting parts, systems tend to respond in regularized ways; their actions have patterns. Boundaries separate one system from another, but there can be exchanges across these boundaries. A system can break down when changes within it become so significant that in effect a new system emerges.

In the 1950s, the behavioral revolution in the social sciences and the growing acceptance of political realism in international relations led scholars to conceptualize international politics as a system, using the language of systems theory. Beginning with the supposition that people act in regularized ways and that their patterns of interaction with each other are largely habitual, both realists and behavioralists made the conceptual leap that international politics is a system whose major actors are individual states.[1] This notion of a system is embedded in ideas of the major theoretical schools of international relations. Of particular interest is how change occurs.

The International System According to Realists

Political realists have clear notions of the international system and its essential characteristics. All realists characterize the international system as anarchic. No authority exists above the state; the state is sovereign. This anarchic structure constrains the actions of decision makers and affects the distribution of capabilities among the various actors. Realists differ among themselves, however, about the degree of a state's autonomy in the international system. Traditional realists acknowledge that states act and shape the system, whereas neorealists believe that states are constrained by the structure of the system. Yet for both, anarchy is the basic ordering principle. Each state in the system must, therefore, look out for its own interests above all.

Realists differentiate the international system largely along the dimension of polarity. System polarity simply refers to the number of blocs of states that exert power in the international system. Realists are particularly interested in polarity because of its focus on power. There are three types of system polarity: multipolarity, bipolarity, and hegemony (or sometimes unipolarity) (see Figure 4.1).

If there are a number of influential actors in the international system, a balance-of-power, or multipolar, system is formed. In a classical balance of power, the actors are exclusively states, and there should be at least five of them. The nineteenth-century balance of power—among Great Britain, Russia, Prussia, France, and Austria—is the real-world antecedent discussed in Chapter 2. In multipolar systems, several states—at least three or more—enjoy relative power parity.

FIGURE 4.1 | Polarity in the International System

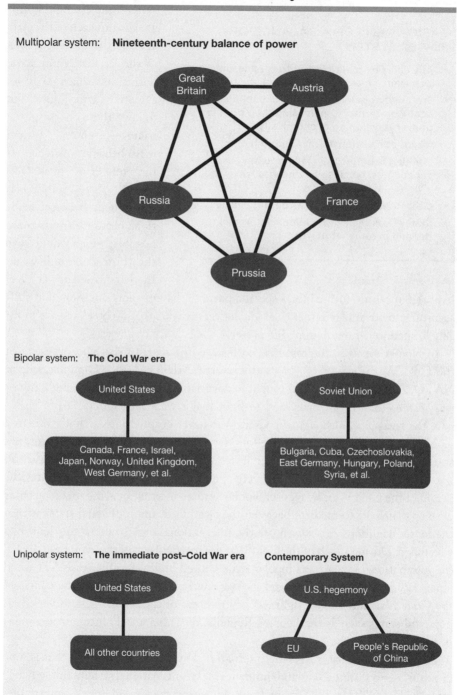

Multipolar system: **Nineteenth-century balance of power**

Bipolar system: **The Cold War era**

Unipolar system: **The immediate post–Cold War era**   **Contemporary System**

In Focus ◉ ███████████

BASIC NORMS OF A BALANCE-OF-POWER SYSTEM

- Any actor or coalition that tries to assume dominance must be constrained.
- States want to increase their capabilities by acquiring territory, increasing their population, or developing economically.
- Negotiating is better than fighting.
- Fighting is better than failing to increase capabilities, because no one else will protect a weak state.
- Other states are viewed as potential allies.
- States seek their own national interests, defined in terms of power.

In a balance-of-power system, the essential norms are clear to each of the state actors. The In Focus box to the left lists those basic norms of behavior. If an essential actor does not follow these norms, the balance-of-power system may become unstable. If the number of states declines to three, stability is threatened, because coalitions between any two are possible, which would leave the third alone and weak. In balance-of-power systems, alliances are formed for a specific purpose, have a short duration, and shift according to advantage rather than ideology. Any wars that do break out are probably limited in nature, designed to preserve the balance of power.

In bipolar systems, the essential norms are different. In the bipolar system of the Cold War, each of the blocs (the North Atlantic Treaty Organization, or NATO, and the Warsaw Pact) sought to negotiate rather than fight, to fight minor wars rather than major ones, and to fight major wars rather than fail to eliminate the rival bloc, although the Cold War never erupted into a "hot" war. In a bipolar system, alliances tend to be long term, based on relatively permanent, not shifting, interests. In a tight bipolar system, international organizations either do not develop or are completely ineffective, as the United Nations was during the height of the Cold War. In a looser bipolar system, international organizations may develop primarily to mediate between the two blocs, and individual states within the looser coalitions may try to use the international organizations for their own advantage. During much of the Cold War era, particularly in the 1950s and 1960s, the international system was bipolar—the United States, its allies in NATO, and Japan faced the Soviet Union and its Warsaw Pact allies. But over the course of the Cold War, the relative tightness or looseness of the bipolar system varied, as powerful states such as the People's Republic of China and France pursued independent paths.

Another possibility is that the international system is hegemonic; that is, one group or even one state commands influence in the international system. Immediately after the Gulf War in 1991, many states, including the United States' closest allies and virtually all developing states, grew concerned that the international system had actually become unipolar. After all, the defense expenditures of the United States were greater than those of the next fifteen states combined; its economy was three times stronger than those of the next three rivals combined. With that superiority, other states were concerned that there might be no effective counterweight to the power of the United States. Yet fifteen years later, the description of unipolarity has been replaced by one of hegemony. Although in military expenditures the United States remains dominant, other states

During the Cold War, the international system was bipolar, with two blocs of countries allied with either the United States or the Soviet Union. Each side sought to counter the other's power, through military and other means. In this 1968 photo, Soviet missiles are set up, ready to respond to any threat from the U.S. and its allies.

such as China and Japan and groups such as the European Union are rising in economic terms. So is a group of emerging economies such as Brazil. The trend clearly suggests that although the United States remains the hegemon in absolute terms, challengers are emerging.

The type of international system in place at any given time has implications for system management and stability. Are certain polarities more manageable and hence more stable than others? Are wars more likely to occur in bipolar systems, multipolar systems, or hegemonic systems? These questions have dominated much of the discussion among realists, but the studies of these relationships are inconclusive.

Bipolar systems are very difficult to regulate formally, because neither uncommitted states nor international organizations are able to direct the behavior of either of the two blocs. Informal regulation may be easier. If either of the blocs is engaged in disruptive behavior, the consequences are immediately evident, especially if one of the blocs gains in strength or position as a result. Kenneth Waltz, for one, argues that because of this visibility, the bipolar international system is the most stable structure in the long run: the two sides are "able both to moderate the other's use of violence and to absorb possibly destabilizing changes that emanate from uses of violence that they do not or cannot control."[2] In such a system, there is a clear difference in the amount of power held by each pole compared with that held by the other state actors. Because of the power disparity, each of the two sides is able to focus its activity almost exclusively on the other. Each can anticipate the other's actions and accurately predict its responses because of their history of repeated interactions. Each tries to preserve this balance of power in order to preserve itself and the bipolar system.

Pointing to the stability attained in the bipolar Cold War system, John Mearsheimer provoked controversy by suggesting that the world would miss the stability and predictability that the Cold War forged. With the end of the Cold War bipolar system, Mearsheimer argued, more specific inter-state conflicts would develop and hence more possibilities for war. He felt that deterrence would be more difficult and miscalculations more probable. He drew a clear policy implication: "The West has an interest in maintaining peace in Europe. It therefore has an interest in maintaining the Cold War order, and hence has an interest in the continuation of the Cold War confrontation; developments that threaten to end it are dangerous. The Cold War antagonism could be continued at lower levels of East-West tension than have prevailed in the past; hence the West is not insured by relaxing East-West tension, but a complete end to the Cold War would create more problems than it would solve."[3] Most analysts do not agree with this provocative conclusion, partly because factors other than polarity can affect system stability.

Theoretically, in multipolar, or balance-of-power, systems, the regulation of system stability ought to be easier than in bipolar systems. The whole purpose of the balancer, as Great Britain was in the nineteenth century, is to act as a regulator for the system, stepping in to correct a perceived imbalance. For example, Great Britain intervened in the Crimean War of 1854–55, opposing Russia on behalf of Turkey. Under multipolarity, numerous interactions take place among all the various parties, and thus each has less opportunity to dwell on a specific relationship. Interaction by any one state actor with other states leads to crosscutting loyalties and alliances and therefore moderates hostility or friendship with any other single state actor. States are less likely to respond to the arms buildup of just one party in the system, and so war becomes less likely.

Hegemonic stability theorists claim that unipolarity, or dominance by a hegemon, leads to the most stable international system. In *The Rise and Fall of the Great Powers*, the historian Paul Kennedy argues that it was the hegemony (though not unipolarity) of Britain in the nineteenth century and that of the United States in the immediate post–World War II era that led to the greatest stability.[4] Other proponents of this theory, such as Robert O. Keohane, contend that hegemonic states are willing to pay the price of enforcing norms, unilaterally if necessary, to ensure the continuation of the system that benefits them. When the hegemon loses power and declines, then system stability is jeopardized.[5]

POLICY DEBATE

Will the international system with the U.S. as hegemon persist?

Yes

- The United States has unprecedented military power, which it can project around the world; its defense expenditures are greater than those of the next fifteen states combined.
- The United States is the premier innovator in information technology.
- As a leading land power, the United States is unlikely to provoke balancing conditions from other contending powers.
- The U.S. economy is three times stronger than those of the next three rivals combined.
- Once viewed as an economic rival, Japan has an aging population; its economic growth rates have slowed dramatically.
- Though enjoying high economic growth rates, China still has a large rural sector that has a long way to go to catch up.
- U.S. soft power—its examples of democracy and human rights activities and cultural hegemony—has no rival.

No

- U.S. military power is ill suited to twenty-first-century warfare and aggression. The wars in both Iraq and Afghanistan have each lasted longer than World War II.
- With its 27 member states, its population of almost 500 million, and its $14 trillion economy, the European Union is exerting increasing influence in world affairs.
- In economic terms, the U.S. has been in relative decline. China and the emerging economies of India and Brazil have made startling advances.
- U.S. soft-power leadership has suffered from allegations of torture and rendition of terrorist suspects, its failure to lead on transnational issues such as global warming, and economic missteps that are now widely blamed for the global economic crisis of 2008–09.
- U.S. domestic politics has become gridlocked.
- The U.S. population no longer is willing to bear the costs of being the hegemon in the international system.

It is clear, then, that realists do not agree among themselves on how polarity matters. Individual and group efforts to test the relationship between polarity and stability have been inconclusive. The Correlates of War project (discussed in Chapter 1) did test two hypotheses flowing from the polarity-stability debate. J. David Singer and Melvin Small hypothesized that the greater the number of alliance commitments in the system, the more war the system will experience. They also hypothesized that the closer the system is to bipolarity, the more war it will experience. On the basis of the data between 1815 and 1945, however, neither argument was proven valid across the whole time span. During the nineteenth century, alliance commitments prevented war, whereas in the twentieth century, proliferating alliances seemed to predict war.[6]

Other evidence from the 1970s suggest that although U.S. economic prowess declined in relative terms, the hegemonic system itself remained stable. Those findings suggest that system stability is not dependent solely on hegemonic power.[7] The behavioral evidence drawn from the analysis of realists themselves regarding the relationship between polarity and system stability is, therefore, inconclusive.

Realists and International System Change

Although realists value the continuity of systems, they recognize that international systems do change, as described above. Why do systems change? Realists attribute system change either to changes in the actors and hence the distribution of power or to exogenous changes, those emanating from outside the system.

Changes in either the number of major actors or the relative power relationship among those actors may result in a fundamental change in the international system. Wars are usually responsible for such fundamental changes in power relationships. For example, the end of World War II brought the relative decline of Great Britain and France, even though they were the victors. The war also signaled the end not only of Germany's and Japan's imperial aspirations but of their basic national capabilities as well. Their militaries were soundly defeated; their civil society was destroyed and their

THEORY IN BRIEF

The Realist Perspective on the International System

CHARACTERIZATION	Anarchic
ACTORS	State is primary actor
CONSTRAINTS	Polarity
POSSIBILITY OF CHANGE	Slow change when the balance of power shifts or technological change occurs

infrastructure demolished. Two other powers emerged into dominant positions—the United States, now willing to assume the international role that it had shunned after World War I, and the Soviet Union, buoyed by its victory although economically weak. The international system had fundamentally changed; the multipolar world had been replaced by a bipolar one.

Robert Gilpin, in *War and Change in World Politics,* sees another form of system change, whereby states act to preserve their own interests and thus change the international system. Such changes can occur because states respond at different rates to political, economic, and technological developments. For example, the rapidly industrializing East Asian states—South Korea, Taiwan, and Hong Kong (though now part of China)—have responded to technological change the fastest. By responding rapidly and with single-mindedness, these states have improved their relative positions in terms of system stratification. Thus, characteristics of the international system can be changed by the actions of a few.[8]

Exogenous changes may also lead to a shift in the international political system. Advances in technology—the instruments for oceanic navigation, the airplane for transatlantic crossings, and satellites and rockets for the exploration of space, for example—not only have expanded the boundaries of accessible geographic space, but also have brought about changes in the boundaries of the international political system. With these came an explosion of new state actors, reflecting different political interests and different cultural traditions.

No technological change has had more of an impact on the international system than the development of nuclear weapons and their use in warfare. The destructiveness of these weapons, their inability to discriminate between combatants and civilians, and their evident harm to future generations are all characteristics that have led policy makers to change the rules of the game. During the Cold War this meant that the superpowers did not fight directly but preferred to spar through non-nuclear proxies using conventional military technology. Since nuclear weapons have not been used since 1945, they are no longer seen as credible in some circles. Nevertheless, they remain greatly feared, and efforts by non-nuclear states to develop such weapons, or even the threat to do so, have met sharp resistance, as occurred when North Korea and Iran announced their intentions to become nuclear. The nuclear states do not want a change in the status quo; in their view, nuclear proliferation, particularly in the hands of rogue states such as North Korea and Iran, leads to international system instability.

Thus, in the view of realists, international systems can change, yet the inherent bias among realist interpretations is for continuity. All realists agree that there are patterns of change in the system, although they may disagree about what time frame to look at in order to study the changes. Efforts by realists to test many of the ideas arising from their notions about the international system have proven inconclusive.

The International System According to Liberals

The international system is less consequential as an explanatory level of analysis in the view of liberals. It is therefore not surprising to find at least three different conceptions of the international system in liberal thinking.

The first conception sees the international system not as a structure but as a process, in which multiple interactions occur among different parties and where various actors learn from the interaction. Actors in this process include not only states but also international governmental organizations (such as the United Nations), nongovernmental organizations (such as Human Rights Watch), multinational corporations, and substate actors (such as parliaments and bureaucracies). Each different type of actor has interactions with all of the others. With so many different kinds of actors, a plethora of national interests defines the liberal international system. Although security interests, so dominant for realists, are also important to liberals, other interests such as economic and social issues are considered, depending on the time and circumstance. In their book *Power and Interdependence,* the political scientists Robert Keohane and Joseph Nye describe the international system as an interdependent system in which the different actors are both sensitive to (affected by) and vulnerable to (suffering costly effects from) the actions of others. Interdependent systems have multiple channels connecting states; these channels exist between governmental elites and among nongovernmental elites and transnational organizations as well. Multiple issues and agendas arise in the interdependent system. Military force may be useful in some situations, but is not useful for all issues.[9]

A second liberal conception of the international system comes from the English tradition of international

THEORY IN BRIEF

The Liberal Perspective on the International System

CHARACTERIZATION	Three liberal interpretations: interdependence among actors, international society, and anarchy
ACTORS	States, international governmental institutions, nongovernmental organizations, multinational corporations, substate actors
CONSTRAINTS	From anarchy and interdependence
POSSIBILITY OF CHANGE	Low likelihood of radical change, but may occur; constant incremental change as actors are involved in new relationships

society. According to two of the principal architects of this tradition, the scholars Hedley Bull and Adam Watson, although the international system comprises a group of independent political communities, an **international society** is more than that. In an international society, the various actors communicate; they consent to common rules and institutions and recognize common interests. Actors in international society share a common identity, a sense of "we-ness"; without such an identity, a society cannot exist. This conception of the international system has normative implications: liberals view the international system as an arena and a process for positive interactions.[10]

A third liberal view of the international system is that of neoliberal institutionalism, a view that comes closer to realist thinking. Neoliberal institutionalists see the international system as an anarchic one in which each individual state acts in its own self-interest. But unlike many realists, they see the product of the interaction among actors as a potentially positive one, where institutions created out of self-interest moderate state behavior, because states realize they will have future interactions with the other actors involved. Thus, in the neoliberal view, institutions provide a framework for interactions; they are focal points for coordination, helping to reduce cheating and facilitating transparency.

Liberals and International System Change

All liberals acknowledge and welcome incremental change in the international system. Liberals see change as coming from several sources. First, changes in the international system occur as the result of exogenous technological developments, that is, progress occurring independently, or outside the control of actors in the system. For example, changes in communication and transportation are responsible for the increasing level of interdependence among states within the international system.

Second, change may occur because of changes in the relative importance of different issue areas. Although realists give primacy to issues of national security, liberals identify the relative importance of other issue areas. Specifically, in the last decades of the twentieth century, economic issues replaced national security issues as the leading topic of the international agenda. In the twenty-first century, transnational issues such as human rights and the environment may assume primacy. These are fundamental changes in the international system, according to liberal thinking.

Third, change may occur when new actors, including multinational corporations, nongovernmental organizations, or other participants in global civil society, augment or replace state actors. The various new actors may enter into new kinds of relationships and may alter both the international system and state behaviors.

These types of changes are compatible with liberal thinking and are discussed by liberal writers. Yet, like their realist counterparts, liberal thinkers also acknowledge that change may occur in the overall power structure among the states. Although liberals posit that change may occur in the overall power structure, radicals advocate major changes.

The International System According to Radicals

Whereas realists define the international system in terms of its polarity and stability, radicals seek to describe and explain the structure in terms of stratification. The system that they see is totally different from that described by liberals and realists. Hence the radicals advocate for a different future.

Radicals describe the structure of the international system by stratification. **Stratification** refers to the uneven division of resources among different groups of states. The international system is stratified according to which states have vital resources, such as oil or military strength or economic power. Stratification is the key to understanding the radical notion of the international system.

Different international systems have had varying degrees of stratification. Indeed, system stratification is strong. According to one set of measures, several of the world's powers (the United States, Japan, Germany, France, Britain, Russia, and China) accounted for about one-half of the world's total gross domestic product (GDP). The other 180 plus states shared the other half (see Figure 4.2). From the stratification of power and resources comes the division between the haves, loosely characterized as the **North,** and the have-nots, states largely located in the **South.** This distinction is vital to the discussion of international political economy found in Chapter 9.

Stratification of influence and resources has implications for the ability of a system to regulate itself, as well as for system stability. When the dominant powers are challenged by those states just below them in terms of access to resources, the system may become highly unstable. For example, Germany's and Japan's attempts to obtain and reclaim resources during the 1930s led to World War II. Such a group of second-tier powers has the potential to win a confrontation, but the real underdogs in a severely stratified system do not (although they can cause major disruptions). The rising powers, especially those that are acquiring resources, seek first-tier status and are willing to fight wars to get it. If the challengers do not begin a war, the top powers may do so to quell the threat of a power displacement.

For Marxists, as well as most other radicals, crippling stratification in the international system is caused by capitalism. Capitalism structures the relationship

FIGURE 4.2 | **Stratification in the International System**

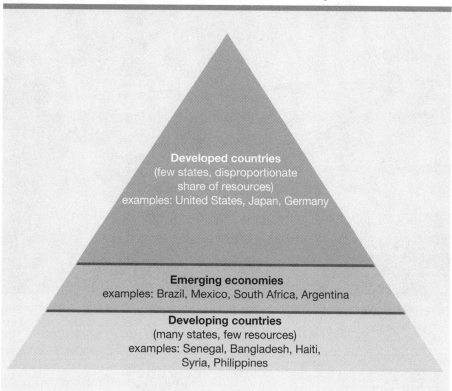

Developed countries
(few states, disproportionate
share of resources)
examples: United States, Japan, Germany

Emerging economies
examples: Brazil, Mexico, South Africa, Argentina

Developing countries
(many states, few resources)
examples: Senegal, Bangladesh, Haiti,
Syria, Philippines

between the advantaged and the disadvantaged, empowering the rich and disenfranchising the weak. Marxists assert that capitalism breeds its own instruments of domination, including international institutions whose rules are structured by capitalist states to facilitate capitalist processes, multinational corporations whose headquarters are in capitalist states but whose loci of activity are in dependent areas, and even individuals (often leaders) or classes (the national bourgeoisie) residing in weak states who are co-opted to participate in and perpetuate an economic system that places the masses in a permanently dependent position.

Radicals believe that the greatest amount of resentment will arise in systems where the stratification is most extreme. There, the poor are likely to be not only resentful but also aggressive. They want change, but the rich have very little incentive to change their behavior. The call for the **New International Economic Order (NIEO)** was voiced by radicals (and some liberal reformers) in the 1970s in most developing countries. The poorer, developing states of the South, underdogs with a dearth of resources, sought fundamental changes that would enhance their

Radicals believe that capitalism makes the international system inherently unequal. Developing countries, such as those in much of Africa, may be unable to increase their power in a system that is biased in favor of rich, capitalist countries.

economic development and control over their own natural resources, thus increasing their relative power over the North.

In short, radicals believe that great economic disparities are built into the structure of the international system and that all actions and interactions are constrained by this structure. But some radicals recognize that transitions may occur. The hegemonic Dutch of the eighteenth century were replaced by the British in the nineteenth century and by the Americans in the twentieth. Change may occur in the semiperiphery and periphery, as states change their positions relative to each other. Capitalism goes through cycles of growth and expansion,

THEORY IN BRIEF

The Radical Perspective on the International System

CHARACTERIZATION	Highly stratified
ACTORS	Capitalist states vs. developing states
CONSTRAINTS	Capitalism; stratification
POSSIBILITY OF CHANGE	Radical change desired but limited by the capitalist structure

as occurred during the age of colonialism and imperialism, followed by periods of contraction and decline. So capitalism itself is a dynamic force for change, though radicals do not view those changes in a positive light.

But can the capitalist system itself be changed? In other words, is system transformation—such as the change from the feudal to the capitalist system— possible? Here, the radicals differ among themselves. Some are quite pessimistic, others more optimistic. Just as realists disagree among themselves about policy implications, radicals disagree about the likelihood that the system stratification that they all abhor can be altered.

Constructivism and Change

Constructivists argue that the whole concept of an international system is a European idea. They hold that nothing can be explained by international material structures alone. Martha Finnemore suggests that there have been different international orders with changing purposes, different views of threat, and reliance on different ways to maintain order. She traces at least four European international orders: an eighteenth-century balance order, a nineteenth-century concert one, a sphere-of-influence system for much of the twentieth century, and after the end of the Cold War an evolving new order whose purposes are the promotion of liberal democracy, capitalism, and human rights. Yet as she admits, at any given time the distribution of power may not be evident: "[W]hat made 1815 a concert and 1950 a cold war was not the material distribution of capabilities but the shared meanings and interpretations participants imposed on those capabilities."[11] Thus, the meaning of various system descriptions can change over time. Indeed, the whole notion of anarchy is socially constructed—as explained in Chapter 3, it is what states make of it.

Constructivists believe that what does change are social norms, although not all norm changes will be transforming. Social norms can be changed through both actions of the collective and through individuals. Collectively, norms may change through coercion, but most likely through international institutions, law and social movements. At the individual level, change occurs through persuasion and through internationalization of the new norms. So although material capabilities do matter in explaining change, just as the realists and many liberals argue, and those conditions set the constraints of what order is possible, "why one order emerges rather than another," can only be seen, Finnemore argues, "by examining the ideas, culture, and social purpose of the actors involved." [12]

Constructivists, then, are interested in analyzing the major changes in the normative structure: how the use of force has evolved over time, how the view of who is human has changed, and how ideas about democracy and human rights have internationalized and how states have been socialized in turn.

Advantages and Disadvantages of the International System as a Level of Analysis

For adherents of all theoretical perspectives, using the international system as a level of analysis has clear advantages. The language of systems theory allows comparison and contrasts between systems: the international system at one point in time may be compared with one at another point in time; international systems may be compared with internal state systems; political systems may be contrasted with social or even biological systems. How these various systems interact is the focus of both the social and the natural sciences.

For all the sciences, two of the most significant advantages to this level of analysis lie in the comprehensiveness of systems theory. First, important aspects of the whole are more difficult to understand by reference to their parts. If systems interest you, then trying to understand them entirely by reference to their parts will prove misleading. Second, it enables scholars to organize the seemingly disjointed parts into a whole; it allows them to hypothesize about and then to test how the various parts, actors, and rules of the system are related and to show how change in one part of the system results in changes in other parts. In this sense, the notion of a system is a significant research tool.

In short, systems theory is a holistic, or top-down, approach. Although it cannot describe events at the micro level (such as why a particular individual acts a certain way), it does allow plausible explanations at the more general level. For the realists, generalizations derived from systems theory provide the fodder for prediction, the ultimate goal of all behavioral science. For liberals and radicals, these generalizations have definite normative implications; in the former case they affirm movement toward a positive system, and in the latter case they confirm pessimistic assessments about the place of states in the economically determined international system.

But systems theory also has some glaring weaknesses and inadequacies. The emphasis at the international system level means that politics is often neglected. The generalizations are broad and sometimes obvious. Who disputes that most states seek to maintain their relative capability or that most states prefer to negotiate rather than fight under all but a few circumstances? Who doubts that some states occupy a preeminent economic position that determines the status of all others?

International system theorists have always been hampered by the problem of boundaries. If they use the notion of the international system, do they mean the international *political* system? What factors lie outside of the system? In fact, much realist theory systematically ignores this critical question by differentiating several different levels within the system but only one international-system-level construct. Liberals do better, differentiating factors external to the system and even incorporating those factors into their expanded notion of an interdependent international system. Yet if you cannot clearly distinguish between what is inside and what is outside of the system, do you in fact have a system? Even more important, what shapes the system? What is the reciprocal relationship between international system constraints and unit (state) behavior? By way of contrast, constructivists do not acknowledge such boundaries. They argue that there is no natural or necessary distinction between the international system and the state or between international politics and domestic politics and no distinction between endogenous and exogenous sources of change.

Just as any systems theory has weaknesses, so is the testing of such theories very difficult. In most cases, theorists are constrained by a lack of historical information. After all, few systems theorists besides some radical and cyclical theorists discuss systems predating 1648. In fact, most begin with the nineteenth century. Those using earlier time frames are constrained both by a poor grounding in history and by glaring lapses in the historical record. Although these weaknesses are not fatal, they restrict scholars' ability to generalize their findings.

Perhaps the most fundamental critique is the attention paid to one international system in particular. Is not the idea of one international system really a Eurocentric notion? Here, the critics have a valid point. The idea of an international system evolved out of the statecentric, post-Westphalian world. In that world, the international system consisted of sovereign European states that shared common pre-Westphalian traditions: the Roman Empire, which had imposed order and unity by force on a large geographic expanse and used a common language and the Christian tradition, as exemplified by the Catholic Church of the medieval era with its authority and law. From those common social roots, the idea of the international system arose. Some scholars, the so-called English school, call this system an international society, because it is grounded in a common culture that was a foundation for common rules and institutions.

Yet were there not international systems—or more accurately international societies—beyond the European world? Perhaps those societies were based on other sets of rules and institutions. For example, various kingdoms flourished in China for centuries before unification in 200 BCE. Imperial China endured for two thousand years, united around a common culture that the Chinese thought was the center of the universe. The Islamic peoples, too, shared a common identity as Islam spread across the Middle East to Africa, Asia, and even Europe. That social identity can be seen in the belief in the *umma*, or community of believers.

The International System: A View from China

Realists posit that the international system changes as great powers gain or lose power relative to other states. As China's economic and political power has grown, many scholars have speculated whether China will catch up to the United States, leading to a new bipolarity, or surpass the United States in a new unipolar system. Chinese government officials have stated their intentions.

Following almost a century of seeing itself as a victim of the great powers and after decades of internal revolution when it was closed to the world, China is becoming a confident great power. The country wields considerable economic and political influence through both bilateral and multilateral diplomacy. Chinese foreign policy objectives and interests have become closely aligned to those of other major powers, and the country now operates within the rules of the contemporary international system.

The economic revolution in China, its embrace of free market capitalism, and its opening to foreign investment and enterprise, have led to three decades of unprecedented economic growth of more than 9 percent per year. Deng Xiaoping and the Chinese Communist party learned from the policy mistakes of the Cultural Revolution and focused on economic liberalization as a path out of poverty for China's 1.3 billion citizens. Now it is the world's third largest economy, surpassing Germany's. China's economic growth has taken place peacefully, and it is in China's interest to continue this peaceful growth. This "peaceful rise," or *zhongguo heping jueqi*, benefits China as well as its regional and global partners, including the advanced capitalist countries of the West.

The peaceful rise has not only propelled hundreds of millions of Chinese out of poverty but has also led to better political and economic relationships with states around the world, regardless of political ideology or level of development. Although these new relationships are

clearly in China's self-interest, they also illustrate its responsibilities as a global power. China has embraced this new role through joining global and regional institutions that address and manage common problems such as trade agreements, regional security, and international financial stability.

China's participation in world trade regimes has increased its global presence to the benefit of all parties. China's accession to the World Trade Organization (WTO) and its Free Trade Agreement with the United States has allowed it to maximize economic output while demonstrating to the world that it can adhere to WTO regulations such as nondiscrimination policies, elimination of price controls, and revision of domestic laws to comply with WTO obligations. China is also now actively engaged in regional trade and economic agreements. Negotiations have continued since 2001 on the establishment of a free-trade area between members of the Association of South East Asian Nations (ASEAN) and China. The China-ASEAN exposition in 2009 focused on economic and trade cooperation in the region. Similarly, China's involvement in Asia-Pacific Economic Cooperation (APEC) seeks to foster peaceful relations among Pacific Rim countries. In the photo on the next page, Chinese president Hu Jintao addresses the 2009 APEC conference.

China has similarly sought greater participation in international financial institutions such as the World Bank and the International Monetary Fund (IMF). China

took an active role in the meetings during the 2008–09 international financial crisis. In fact, many proposals for developing a new financial architecture following the crisis include greater participation and involvement of China.

To continue economic growth, China needs peaceful relations with its neighbors. Through organizations such as the Shanghai Cooperation Organization (SCO), China has committed itself to this path as the SCO addresses the issues of terrorism, economic security, and energy. China's participation in talks on the future of the Korean peninsula and on North Korea's nuclear standoff are further evidence of a commitment to a stable order.

China is also building relations with African countries by investment in infrastructure, technology, and natural resources. Whereas the West colonized these lands and often stripped them of their resource wealth, China seeks a peaceful, mutually beneficial relationship with African states. China does not interfere in the domestic affairs of states or impose unwanted conditions on issues that are within the state's own responsibility. This has led to criticism of China over its investment in energy infrastructure in Sudan, for example.

China is involved in a diverse array of organizations, agreements, and regional forums that all have one common thread: they have all taken place in a period of growth unprecedented in human history. China is proud of its accomplishments and appreciates that the factors influencing such change are not all domestic. Indeed, China relies on many countries around the world to secure its own economic future and needs open overseas markets to sell its goods. China also acknowledges the relationship between economic development and the environment. Although as a developing country, it was not a party to the Kyoto Protocol on climate change, China is seizing the initiative in using fossil fuels more efficiently and improving technology for solar energy.

China sees the economic, political, and social benefits of market liberalization. It also understands that the cornerstone of market liberalization is international cooperation. For this reason, China will likely remain a harmonious, responsible, and active participant in the international system.

China is not likely to seek territorial expansion or world hegemony, but it will defend the one-China policy concerning those lands historically part of China, including Taiwan. China is aware of the security benefits that accrue to an economic and trading power. Of particular concern are Japanese ambitions in East Asia and North Korean economic refugees. China's wealth and influence appear likely to help with both issues without upsetting the status quo of the international system.

For Critical Analysis

Answer these questions on wwnorton.com/studyspace

1. *Why does China have an interest in sustaining the contemporary international system even if it does not dominate it?*

2. *How would an offensive realist react to China's explanation of its role in the international system?*

3. *China has consistently argued in favor of sovereignty and noninterference in the domestic affairs of states. How does this position support China's international role?*

4. *Constructivists argue that changes in norms lead to system change. Has China learned new norms? Or is it merely acting in its own self-interest, as realists suggest?*

THEORY IN BRIEF

Contending Perspectives on the International System

	LIBERALISM / NEOLIBERAL INSTITUTIONALISM	REALISM / NEOREALISM	RADICALISM / DEPENDENCY THEORY	CONSTRUCTIVISM
CHARACTERIZATION	Three liberal interpretations: interdependence among actors, international society, and anarchy	Anarchic	Highly stratified	International system exists as social construct
ACTORS	States, international governmental institutions, nongovernmental organizations, substate actors	State is primary actor	Capitalist states vs. developing states	Individuals matter; no deliniation between international and domestic
CONSTRAINTS	None; ongoing interactions	Polarity; distribution of power	Capitalism; stratification	Ongoing interactions
POSSIBILITY OF CHANGE	No possibility of radical change; constant incremental change as actors are involved in new relationships	Slow change when the balance of power shifts	Radical change desired but limited by the capitalist structure	Emphasis on change in social norms and identities

The *umma* was symbolized by the institution of the caliphate, the Islamic political authority, and was an identity that overrode tribe, race, and even the state itself. That unity broke down in the division between Sunni and Shia, a dispute over who was the rightful successor to the Prophet Muhammad. Some advocate restoration of the caliphate as a renewal of Islamic civilization's former historical greatness. International relations scholars have often paid too little attention to non-European international societies.

As the Europe-based international system emerged as the most powerful and dominant one, how did other regions become part of it? Colonialism and the spread of capitalism by the European powers brought many areas into the new system.

Struggles persist among these different international societies. The political scientist Samuel Huntington identified them as civilizational, positing that there was not one international system sharing common culture and traditions, but different societies, or civilizations. That variety would be the basis of international conflict.[13]

Thus, although the notion of one international system may reflect power realities from the nineteenth century to the early years of the twenty-first, that idea is disputed because of its Eurocentric bias, its neglect of the international systems of "others," and the empirical difficulties involved in differentiating the international system and its component parts.

In Sum: From the International System to the State

Of all the theoretical approaches, the international system level of analysis receives the most attention from realists and radicals. For realists, the defining characteristic of the international system is polarity; for radicals, it is stratification. In both perspectives, the international system constrains state behavior. Realists generally view such constraints as positive, depending on the distribution of power, whereas for radicals the constraints are negative, preventing economically depressed states from achieving equality and justice. Liberals view the international system from a more neutral perspective as an arena and process for interaction. Constructivists take an evolutionary approach, emphasizing how changes in norms and ideas shape the system, seeing little differentiation between international and domestic systems and discounting the importance that other theorists attach to international system structure.

States and foreign policy decision makers operate within the confines of the international system. In the next chapter we examine the state, models of state decision making, and challenges to the state.

DISCUSSION QUESTIONS

1. Is the international system like other physical or biological systems? How are these systems similar? How are they different?

2. The realist view of the international system has been criticized as oriented to the status quo. To what extent is that critique valid? Is that characteristic desirable or not?

3. Neorealists and neoliberals agree on an essential characteristic of the international system. How do they disagree? Why is that disagreement important?

4. After the collapse of the Soviet Union, some theorists argued that Marxism had been discredited and was, in fact, dead. Is that true? How can radicalism help us explain anything about the international system?

KEY TERMS

international society, p. 103
New International Economic Order
    (NIEO), p. 105
North, p. 104

South, p. 104
stratification, p. 104
system, p. 93

 Find chapter outlines, practice quizzes, flashcards, and other study and
review materials for this chapter at wwnorton.com/studyspace.

05

The State

- How is the state, the major actor in international relations, defined?
- What are the different views of the state held by the various theoretical perspectives?
- How is state power measured?
- What methods do states use to exercise their power?
- Do democracies behave differently from nondemocracies?
- What models help us explain how states make foreign-policy decisions?
- What are the major contemporary challenges to the state?

IN THINKING ABOUT INTERNATIONAL relations, the state is central. Much of the history traced in Chapter 2 was the history of how the state developed, emerging from the post-Westphalian framework, and how the state, sovereignty, and the nation developed in tandem. Two of the theoretical perspectives—realism and liberalism—acknowledge the primacy of the state. Yet despite this emphasis on the state, it is inadequately conceptualized. As the scholar James Rosenau laments, "All too many studies posit the state as a symbol without content, as an actor whose nature, motives, and conduct are so self-evident as to obviate any need for precise conceptualizing. Often, in fact, the concept seems to be used as a residual category to explain that which is otherwise inexplicable in macro politics."[1] We need to do better.

The State and the Nation

For an entity to be considered a **state**, four fundamental conditions must be met. First, a state must have a territorial base, geographically defined boundaries. Second, within its borders, a stable population must reside. Third, there should be a government to which this population owes allegiance. Finally, a state has to be recognized diplomatically by other states.

These legal criteria are not absolute. Most states do have a territorial base, though the precise borders are often the subject of dispute. Until the Palestinian Authority was given a measure of control over the West Bank and Gaza, for instance, Palestine was not territorially based. It was, however, given special observer status in international bodies and was viewed as a quasi state. Most states have a stable population, but migrant communities and nomadic peoples cross borders, as the Masai peoples of Kenya and Tanzania do, undetected by state authorities. Most states have some type of institutional structure for governance, but whether the people are obedient to it can be unknown, because of lack of information, or it can be problematic, because the institutional legitimacy of the government is constantly questioned. A state need not have a particular form of government, but most of its people must acknowledge the legitimacy of that government. In 1997, the people of Zaire (now the Democratic Republic of Congo) told the rest of the international community that they no longer recognized the legitimacy of the government led by Mobutu Sese Seko, thus plunging the country into a civil war. Finally, other states must recognize the state diplomatically; but how many states' recognition does it take for this criterion to be fulfilled? The Republic of Transkei—a tiny piece of real estate carved out of South Africa—was recognized by just one state, South Africa. This action, designed to quell international outrage over South Africa's racist apartheid policy, proved insufficient to give Transkei status as a state, and the territory was soon reincorporated into South Africa. So although the legal conditions for statehood provide a yardstick, that measuring stick is not absolute. Other states remain contested. In early 2008, Kosovo, once a semiautonomous part of Yugoslavia and later a province of Serbia, declared unilateral independence from Serbia. A constitution was accepted and a ministry of foreign affairs established. By the end of the same year over fifty countries had recognized Kosovo as an independent state. Serbia objected to the declaration and appealed to the United Nations General Assembly to request an advisory opinion from the International Court of Justice to review the legality of Kosovo independence. Although any opinion will be nonbinding, the actions illustrate the contested fact of statehood. Some entities that do not fulfill all the legal criteria are still states.

The definition of a state differs from that of a **nation**. A nation is a group of people who share a set of characteristics. Do a people share a common history and heritage, a common language and customs, or similar lifestyles? If so, then the people make up a nation. It was this feeling of commonality, of people uniting together for a cause, that provided the foundation for the French Revolution and spread to Central and South America and to central Europe. It was nationalism—the belief that nations should form their own states—that propelled the formation of a unified Italy and Germany in the nineteenth century. At the core of the concept of a nation is the notion that people with commonalities owe their allegiance to the nation and to its legal representative, the state. The recognition of commonalities among people (and hence of differences from other groups) spread with new technologies and education.

The Palestinian people seek to establish a new state in territories occupied by Israel, including the West Bank. Here, the Palestinian prime minister Salam Fayyad planted trees in the West Bank in 2010 "to establish our presence on our land."

When the printing press became widely used, the masses could read in their national languages; with improved methods of transportation, people could travel, witnessing firsthand similarities and differences among other groups. With better communications, elites could use the media to promote unity or sometimes to exploit differences.

Some nations, like the Danes and Italians, formed their own states. That coincidence between state and nation, the **nation-state**, is the foundation for national self-determination, the idea that peoples sharing nationhood have a right to determine how and under what conditions they should live. Other nations are spread among several states. For example, Germans resided and still live not only in a united Germany but in the far-off corners of eastern Europe; Somalis live in Kenya, Ethiopia, and Djibouti as well as in Somalia. Still other states have within their borders several different nations—India, Russia, and South Africa are prominent examples. In these cases, the state and the nation do not coincide. Sometimes, there is a congruence between state and nation, as in Denmark and Italy. A state

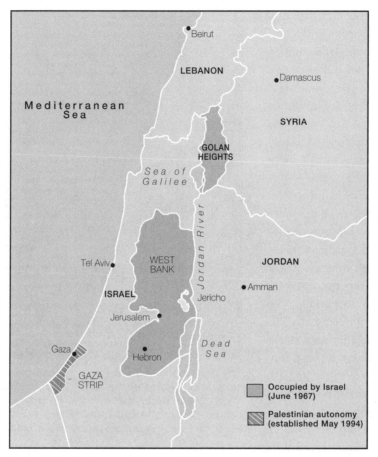

Central Middle Eastern Region, 2010

may contain several nations, as do South Africa and India. The United States and Canada present yet another form. In each, a number of different Native American nations are a part of the state, as are multiple immigrant communities. The state and the nation do not coincide. Yet over time, a common identity and nationality are forged, even in the absence of religious, ethnic, or cultural similarity. In the case of the United States, national values reflecting commonly held ideas are expressed in public rituals including reciting the Pledge of Allegiance, singing the national anthem, and civic volunteerism.[2] States are both complex and constantly evolving.

Some of the hundreds of national subgroups (and 900 million people) around the world identify more with a particular culture or religion than with a particular state, often experiencing discrimination or persecution because of their identity. This situation is not new. The gradual disintegration of the

Ottoman Empire between the 1830s and World War I reflected increasing ethnic demands for self-determination from Egypt and Greece to Albania, Montenegro, and Bulgaria.

Yet not all ethnonationalists aspire to the same goals. Some want recognition of a unique status, the right to speak and write a particular language or practice their religion, or special seats in representative bodies, as the Basques in Spain and France desire. Some seek solutions in federal arrangements, hoping to guarantee autonomy within an established state, as the Kurds have sought in Iraq. Yet the Kurds' new 2009 constitution, proclaiming exclusive rights to oil and gas resources beneath their territory, suggests they may want more authority. Still other groups seek separation and the right to form their own state. A few prefer **irredentism**, joining with fellow ethnonationalists in other states and creating with them another state or joining with another state that is populated by fellow ethnonationalists.

Disputes over state territories and the desires of nations to form their own states have been major sources of instability and even conflict since the end of colonialism in Africa, and most recently after the breakup of the Soviet Union and Yugoslavia. Of these conflicts none has been as intractable as that between Israeli Jews and Palestinian Arabs, who each claim the same territory. This conflict has been complicated by several factors—that Jews, Christians, Muslims, and Bahais each claim land or some monuments as sacred, the intense opposition from Arab states to the existence of the state of Israel, and Israel's gradual expansion of its territory through war and settlements. Since the founding of Israel in 1948, the Arab and Jewish peoples of Palestine have been involved in six interstate wars and three popular uprisings. Civilians on both sides have been harmed or killed, and many continue to live as refugees. This leads to a major debate: Should Palestine be divided into two separate independent states?

Contending Conceptualizations of the State

Just as the nation is more than a historic entity, the state is more than a legal entity. There are numerous competing conceptualizations of the state, many of which emphasize ideas absent from the legalistic approach.

Other concepts of the state include: the state is a normative order, a symbol for a particular society and the beliefs that bind the people living within its borders. It is also the entity that has a monopoly on the legitimate use of violence within a society. The state is a functional unit that takes on a number of important responsibilities, centralizing and unifying them. The perspectives of the state parallel the general theories discussed in Chapters 3 and 4. For two of these theoretical perspectives, the state is paramount.

POLICY DEBATE

Should Israel and the Palestinian territories be divided into two separate independent states?

Yes

- A Palestinian state would reinforce the democratic commitment to the principle of self-determination.
- A Palestinian state would provide greater stability in the region. With the Palestinian dream realized, Arab states would have achieved an important foreign policy objective.
- A Palestinian state could encourage the return of refugees who fled the territory during the wars between the Arabs and Israel, reuniting the Palestinian diaspora.
- The establishment of a Palestinian state would frustrate the rise of more extremist factions within Hamas or Hezbollah.
- The end of Israeli occupation of the West Bank would shift the burden of governing the people there from Israel to the Palestinians.
- Palestinians living is Israel may choose to move to the newly created Palestine, decreasing religious and ethnic conflict in Israel.
- The two-state solution is the only moderate solution likely to lead to the end of hostilities between the Israelis and Palestinians.
- All other alternatives would be worse for both Israelis and Arabs.
- The two-state solution enjoys considerable international political support.

No

- Israel's security would be jeopardized by the increased military capability of the newly created state of Palestine.
- Israel's internal security could be compromised if right-wing Jewish settlers are forced to move from territory handed back to the Palestinians. Extremists could cause unrest as they compete for scarce land.
- Separate states could result in a massive population transfer, making war more likely when ethnic tensions erupt.
- Separate states can be maintained only with a third-party buffer between Israel and Palestine.
- Too many issues need to be resolved: determination of borders; the status of Jerusalem and other religious sites; the status of Israeli settlements; water rights. No consensus on these issues exists.

The Realist View of the State

Realists generally hold a statist, or state-centric, view. They believe that the state is an autonomous actor constrained only by the structural anarchy of the international system. The state enjoys sovereignty, that is, the authority to govern matters that are within its own borders and that affect its people, economy, security, and form of government. As a sovereign entity, the state has a consistent set of goals—that is, a national interest—defined in terms of power. Different kinds of power can be translated into military power. Although power is of primary importance to realists, as we will see later in this chapter, ideas also matter in their estimation; ideology, for example, can determine the nature of the state, as with the North Korean state under communism. But in international relations, once the state (with power and ideas) acts, according to the realists, it does so as an autonomous, unitary actor.

In Focus

THE REALIST VIEW OF THE STATE

The state is:

- an autonomous actor.
- constrained only by the anarchy of the international system.
- sovereign.
- guided by a national interest that is defined in terms of power.

The Liberal View of the State

In the liberal view, the state enjoys sovereignty but is not an autonomous actor. Just as liberals believe the international system is a process occurring among many actors, they see the state as a pluralist arena whose function is to maintain the basic rules of the game. These rules ensure that various interests (both governmental and societal) compete fairly and effectively in the game of politics. There is no single explicit or consistent national interest; there are many. These interests often compete against each other within a pluralistic framework. A state's national interests change, reflecting the interests and relative power positions of competing groups inside and sometimes also outside of the state.

In Focus

THE LIBERAL VIEW OF THE STATE

The state is:

- a process, involving contending interests.
- a reflection of both governmental and societal interests.
- the repository of multiple and changing national interests.
- the possessor of fungible sources of power.

In Focus ◎ ▮▮▮▮▮▮▮▮▮▮▮▮▮▮▮▮

THE RADICAL VIEW OF THE STATE

The state is:

- the executing agent of the bourgeoisie.
- influenced by pressures from the capitalist class.
- constrained by the structure of the international capitalist system.

The Radical View of the State

Radicals offer two alternative views of the state, each emphasizing the role of capitalism and the capitalist class in the formation and functioning of the state. The *instrumental* Marxist view sees the state as the executing agent of the bourgeoisie. The bourgeoisie reacts to direct societal pressures, especially to pressures from the capitalist class. The *structural* Marxist view sees the state as operating within the structure of the capitalist system. Within that system, the state is driven to expand, not because of the direct pressure of the capitalists but because of the imperatives of the capitalist system. In neither view is there a national interest: state behavior reflects economic goals. In neither case is real sovereignty possible, because the state is continually reacting to external (and internal) capitalist pressures.

The Constructivist View of the State

Because constructivists see both national interests and national identities as social constructs, the state is conceptualized very differently from any of the other theoretical perspectives. To constructivists, national interests are neither material nor given. They are ideational and ever-changing and evolving, both in response to domestic factors and in response to international norms and ideas. States share a variety of goals and values, which they are socialized into by international and nongovernmental organizations. Those norms can change state preferences, which in turn can influence state behavior. So, too, do states have multiple identities, including a shared understanding of national identity, which also changes,

In Focus ◎ ▮▮▮▮▮▮▮▮▮▮▮▮▮▮

THE CONSTRUCTIVIST VIEW OF THE STATE

The state is:

- a socially constructed entity.
- the repository of national interests that change over time.
- shaped by international norms that change preferences.
- influenced by changing national interests that shape and reshape identities.
- socialized by IGOs and NGOs.

altering state preferences and hence state behavior. In short, the state "makes" the system and the system "makes" the state.[3]

Contrasting the Various Views of the State

Conceptualizations of the state can be easily contrasted using the example of an important primary commodity—oil.[4]

A realist interpretation posits a uniform national interest that is articulated by the state. Oil is a key strategic commodity that is vital for national security. Thus, the state desires stability in the availability and prices of primary commodities. For example, the United States needs to be assured of a safe and secure supply of oil and seeks to obtain it at relatively uniform prices. When the United States negotiates in international forums, with individual supplier states, or with multinational companies, the national interest of the state defined in strategic terms is the bottom line of the negotiations. This is also the case with China. Oil is the engine of its rapidly expanding economy, and therefore it has forged strong bilateral ties with oil-exporting states such as Iran, Sudan, and Angola.

Liberals believe that multiple national interests influence state actions: consumer groups desire the oil at the lowest price possible; manufacturers, who depend on bulk supplies to run their factories, prefer a stable supply of oil, otherwise they risk losing their jobs; producers of oil, including domestic producers, want high prices, so that they will make profits and have incentives to reinvest in drilling. The state itself reflects no consistent viewpoint about the oil; its task is to ensure that the "playing field is level" and that the procedural rules are the same for the various players in the market. The substantive outcome of the game—which group's interests predominate—changes depending on circumstances and is of little import to the state. When negotiations occur, the state ensures that the various interests have a voice and provides a forum for the interactions. There is no single or consistent national interest: at times, it is low consumer prices; at other times, stability of prices; and at still other times, high prices in order to stimulate domestic production.

In the radical perspective, primary commodity policy reflects the interests of the owner capitalist class aligned with the bourgeoisie (in the instrumental Marxist view) and reflects the structure of the international capitalist system (in structural Marxist thinking). Both views would more than likely see the negotiating process as exploitative, where the weak (poor and dependent groups or states) are exploited for the advancement of strong capitalists or capitalist states. According to radical thinking, the international petroleum companies are the capitalists, aligned with hegemonic states. They are able to negotiate favorable prices, often to the detriment of developing, oil-producing states such as Mexico or Nigeria. Radicals may explain U.S. and European interests in the Middle East in terms of the need for a reliable petroleum and natural gas supply.

By way of contrast, although constructivists may pay little heed to materialist conceptions of power defined in terms of oil resources, they may try to tease out how the identities of states are forged by having such a valuable resource. Saudi Arabia and the Persian Gulf states have developed an identity based on seemingly limitless, valuable resources. Oil permits them to merge that identity with their identity as Islamic states that export the faith to other countries.

Thus, each theory holds a different view about the state. These differences can be seen in four topic areas: the nature of state power (what is power? what are important sources of power?), the exercise of state power (the relative importance of different techniques of statecraft), how foreign policy is made (the statist versus the bureaucratic or the pluralist view of decision making), and the determinants of foreign policy (the relative importance of domestic versus international factors).

The Nature of State Power

States are critical actors because they have **power**, which is the ability not only to influence others but also to control outcomes so as to produce results that would not have occurred naturally. States have power with respect to each other and with respect to those actors within the state. All theoretical perspectives acknowledge the importance of power. But each pays attention to different types of power. Realists, liberals, and radicals all conceptualize power in materialist terms, realists and radicals primarily in natural and tangible sources, with liberals paying more attention to intangible sources, though not exclusively. Constructivists emphasize the nonmaterialist sources found in the power of ideas, one of the intangible sources. All agree that power is multidimensional, dynamic, and situational.

Natural Sources of Power

Through the exercise of power, states have influence over others and can control the direction of policies and events. Whether power is effective at influencing outcomes depends, in part, on the **power potential** of each party. A state's power potential depends in part on its natural sources of power, each of which is critical to both realist and radical perspectives. The three most important natural sources of power are geographic size and position, natural resources, and population.

Geographic size and position are the natural sources of power recognized first by international relations theorists. A large geographic expanse gives a state automatic power (when we think of power, we think of large states—Russia, China, the United States, Australia, India, Canada, or Brazil, for instance). Long borders, however, may be a weakness: they must be defended, an expensive and often problematic task.

Two different views about the importance of geography in international relations emerged at the turn of the century within the realist tradition. In the late 1890s, the naval officer and historian Alfred Mahan (1840–1914) wrote of the importance of controlling the sea. He argued that the state that controls the ocean routes controls the world. To Mahan, sovereignty over land was not so critical as having access to and control over sea routes.[5] In 1904, the British geographer Sir Halford Mackinder (1861–1947) countered this view. To Mackinder, the state that had the most power was the one that controlled the Eurasian geographic "heartland": "He who rules Eastern Europe commands the Heartland of Eurasia; who rules the Heartland commands the World Island of Europe, Asia, and Africa, and who rules the World Island commands the world."[6]

Both views have empirical validity. British power in the eighteenth and nineteenth centuries was determined largely by its dominance on the seas, a power that allowed Britain to colonialize distant places, including India, much of Africa, and North and Central America. Russia's lack of easy access to the sea and its resultant inability to wield naval power have been viewed as persistent weaknesses in that country's power potential. Control of key oceanic choke points—the Straits of Malacca, Gibraltar, and Hormuz; the Dardanelles; the Persian Gulf; and the Suez and Panama Canals—is viewed as a positive indicator of power potential.

Yet geographic position in Mackinder's heartland of Eurasia has also proven to be a significant source of power potential. More than any other country Germany has acted to secure its power through its control of the heartland of Eurasia, acting very clearly according to Mackinder's dictum, as interpreted by the German geographer Karl Haushofer (1869–1946). Haushofer, who had served in both the Bavarian and the German armies, was disappointed by Germany's loss in World War I. Arguing that Germany could become a powerful state if it could capture the Eurasian heartland, he set out to make geopolitics a legitimate area for academic inquiry. He founded an institute and a journal, thrusting himself into a position as the leading supporter and proponent of Nazi expansion.

But geographic power potential is magnified or constrained by natural resources, a second source of natural power. Controlling a large geographic expanse is not a positive ingredient of power unless that expanse contains natural resources. Petroleum-exporting states such as Kuwait, Qatar, and the United Arab Emirates, which are geographically small but have a crucial natural resource, have greater power potential than their sizes would suggest. States need oil and are ready to pay dearly for it, and will even go to war when access to it is denied. States that have such valuable natural resources, regardless of their geographic size, wield power over states that do not. The United States, Russia, and South Africa exert vast power potential because of their diverse natural resources—oil, copper, bauxite, vanadium, gold, and silver. Since 2006, Russia has used that power potential, cutting off natural gas supplies to Ukraine and hence slowing supplies to Europe,

Natural resource wealth can contribute to state power, but it may also invite aggressive action by other states. In 1990, Iraq invaded Kuwait in the hope of seizing control of some of its oil reserves. When their invasion failed, the retreating Iraqi forces set Kuwaiti oil fields on fire.

which gets one-quarter of its gas through Ukraine. Though it began as a commercial dispute over pricing, the conflict has become a tool Russia can use to punish Ukraine for bringing an anti-Russian government into power during the 2005 "Orange Revolution" and for its rapprochement with the West.

Of course, having a sought-after resource may prove a liability, making states targets for aggressive actions, as Kuwait soberly learned in 1990. The absence of natural resources does not mean that a state has no power potential, however; Japan is not rich in natural resources, but it has parlayed other elements of power so as to make itself an economic powerhouse.

Population is a third natural source of power. Sizable populations, such as those of China (1.3 billion people), India (1.2 billion), the United States (307 million), and Russia (142 million), automatically give power potential, and often great power status, to a state. Although a large population produces a variety of goods and services, characteristics of that population (health status, age distribution, level of social services) may magnify or constrain state power. States with small, highly educated, skilled populations, such as Switzerland, Norway, Austria, and Singapore, can fill disproportionately large economic and political niches. States with large but relatively poor populations, such as

FIGURE 5.1 | **Ingredients of State Power Potential**

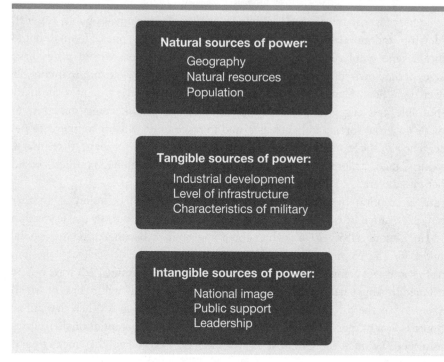

Ethiopia (with 79 million people but a gross national product of only $800 per capita), can exercise less power.

These natural sources of power are modified by the use and organization of power into tangible and intangible sources. These sources are used to enhance, modify, or constrain power potential, as shown in Figure 5.1.

Tangible Sources of Power

Among the tangible sources of power, industrial development, economic diversification, level of infrastructure, and characteristics of the military are among the most critical. With an advanced industrial capacity, the advantages and disadvantages of geography diminish. Air travel, for example, makes geographic expanse less of a barrier to commerce, yet at the same time makes even large states militarily vulnerable. With industrialization, the importance of population is modified, too. Large but poorly equipped armies are no match for small armies with advanced equipment. Industrialized states generally have higher educational levels, more advanced technology, and more efficient use of capital, all of which add to their tangible power potential.

Intangible Sources of Power

Intangible power sources—national image, quality of government, public support, leadership, and morale—may be as important as the tangible ones, although not to radicals, who emphasize material sources of power. People within states have images of their own state's power potential—images that translate into an intangible power ingredient. Canadians have typically viewed themselves as internationally responsible and eager to participate in multilateral peacekeeping missions, to provide generous foreign aid packages, and to respond unselfishly to international emergencies. The state has acted on and, indeed, helped to shape that image, making Canada a more powerful actor than its small population (33 million) would otherwise dictate.

The perception by other states of public support and cohesion is another intangible source of power. China's power was magnified during the leadership of Mao Zedong (1893–1976), when there appeared to be unprecedented public support for the communist leadership and a high degree of societal cohesion. Israel's successful campaigns in the Middle East in the 1967 and 1973 wars can be attributed in large part to strong public support, including the willingness of Israeli citizens to pay the cost and die for their country when necessary. When that public support is absent, particularly in democracies, the power potential of the state is diminished. Witness the U.S. loss in the Vietnam War, when challenges to and disagreement with the war effort undermined military effectiveness. Loss of public support may also inhibit authoritarian systems. In both the 1991 Gulf War and the 2003 Iraq War, Saddam Hussein's support from his own troops was woefully inadequate: many were not ready to die for the Iraqi regime and fled.

Leadership is another source of intangible power. Visionaries and charismatic leaders, such as India's Mohandas Gandhi, France's Charles de Gaulle, the United States' Franklin Roosevelt, Germany's Otto von Bismarck, and Britain's Winston Churchill, were able to augment the power potential of their states by taking bold initiatives. Poor leaders, those who squander public resources and abuse the public trust, such as Libya's Muammar Qaddafi, Zimbabwe's Robert Mugabe, and Iraq's Saddam Hussein, diminish the state's power capability and its capacity to exert power over the long term. Liberals, in particular, pay attention to leadership: good leaders can avoid resorting to war; bad leaders may not be able to prevent it.

More generally, intangible power characteristics can be exercised. Joseph S. Nye labeled such power **soft power**, the ability to attract others because of the legitimacy of the state's values or its policies.[7] Rather than exerting its natural and tangible power, such a state influences other states by being what it is. In the case of the United States, its soft power resources may include its model of soft-functioning democracy and commitment to political and civil rights.

Clearly, when coupled with the tangible, intangible power sources either augment a state's capacity or diminish its power. Liberals, who have a more expansive notion of power, would more than likely place greater importance on these intangible ingredients, because several are characteristics of domestic processes. Yet different combinations of the sources of power may lead to varying outcomes. The victory by the NATO alliance over Slobodan Milošević's Yugoslavian forces in 1999 can be explained by the alliance's overwhelming natural sources of power coupled with its strong tangible sources of power. But how can Afghanistan's victory over the Soviet Union in the early 1980s be explained, or the North Vietnamese victory over the United States in the 1970s, or the Algerian victory over France in the early 1960s? In those cases, countries with limited natural and tangible sources of power were able to prevail over those with strong natural and tangible power resources. In these cases, the intangible sources of power, including the willingness of the populations to continue to fight against overwhelming odds, explains victory by the objectively weaker side.[8] Success in using various forms of state power clearly depends on the specific context.

Constructivists, in contrast, offer a unique perspective on power. They argue that power includes not only the tangible and intangible sources. In addition, it includes the power of ideas and language—as distinguished from ideology, which fueled the unlikely victory of the objectively weaker side in the cases described above. It is through the power of ideas and norms that state identities and nationalism are forged and changed.

The Exercise of State Power

In all theoretical perspectives, power is not just to be possessed, it is to be used. Using state power is a difficult task.

States use a variety of techniques to translate power potential into effective power, namely, diplomacy, economic statecraft, and force. In a particular situation, a state may begin with one approach and then try a number of others to influence the intended target. In other cases, several different techniques may be utilized simultaneously. Which techniques political scientists think states emphasize varies across the theoretical perspectives. Different types of states may make different choices.

The Art of Diplomacy

Traditional **diplomacy** entails states' trying to influence the behavior of other actors by negotiating, by taking a specific action or refraining from such an action, or by conducting public diplomacy.

According to Harold Nicolson, a British diplomat and writer, diplomacy usually begins with negotiation, through direct or indirect communication, in an attempt to reach agreement on an issue. This negotiation may be conducted tacitly among the parties, each of which recognizes that a move in one direction leads to a response by the other that is strategic. The parties may conduct open, formal negotiations, where one side offers a formal proposal and the other responds in kind; this is generally repeated many times until a compromise is reached. In either case, reciprocity usually occurs, whereby each side responds to the other's moves in kind.

Yet for negotiations to be successful, each party needs to be credible, that is, each party needs to make believable statements, assume a likely position, and be able to back up its position by taking action. Well-intentioned and credible parties will have a higher probability of engaging in successful negotiations.

States seldom enter diplomatic bargaining or negotiations as power equals. Each knows its own and its opponent's power potential, as well as knowledge of its own goals, even though information about the opponent may be imperfect, incomplete, or even just wrong. Thus, although the outcome of the bargaining is almost always mutually beneficial (if not, why bother?), that outcome is not likely to please the parties equally. And the satisfaction of each party may change as new information is revealed or as conditions change over time.

Bargaining and negotiations are complex processes, complicated by at least two critical factors. First, most states carry out two levels of bargaining simultaneously: international bargaining between and among states and the bargaining that must occur between the state's negotiators and its various domestic constituencies, both to arrive at a negotiating position and to ratify the agreement reached by the two states. The political scientist Robert Putnam refers to this as the "two-level game."[9] International trade negotiations within the World Trade Organization are such a two-level game. For example, Japan and South Korea bargain with the United States over the liberalization of rice markets. The United States supports liberalization in order to improve the balance of trade between it and the respective Asian powers; by advocating this position, the United States supports its own domestic rice producers, located in the key electoral states of California and Texas. Japan and South Korea have powerful domestic interests opposing liberalization, including rice farmers strategically located in virtually all voting constituencies. Thus, in each case, the United States and Japan or South Korea are each conducting two sets of negotiations: one with the foreign state and the other within the domestic political arena. What makes the game unusually complex is that "moves that are rational for one player at one board . . . may be impolitic for that same player at the other board."[10] The negotiator is the formal link between the two levels of negotiation. Realists see the two-level game as constrained primarily by the structure of the international system, whereas liberals more readily acknowledge domestic pressures and incentives.

Second, bargaining and negotiating are, in part, a culture-bound activity. Approaches to bargaining vary across cultures—a view accepted among liberals, who place importance on state differences. At least two styles of negotiations have been identified.[11] These two different styles may lead to contrasting outcomes.

In the negotiations during the 1970s for the New International Economic Order (NIEO), for example, the South argued in a deductive style—from general principles to particular applications. This approach conveniently masked conflict over details until a later stage. The South's approach contrasted sharply with that preferred by the United States and Great Britain, which favored discussion of concrete detail, eschewing grand philosophical debate, addressing concrete problems, and resolving specific issues before broader principles were crystallized. These differences in negotiating approaches led, in part, to a stalemate in negotiations and eventually the failure to achieve any meaningful concessions.[12]

The use of **public diplomacy** is an increasingly popular diplomatic technique in a communication-linked world. Public diplomacy involves targeting both foreign publics and elites, attempting to create an overall image that enhances a country's ability to achieve its diplomatic objectives. For instance, the former First Lady and current secretary of state Hillary Rodham Clinton's international travels highlight the role of women, promoting values, democracy, and human rights.

Before and during the 2003 Iraq War, public diplomacy became a particularly useful diplomatic instrument. American administration officials, notably Secretary of State Colin Powell, National Security Advisor Condoleezza Rice, and Secretary of Defense Donald Rumsfeld, not only made the case for war to the American people in news interviews and newspaper op-ed pieces, but also lobbied friendly and opposing states both directly in negotiations and indirectly through various media outlets, including independent Arab media such as the Al Jazeera television network. The Department of State established the Middle East Radio Network, comprising both Radio Sawa and Alhurra. Radio Sawa broadcasts both Western and Middle Eastern popular music with periodic news briefs. The more controversial Alhurra presents the American perspective on foreign policy in the Middle East. It has been criticized for failing to meet high journalistic standards, its escalating budget ($113 million for 2010), and its falling ratings. Although Al Jazeera is the number one news source for an estimated 55 percent of the Arab world, Alhurra attracts less than 1 percent of the Arab market. Although in the communications age, states have another diplomatic instrument, it may be more difficult to succeed in changing "hearts and minds."

But diplomacy may need to include more than negotiations. Negotiators may find they need to utilize other measures of statecraft, including positive incentives such as diplomatic recognition, foreign aid in return for desired actions, and the threat of negative consequences (reduction or elimination of foreign aid, severance of diplomatic ties, use of coercive force) if the target state continues to move in a specific direction. The tools of statecraft are both economic and military. Although greater powers have the ability to exercise multiple means of statecraft, other states may choose **niche diplomacy**, concentrating their resources in a few areas. Since the 1990s, Canada has adopted niche diplomacy, specializing in multilateral peacekeeping training and concentrating on human security issues such as the use of child soldiers, women's rights, and global warming.

Economic Statecraft

States use more than words to exercise power. They may use economic statecraft—both positive and negative **sanctions**—to try to influence other states.[13] Positive sanctions involve offering a "carrot," enticing the target state to act in the desired way by rewarding moves made in the desired direction. The assumption is that positive incentives will lead the target state to change its behavior. Negative sanctions, however, may be imposed more often: threatening to act or actually taking actions that punish the target state for moves made in the direction not desired. The goal of using the "stick" (negative sanctions) may be to punish or reprimand the target state for actions taken or may be to try to change the future behavior of the target state. Table 5.1 provides examples of positive and negative sanctions used in economic statecraft.

A state's ability to use these instruments of economic statecraft depends on its power potential. States with a variety of power sources have more instruments at their disposal. Clearly, only economically well-endowed countries can grant licenses, offer investment guarantees, grant preferences to specific countries, house foreign assets, or boycott effectively. Radicals often point to this fact to illustrate the hegemony of the international capitalist system.

Although radicals deny it, liberals argue that developing states do have some leverage in economic statecraft under special circumstances. If a state or group of states controls a key resource whose production is limited, their power is strengthened. Among the primary commodities, only petroleum has this potential, and it gave the Arab members of the Organization of the Petroleum Exporting Countries (OPEC) the ability to impose oil sanctions on the United States and the Netherlands when those two countries strongly supported Israel in the 1973 Arab-Israeli War.

South Africa illustrates a case of relative success in the use of economic sanctions. When positive sanctions in the form of the Reagan administration's "constructive engagement" policy failed to work, the U.S. Congress approved harsh sanctions against South Africa's apartheid regime in 1986, over a presidential veto. Under the Comprehensive Anti-Apartheid Act, the United States joined with other countries and the United Nations, which had already imposed economic sanctions. In 1992, the white-controlled South African regime announced a political opening that led

TABLE 5.1

Types of Sanctions in Economic Statecraft

TYPE	SANCTION	EXAMPLE
POSITIVE	Give the target state the same trading privileges given to your best trading partner (most-favored-nation [MFN] status) as incentive for policy change.	U.S. granted MFN status to China, in spite of that country's poor human rights record.
	Allow sensitive trade with target state, including militarily useful equipment.	France and Germany export equipment to Iran, even though Iran's government is hostile to the West.
	Give corporations investment guarantees or tax breaks as incentives to invest in target state.	U.S. offered insurance to U.S. companies willing to invest in post-apartheid South Africa.
	Allow importation of target state's products into your country at best tariff rates.	Industrialized states allow imports from developing countries at lower tariff rates.
NEGATIVE	Freeze target state's assets.	U.S. froze Iranian assets during 1979 hostage crisis; UN froze Libyan assets 1993–99; UN froze Afghanistan's assets under Taliban 1999–2001.
	Blacklist target state.	Arab states blacklisted companies that conducted business in Israel.
	Boycott goods and services of target states.	South Africa was boycotted for apartheid policy in 1970s and 1980s; exports of dual-use technologies were prohibited to Iraq, Iran, Syria, Libya, North Korea, Sudan in the 1990s and after because of their support of terrorism.
	Ban importation of one or all products of target state.	Iraq was forbidden to sell oil internationally 1991–2003 as punishment for the 1991 Gulf War; UN sanctions were imposed against Haiti 1990, 1993–94 to try to overthrow the military government there.

to the end of apartheid and white-minority rule. Most commentators conclude that sanctions probably had an important effect on the regime's decision to change policy. In fact, the 1990s have been referred to as the sanctions decade.[14]

In general, however, economic sanctions have not been very successful. In the short term, the public often rallies around a leader who is threatened from outside. States gradually make economic changes to compensate for the sanctions. Over the long term, it is difficult to maintain international cohesion, because states imposing the sanctions find it ultimately advantageous to bust them, thereby gaining economically.

Increasingly since the mid-1990s, states have imposed **smart sanctions**, including freezing assets of governments and/or individuals and imposing commodities sanctions (oil, timber, diamonds). Targeting has involved not just "what" but also "who," as the international community has tried to affect specific individuals and rebel groups, reduce ambiguity and loopholes, and avoid the high humanitarian costs of general sanctions. With these modifications, liberal theorists continue to place special emphasis on the diplomatic, economic, and less coercive avenues of power, because they view power as multidimensional. Realist theorists believe it is necessary in exercising power to resort to or threaten to use force on a more regular basis.

The Use of Force

Force (and the threat of force) is another critical instrument of statecraft and is central to realist thinking. Like economic statecraft, force or its threat may be used either to get a target state to do something or to undo something that state has done—compellence—or to keep an adversary from doing something—deterrence.[15] Liberal theorists are more likely to advocate compellent strategies, moving cautiously to deterrence, whereas realists promote deterrence.

With the strategy of **compellence**, a state tries, by threatening to use force, to get another state to do something or to undo an act that it has undertaken. The prelude to the 1991 Gulf War is an excellent example. The United States, the United Nations, and coalition members tried to get Saddam Hussein to change his actions with the compellent strategy of escalating threats. Iraq's invasion of Kuwait was initially widely condemned. Formal UN Security Council measures gave multilateral legitimacy to the condemnation. Next, Iraq's external economic assets were frozen and economic sanctions were imposed. Finally, U.S. and coalition military forces were mobilized and deployed, and specific deadlines were given for Iraq to withdraw from Kuwait. At each step of the compellent strategy of escalation, one message was communicated to Iraq: withdraw from Kuwait or more coercive actions will follow. Similarly, the Western alliance sought to get Serbia to stop abusing the human rights of Kosovar Albanians and to withdraw its military forces from the region. Compellence was also used before the 2003 Iraq War, when the United States and others threatened Saddam Hussein that if certain actions were not taken, then war would follow. Threats began when George W. Bush labeled Iraq a member of the "axis of evil"; they escalated when the United Nations found Iraq to be in material breach of a UN resolution. Then in March 2003, Great Britain, one of the coalition partners, gave Iraq ten days to comply with the UN resolution. And on March 17, the last compellent threat was issued:

U.S. president George W. Bush gave Saddam's Baathist regime forty-eight hours to leave Iraq as its last chance to avert war. In all of these cases, it was necessary to resort to an invasion because compellence via an escalation of threats failed. Note that compellence ends once the use of force begins.

With the strategy of deterrence, states commit themselves to punishing a target state if that state takes an undesired action. Threats of actual war are used as an instrument of policy to dissuade a state from pursuing certain courses of action. If the target state does not take the undesired action, deterrence is successful and conflict is avoided. If it does choose to act despite the deterrent threat, then the first state will presumably deliver a devastating blow.

Since the advent of nuclear weapons in 1945, deterrence has taken on a special meaning. Today if a state chooses to resort to violence against a nuclear state, it is possible that nuclear weapons will be launched against it in retaliation. If this happens, the cost of the aggression will be unacceptable, especially if both states have nuclear weapons, in which case the viability of both societies will be at stake. Theoretically, therefore, states that recognize the destructive capability of nuclear weapons and know that others have a **second-strike capability**—the ability to retaliate even after an attack has been launched by an opponent—will refrain from taking aggressive action, using its **first-strike capability**. Deterrence is then successful.

For either compellence or deterrence to be effective, states have to lay the ground-work. They must clearly and openly communicate their objectives and capabilities, be willing to make good on threats or to fulfill promises, and have the capacity to follow through with their commitments. In short, a state's credibility is essential for compellence and deterrence. Yet this is not a one-sided, unilateral process; it is a strategic interaction where the behavior of each state is determined not only by one's own behavior, but by the actions and responses of the other.

Compellence and deterrence can fail, however. If compellence and deterrence fail, states may go to war, but even during war, states have choices. They choose the type of weaponry (nuclear or nonnuclear, strategic or tactical, conventional or chemical and biological), the kind of targets (military or civilian, urban or rural), and the geographic locus (city, state, region) to be targeted. They may choose to respond in kind, to escalate, or to de-escalate. In war, both implicit and explicit negotiation takes place, over both how to fight the war and how to end it. We will return to a discussion of war in Chapter 8.

Democracy and Foreign Policy

Although all states use diplomacy, economy, and force to conduct foreign policy, do policy choices vary by type of government? Specifically, do democratic states conduct foreign policy and make policy choices that are any different from the choices and policies made by authoritarian states and leaders? We might expect that in democratic states, the intangible sources of power—national image, public support, and leadership—would matter more, because the leaders are responsible to the public through elections. If that is true, then is the foreign policy behavior of democratic states any different from the behavior of nondemocratic or authoritarian states?

This question has occupied philosophers, diplomatic historians, and political scientists for centuries. In *Perpetual Peace* (1795), Immanuel Kant argued that the spread of democracy would change international politics by eliminating war. He reasoned that the public would be very cautious in supporting war because they, the public, are likely to suffer the most devastating effects. Thus, leaders will act in a restrained fashion and tend to abstain from war because of domestic constraints.[16] Since Kant's time, other explanations have been added to the democratic peace hypothesis. Perhaps democracies are simply more satisfied with the status quo and unwilling to support change. Perhaps democracies are simply more likely to be allies of each other because they share similar values. Many of these ideas found resonance with Woodrow Wilson, a major advocate of the democratic peace.

Political scientists have developed an extensive research agenda related to the **democratic peace** theory. Are democracies more peaceful than nondemocracies? More specifically, do democracies fight each other less than nondemocracies do? Do democracies fight nondemocracies more than they fight each other? Gathering data on different kinds of warfare over several centuries, researchers have addressed these questions. One study has confirmed the hypothesis that democracies do not go to war against each other: since 1789 no wars have been fought strictly between independent states with democratically elected governments. Another study has found that wars involving democracies have tended to be less bloody but more protracted, although between 1816 and 1965, democratic governments were not noticeably more peaceable or passive.[17] But the evidence is not that clear-cut, and explanations are partial. Why are states in the middle of transitions to democracy more susceptible to conflict? How can we explain that when democratic states have not gone to war, it may have had little to do with their democratic character?

Why have some of the findings on the democratic peace been so divergent? Even within a single research program there may be serious differences in conclusions, based on the assumptions made by researchers and the methods used. Scholars who use the behavioral approach themselves point to some of the difficulties. Some researchers analyzing the democratic peace use different definitions of the key variables, democracy and war. Some researchers distinguish between liberal democracies (for example, the United States and Germany) and illiberal democracies (Yugoslavia in the late 1990s). Also, the data for war would be different if wars with fewer than one thousand deaths were included, as they are in some studies. And other studies of the democratic peace examine different time periods.

Such differences in research protocols might well lead to different research findings. Yet even with these qualifications, the basic finding from the research is that democracies do not engage in militarized disputes against each other. That finding *is* statistically significant; that is, it does not occur by random chance. Overall, democracies are not more pacific than nondemocracies; democracies simply do not fight *each other*. In fact, autocracies are just as peaceful with each other as are democracies, so one could also talk of an autocratic peace.

Models of Foreign Policy Decision Making

How are specific foreign policy decisions actually made? Do democracies make foreign policy choices differently from nondemocracies? How do the different theories view the decision-making process? Differences depend in large part on how subnational actors—interest groups, **nongovernmental organizations (NGOs)**, and businesses—are viewed.

The Rational Model

Most policy makers, particularly during crises, and most realists begin with the rational model, which conceives of foreign policy as actions chosen by the national government that maximize its strategic goals and objectives. The state is assumed to be a unitary actor with established goals, a set of options, and an algorithm for deciding which option best meets its goals. The process is relatively straightforward, as shown in Figure 5.2. Taking as our case the 1996 incident in which China was testing missiles by launching them over Taiwan, a rational approach would view Taiwan's decision making process about how to respond in the following manner (the numbers correspond to the numbered steps in Figure 5.2):

1. The People's Republic of China was testing missiles over Taiwan, in direct threat to the latter's national security and just prior to Taiwan's first democratic election.

2. The goal of both Taiwan and its major supporter, the United States, was to stop the firings immediately.

3. The Taiwanese had several options: do nothing; wait until after the Taiwanese elections, hoping that the Chinese will then stop; issue diplomatic protests; bring the issue to the UN Security Council; threaten or conduct military operations against China by bombing its missile sites or mounting a land invasion; or threaten or use economic statecraft (cut trade, impose sanctions or embargoes).

FIGURE 5.2 | **The Rational Model of Decision Making**

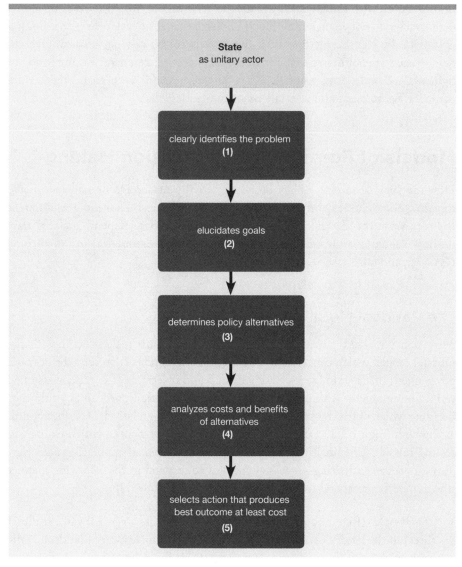

4. The Taiwanese government analyzed the benefits and costs of these options. Mounting an invasion, for example, may eliminate the problem but would likely result in the destruction of Taiwan, an unacceptable side effect.

5. Taiwan, with U.S. support, chose as a first step diplomatic protest, in the hope that the antagonistic firing would cease after the election. Doing nothing clearly would have suggested that the missile testing was acceptable, which it was not. Military action against China was too extreme, with possibly disastrous consequences.

In times of crisis, when decision makers are confronted by a surprising, threatening event and have only a short time to make a decision about how to respond, using the rational model as a way to assess the other side's behavior is an appropriate choice. Often in such a crisis, there is little time for substate actors to have much influence. If a state knows very little about the internal domestic processes of another state—as the United States knew little about mainland China during the era of Mao Zedong—then decision makers have little alternative but to assume that the other state will follow the rational model. Indeed, in the absence of better information, most U.S. assessments of decisions taken by the Soviet Union during the Cold War were based on a rational model: the Soviet Union had a goal, its alternatives were clearly laid out, and decisions were taken to maximize its achievement of that goal. Only after the opening of the Soviet governmental archives following the end of the Cold War did historians find that, in fact, the Soviets had no concrete plans for turning Poland, Hungary, Romania, or other East European states into communist dictatorships or socialist economies, as the United States believed. The Soviets appear to have been guided by events happening in the region, not by a specific rational plan or ideology.[18] The United States was incorrect in imputing the rational model to Soviet decision making, but in the absence of complete information, this was the least risky approach: the anarchy of the international system means that a state assumes that its opponent engages in rational decision making.

THEORY IN BRIEF	
The Realist Perspective on State Power and Policy	
NATURE OF STATE POWER	Emphasis on power as key concept in international relations; geography, natural resources, population especially important
USING STATE POWER	Emphasis on coercive techniques of power; use of force acceptable
HOW FOREIGN POLICY IS MADE	Emphasis on rational model of decision making; unitary state actor assumed once decision is made
DETERMINANTS OF FOREIGN POLICY	Largely external/international determinants

The Bureaucratic/Organizational Model

Not all decisions occur during crises, and not all decisions are taken with so little knowledge of domestic politics in other countries. So foreign policy decisions may be products of either subnational governmental organizations or bureaucracies (departments or ministries of government). **Organizational politics** emphasizes

FIGURE 5.3 | The Organizational / Bureaucratic Model of Decision Making

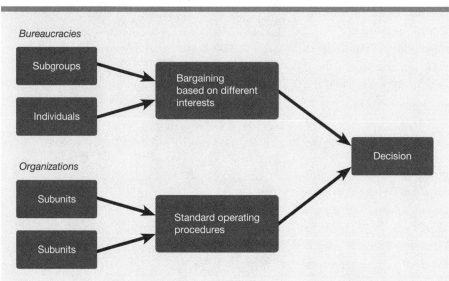

the standard operating procedures and processes of an organization. Decisions arising from organizational processes depend heavily on precedents; major changes in policy are unlikely. Conflicts can occur when different subgroups within the organization have different goals and procedures. Often those different goals have been strongly influenced by particular interest groups or NGOs.

Bureaucratic politics, on the other hand, occurs among members of the bureaucracy representing different interests. Decisions determined by bureaucratic politics flow from the push and pull, or tug-of-war, among these departments, groups, or individuals. In either political scenario, the ultimate decision depends on the relative strength of the individual bureaucratic players or the organizations they represent (see Figure 5.3).

Trade policy is a ripe area for seeing the bureaucratic/organizational model of decision making at work. For example, South Korean agricultural markets were traditionally closed to foreign imports. This closure was designed to protect South Korean producers of major agricultural products, including rice, beef, and tobacco. In the 1980s, pressure from the United States to open these markets grew. The South Korean Ministry of Agriculture, Forestry, and Fisheries strongly opposed the opening of agricultural markets, arguing that South Korean farmers would be put out of work. But the Ministry of Finance and the Ministry of Trade and Industry were concerned about retaliatory measures that the United States might take against South Korean manufacturers entering the U.S. market. Policy change resulted from the push and pull among these various ministries. The Ministry of Agriculture capitulated on tobacco, opening the market to full liberalization, but for rice, whose producers were the strongest and the best organized politically, movement toward liberalization was very slow.

Noncrisis situations, such as the South Korean foreign trade policy issue just described, are likely to reflect the bureaucratic/ organizational model. When time is no real constraint, informal bureaucratic groups and departments are free to mobilize. They hold meetings, hammering out positions that satisfy all the contending interests. The decisions arrived at are not always the most rational ones; rather the groups are content with **satisficing** — that is, satisfying the most different constituents without ostracizing any.

Liberals especially turn to this model of decision making behavior in their analyses, because for them the state itself is only the playing field; the actors are the competing interests in bureaucracies and organizations. The model is most relevant in large, democratic countries, which usually have highly differentiated institutional structures for foreign policy decision making and where responsibility and jurisdiction are divided among a number of different units. For example, most foreign-trade decisions made by the United States, Japan, or the governments of European Union countries closely approximate the bureaucratic/organizational model. But to use this model in policy making circles to analyze or predict other states' behavior or to use it to analyze decisions for scholarly purposes, one must have detailed knowledge of a country's foreign policy structures and bureaucracies. In the absence of such information and in a crisis situation where policy must be determined quickly, the rational model is the best alternative.

THEORY IN BRIEF

The Liberal Perspective on State Power and Policy

NATURE OF STATE POWER	Multiple power sources; tangible and intangible sources
USING STATE POWER	Broad range of power techniques; preference for noncoercive alternatives
HOW FOREIGN POLICY IS MADE	Organizational/bureaucratic and pluralist models of decision making
DETERMINANTS OF FOREIGN POLICY	Largely domestic determinants

The Pluralist Model

The pluralist model, in contrast to the other two alternatives, attributes decisions to bargaining conducted among domestic sources—the public, interest groups, mass movements, and multinational corporations (see Figure 5.4). In noncrisis situations

FIGURE 5.4 | **The Pluralist Model of Decision Making**

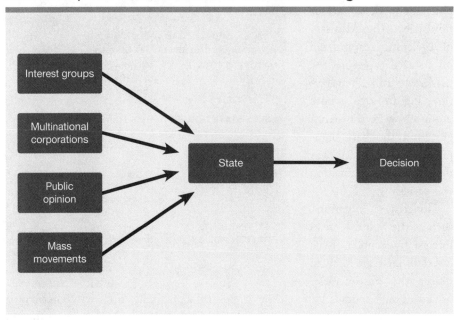

and on particular issues, especially economic ones, societal groups may play very important roles. No one doubts the power of the rice farmer lobbies in both Japan and South Korea in preventing the importation of cheap, U.S.-grown rice. No one disputes the success of French winegrowers in preventing the importation of cheap Greek or Spanish wines by publicly dumping their product for media attention. No one denies the power of U.S. shoe manufacturers in supporting restrictions on the importation of Brazilian-made shoes into the United States, despite U.S. governmental initiatives to allow imports of products from developing countries.

Societal groups have a variety of ways of forcing decisions in their favor or constraining decisions. They can mobilize the media and public opinion, lobby the government agencies responsible for making the decision, influence the appropriate representative bodies (the U.S. Congress, the French National Assembly, the Japanese Diet), organize transnational networks of people with comparable interests, and, in the case of high-profile heads of multinational corporations, make direct contacts with the highest governmental officials. The decision made will reflect these diverse societal interests and strategies—a result that is particularly compatible with liberal thinking. The movement to ban land mines in the 1990s is an example of a societally based pluralist foreign policy decision, a process reflecting democratic practices.

Both realists and liberals acknowledge that states have real choices in foreign policy, no matter which model explains the behavior; radicals, however, see fewer real choices. In the radical view, capitalist states' interests are determined by the structure of the international system, and their decisions are dictated by the economic imperatives of the dominant class. Internal domestic elites have been co-opted by international capitalists such as multinational corporations.

THEORY IN BRIEF

The Radical Perspective on State Power and Policy

NATURE OF STATE POWER	Economic power organized around classes
USING STATE POWER	Weak having few instruments of power
HOW FOREIGN POLICY IS MADE	States having no real choices; decisions dictated by economic capitalist elites
DETERMINANTS OF FOREIGN POLICY	Largely external determinants; co-opted internal elements

Constructivists hold that foreign policy decisions are based on the decision makers' adherence to international norms. Because elite socialization with international norms is evident to the public (in contrast to the power-driven interests that neorealists and neoliberals, assume to underlie decisions), leaders are inclined to build policies through processes open to domestic and international civil society, the mass media, and international partners. Foreign policy decisions are determined by leaders' beliefs that their actions are congruent to the international norms that they have appropriated.

Each alternative model offers a simplification of the foreign-policy decision-making process. Each provides a window on how groups (both governmental and nongovernmental) influence the foreign policy process. But these models do not provide answers to other critical issues. They do not tell us the content of a specific decision or indicate the effectiveness with which the foreign policy was implemented.

THEORY IN BRIEF

The Constructivist Perspective on State Power and Policy

NATURE OF STATE POWER	Power is subject to norm socialization
USING STATE POWER	Power is tool of elite for socializing societies through norms
HOW FOREIGN POLICY IS MADE	Decisions based on norms that regulate policy sector
DETERMINANTS OF FOREIGN POLICY	External determinants in combination with domestic civil society

Challenges to the State

The state, despite its centrality, is facing challenges from the processes of globalization, religiously and ideologically based transnational movements, and ethnonational movements (see Table 5.2). As Jessica Matthews succinctly explains in her seminal *Foreign Affairs* article of 1997, there has been a power shift: "The steady concentration of power in the hands of states that began in 1648 with the Peace of Westphalia is over, at least for a while."[19]

Globalization

Externally, the state is buffeted by **globalization**, the growing integration of the world in terms of politics, economics, communications, and culture, a process that increasingly undermines traditional state sovereignty. In political terms, the state is confronted by transnational issues—environmental degradation and disease—that governments cannot manage alone. Such issues require unprecedented political cooperation, as illustrated by the 2003 SARS (Severe Acute Respiratory Syndrome) threat, when the governments of the developed world had to respond to a growing epidemic in China, whose national authorities did not have the capacity to address the issue. More and more, such cooperative actions require states to compromise their sovereignty. In economic terms, states and financial markets are increasingly tied inextricably together; multinational corporations and

TABLE 5.2

Challenges to State Power

FORCES	EFFECTS ON THE STATE
GLOBALIZATION—political, economic, cultural	Undermines state sovereignty; interferes with state exercise of power
TRANSNATIONAL CRIME	State is unable to curb due to expansion of communication networks
TRANSNATIONAL MOVEMENTS	
Religious/ideological	Seek loyalty and commitment of individuals beyond the state; want to transform the ideology of the state
Political	Change state behavior on a specific problem or issue
ETHNONATIONAL MOVEMENTS	Seek own state; attempt to replace current government with one representing the interests of the movement

the internationalization of production and consumption make it ever more difficult for states to regulate their own economic policies, as discussed in Chapter 9. National cultures are changing as new and intrusive technologies—e-mail, Facebook, Twitter, cell phones with cameras, fax machines, direct satellite broadcasting, worldwide television networks such as CNN—increasingly undermine the state's control over information and hence its control over its citizenry. Countries such as Saudi Arabia and others in the Persian Gulf region have fought losing battles trying to "protect" their populations from what they see as crass Western values transmitted through modern media. China, too, is losing

States may find it difficult to maintain total control over their territories in a globalizing world. For example, multinational corporations like Google have complicated the Chinese government's efforts to control its citizens' access to information.

the battle to limit information coming into the country via the Internet. As Jessica Matthews explains, "The most powerful engine of change in the relative decline of the state and the rise of non-state actors is the computer and telecommunications revolution, whose deep political and social consequences have been almost completely ignored. . . . In every sphere of activity, instantaneous access to information and the ability to put it to use multiplies the number of players who matter and reduces the number who command great authority."[20]

Transnational Crime

Nowhere is this challenge to the state more evident than in the rise of transnational crime—illicit activities made easier by globalization. Growing in value, extending in scope, and becoming highly specialized, these activities have been facilitated by more and faster transportation routes, rapid communication, and electronic financial networks. Transnational crime has led to the accelerating movement of illegal drugs, counterfeit goods, smuggled weapons, laundered money, trade in body parts, piracy, and trafficking in poor and exploited people. (This is further explained in Chapter 10.) Organized around flexible networks and circuitous trafficking routes, and lubricated by electronic transfer of funds, transnational crime has created new businesses while distorting national and regional economies. States and governments are largely incapable of responding: rigid bureaucracies, laborious procedures, interbureaucratic fighting, and corrupt officials undermine states' efforts. In fact, some states—such as China, North Korea, and Nigeria—actively participate in these illicit activities or do nothing to stop them because key elites are making major profits.[21]

Other states such as Mexico have made concerted efforts to stop transnational crime. When Felipe Calderón assumed the Mexican presidency in 2006, he launched a major effort to break up the drug cartels. That effort has escalated in violence, particularly in the central region, with over six thousand killed in 2008 alone, as the cartels fight both each other and the Mexican authorities. The effort has had transnational implications. Small arms smuggled into Mexico from the United States fuel the violence; gang violence crosses the border into American cities; American tourists are staying away from Mexican resorts, with adverse effects on the economy. Many states are finding it very difficult to control and punish the transgressors, undermining their own sovereignty and that of their neighbors.

Transnational Movements

Other products of globalization and now political forces that in their own right challenge the state are **transnational movements**, particularly religious and ideological movements. These extremist movements are antisecular and antimodern. Members of Christian cults, for example, have posed serious problems for state authority. One such group, The Covenant, the Sword, and the Arm of the Lord, is examined in Jessica Stern's revealing book, *Terror in the Name of God.*[22] The cult began as a commune, with members living under primitive conditions and sharing Bible readings and prayer, but the group gradually cut itself off from the outside world. Members came to believe that Zionists, socialists, communists, and others had taken over the United States, as exemplified in the UN, the IMF, and the Council on Foreign Relations—all indications of Satan's power. Joining forces with other right-wing groups, they planned—as directed by God—to poison residents in American cities and to destroy the so-called Zionist Occupied Government. Although federal authorities foiled the plot, the group has since joined with Identity Christianity, the major group of the racist right wing. Among its adherents were Timothy McVeigh, responsible for the Oklahoma City Federal Building bombing in 1995.

States are also confronted with extremist **Islamic fundamentalism**. Although Islamic fundamentalists come from many different countries and support different strategies for reaching their end goal, believers are united by wanting to change states and societies by basing them on interpretations of the Koran. This movement presents both a basic critique of what is wrong in many secular states, and solutions that call for radical state transformation. Islamic fundamentalists see a long-standing discrepancy between the political and economic aspirations of states and the actual conditions of uneven economic distribution and rule by corrupt elites. Some advocate violence as the means to overthrow these corrupt rulers and to fight for their Palestinian brethren, who they believe have been wronged by Israel and its Western supporters; others suggest that change can occur without the use of violence.

The fight by the Afghans and their Islamic supporters against the Soviet Union in the 1980s proved to be a galvanizing event for extremist Islamic fundamentalism. It brought together religiously committed yet politically and economically disaffected young Islamists from all over the world; fighting the "godless" enemy forged group cohesion; and fighting the better-equipped Soviet military allowed them to hone their guerrilla tactics. These *mujahideen* (holy warriors) gained confidence by beating the Soviets into retreat. When they returned to their homelands in Saudi Arabia, Egypt, and other parts of the Middle East, they were imbued with a mission—to wage *jihad* (holy war) against what they view as illegitimate regimes. During the fight in Afghanistan, Osama bin Laden, a Saudi national, emerged as a charismatic leader. When the Taliban assumed power in Afghanistan in 1996, bin Laden and what remained of the *mujahideen* formed Al Qaeda. Yet, as we will see in Chapter 8, Al Qaeda is just one of many Islamic fundamentalist groups, although its successful terrorist attacks on September 11, 2001, have made it the most widely known. Although Islamic fundamentalists are only a small proportion of the over 1.5 billion Muslims worldwide, theirs is still a powerful transnational movement and a challenge to states from the Philippines and Indonesia, to Nigeria and Algeria, to Saudi Arabia, Iran and Pakistan. As terrorist attacks in Israel, Europe, Asia, and the United States show, these areas, too, are the targets of Islamic fundamentalists. These attacks have led many to believe that the next great international conflict would be a "clash of civilizations" arising from underlying differences between Western liberal democracy and Islamic fundamentalism.[23]

Not all transnational movements pose such direct challenges to the state. Indeed, many such movements, rather than forming around major cleavages such as religion or ideology as discussed above, develop around progressive goals such as the environment, human rights, and development, or around conservative goals such as opposition to abortion, family planning, or immigration. Often organized around nongovernmental organizations that frame the issue and mobilize resources, these

The Taliban in Pakistan: A Challenge to the Pakistani State?

Governing Pakistan is difficult. Both military and strong civilian rulers have tried different approaches since independence from Britain in 1947. Yet in 2010 Pakistan finds itself
not only faced with internal threats to its territorial integrity, but also in the middle of a
more militarized region.

The Islamic State of Pakistan (population 176 million) includes followers of both Sunni (75 percent) and Shia (20 percent) Islam. Two of Pakistan's provinces, the North West Frontier Province (whose capital is Peshawar) and Baluchistan (whose capital is Quetta), include tribal areas that are self-governing, though often described as lawless. Over sixty languages are spoken in this ethnically diverse land. Pakistan is also a poor country, with 20 percent of its people living below the poverty line of $1.25 a day. With state resources stretched thin, the poor often receive their education in a large network of religious schools, the *madrassas*, viewed by many as sources of radical religious indoctrination.

Pakistan is located in a region rife with tension, with India, its long-time enemy to the east; Afghanistan to the west, where by the middle of the 2010, ninety eight thousand American troops and fifty two thousand NATO troops were fighting an insurgency; the fundamentalist, Shia Iran in the southwest; and the resurgent China to the north.

In the war on terrorism, Pakistan is a key U.S. ally and has reaffirmed its commitment to fighting the Taliban insurgency within its own borders and to rooting out the Taliban and Al Qaeda operatives who fled there from Afghanistan following the 2001 U.S. invasion. In the view of the United States, those groups enjoy support in the tribal regions and continue to provide material assistance to the insurgency in Afghanistan. But given both the historical background and the geographic and political divisions within Pakistan itself, the task of the Pakistan government is not an easy one.

Al Qaeda has its roots in the 1979-88 Soviet-Afghan War. The United States supported the Afghan resistance (the *mujahideen*, or "holy warriors") by funneling funds through the Pakistani intelligence service, the ISI. The mujahideen were also supported by several international Muslim groups, including those linked to both Saudi Arabia and Osama bin Laden.

The Pakistani government has tried different approaches to address the security situation. Pakistan is the home of the Quetta Shura, the central Taliban Council in Quetta. In 2006, the government signed a peace treaty with seven of the more militant groups, which together are called the Pakistan Taliban. Pakistan's army agreed to withdraw from the area and permit the Taliban to govern themselves as long as they did not attack Pakistanti troops or cross the border into Afghanistan. The United States, which provides critical economic and military aid to the Pakistani government, opposed the agreement, believing that it would provide a safe haven for the Taliban.

Pakistan itself was shocked when in the spring of 2009 those same groups moved into strategic locations as close as 60 miles to the capital city of Islamabad, abducted Pakistani military officers, and executed them. Suicide attacks aimed at the security forces and bombings in installations near the capital mobilized the Pakistani government. However, it was the Taliban's increasing influence in

Baluchistan and in the Swat and Buner valleys, and its expressed intention to impose fundamentalist Sharia law that have mobilized the Pakistani army. As thousands of Pakistanis fled the Taliban and massed in refugee camps, the army mobilized eighty thousand troops.

Increasingly the government has taken targeted action against Taliban leaders and have been successful, either killing or injuring many. Occasionally, those operations have included CIA drone missiles, which are quietly tolerated by Pakistan's government. But that has opened up the government to accusations that it is allowing foreigners to violate Pakistan's sovereignty. Some of those successful attacks have also resulted in civilian casualties, further alienating the population. Yet, Pakistan's army has also not only targeted the Taliban but has increasingly provided more security to the population, aiding in the return of 1.65 million displaced people, working to remove Taliban in the Swat region, and returning that area to civilian rule.

Pakistan is trying to act responsibly. The terrorists carrying out the attacks in Mumbai, India in 2008 were Pakistani. Pakistan put the last surviving terrorist of that group under house arrest with the intention of prosecuting him. It acknowledges the nationality of the attacker and is bringing him to justice using national laws. This gives the Pakistani government legitimacy in the international community.

Pakistan expects to be rewarded for its success in the global war on terrorism. It has received almost $11 billion in U.S. aid since 2001. Some government leaders argue that more sophisticated military technology is also needed. But so, too, is more economic aid. The U.S. Congress approved an economic aid package of $1.5 billion annually to help this struggling democracy better meet the needs of its people.

Yet the Pakistani government remains ambivalent in its opposition to the Taliban and its support of the global war on terrorism. The ISI still contains Taliban sympathizers; thus, the United States is reluctant to share intelligence information with the agency. Pakistan's leaders remain divided as well. Some see the Taliban as righteous underdogs and believe tacit support of the Taliban will preserve a useful strategic weapon against Pakistan's enemies in the disputed Kashmir region. Others worry that by supporting the Taliban, Pakistan is riding a tiger; they fear that continuing to support the Taliban will one day cause them to end up inside it.

Still others in the Pakistani government fear growing U.S. influence in their country. As Jahangir Tareenh, a member of Parliament, explains, "Some people think that the United States is out to get Pakistan, to defang Pakistan, to destroy the army as it exists so it can't fight India and to break down the ISI's ability to influence events in India and Afghanistan. Everyone is saying about the Americans, 'Told you so.'"[a]

1. *Why is it difficult to determine the national interests of Pakistan?*

2. *Which decision-making model best helps us understand Pakistan's domestic situation?*

3. *Both international and internal factors can threaten a state's survival. Explain in relation to Pakistan.*

4. *What kind of influence does the United States have over Pakistan? What are the limits to that influence?*

[a] Quoted in Jane Perlez, "U.S. Push to Expand in Pakistan Meets Resistance," *New York Times*, October 6, 2009, A6.

social movements want change, developing new approaches to problems and seeking to push governments to take action, but these movements are generally not undermining state sovereignty.

Cases of Ethnonational Movements: Kashmir and the Uighurs

Another dramatic challenge to the state is found in **ethnonational movements**. The end of the Cold War and the demise of multiethnic states such as the Soviet Union and Yugoslavia, along with the communications revolution of fax, cell phone, and Internet, have led to increasing demands by ethnonational movements.

One of the more complex ethnonational movements with international implications involves Kashmir—a mountainous area at the intersection of India, Pakistan, and China—and the Kashmiris, a people who are overwhelmingly Muslim but who have traditionally been ruled by Hindus. When India (dominated by Hindus) and Pakistan (dominated by Muslims) separated into two independent states in 1947, the maharaja of Kashmir, Hari Singh, opted to join India, much to the displeasure of the majority population, which wanted national affiliation with Pakistan. In 1947–48 and again in 1965, India and Pakistan fought over the territory, which has been plagued ever since by tensions and periodic skirmishes. A Line of Control (LOC) was reestablished in 1972, dividing Kashmir into India-administered Kashmir to the east and south, with 9 million people, and Pakistan-administered Kashmir to the north and west, with 3 million people. Besides the rival claims of India and Pakistan, since 1989 a growing violent separatist movement has fought against Indian rule in Kashmir. The most prominent separatist group is the pro-Pakistani Hizbul Mujahideen, seeking union with Pakistan. The largest pro-independence group is the Jammu and Kashmir Liberation Front, but its influence has been declining. The Kashmiri ethnonational conflict has been particularly difficult because its factions are not only fighting for control of territory but are also tied into the larger conflict between India and Pakistan. In 2003, India and Pakistan signed a cease-fire along their borders in Kashmir and established diplomatic ties. But violence in the region has continued, and the 2005 earthquake centered in the Pakistan-administered region of Kashmir has turned international efforts to relief and reconstruction.

Ethnonationalist movements pose a challenge even to the strongest states. China has been confronted by ethnic uprisings within the Muslim Uighur minority in the Xinjiang Uighur Autonomous Region, the northwestern most province, over the past several decades. Today, Xinjiang (a name the Uighurs find offensive), one-sixth of China's land area, is home to 20 million people and thirteen ethnic groups. Of these, 45 percent are Uighurs and 40 percent ethnic Han. The Uighurs migrated into the Chinese border region from the Mongolian steppe in the tenth century. They are a Turkic-speaking race that follows a branch of Sunni Islam. Their diaspora is centered in this area, but Uighurs also live in Kazakhstan, Kyrgyzstan, and Uzbekistan, with smaller numbers in Mongolia and Afghanistan. They have had a long history of fighting for independence as Uighuristan or East Turkestan.

When vast mineral and oil deposits were found, Han Chinese began to move into the region in 1956, responding to Mao Zedong's call to "open

Kashmir, 2005

Note: The Line of Control separates the two sides in the Kashmir conflict.

up the West," the borderland that for centuries had opposed Chinese central government subjugation. The government promised its youth factory jobs and infrastructure, and settlers answered Mao's call. But to the Uighurs, the ethnic Han Chinese migrants are colonists; their Islamic faith, traditional language, and economic prosperity are being repressed by the official Han policies.

Following 9/11, the Chinese government began to refer to Uighurs as terrorists, and greater repression has followed. Demonstrations broke out in the summer of 2009 when police tried to stop one thousand Uighurs from demonstrating to protest judicial discrimination. Uighurs attacked Han Chinese, who in return took up violence against the Uighurs. Over two hundred people were killed and two thousand people wounded. The Chinese government is concerned about ethnic revolts and instability within its borders. Fearing the "Kosovo effect" (referring to the breakaway state contested by Serbia), it accuses its rioting ethnic minorities of seeking Western and broader international support while justifying its own response as a war against terrorism.

Chinese policy toward minorities is one of official recognition, granting limited autonomy with an extensive effort at central control. Although only 9 percent of China's population consists of ethnic minorities, those minorities are spread across resource-rich areas. They are actually the majorities in the strategically important border areas of not only Xinjiang but also Tibet, Inner Mongolia, and Yunan. These minorities also have higher birthrates than the Han Chinese, due to policies that permit the minorities more children.

TABLE 5.3

Ethnonational Challengers

STATE	ETHNONATIONAL GROUPS
INDONESIA	Timorese, Papuans, Moluccans
SPAIN	Basques
PEOPLE'S REPUBLIC OF CHINA	Tibetans, Uighurs, Manchus
NIGERIA	Yorubas, Ibos
BURUNDI, RWANDA	Hutus, Tutsis
SYRIA, IRAQ, IRAN, TURKEY	Kurds
MOLDOVA	Ukranians, Russians
SERBIA, MACEDONIA	Albanians
MEXICO, GUATEMALA	Maya, Zapotecs, Mixtecs
BURMA, THAILAND	Karens
CANADA	Quebecois
INDIA	Kashmiris
AFGHANISTAN	Pashtuns, Hazaras, Tajiks, Uzbeks, Turkmens
GEORGIA	Abkhaz, Ossetes

The government's suppressions of Tibet in 1959 and 2008 and of Xinjiang in 2009 demonstrate Beijing's determination to exert dominance and authority across the entire country. However, with increasing economic problems and the internal struggle for succession, the state may continue to be challenged by ethnic minorities.

Some ethnonational challenges lead to civil conflict and even war, as the case of Kashmir illustrates. The political scientist Jack Snyder has identified the causal mechanism whereby ethnic nationalists challenge the state on the basis of the legitimacy of their language, culture, or religion. Particularly when countervailing institutions are weak, elites within these ethnonational movements may be able to incite the masses to war.[24] Table 5.3 lists some of the ethnonational challengers in the world today.

THEORY IN BRIEF

Contending Perspectives on State Power and Policy

	REALISM / NEOREALISM	LIBERALISM / NEOLIBERAL INSTITUTIONALISM	RADICALISM / DEPENDENCY THEORY	CONSTRUCTIVISM
NATURE OF STATE POWER	Emphasis on power as key concept in international relations; geography, natural resources, population especially important	Multiple power sources; tangible and intangible sources	Economic power organized around classes	Power is subject to norm socialization
USING STATE POWER	Emphasis on coercive techniques of power; use of force acceptable	Broad range of power techniques; preference for noncoercive alternatives	Weak having few instruments of power	Power is tool of elite for socializing societies through norms
HOW FOREIGN POLICY IS MADE	Emphasis on rational model of decision making; unitary state actor assumed once decision is made	Organizational/ bureaucratic and pluralist models of decision making	States having no real choices; decisions dictated by economic capitalist elites	Decisions based on norms that regulate policy sector
DETERMINANTS OF FOREIGN POLICY	Largely external/ international determinants	Largely domestic determinants	Largely external determinants; co-opted internal elements	External determinants in combination with domestic civil society

In Sum: The State and Challenges Beyond

The centrality of the state in international politics cannot be disputed. In this chapter, we have conceptualized the state according to the contending theoretical perspectives. We have looked inside the state to describe the various forms of state power. We have discussed the ways that states are able to use power through the diplomatic, economic, and coercive instruments of statecraft. We have explored the question of whether certain kinds of governments—democracies, in particular—behave differently from nondemocracies. We have disaggregated the subnational actors within the state to identify different models of foreign policy decision making. And we have examined the ways in which globalization, transnational crime, transnational movements, and ethnonationalist movements pose threats to state sovereignty and to the stability of the international system. Such movements, however, depend on individuals; it is individuals who lead the challenge. Some are elites who are charismatic and powerful leaders in their own right. Some are part of a mass movement. It is these individuals to whom we now turn.

DISCUSSION QUESTIONS

1. You are the leader of an emerging economy such as Brazil. What tools of state-craft do you have at your disposal to influence your neighbors? A hegemon like the United States?

2. Find two newspaper articles that suggest use of soft power. How can you tell whether soft power "works"?

3. Transnational criminal activities—money laundering, drug trafficking—undermine the effectiveness of governments and control by the state. Choose a state where such activities flourish and discuss the government's approach to addressing such problems.

4. Ethnic conflict is a major source of state instability. Compare two recent cases of such conflict. How are the respective states addressing the issue? Or are they?

KEY TERMS

bureaucratic politics, p. 140
compellence, p. 134
democratic peace, p. 136
diplomacy, p. 129
ethnonational movements, p. 150
first-strike capability, p. 135
globalization, p. 144
irredentism, p. 119
Islamic fundamentalism, p. 147
nation, p. 116
nation-state, p. 117
niche diplomacy, p. 132
nongovernmental organizations
   (NGOs), p. 137

organizational politics, p. 139
power, p. 124
power potential, p. 124
public diplomacy, p. 131
sanctions, p. 132
satisfice, p. 141
second-strike capability, p. 135
smart sanctions, p. 134
soft power, p. 128
state, p. 116
transnational movements, p. 146

Find chapter outlines, practice quizzes, flashcards, and other study and review materials for this chapter at wwnorton.com/studyspace.

06

The Individual

- Which individuals matter most in international relations?
- What psychological factors have an impact on elites making foreign policy decisions?
- What roles do other private individuals play in international relations?
- What roles do mass publics play in foreign policy?
- According to the various theoretical perspectives, how much do individuals matter?

INTERNATIONAL RELATIONS CERTAINLY AFFECTS the lives of individuals, as discussed in Chapter 1. Are individuals merely passive recipients of actions taken by the state or for events emerging out of the structure of the international system? Or are individuals actors too, and as such, represent the third level of analysis? Individuals head governments, multinational corporations, and international bodies. Although individuals fight wars and make the daily decisions that shape the international political economy, they are viewed differently by the theorists.

Recall the possible explanations given in Chapter 3 for why the United States invaded Iraq in 2003. One explanation pointed to the beliefs of President George W. Bush and his security advisers and to their response to Saddam Hussein, his personal characteristics, and his advisers. Clearly, one group of individuals that makes a difference is leaders. But individuals holding more informal roles can also have significant influence, as can the mass public.

Foreign Policy Elites: Individuals Who Matter

Do individuals matter in the making of foreign policy? Liberals are particularly adamant that leaders do make a difference. Whenever there is a leadership change in a major power such as the United States or Russia, speculation always arises about possible changes in the country's foreign policy. This speculation reflects the general belief that individual leaders and their personal characteristics do make a difference in foreign policy, and hence in international relations. Ample empirical proof has been offered for this position. For instance, in March 1965 Nicolae Ceauşescu became the new leader of the Communist party of Romania. During his twenty-two years as Romania's head of state, the course of Romanian security policy changed significantly, reflecting the preferences and skills of Ceauşescu himself. Romania's security policy became more independent of the Soviet Union's foreign policy. Ceauşescu established diplomatic relations with Israel, denounced the 1968 Soviet invasion of Czechoslovakia, and strengthened ties with both Yugoslavia and China, despite those states' hostile relations with the Soviet Union. In short, Ceauşescu, a strong leader, significantly changed Romania's foreign policy, moving it in a direction that deviated from the preferences of its closest ally.

The example of the Soviet leader Mikhail Gorbachev also illustrates the fact that leaders can effect real change. Soon after coming to power in 1985, Gorbachev asked penetrating questions about the failures of the Soviet Union in Afghanistan and examined the reasons for the dismal performance of the Soviet economy. He began to frame the problems of the Soviet Union differently, identifying the Soviet security problem as part of the larger problem of weakness in the Soviet economy. Through a process of trial and error, and by living through and then studying failures, Gorbachev came to a new conceptualization of the Soviet security problem. He determined that the economic system had to be reformed in order to improve the country's security. In initiating that policy change, he needed to decide when and how change would happen, and how far it would go. Gorbachev's leadership made a difference in starting and sustaining broad economic reform in the Soviet Union, although he eventually lost power.

Constructivists attribute the policy shift in the Soviet Union to its "New Thinking." They credit not only the changes in calculations made by Gorbachev himself but more subtly the changes caused by the policy entrepreneurs, the networks of Western-oriented reformists and international affairs specialists who promoted new ideas.[1]

For realists, individuals are of little importance. Their position comes from the realist assumption of a unitary actor. Thus, states are not differentiated by their government type or personalities or styles of leaders in office but by the relative power they hold in the international system. Hans J. Morgenthau explained as follows:

> The concept of national interest defined as power imposes intellectual discipline upon the observer, infuses rational order into the subject matter of politics, and thus makes the theoretical understanding of politics possible. On the side of the actor, it provides for rational discipline in action and creates the astounding continuity in foreign policy which makes American, British, or Russian foreign policy appear as an intelligible, rational continuum, by and large consistent with itself, regardless of the different motives, preferences, and intellectual and moral qualities of successive statesmen.[2]

Yet, sometimes, individual motives and preferences do make a difference. *Glasnost* and *perestroika* were introduced in the Soviet Union beginning in 1986, Romania did carve a foreign policy niche independent of the Soviet Union during the 1970s, and the Chinese leader Deng Xiaoping established himself as the architect of the new China after 1978. Under his socialist market economy, the state permitted limited private competition and gradually opened itself economically to the outside world. Were these individuals responsible for these major changes, or did individual leaders just happen to be the right (or wrong) people at the time? Given the same situation, would different individuals have made different decisions, thus charting different courses through international relations?

Two questions are most pertinent to determining the role of individuals in international relations: When are the actions of individuals likely to have a greater or lesser effect on the course of events? And under what circumstances do different actors (in terms of their personal characteristics) behave differently?

The Impact of Elites: External Conditions

An individual's actions affect the course of events when at least one of several factors is present (see Figure 6.1 on p. 159). When political institutions are unstable, young, in crisis, or collapsed, leaders are able to provide powerful influences. Founding fathers, be they the United States' George Washington, Kenya's Jomo Kenyatta, India's Mohandas Gandhi, Russia's Vladimir Lenin, or the Czech Republic's Václav Havel, have a great impact because they lead in the early years of their nation's lives, when institutions and practices are being established. Adolf Hitler, Franklin Roosevelt, Mikhail Gorbachev, and Vladimir Putin had more influence precisely because their states were in economic crises when they were in power.

Individual leaders can have a powerful influence on their country and its relations with the rest of the world. Mohandas Gandhi led the Indian movement for independence from Britain and helped establish India as an independent state. Here, Gandhi visits the British prime minister's residence in London in 1931.

Individuals also affect the course of events when they have few institutional constraints. In dictatorial regimes, top leaders are relatively free from domestic constraints such as societal inputs and political opposition, and thus are able to chart courses and implement foreign policy relatively unfettered. In democratic regimes, too, occasionally top decision makers are able to change policy in a dramatic fashion. For example, U.S. president Richard Nixon in 1972 was able to engineer a complete foreign policy reversal in relations with the People's Republic of China, secretly sending his top foreign policy adviser, Henry Kissinger, for several meetings with the Chinese premier Zhou Enlai and his advisers. These moves were an unexpected change, given Nixon's Republican party affiliation and prior anti-communist record. Bureaucratic and societal constraints mattered little, even in such a relatively open democracy.

The specifics of a situation also determine the extent to which individuals matter. Decision makers' personal characteristics have more influence on outcomes when the issue is peripheral rather than central, when the issue is not routine—that is, standard operating procedures are not available—or when the situation is ambiguous and information is unclear. Crisis situations, in particular, when information is in short supply and standard operating procedures are inapplicable, create scenarios in which a decision maker's personal characteristics count most. Such a scenario arose during the Cuban missile crisis, when President John F. Kennedy's personal openness to alternatives and attention to group dynamics paid off.

FIGURE 6.1 | **The Impact of Individual Elites**

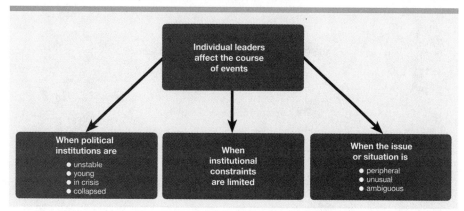

The Impact of Elites: The Personality Factor

Even among elite leaders working amid similar external conditions, some individuals seem to have a greater impact on foreign policy than others; this leads us to examine both the personal characteristics that matter and the thought processes of individuals.

The political psychologist Margaret Hermann has found a number of personality characteristics that affect foreign policy behaviors. Because top leaders do not generally take personality tests, Hermann used a different research strategy. She systematically collected spontaneous interviews and press conferences with eighty heads of state holding office in thirty-eight countries between 1959 and 1968. From these data, she found key personality characteristics that she felt influence a leader's orientation toward policy.[3] Those characteristics are listed in the top section of Figure 6.2.

These personality characteristics orient an individual's view of foreign affairs. Two orientations emerge from the personality traits. One group, leaders with high levels of nationalism, a strong belief in their own ability to control events, a strong need for power, low levels of conceptual complexity, and high levels of distrust of others, tend to develop an independent orientation to foreign affairs. The other group, leaders with low levels of nationalism, little belief in their ability to control events, a high need for affiliation, high levels of conceptual complexity, and low levels of distrust of others, tended toward a participatory orientation in foreign affairs. (The bottom of Figure 6.2 illustrates these orientations.) Then Hermann tested whether these personal characteristics and their respective orientations were related to both the foreign policy style and the behavior of the leaders.

Both Hermann and subsequent researchers using the same schema have found that they did. For example, one study considered the personality characteristics of the former British prime minister Tony Blair by using Hermann's categories to

FIGURE 6.2 | Personality Characteristics of Leaders

Personality Characteristics of Leaders

Nationalism: strong emotional ties to nation; emphasis on national honor and dignity

Perception of control: belief in ability to control events: high degree of control over situations; governments able to influence state and nation

Need for power: need to establish, maintain, and project power or influence over others

Need for affiliation: concern for establishing and maintaining friendly relationships with others

Conceptual complexity: ability to discuss with other people places, policies, ideas in a discerning way

Distrust of others: feelings of doubt, uneasiness about others; doubt about motives and actions of others

Foreign Policy Orientations

Independent leader:......... high in nationalism

high in perception of control

high in need for power

low in conceptual complexity

high in distrust of others

Participatory leader:......... low in nationalism

low in perception of control

high in need for affiliation

high in conceptual complexity

low in distrust of others

Source: Margaret G. Hermann, "Explaining Foreign Policy Behavior Using the Personal Characteristics of Political Leaders," *International Studies Quarterly* 24:1 (March 1980): 7–46.

organize Blair's foreign policy answers to questions posed in the House of Commons.[4] The researcher found that Blair had a high belief in his own ability to control events and a high need for power, accompanied by a low conceptual complexity. These personality findings go a long way toward explaining British foreign policy toward the 2003 Iraq War, a policy that many in the government and the British public opposed. Thus, even in democracies, where institutional constraints are high, individual personality characteristics influence foreign policy orientation and behavior.

Professor Betty Glad of the University of South Carolina has developed a profile of the former president Jimmy Carter that suggests how his personality characteristics played a key role in influencing the course of U.S. policy during the 1979–81 hostage crisis. The crisis began when Iranian militants kidnapped more than sixty Americans and held them for more than a year. Carter personalized the hostage taking. He was humiliated, obsessed, wanting above all to have *his* decisions vindicated. After an attempted helicopter rescue mission failed, he rationalized the failure as a "worthy effort," feeling that some action was better than nothing. Glad points to Carter's personality characteristics:

> Carter's subsequent difficulty in admitting that he made mistakes in this situation was based on his more general need to be right. He had always had difficulty in learning from his mistakes. In this instance the psychic costs to the United States of its importance in a crisis upon which the entire people and government focused for several months, as well as the political price Carter had to pay for that fixation, would make it particularly difficult for him to see where he had gone wrong.[5]

Personality characteristics affect the leadership of dictators more than that of democratic leaders because of the absence of effective institutional checks, as Glad has also investigated. She analyzed the personalities of tyrants—those who rule without attention to law, who capitalize on grandiose self-presentations and projects, look for every advantage, and utilize cruel, often extreme tactics. Comparing Hitler, Stalin, and Saddam Hussein, she labels them as having malignant narcissism syndrome. Glad explains how "project over-reach and creation of new enemies leads to increasing vulnerability, a deepening of the paranoiac defense, and volatility in behavior."[6] The North Korean leader Kim Jong-Il (the "Dear Leader") and his father, Kim Il-Sung (the "Great Leader"), exhibit some of these same characteristics. Kim Il-Sung erected more than thirty-four thousands monuments to himself during his fifty-year rule, and his photo was prominently displayed in buildings and other public places. Kim Jong-Il expresses his megalomania with gigantic pictures of himself, spending millions of dollars on spectacles of historical themes while more than a million of his people are starving. One former

A View from Venezuela: Hugo Chávez

Leaders are usually more complex than the simplistic labels that are attached to them: "good" or "bad," "weak" or "strong," "democrat" or "tyrant." President Hugo Chávez of Venezuela is one such leader: he is a complicated individual who supports populist domestic policies and revolutionary policies abroad.

President Hugo Chávez is the charismatic, democratically elected authoritarian leader of Venezuela. After mounting a failed coup attempt in 1992, he decided that the way to win power was through the ballot box. Chávez was elected in 1998. Inspired by Simón Bolívar, Che Guevara, the Chilean socialist president Salvador Allende, and Fidel Castro, Chávez has adopted a style and policies that put Venezuela on a new course.

Arguing that the model of economic development imposed on Latin American governments by the United States has failed, Chávez calls his approach a new "socialism of the twenty-first century." Inspired by the teachings of Jesus, he has spent large amounts of money on social programs such as housing and health care. Cuban doctors run neighborhood clinics, bringing free primary care to the poorest areas. Price controls have been placed on over four hundred food items, with soup kitchens providing food for the poorest. In one year alone, state spending for such programs increased by more than 30 percent. Chávez's Bolivarian Missions (named after Bolívar) work to combat disease, illiteracy, and poverty. According to government statistics, between 2000 and 2007, extreme poverty was cut in almost half, from 17 percent to 8 percent. Chávez has provided more for the poor than any other Venezuelan leader. As Alberto Müller Rojas, a leader of Chávez's United Socialist Party of Venezuela, argues, "A social consciousness has been created. It's improbable that we will regress to the way it was before."[a]

These programs benefitted from escalating export revenues earned from petroleum since 1999. During these years economic growth was strong. By 2004, the government had full control over the oil industry through the takeover of Venezuela's national oil company, PDVSA, by Chávez loyalists. Yet several government policies regarding oil have proven counterproductive. Although world petroleum prices remained high at least midway through 2008, Venezuela's production costs increased due to declining technical capacity. Policies that require PDVSA to supply cheap oil to other countries in the region have also led to an overall decline in revenue.

During his tenure, Chávez has been able to exercise his democratic authority by reducing the size of the political center and confronting his political opposition, but not banning them. He lavishes his supporters with gifts and withholds resources from those who oppose him. He has increased his control over the judiciary, the institution that supervises elections, as well as his control over the petroleum industry. This strategy, sometimes called "Chavenomics," entails the overwhelming presence of the state in the economy and presidential involvement in state management.

Chávez has broadened popular political participation through the Bolivarian Circles, grassroots political and social groups. That participation can be seen both in poor neighborhoods around the capital and in rural areas. Bringing technology to these areas has connected

people and given them a means of political participation.

Chávez's policies are popular, especially among the poor, who have benefited from his social programs. He has won fourteen elections and referenda over the last decade. A referendum to eliminate term limits for the president was passed in 2009. Chávez can now run for the office an unlimited number of times. In his own words, "There's still much to do; I need more time."[b]

Chávez's anti-imperialist and anti-American rhetoric also makes him extremely popular throughout Latin America. With his brand of democratically legitimized authoritarianism, he inspires other left-leaning leaders in the region. His well-publicized visits to Cuba to be at the bedside of the ailing Fidel Castro, and to Bolivia and Peru to support their populist leaders, have included foreign aid packages that strengthen those sympathetic leftist movements.

Chávez saves his most radical criticisms for the United States. He is a strong critic of U.S. neoliberal economic policies and has even provided grants to local organizations based in New York City, widely publicizing such programs to help the impoverished in the United States. Calling former president Bush both a donkey and a devil, he taps a deep animosity toward the United States in Latin America and beyond. In 2009, Venezuela and Russia signed an agreement for a joint venture in oil exploration, a measure designed to revive the petroleum industry.

Chávez has also forged relationships with other oil-producing countries, visiting both Iran and Libya and defending their policies. He has also chosen to deepen his strategic alliance with Russia. Cooperation between the two countries is currently increasing in the areas of military hardware and nuclear technology acquisition and development. Chávez has purchased more than $4 billion worth of Russian arms, including jet fighters and assault rifles. He plans to buy more Russian tanks, fearing escalating violence with and U.S. support for Colombia, with which Venezuela shares an extensive border.

But Chávez's popularity may be waning as Venezuela's economic situation becomes more difficult. Reports of empty shelves in stores and the deteriorating quality of medical and educational services illustrate that decline. The fall in oil prices, particularly since mid-2009, makes Chávez's situation more problematic, because revenue from oil experienced a precipitous drop.

For Critical Analysis

Answer these questions on wwnorton.com/studyspace

1. *Using Hermann's personality characteristics, how would you describe Hugo Chávez?*

2. *Is it personality or policies that has made Chávez both popular and powerful?*

3. *How has Chávez augmented the power and reach of the Venezuelan state?*

4. *Realists argue that individuals themselves are not key actors. Explain that viewpoint, using this case.*

---

[a] Quoted in Sara Miller Llana, "Where Has Chávez Taken Venezuela?" *Christian Science Monitor*, February 2, 2009, www.csmonitor.com/World/Americas/2009/0202/p01s03-woam.html (accessed 1/15/09).
[b] Llana, "Chávez."

CIA psychiatrist has suggested that Kim Jong-Il is self-absorbed, lacks an ability to empathize, and is capable of "unconstrained aggression." The "Dear Leader," he warns, "will use whatever aggression is necessary, without qualm of conscience, be it to eliminate an individual or to strike at a particular group."[7]

Personality characteristics, then, partly determine what decisions individual leaders make. But those decisions also reflect the fact that all decision makers are confronted with the task of putting divergent information into an organized form.

Individual Decision Making

The rational model of decision making that we discussed in Chapter 5 suggests that the individual possesses all the relevant information, stipulates a goal, examines the relevant choices, and makes a decision that best achieves that goal. In actuality, however, individuals are not perfectly rational decision makers. Confronted by information that is neither perfect nor complete, and often overwhelmed by a plethora of information and conditioned by personal experience, the decision maker selects, organizes, and evaluates incoming information about the surrounding world.

Individuals use a variety of psychological techniques to process and evaluate information. In perceiving and interpreting new and often contradictory information, individuals rely on existing perceptions, usually based on prior experiences. Such perceptions are the "screens" that enable individuals to process information selectively; these perceptions have an integrating function, permitting the individual to synthesize and interpret the information. Perceptions also serve an orienting function, providing guidance about future expectations and expediting planning for future contingencies. If those perceptions form a relatively integrated set of images, then they are called a **belief system.**

International relations scholars have devised methods to test the existence of elite images, although research has not been conducted on many individuals, for reasons made obvious below. Professor Ole Hosti of Duke University systematically analyzed 434 of the publicly available statements of Secretary of State John Foster Dulles concerning the Soviet Union during the years 1953–54. His research showed convincingly that Dulles held a very specific and unwavering image of the Soviet Union, one focused on atheism, totalitarianism, and communism. To Dulles, the Soviet people were good, but their leaders were bad; the state was good, the Communist party bad. This image was unvarying; the character of the Soviet Union in Dulles's mind did not change. Whether this image, gleaned from Dulles's statements, affected U.S. decisions during the period cannot be stated with certainty. He was, after all, only one among a group of top leaders. Yet a plethora of decisions taken during that time are consistent with the image.[8]

The political scientists Harvey Starr and Stephen Walker both completed similar empirical research on Henry Kissinger.[9] Elucidating Kissinger's operational code (the rules he operated by) from his scholarly writings, Walker found that the conduct of the Vietnam War, orchestrated in large part by Kissinger between 1969 and 1973, was congruent with the premises of his operational code and his conception of mutually acceptable outcomes. He wanted to negotiate a mutual withdrawal of external forces and to avoid negotiating about the internal structure of South Vietnam. He used enough force, applied in combination with generous peace terms, so that North Vietnam was faced with an attractive peace settlement versus unpalatable alternatives—stalemate or escalation.

These elite mind-set studies were possible because the particular elites left behind extensive written records from before, during, and after they held key policy making positions. Since few leaders leave such a record, however, our ability empirically to reconstruct elite images, perceptions, or operational codes is limited, as is our inability to state with certainty their influence on a specific decision.

Information-Processing Mechanisms

Our image and perception of the world are continually bombarded by new, sometimes overwhelming, and often discordant information. Images and belief systems, however, are not generally changed, and almost never are they radically altered. Thus, individual elites utilize, usually unconsciously, a number of psychological mechanisms to process the information that forms their general perceptions of the world. These mechanisms are summarized in Table 6.1.

First, individuals strive for **cognitive consistency,** ensuring that images hang together consistently within their belief systems. For example, individuals like to believe that the enemy of an enemy is a friend and the enemy of a friend is an enemy. Because of the tendency to be cognitively consistent, individuals select or amplify information that supports existing beliefs and ignore or downplay contradictory information. For example, because both Great Britain and Argentina were friends of the United States prior to their war over the Falkland/Malvinas Islands in 1982, U.S. decision makers denied the seriousness of the conflict at the outset. The United States did not think that its friend, the "peaceful" Britain, would go to war with Argentina over a group of barren islands thousands of miles from Britain's shores. The United States underestimated the strength of public support for military action in Britain, as well as misunderstanding the precarious domestic position of the Argentinian generals, who were trying to bolster their power by diverting attention to a popular external conflict.

Elites in power also perceive and evaluate the world according to what they have learned from past events. They look for details of a present episode that look like those of a past one, perhaps ignoring the important differences. Such similar details

TABLE 6.1

Psychological Mechanisms Used to Process Information

TECHNIQUE	EXPLANATION	EXAMPLE
COGNITIVE CONSISTENCY	Tendency to accept information that is compatible with what has previously been accepted, often ignoring inconsistent information. Desire to be consistent in attitude.	Just prior to the Japanese attack on Pearl Harbor, military spotters saw unmarked planes approaching Hawaii. Not believing the evidence, they discounted the instructions.
EVOKED SET	Details in a present situation that are similar to information gleaned from past situations. The tendency to look for an evoked set leads one to conclusions that are similar to those of the past.	During the Vietnam War, U.S. decision makers saw the Korean War as a precedent, although there were critical differences.
MIRROR IMAGE	Seeing in one's opponent the opposite of characteristics seen in oneself. Opponent is viewed as hostile and uncompromising, whereas one views oneself as friendly and compromising.	During the Cold War, both U.S. elites and masses viewed the Soviet Union in terms of their own mirror image: the United States was friendly, the Soviet Union hostile.
GROUPTHINK	Thought process whereby small groups to form consensus and resist criticism of that core position, often disregarding contradictory information.	During the U.S. planning for the Bay of Pigs operation against Cuba in 1961, opponents were ostracized from the planning group.
SATISFICING	Tendency for groups to search for a "good enough" solution, rather than an optimal one.	Decision of NATO to bomb Kosovo in 1999 in an attempt to stop the ethnic cleansing against the Albanian Kosovars, rather than sending in ground troops.

are often referred to as an **evoked set.** During the 1956 Suez crisis, for instance, the British prime minister Anthony Eden saw Egyptian president Gamal Abdel Nasser as another Hitler. Eden recalled Prime Minister Neville Chamberlain's failed effort to appease Hitler with the Munich agreement in 1938 and thus believed that Nasser, likewise, could not be appeased.

Individual perceptions are often shaped in terms of **mirror images:** whereas one considers one's own actions good, moral, and just, the enemy's actions are automatically found to be evil, immoral, and unjust. Mirror imaging often exacerbates conflicts, making it all the more difficult to resolve a contentious issue.

The psychological mechanisms that we have discussed so far affect the functioning of both individuals and small groups. But small groups themselves also have psychologically based dynamics that undermine the rational model. The psychologist Irving Janis called this dynamic **groupthink.** Groupthink, according to Janis, is "a mode of thinking that people engage in when they are deeply involved in a cohesive in-group, when members' strivings for unanimity override their motivation to realistically appraise alternative courses of action."[10] The dynamics of the group, which include the illusion of invulnerability and unanimity, excessive optimism, the belief in the group's own morality and the enemy's evil, and pressure placed on dissenters to change their views, leads to groupthink. During the Vietnam War, for example, a top group of U.S. decision makers, unified by bonds of friendship and loyalty, met in what they called the Tuesday lunch group. In the aftermath of President Lyndon Johnson's overwhelming electoral win in 1964, the group basked in self-confidence and optimism, rejecting out of hand pessimistic information about North Vietnam's military buildup. When information mounted about increasing South Vietnamese and American casualties, the group pulled even more tightly together; as the external stress intensified, the group further closed ranks, its members taking solace in the security of the group. New information was inserted only into old perceptions; individuals not sharing the group's thinking were both informally and formally removed from the group, as their contradictory advice fell on deaf ears.

Participants in small groups, then, are likely to employ the same psychological techniques, such as the evoked set and the mirror image, to process new incoming information at the individual level. But additional distorting tendencies affect small groups, such as the pressure for group conformity and solidarity. Larger groups seeking accommodation look for what is possible within the bounds of their situation, searching for a "good enough" solution, rather than an optimal one. Herbert Simon has labeled this trait *satisficing*.[11]

The political scientist Robert Jervis offers suggestions on how decision makers can safeguard their thinking and minimize mistakes due to various kinds of misperceptions.[12] They need to make their assumptions and beliefs as explicit as possible; be cognizant of the pitfall of interpreting data only as consistent with one's own theory; and be willing to play with information from different angles. Yet even doing all these things does not necessarily lead to a rational model of decision making. It is not just the tyrants (Germany's Adolf Hitler, North Korea's Kim Jong-Il, Uganda's Idi Amin, Cambodia's Pol Pot, or Zimbabwe's Robert Mugabe), but also the visionaries (Tanzania's Julius Nyerere, India's Mohandas Gandhi, South Africa's Nelson Mandela) and the political pragmatists (Great Britain's Margaret Thatcher, the Philippines' Corazon Aquino, Russia's Vladimir Putin, or Liberia's Ellen Johnson Sirleaf) who make an impact on the basis of their perceptions and misperceptions.

After the devastating reigns of corrupt authoritarian leaders such as Saddam Hussein in Iraq, Mobutu Sese Seko in Congo (formerly Zaire), and Robert Mugabe in Zimbabwe, whose people have been unwitting hostages, some pundits and politicians have suggested that "bad" or "corrupt" leaders should be removed by the international community.[13] That debate brings up numerous normative and pragmatic issues for students of international relations.

Private Individuals

Although leaders holding formal positions have more opportunity not only to participate in but to shape international relations, private individuals can and do play key roles. Private individuals, independent of any official role, may by virtue of circumstances, skills, or resources carry out independent actions in international relations. Less bound by the rules of the game or by institutional norms, such individuals engage in activities in which official representatives are either unable or unwilling to participate. The donations by Microsoft's founder Bill Gates and his wife, Melinda, to global vaccination, immunization, and AIDS programs is one such example.

In the area of conflict resolution, for instance, private individuals increasingly play a role in so-called **track-two diplomacy.** Track-two diplomacy utilizes individuals outside of governments to carry out the task of conflict resolution. High-level track-two diplomacy has met with some success. In the spring of 1992, for example, Eritrea signed a declaration of independence, seceding from Ethiopia after years of both low- and high-intensity conflict. The foundation for the agreement was negotiated in numerous informal meetings in Atlanta, Georgia, and elsewhere between the affected parties and former president Jimmy Carter, acting through the Carter Center's International Negotiation Network at Emory University. In the fall of 1993, the startling framework for reconciliation between Israel and the Palestine Liberation Organization was negotiated through track-two informal and formal techniques initiated by Terje Larsen, a Norwegian sociologist, and Yossi Beilin of the opposition Labor party in Israel. A series of preparatory negotiations was conducted over a five-month period in total secrecy. Beginning unofficially, the talks gradually evolved into official negotiations, building up trust in an informal atmosphere and setting the stage for an eventual agreement.[14]

Such high-level track-two diplomatic efforts are not always well received. For example, Jimmy Carter's eleventh-hour dash in 1994 to meet with North Korea's Kim Il-Sung to discuss the latter's nuclear buildup was met by a barrage of probing questions. Was the U.S. government being preempted? For whom did Carter speak? Could the understandings become the basis of a formal intergovernmental

POLICY DEBATE

Should "bad" or "corrupt" leaders be forcibly removed by the international community?

Yes

- Removal of "bad" leaders by the international community potentially averts war and continued humanitarian abuses, saving lives and money in the long term.
- Forcible removal of leaders not only punishes those individuals but serves as a deterrent to the misbehavior of other leaders.
- International intervention to remove tyrannical leaders shows that the international community will act, even using force if necessary.
- Under the principle of universal jurisdiction by the international community over the criminal acts of individuals, the removal of bad or corrupt leaders from office is a way to punish those individuals and is legal.

No

- Removal of leaders from office by the international community undermines traditional notions of sovereignty and noninterference in the domestic affairs of states.
- Deciding which leaders are so dangerous to the state and the international community is a highly charged political question, subject to abuse and unfair selectivity.
- There is a contradiction between the international community's responsibility to ensure international peace and security and the decision to use force, coercion, or even assassination to remove a corrupt leader.

agreement? Despite the misgivings and the eventual unraveling of North Korea's promises, Carter received the Nobel Peace Prize in 2002 for this and other efforts to promote peace around the world. Similar objections were raised when former president Bill Clinton journeyed to North Korea in 2009 to facilitate the release of two jailed American journalists. Did Clinton's meeting with the North Korean leader amount to negotiations with the errant regime? Was this private citizen actually speaking on behalf of the U.S. administration? The fact that Clinton is a former president and his wife the current U.S. secretary of state added to the confusion.

In 2009, former president Bill Clinton played an instrumental role in arranging the release of two American journalists being held by North Korea. Private individuals, including former leaders who no longer hold any government position, can sometimes shape international relations.

Other types of track-two diplomacy involve a lengthier process, a sustained dialogue.[15] In some cases, unofficial individuals from different international groups are brought together in small problem-solving workshops in order to develop personal relationships and understanding of the problems from the perspective of others. It is hoped that these individuals will then seek to influence public opinion in their respective states, trying to reshape, and often rehumanize, the image of the opponent. This approach has been used to address the conflict between Protestants and Catholics in Northern Ireland and the Arab-Israeli dispute. Problem-solving workshops have been conducted over two decades and cooperative activities encouraged.

Other private individuals have played linkage roles between different countries. Armand Hammer, a U.S. corporate executive, was for years a private go-between for the Soviet Union and the United States. His long-standing business interests in the Soviet Union and his carefully nurtured friendships with both Soviet economic and political leaders and U.S. officials provided a channel of communication at a time when few informal contacts existed between the two countries. In the immediate aftermath of the 1986 Chernobyl nuclear plant explosion, Hammer convinced Gorbachev to accept U.S. medical personnel and expertise.

The Cases of A. Q. Khan and Aung San Suu Kyi

Sometimes individuals are propelled into the international arena by virtue of their actions. A. Q. (Abdul Qadeer) Khan, the scientist dubbed the father of Pakistan's atomic bomb, confessed to selling nuclear technology and components to Libya, Iran, and North Korea in 2004. Under pressure from the West, the Pakistani government placed Khan in house detention but released him in 2009. By his activities Khan has enabled nuclear proliferation, making, in the view of many, the world a less secure place.

COURTESY PTV

The Pakistani nuclear scientist A.Q. Khan influenced international relations when he and a network of associates secretly sold nuclear technology to Iran, Libya, and North Korea—setting back international efforts toward nuclear nonproliferation. Khan confessed on Pakistani television in 2004 and was pardoned by the Pakistani president.

Aung San Suu Kyi became a different symbol: the face of the opposition movement to the repressive military government of Myanmar (formerly Burma). Her father, General Aung San, negotiated that country's independence from Great Britain in 1947. Assassinated the same year, he is viewed by many as the father of modern-day Burma. His daughter's public acts began after the 1962 military coup. Defying a ban on political gatherings, she spoke to large crowds, demanding democratic government.

Having spent many years outside of the country, she returned to Burma in 1988 and became the secretary-general of the newly formed National League for Democracy. Advocating nonviolence and civil disobedience, she traveled across the country, speaking to large audiences. In 1989, the government placed her under house arrest without charge or trial. She has spent most of the time since in confinement in her home.

Awarded the Nobel Peace Prize in 1991, Aung San Suu Kyi is the international symbol of the opposition, though not the only one. Buddhist monks actively opposed British colonialism and the military dictatorship. In 2007, that opposition, led by the monks, took to the streets after the regime raised fuel prices. Their demands included the release of political prisoners and broader political change.

When the government fired on the monks, the public was outraged. Various UN negotiators and groups have worked for change. The United States has proposed reducing existing sanctions if Ms. Aung San Suu Kyi is freed and the country's human rights record improves. Yet neither the international support for Ms. Aung San Suu Kyi nor the Western-imposed sanctions have had an obvious effect on policy. China, the country's largest trading partner, remains protective of the regime. China claims that Myanmar's internal politics are not a concern of the international community. So although a famous individual can galvanize an issue, that individual may not be able to change policy. That conclusion is consistent with the realist position that individuals matter little.

Alternative critical and postmodernist approaches are attempting to draw mainstream theorists' attention to these other stories, because they, too, are part of the fabric of international relations. Feminist writers in particular have sought to bring attention to the role of private individuals and especially women. In *Bananas, Beaches, and Bases,* the political scientist Cynthia Enloe shows strikingly how "the personal is international" by documenting the many ways that women influence international relations. She points to women in economic roles participating in the international division of labor, as seamstresses, light-industry "girls," nannies, and fashion models. She also identifies women more directly involved in foreign policy—the women living around military bases, diplomatic wives, domestic servants, and women in international organizations.[16] Theirs are the untold stories of marginalized groups that critical theorists, postmodernists, and constructivists are increasingly bringing to light.

Mass Publics

Mass publics have the same psychological tendencies as elite individuals and small groups. They think in terms of perceptions and images, they see mirror images, and they use similar information-processing strategies. For example, following the seizure of the U.S. embassy in Iran in November 1979, public-opinion surveys showed the prevalence of mirror images. The majority of U.S. respondents attributed favorable qualities to the United States and its leader and unfavorable ones to Iran and its leader. The United States was strong and brave; Iran, weak and cowardly. The United States was deliberate and decisive; Iran, impulsive and indecisive. President Carter was safe; the Ayatollah Khomeini, dangerous; Carter, humane; Khomeini, ruthless. In a relatively short period of time, under crisis conditions, the public's perception of Iran had crystallized. Yet whether this had an impact on top decision makers is unclear.[17] President Carter focused almost exclusively on the hostages, becoming obsessed with his mission of freeing them. But was this because of the public attention being paid to the hostages? Or did Carter's personality characteristics predispose him to focus so exclusively and so passionately on the hostages?

FIGURE 6.3 | Public Influence on Foreign Policy

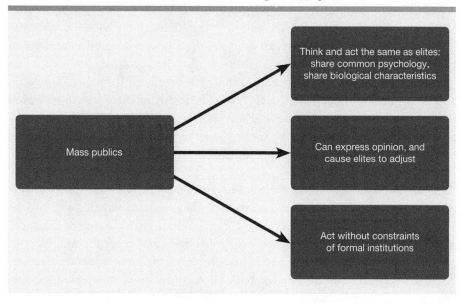

The influence that mass publics have on foreign policy can be explained in three ways. First, it can be argued that elites and masses act the same because they share common psychological and biological characteristics. Second, the masses have opinions and attitudes about foreign policy and international relations, both general and specific, that are different from those of the elites. If these differences are captured by public-opinion polls, will the elites listen to these opinions? Will policy made by the elites reflect the public's attitudes? The third possibility is that the masses, uncontrolled by formal institutions, may occasionally act in ways that have a profound impact on international relations, regardless of anything that the elites do. These three possibilities are illustrated in Figure 6.3.

Elites and Masses: Common Traits

Some scholars argue that there are psychological and biological traits common to every man, woman, and child and that societies reflect those characteristics. For example, individuals, like animals, are said to have an innate drive to gain, protect, and defend territory—the "territorial imperative." This, according to some, explains the preoccupation with defending territorial boundaries, such as Britain's determination in 1982 to defend its position on the Falkland Islands, a desolate archipelago 8,000 miles from Britain's shores. Individuals and societies also share the frustration-aggression syndrome: when societies become frustrated, just like individuals, they become aggressive. Frustration, of course, can arise from a number of different sources—economic shocks such as those Germany suffered after World War I or those Russia experienced in the 1990s, or failure to possess what is felt to be rightfully one's own, for example, the Palestinian claim to territory of the Israeli state.

The problem with both the territorial imperative and the frustration-aggression notion is that even if all individuals and societies share these innate biological predispositions, not all leaders and all peoples act on these predispositions. So general predispositions of all societies or the similarities in predispositions between elites and masses cannot explain the extreme variation found in individual behavior.

Another possibility is that elites and masses share common traits differentiated by gender. Male elites and masses possess characteristics common to each other, whereas female elites and masses share traits different from the males'. These differences can explain political behavior. Although there is considerable interest in this possibility, the research is sketchy. One much-discussed difference is that males, both elites and masses, are power seeking, whereas women are consensus builders, more collaborative, and more inclined toward compromise. One study, for example, sees the direct implications of these gender differences for peace negotiations. Because women often come to the negotiating table with experience in civic activism, nongovernmental organizations, and citizen-empowering movements, they bring different attitudes and skill-sets to the table. Drawing on this research, the European Union (EU) has mandated that 40 percent of all peacekeeping, reconciliation, and peace-building posts be given to women, and the United Nations and the Organization of Security and Cooperation in Europe have both tried to include more women in peace processes, in anticipation that gender differences may lead to better outcomes.[18]

If there are differences in male and female attitudes and behavior, are these differences rooted in biology or are they learned from the culture? Most feminists, particularly the constructivists, contend that these differences are socially constructed products of culture and can thus be reconstructed over time. Yet, once again, these general predispositions, whatever their origin, cannot explain extreme variation in individual behavior.

The Impact of Public Opinion on Elites

Publics do have general foreign-policy orientations and specific attitudes about issues that can be revealed by public-opinion polls. Sometimes these attitudes reflect a perceived general mood of the population that leaders can detect.

President Johnson probably accurately gauged the mood of the U.S. people toward the Vietnam War when he chose not to run for reelection in 1968. President George H. W. Bush was able to capitalize internationally on the positive public mood in the aftermath of victory in the 1991 Gulf War, although the domestic effect was short lived; he did not win reelection. Even leaders of authoritarian regimes pay attention to dominant moods, since these leaders also depend on a degree of legitimacy.

More often than not, however, publics do not express a single, dominant mood; top leaders are usually confronted with an array of public attitudes. These opinions are registered in elections, but elections are an imperfect measure of public opinion because they merely select individuals for office—individuals who share voters' attitudes on some issues but not on others.

Occasionally and quite extraordinarily, the masses may vote directly on an issue with foreign policy significance. For example, following the negotiation of the 1992 Maastricht Treaty, which detailed closer political cooperation among members of the European Union (EU), some states used popular referendums to ratify the treaty. At first, the Danish population defeated the referendum, thus choosing not to join the EU, despite the fact that the measure had support from most societal groups. Subsequently, Danes approved the referendum. The Norwegian public chose by a referendum to remain outside of the EU, another rare instance of direct public input on a foreign policy decision. Similarly, in 2002 the Swiss people voted to join the United Nations. In 2005, both French and Dutch voters failed to approve the referendum on the European Union Constitution. Ireland voted down the Lisbon Treaty, the new draft constitution in 2007, but reversed itself in 2009.

In most democratic regimes, public-opinion polling, a vast and growing industry, provides information about public attitudes. The European Union, for example, conducts the Eurobarometer, a scientific survey of public attitudes on a wide range of issues in EU countries. Because the same questions are asked during different polls over time, both top leaders in member states and the top leadership of the EU have amassed sophisticated data concerning public attitudes. But do they make policy with these attitudes in mind? Do elites change policy to reflect the preferences of the public?

Evidence from the United States suggests that elites do care about the preferences of the public, although they do not always directly incorporate those attitudes into policy decisions. Presidents care about their popularity because it affects their ability to work; a president's popularity is enhanced if he or she follows the general mood of the masses or fights for policies that are generally popular. Such popularity gives the president more leeway to set a national agenda. But mass attitudes may not always be directly translated into policy. For example, opinion polls suggest that U.S. elites, including top decision makers, are more supportive of an activist international agenda and of free trade and less supportive of economic protectionism than the mass public is. Thus, elite-made policy is not a direct reflection of public attitudes; the relationship between elite and mass public opinion is a complex one.

Mass Actions by a Leaderless Public

The mass public does not always have articulated opinions, nor is it always able to vote at the polls. Nor are groups of elites always able to control events. At times, the masses, essentially leaderless, take collective actions that have significant effects on the course of world politics.

Individuals act to improve their own political and economic welfare. An individual making such decisions alone usually will not have much impact on international relations. However, when hundreds or even thousands of individuals act, the repercussions can be dramatic. It was the individual acts of thousands fleeing East Germany that led to the construction of the Berlin Wall in 1961. Twenty-eight years later, it was the spontaneous exodus of thousands of East Germans through Hungary and Austria that led to the tearing down of the wall in 1989. The spontaneous movement of "boat people" fleeing Vietnam and the ragged ships leaving Cuba and Haiti for the U.S. coast resulted in changes in U.S. immigration policy. The spontaneous mass uprising against Philippine president Ferdinand Marcos in 1986 signaled the demise of his regime. The "Velvet Revolution" of the masses in Czechoslovakia in the 1990s brought the end of the communist regime in that country. Iranian students marching against the current regime, likewise, seek more social and economic freedom and an end to religious rule.

The scenario of dramatic changes initiated by the masses is vividly illustrated by the "people's putsch" during October 2000 against the Yugoslavian leader Slobodan Milošević. After thirteen years of rule, people from all walks of Serbian life joined seven thousand striking miners, crippled the economic system, blocked transportation routes, and descended on Belgrade, the capital. Aided by new technology such as the cell phone, they were able to mobilize citizens from all over the country, driving tractors into the city, attacking the parliament, and disrupting Milošević's radio and TV stations. As *Time* reported, "Years of pent-up frustration under Milošević's blighting misrule had finally erupted in a tumultuous showdown, as each new success taught Serbs to see they had the power to change their future. The revolution ran at cyberspeed from the disputed election two weeks ago, ending victoriously in the dizzying events of one day. Just like that, the Serbs took back their country and belatedly joined the democratic tide that swept away the rest of Eastern Europe's communist tyrants a decade ago."[19]

Mass publics can influence politics at home and abroad. In 2009, tens of thousands of Iranians protested elections that they believed to be unfair—and spread the word to the rest of the world via text messages and Twitter.

The people's revolution in Serbia against Milošević (the "Bulldozer Revolution") has proven to be a blueprint for action in other states of the post-communist world. In Georgia, in 2003, the "Rose Revolution" brought to power President Mikheil Saakashvili, and a political dynasty was broken. In the Ukraine in 2004, after seventeen days of demonstrations in bitter cold, the opposition leader Viktor Yushchenko won a hotly contested election in the "Orange Revolution." In March 2005, the old-style dictator of Kyrgyzstan was forced to flee to Moscow after holding power since the independence of that tiny republic in Central Asia in the "Tulip Revolution." Although these events were vivid illustrations of the power of the masses and of mass communications, their long-term impact remains in doubt. In several color-revolution states, newly instituted reforms have subsequently been curbed and the NGOs that they spawned have been severely restricted (see the Global Perspectives box in Chapter 7).

Iran is another case where mass opposition to a regime is strong, but whose outcome is unclear. The contested elections of June 2009, which gave victory to the incumbent president Mahmoud Ahmadinejad over his principal rival, Mir Hussein Moussavi, was the immediate trigger for mass demonstrations. Believing the elections were corrupt and unfair, tens of thousands of demonstrators, wearing bright green, marched in Tehran, the capital, along with prominent members of the opposition. For the first time events were communicated to the rest of the world via Twitter. When groups were prohibited from congregating, individuals were arrested, imprisoned, and reportedly raped and tortured by authorities. Yet three months later that "green" mass opposition demonstrated again, hijacking government-organized anti-Israeli demonstrations and voicing opposition to the Ahmadinejad regime and, by implication, opposition to Iran's supreme leader, Ayatollah Ali Khamenei. In this case, the rebellious actions of the discontented masses mirror real internal challenges to religious and political elites.

In Sum: How Much Do Individuals Matter?

For liberals, the actions of individuals matter. Individual elites can make a difference: they have choices in the kind of foreign policy they pursue and therefore can affect the course of events. Thus, we need to pay attention to

THEORY IN BRIEF

Contending Perspectives on the Individual

	LIBERALISM / NEOLIBERAL INSTITUTIONALISM	REALISM / NEOREALISM	RADICALISM / DEPENDENCY THEORY	CONSTRUCTIVISM
FOREIGN-POLICY ELITES	Significant impact on international relations through choices made and personality factors	Constrained by anarchic international system and national interests	Constrained by international capitalist system	Shape popular understanding and incorporation of events and processes
PRIVATE INDIVIDUALS	Secondary role, but may be involved in track-two diplomacy and may fund important initiatives	Actions of private individuals have effect only in aggregate, as reflected in national interest	Individual capitalists may be influential	Actions of individuals less important than beliefs
MASS PUBLICS	May affect international relations through mass actions that pressure state decision makers	Actions may be reflected in national interest	Agents of potential revolutionary change	Agents of potential change through discourse

personality characteristics and understand how individuals make decisions, how they employ various psychological mechanisms to process information, and what impact these processes have on individual and group behavior. Mass publics matter to liberals because liberals believe they help formulate the state's interests. Private individuals also matter, although they are clearly of secondary importance even in liberal thinking. Only in more recent postmodernist and constructivist scholarship, especially in feminist scholarship, have private individuals' stories found salience.

Constructivists do see individuals as important. Individuals form collective identities; elites can be key policy entrepreneurs who can promote change through ideas.

Realists and radicals do not recognize individuals as important, independent actors in international relations. They see individuals primarily as constrained by the international system and by the state. To realists, individuals are constrained by an anarchic international system and by a state seeking to project power consonant with its national interest. Similarly, radicals see individuals only as members of a class often misled or deluded by elites of the international capitalist system and within a state driven by economic imperatives. In neither case are individuals believed to be sufficiently unconstrained to be considered at the same level of analysis as either the international system or the state.

Individuals and states are not only important in themselves. They form into groups and operate in both international organizations and nongovernmental organizations, within a framework of international law. We turn to these actors in the next chapter.

DISCUSSION QUESTIONS

1. Leaders such as Fidel Castro, Robert Mugabe, or Muammar Qaddafi, are often dismissed as "crazy" or "nuts." What do we mean? What other explanation can be offered for their behavior?

2. You are a top decision maker in a government bureaucracy. What strategies would you use to try to minimize the effects of misperceptions in decision making?

3. If more women held major leadership positions in international affairs, would policies be any different? What theories would explain behavior by women leaders that is similar to or different from that of male leaders?

4. Mass publics are often stimulated by the media and connected by the new technologies. How? Show how the fax, the Internet, cell phones, and Twitter have made a difference.

KEY TERMS

belief system, p. 164
cognitive consistency, p. 165
evoked set, p. 166

groupthink, p. 167
mirror images, p. 166
track-two diplomacy, p. 168

 Find chapter outlines, practice quizzes, flashcards, and other study and review materials for this chapter at wwnorton.com/studyspace.

Intergovernmental Organizations, Nongovernmental Organizations, and International Law

- Why do intergovernmental organizations form?
- What have intergovernmental organizations such as the United Nations contributed to international peace and security?
- How has the European Union changed over time?
- What roles do nongovernmental organizations play?
- What is the role of international law in international relations?
- How do international relations theorists see intergovernmental organizations, nongovernmental organizations, and international law?

STATES AND INDIVIDUALS ARE not the only actors in international politics. **Intergovernmental organizations (IGOs)** and **nongovernmental organizations (NGOs)** also play a role in the international system. In this chapter we examine these actors, their historical development and functions, and their role in international relations. We also trace the development of international law. Understanding these actors and the international legal framework is key to understanding the liberal view of international politics in particular. We explore the strengths and weaknesses of liberal approaches to these elements of international relations and examine realist, radical, and constructivist responses.

Intergovernmental Organizations

The Creation of IGOs

Why have states chosen to organize themselves collectively? The response is found in liberalism; within the framework of institutions and rules, cooperation is possible. International organizations are the arenas where states interact and cooperate to solve common problems. During the 1970s, neoliberal institutionalists in particular revived the study of international organizations, arguing that "even if . . . anarchy constrains the willingness of states to cooperate, states nevertheless can work together and can do so especially with the assistance of international institutions."[1]

Neoliberal institutionalists recognize that continuous interaction among states provides the motivation for states to create international organizations. In turn these organizations moderate state behavior, provide a framework for interactions, establish mechanisms for reducing cheating by monitoring others and punishing the uncooperative, and facilitate transparency for state actions. Organizations are the focal points for coordination and make state commitments more credible, specifying expectations and establishing reputations for compliance.

International organizations are particularly useful for solving two sets of problems. One group of problems arises out of the need to cooperate on technical, often nonpolitical, issues where states are not the appropriate units for resolving these problems. As the scholar David Mitrany writes in *A Working Peace System*, units (states, subnational actors) need to "bind together those interests which are common, where they are common, and to the extent to which they are common."[2] This functional approach advocates building on and expanding the habits of cooperation nurtured by groups of technical experts, outside of formal state channels. This explains why international cooperation began in specific issue areas such as health and communications during the nineteenth century. The expectation, according to functionalist thinking, was that solving problems in these technical areas (curbing epidemics, facilitating international mail and telegraphic

In Focus ◎

FUNCTIONALISM

- War is caused by economic deprivation.
- Economic disparity cannot be solved in a system of independent states.
- New functional units should be created to solve specific economic problems.
- People will develop habits of cooperation, which will spill over from economic cooperation to political cooperation.
- In the long run, economic disparities will lessen and war will be eliminated.

Intergovernmental organizations, such as the United Nations, can play key roles in world politics, including solving problems related to collective goods.

services) would spill over into cooperation in political and military affairs, and new international organizations would form.

International organizations also form around collective goods. In "The Tragedy of the Commons," the biologist Garrett Hardin tells the story of a group of herders who share a common grazing area. Each herder finds it economically rational to increase the size of his own herd, allowing him to sell more in the market. Yet if all herders follow what is individually rational behavior, then the group loses: too many animals graze the land and the quality of the pasture deteriorates, which leads to decreased output for all. As each person rationally attempts to maximize his own gain, the collectivity suffers, and eventually all individuals suffer.[3]

What Hardin describes—the common grazing area—is a **collective good.** The grazing area is available to all members of the group, regardless of individual contribution. The use of collective goods involves activities and choices that are interdependent. Decisions by one state have effects for other states; that is, states can suffer unanticipated negative consequences as a result of the actions of others. In the international case, the decision by wealthy countries to continue the production and sale of chlorofluorocarbons affects all countries through long-term depletion of the ozone layer. With collective goods, market mechanisms break down. Alternative forms of management are needed.

In Focus ◉

COLLECTIVE GOODS

- Collective goods are available to all members of a group regardless of individual contributions.
- Some activities of states involve the provision of collective goods.
- Groups need to devise strategies to overcome problems of collective goods caused by the negative consequences of the actions of others—the "tragedy of the commons."
- Strategies include coercion; changing preferences, for example, by offering positive incentives to refrain from engaging in an activity, and altering the size of the group to ensure compliance.

Hardin proposed several possible solutions to the tragedy of the commons. First, use coercion. Force nations or peoples to control the collective goods. States, for example, could force people to limit the number of children they have in order to prevent a population explosion that harms the environment by drawing heavily on scarce natural resources. Second, restructure the preferences of states through rewards and punishments. Offer positive incentives for states to refrain from engaging in the destruction of the commons; tax or threaten to tax those who fail to cooperate, say, by making it cheaper for a polluter to treat pollutants than to discharge them untreated. Third, alter the size of the group. Smaller groups can more effectively exert pressure, because violations of the commons will be more easily noticed. Small groups can also mobilize collective pressure more effectively. China's population policy of one child per couple is administered at the local level, by individuals residing on the same street or in the same apartment building, or working in the same workplace. Close monitoring by these individuals, coupled with strong social pressure, is more likely to lead to compliance with the one-child policy. These alternatives can also be achieved through international organizations. For many, they are the preferred way to address problems of the commons—the sea, space, the environment. However, not all international problems are collective goods problems.

The Roles of IGOs

Intergovernmental organizations, such as the United Nations, the World Bank, and the International Civil Aviation Organization, can play key roles at each level of analysis, as highlighted in Table 7.1.[4] In the international system, IGOs contribute to habits of cooperation; through IGOs, states become socialized to regular interactions, a development that functionalists advocate. Such regular interactions occur between states in the United Nations. Some programs of IGOs, such as the International Atomic Energy Agency's nuclear monitoring program, establish

TABLE 7.1

Roles of Intergovernmental Organizations

LEVEL	ROLE	EXAMPLE
IN THE INTERNATIONAL SYSTEM	Contribute to habits of cooperation	Work within UN system and specialized agencies
	Engage in information-gathering, surveillance	World Bank gathers economic statistics; International Atomic Energy Agency monitors movement of nuclear materials
	Aid in dispute settlement	World Trade Organization or the International Court of Justice mediate disputes
	Conduct operational activities	Immunization campaigns against childhood diseases, run by World Health Organization; refugee camps, run by UN High Commissioner for Refugees
	Serve as arena for bargaining	European Council of Ministers hosts forums
	Lead to creation of international regimes	International trade regime and international food regime
WITH RESPECT TO STATES	Used by states as instrument of foreign policy	Nordic states use UN to distribute international development assistance
	Used by states to legitimate foreign policy	U.S. legitimates military action in Korea and in first Gulf War through UN
	Enhance information available to states	Small states turn to IGOs in absence of extensive bilateral diplomatic networks
	Punish states for acting in certain ways	Sanctions against South Africa, Rhodesia, Iraq, Serbia, and Iran
WITH RESPECT TO INDIVIDUALS	Place where individuals can be socialized to international norms	UN and EU delegates learn diplomatic norms
	Place where individuals become educated about international similarities and differences	Participants are educated at international meetings

regularized processes of information gathering, analysis, and surveillance that are particularly relevant to collective goods theory. Some IGOs, such as the World Trade Organization, develop procedures for making rules, settling disputes, and punishing those who fail to follow the rules. Other IGOs conduct operational activities that help to resolve major substantive international problems. Some IGOs also play key roles in international bargaining, facilitating the formation of transgovernmental and transnational networks composed of both subnational and nongovernmental actors. And IGOs may be the place where major changes in the international distribution of power are negotiated.

IGOs, along with states, often spearhead the creation and maintenance of international rules and principles based on their common concerns. They establish expectations about the behavior of other states. These rules and principles have come to be known generally as **international regimes.** Charters of IGOs incorporate the norms, rules, and decision-making processes of regimes. By bringing members of the regime together, IGOs help to reduce the incentive to cheat and enhance the value of a good reputation. The principles of the international human rights regime, for example, are articulated in a number of international treaties, including the Universal Declaration of Human Rights. Some IGOs, such as the United Nations (through its Office of the High Commissioner for Human Rights) and the European Union, institutionalize those principles into specific norms and rules. They establish processes designed to monitor states' human rights behavior and compliance with human rights principles. These same organizations provide opportunities for different members of the regime—states, other IGOs, NGOs, and individuals—to meet and evaluate their efforts.

For states, IGOs enlarge the possibilities for foreign policy making and add to the constraints under which states conduct and especially implement foreign policy. States join IGOs to use them as instruments of foreign policy. The IGOs may legitimate a state's viewpoints and policies; thus, the United States sought the support of the Organization of American States during the Cuban missile crisis in 1962. The IGOs increase available information about other states, thereby enhancing predictability in the policy making process. Small states, in particular, use the UN system to gather information about the actions of others. Some IGOs, such as the UN High Commissioner for Refugees and UNICEF, may conduct specific activities. These functions are compatible with or augment state policy.

But IGOs also constrain member states by setting international and hence national agendas and forcing governments to make decisions; by encouraging states to develop specialized decision making and implementing processes to facilitate and coordinate IGO participation; and by creating principles, norms, and rules of behavior with which states must align their policies if they wish to benefit from their membership. Both large and small states are subject to such constraints. For example, members of the UN General Assembly have at times set the international

TABLE 7.2

UN Principles and Contemporary Realities

PRINCIPLES	CHANGING REALITIES
SOVEREIGN EQUALITY OF STATES	Increasing number of members, including micro- and mini-states that contribute little but still have equal votes in the General Assembly
ONLY INTERNATIONAL PROBLEMS WITHIN UN JURISDICTION	Expansion of what is considered international because of changes in transportation, technology, and communication. For example, refugees can easily cross borders, leading states to initiate humanitarian intervention without the consent of other states involved.
PRIMARILY CONCERNED WITH INTERNATIONAL PEACE AND SECURITY	Broadened view of security to include economic and environmental security; international intervention to manage economic instability and to protect from environmental pollution

agenda to the displeasure of the United States, forcing the United States to take a stand it would not have taken otherwise. Small states, likewise, have to organize their foreign policy apparatus to address issues discussed in IGOs.

IGOs also affect individuals by providing opportunities for leadership. As individuals work with or in IGOs, they, like states, may become socialized to cooperating internationally.

Not all IGOs perform all of these functions, and the manner in and extent to which each carries out particular functions varies. Clearly the United Nations has been given an extensive mandate to carry out many functions. Yet the United Nations itself is a product of a historical process, an evolution that permits it to play its designated roles.

The United Nations

BASIC PRINCIPLES AND CHANGING INTERPRETATIONS   The United Nations was founded on three fundamental principles (see Table 7.2). Yet over the life of the organization, each of these principles has been significantly challenged by changing realities.[5]

First, the United Nations is based on the notion of the sovereign equality of member states, consistent with the Westphalian tradition. Each state—the United States, Lithuania, India, or Suriname, irrespective of size or population—is legally the equivalent of every other state. This legal equality is the basis for each state's having one vote in the General Assembly. However, the actual inequality of states is recognized in the veto power given to the five permanent members of the Security Council (China, France, Russia, the United Kingdom,

HISTORICAL PERSPECTIVE

Roots of Contemporary International Organization and Law

ANCIENT TIMES	Treaties concluded between city-states and communities (e.g., Mesopotamia, 3000 BCE)
GREEK AND ROMAN ERAS	Development of different kinds of laws governing states, citizens, and aliens
MIDDLE AGES	Under authority of Catholic church, canon law applies to all believers
SEVENTEENTH AND EIGHTEENTH CENTURIES	Hugo Grotius (1583–1645) writes that international relations is based on the rule of law, making him the father of international law; European writers such as Émeric Crucé (1590–1648) and Abbé de Saint-Pierre (1658–1743) propose that European states meet to discuss conflicts and make plans for a court and league of states
NINETEENTH CENTURY	Concert of Europe: major European powers use multilateral diplomacy to settle problems and coordinate actions, giving special status to great powers; formation of public international unions to address problems of commerce and communications (e.g., Universal Postal Union, 1864; International Telegraphic Union, 1865; functional cooperation in health and sanitary issues)
LATE NINETEENTH AND EARLY TWENTIETH CENTURIES	Development of international legal institutions resulting from conferences in The Hague, Netherlands; both small states and non-European states join with European powers to develop dispute-settlement mechanisms
1918	U.S. president Woodrow Wilson calls for a general association of states in his "Fourteen Points" address to the U.S. Congress
1920	Treaty of Versailles enters into force, and League of Nations is established; International Labor Organization and Permanent Court of International Justice are also established
1945	Representatives of fifty states meet in San Francisco and conclude UN Charter
1946	League of Nations transfers all assets to the United Nations

and the United States), the special role reserved for the wealthy states in budget negotiations, and the weighted voting system used by the World Bank and the International Monetary Fund.

Second is the principle that only international problems fall within the jurisdiction of the United Nations. Indicative of the Westphalian influence, the UN Charter does not "authorize the United Nations to intervene in matters which are essentially within the domestic jurisdiction of any state" (Article 2, Section 7). Over the life of the United Nations, the once-rigid distinction between domestic and international issues has weakened, leading to an erosion of sovereignty. Global telecommunications and economic interdependencies, international human rights, election monitoring, and environmental regulation are among the developments infringing on traditional areas of domestic jurisdiction and hence on states' sovereignty. War is increasingly civil war, which is not legally under the purview of the United Nations. Yet because international human rights are being abrogated, because refugees cross national borders, and because weapons are supplied through transnational networks, such conflicts are increasingly viewed as international, and the United Nations is viewed by some as the appropriate venue for action.

These changes have led to a growing body of precedent for humanitarian intervention without the consent of the host country. In 1992, this precedent was exercised in Somalia, which had no central government to give consent to UN humanitarian relief operations and it also led to debate over whether intervention should occur to stop the atrocities in Darfur, even though the Sudanese government objected. Eventually Sudan accepted international peacekeepers, but in only a limited capacity.

The third principle is that the United Nations is designed primarily to maintain international peace and security. This has meant that member states should refrain from the threat or the use of force, settle disputes by peaceful means, as detailed at the Hague conferences, and support enforcement measures.

Although the foundations of both the League of Nations and the United Nations focused on security in the realist, classical sense—protection of national territory—the United Nations is increasingly confronted with demands for action to support a broadened view of security. Operations to feed the starving populations of Somalia and Rwanda or to provide relief in the form of food, clothing, and shelter for Haitians forced out of their homes are examples of this broadened notion of security—**human security.** Expansion into these newer areas of security collides head on with the domestic authority of states, undermining the principle of state sovereignty. The initial refusal of the Myanmar military to permit international humanitarian aid following the devastating 2008 typhoon Nargis led to discussions of delivering aid through military force in the name of human security, although in the end that option was not needed. The United Nations's founders recognized the tension between the commitment to act collectively against a member state and the affirmation of state sovereignty. But they could not foresee the dilemmas that changing definitions of security would pose.

STRUCTURE The structure of the United Nations was developed to serve the multiple roles assigned by its charter, but incremental changes in that structure have accommodated changes in the international system, particularly the increase in the

TABLE 7.3

Principal Organs of the United Nations

ORGAN	MEMBERSHIP AND VOTING	RESPONSIBILITIES
SECURITY COUNCIL	15 members; 5 permanent with veto; 10 rotating members elected by region	Peace and security: identifies aggressor; decides on enforcement measures
GENERAL ASSEMBLY	192 members; each state has one vote; work in 6 functional committees	Debates any topic within charter's purview; admits states; elects members to special bodies
SECRETARIAT, HEADED BY SECRETARY-GENERAL	Secretariat of 11,000; secretary-general elected for 5-year renewable term by General Assembly and Security Council	Secretariat: gathers information, coordinates and conducts activities; Secretary-general: chief administrative officer, spokesperson
ECONOMIC AND SOCIAL COUNCIL (ECOSOC)	54 members elected for 3-year terms	Coordinates economic and social welfare programs; coordinates action of specialized agencies (FAO, the WHO, UNESCO)
TRUSTEESHIP COUNCIL	Originally composed of administering and nonadministering countries; now made up of 5 great powers	Supervision has ended; proposals have been floated to change function to that of forum for indigenous peoples, NGOs, or nation building
INTERNATIONAL COURT OF JUSTICE	15 judges	Noncompulsory jurisdiction on cases brought by states and international organizations

number of states. The central UN organs comprise six major bodies, as shown in Table 7.3.

The power and prestige of these various organs has changed over time. The **Security Council** was kept small to facilitate swifter decision making in response to threats to international peace and security. Its five permanent members—the United States, Great Britain, France, Russia (successor state to the Soviet Union in 1992), and the People's Republic of China (replaced the Republic of China in 1971)—are key to council decision making, each having veto power on substantive issues where unanimity is required. In the early years of the Cold War, the Security Council became deadlocked by the Soviet Union's frequent use of the veto. Since the 1970s, the United States has used its veto more times than any other permanent member. The majority of these vetoes have concerned the Arab-Israeli-Palestinian conflict.

Since the end of the Cold War, the Security Council has regained power, because the use of the veto has dropped precipitously. The number of annual official meetings has risen, the number of resolutions passed has increased with consensus voting, and informal meetings among the permanent members have been more frequent. With greater cooperation among the permanent powers—especially since 1990, beginning with the council's authorization of force against Iraq after its invasion of Kuwait—the Security Council has taken on more armed conflicts, imposed more types of sanctions in more situations, created war crimes tribunals to prosecute war criminals, authorized protectorates in Kosovo and East Timor, and after 9/11 expanded involvement in antiterrorism activities. But although the Security Council has enormous formal power, it does not have direct control over the means to use that power. It depends on states for funding, personnel, and enforcement of sanctions and military action. A state's willingness to contribute depends on whether it perceives the council as legitimate.

The **General Assembly,** with its growth in membership from 51 to 192, permits debate on any topic under its purview. The bulk of the work of the General Assembly is done in six functional committees: Disarmament and Security; Economic and Financial; Social, Humanitarian, and Cultural; Political and Decolonization; Administrative and Budgetary; and Legal. Debate on resolutions emerging from the committees is organized around regionally based voting blocs, member states using their one vote to coordinate positions and build support for them. Since the end of the Cold War, the General Assembly's work has been increasingly marginalized, as the epicenter of UN power has shifted back to the Security Council and a more active Secretariat, much to the dismay of various caucusing groups, including the **Group of 77**, the coalition of developing states; regional groups (Africa, Asia, Latin America); and some members of the **Group of 20**, a coalition of the emerging economies.

Over the years, the Secretariat has expanded to employ over eleven thousand individuals at UN headquarters and a global staff of almost forty thousand, half of those local personnel in peacekeeping missions. The role of the secretary-general has expanded significantly. Having few formal powers, the secretary-general depends for authority on persuasive capability and an aura of neutrality. With this power, the secretary-general, especially in the post–Cold War era, can potentially forge an activist agenda, as Secretary-General Kofi Annan did until his retirement in 2006. In 1998, at the request of members of the Security Council, he traveled to Baghdad to negotiate a compromise between Iraq and the United States over the authority, composition, and timing of UN inspection teams searching for nuclear, biological, and chemical weapons in Iraq. The secretary-general's negotiated compromise averted a showdown between the two powers at the time.

Annan continued to play a mediator role between Iraq and the rest of the international community. He also implemented significant administrative and budgetary reforms within the organization and worked hard to establish a better relationship with the United States, especially the U.S. Congress, a key body in authorizing funding. Annan used the office to push other initiatives, including the international response to the AIDS epidemic and the promotion of better relations between the private sector and the United Nations. Considered a highly visible secretary-general, he was awarded the Nobel Peace Prize in 2001. It was no wonder that the process to elect a successor in 2006 was such a contentious one, leading to the selection of Ban Ki-moon of the Republic of Korea. Like his predecessor, in his first years in office, he has undertaken strong initiatives on such topics as global warming, Darfur, and preventive diplomacy. He has also set up standby mediation teams to respond to crises. However he has met criticism as a weak leader and ineffective administrator.

Throughout the United Nations, when one organ has increased in importance, others have diminished, most notably the Economic and Social Council (ECOSOC) and the Trusteeship Council, albeit for very different reasons. ECOSOC was originally established to coordinate the various economic and social activities within the UN system through a number of specialized agencies. But the expansion of those activities and the increase in the number of programs has made ECOSOC's task of coordination a problematic one. In addition to covering such broad issues as human rights, the status of women, population and development, and social development, ECOSOC is charged with coordinating the work of the family of UN specialized institutions (discussed below). In contrast, the Trusteeship Council has worked its way out of a job. Its task was to supervise decolonization and to phase out trust territories placed under UN guardianship during the transition of colonies to independent states. Thus, the very success of the Trusteeship Council has meant its demise.

KEY POLITICAL ISSUES The United Nations has always mirrored what is happening in the world, and the world has, in turn, been shaped by the United Nations and its organs. The United Nations played a key role in the decolonization of Africa and Asia. The UN Charter endorsed the principle of self-determination for colonial peoples, and former colonies such as India, Egypt, Indonesia, and the Latin American states seized on the United Nations as a forum to push the agenda of decolonization. By 1960, a majority of the United Nations' members favored decolonization. UN resolutions condemned the continuation of colonial rule and called for annual reports on the progress toward independence of all remaining territories. The United Nations was key to the legitimation of the new international norm that colonialism and imperialism are unacceptable state policies. By the mid-1960s, most of the former colonies had achieved independence with little threat to international peace, and the United Nations had played a significant role in this transformation.

The emergence of the newly independent states transformed the United Nations and international politics more generally. These states formed a coalition of the South, or Group of 77—developing states whose interests lie in economic development, a group often at loggerheads with the developed countries of the North. The split between the North and the South became the basis for the call by the Group of 77 for a New International Economic Order. The North-South conflict continues to be a central feature of world politics and of the United Nations.

PEACEKEEPING Of the issues the United Nations confronts, none is as vexing as peace and security. A new approach, labeled *peacekeeping*, evolved as a way to limit the scope of conflict and prevent it from escalating into a Cold War confrontation. Peacekeeping operations fall into two types, or generations. In **traditional peacekeeping**, multilateral institutions such as the United Nations seek to contain conflicts between two states through third-party military forces. Ad hoc military units, drawn from the armed forces of nonpermanent members of the UN Security Council (often small, neutral members), have been used to prevent the escalation of conflicts and to keep the warring parties apart until the dispute can be settled. Invited in by the disputants, the troops operate under UN auspices, supervising armistices, trying to maintain cease-fires, and physically interposing themselves in a buffer zone between warring parties. Table 7.4 lists some of these traditional UN peacekeeping operations.

In the post–Cold War era, UN peacekeeping has expanded to address different types of conflicts and to take on new responsibilities. Whereas traditional peacekeeping activities primarily address interstate conflict, **complex peacekeeping** activities respond to civil war and ethnonationalist conflicts within states that may not have requested UN assistance. To deal with these new conflicts, peacekeepers have taken on a range of both military and nonmilitary functions. On the military side, they have aided in the verification of troop withdrawal (the Soviet Union from Afghanistan) and have separated warring factions until the underlying issues could be settled (Bosnia). Sometimes resolving underlying issues has meant organizing and running national elections, as in Cambodia and Namibia; sometimes it has involved implementing human rights agreements, as in Central America. At other times UN peacekeepers have tried to maintain law and order in failing or disintegrating societies by aiding in civil administration, policing, and rehabilitating infrastructure, as in Somalia, East Timor, and Afghanistan. (This is often referred to as **peacebuilding**.) And peacekeepers have provided humanitarian aid, supplying food, medicine, and a secure environment in part of an expanded version

TABLE 7.4

Traditional Peacekeeping Operations

OPERATION	LOCATION(S)	DURATION	STRENGTH
UNTSO (UN TRUCE SUPERVISION ORGANIZATION)	Egypt, Israel, Jordan, Syria, Lebanon	June 1948–present	151 military observers; 200 civilians
UNEF I (FIRST UN EMERGENCY FORCE)	Suez Canal, Sinai Peninsula	Nov. 1956–June 1967	3,378 troops
ONUC (UN OPERATION IN THE CONGO)	Congo	June 1960–June 1964	19,828 troops
UNFICYP (UN PEACEKEEPING FORCE IN CYPRUS)	Cyprus	March 1964–present	6,411 military observers
UNEF II (SECOND UN EMERGENCY FORCE)	Suez Canal, Sinai Peninsula	Oct. 1973–July 1979	6,973 troops
UNDOF (UN DISENGAGEMENT OBSERVER FORCE)	Syrian Golan Heights	June 1974–present	1,048 troops; 57 military observers
UNMEE (UN MISSION IN ETHIOPIA AND ERITREA)	Ethiopia/Eritrea border	Sept. 2000–present	4,200 troops; 400 civilians
UNIFIL (UN INTERIM FORCE IN LEBANON)	Southern Lebanon	March 1978–present	11,800 military; 1,000 civilians

Source: United Nations.

of human security in Africa. Table 7.5 lists some representative cases of complex peacekeeping operations.

Complex peacekeeping has had successes and failures, as illustrated by the two African cases of Namibia and Rwanda. Namibia (formerly South-West Africa), a former German colony, was administered by South Africa following the end of World War I. Over the years, pressure was exerted on South Africa to relinquish control of the territory and grant Namibia independence. As long as Soviet-backed Cuban troops occupied neighboring Angola, South Africa refused to consider change, citing security concerns. Finally in 1988, Cuba and Angola agreed to a withdrawal of Cuban troops as part of a regional peace settlement that included

TABLE 7.5

Complex Peacekeeping Operations

OPERATION	LOCATION(S)	DURATION	MAXIMUM STRENGTH
UNTAG (UN TRANSITION ASSISTANCE GROUP)	Namibia, Angola	April 1989–March 1990	4,493 troops; 15,000 police
UNPROFOR (UN PROTECTION FORCE)	Former Yugoslavia (Croatia), Bosnia, Macedonia	March 1992–Dec. 1995	38,000 troops; 4,600 civilians
UNTAC (UN TRANSITION AUTHORITY IN CAMBODIA)	Cambodia	Feb. 1992–Sept. 1993	15,900 troops; 3,600 police; 2,400 civilians
UNOSOM I, II (UN OPERATION IN SOMALIA)	Somalia	Aug. 1992–March 1995	28,000 troops; 2,800 civilians
MONUC (UN MISSION IN DEMOCRATIC REPUBLIC OF CONGO)	Congo	1999–present	16,700 troops; 1000 police; 3,700 civilians
UNMIK (UN INTERIM ADMINISTRATION MISSION IN KOSOVO)	Kosovo	1999–present	3,478 police; 3,591 civilians
UNMISET AND UNMIT (UN MISSIONS IN EAST TIMOR)	Timor-Leste	2002–present	1,588 troops; 1,608 police; 1,200 civilians
UNAMID (AFRICAN UNION/UNITED NATIONS HYBRID OPERATION IN DARFUR)	Darfur	July 2007–present	13,502 troops; 3,200 police; 2,494 civilians

Source: United Nations.

Namibian independence. The United Nations established a major peacekeeping operation in the region, which supervised the cease-fire, monitored the withdrawal of South African forces, supervised the civilian police force, secured the repeal of discriminatory legislation, arranged for the release of political prisoners, and created conditions for free and fair elections. The UN Transition Assistance Group in Namibia (UNTAG) played a vital role in managing the move from war to a cease-fire and then to independence. The operation in Namibia became the model for UN complex peacekeeping and nation building in Cambodia in the early 1990s and in East Timor in the late 1990s.

But not all UN peacekeeping operations have been successful. Rwanda is an example of a situation where a limited UN peacekeeping force proved to be insufficient and where genocide subsequently escalated as the international community watched and did nothing. Rwanda and neighboring Burundi have seen periodic outbreaks of devastating ethnic violence between Hutus and Tutsis since the 1960s. In the 1990s, intermittent fighting once again broke out. A 1993 peace agreement called for a UN force (the UN Assistance Mission in Rwanda, or UNAMIR) to monitor the cease-fire. Yet less than a year later, large-scale violence erupted following the death of the Rwandan president in a plane crash, with Hutu extremists in the Rwandan military and police slaughtering minority Tutsis, resulting in 750,000 Tutsi deaths in a ten-week period. UNAMIR was not equipped to handle the crisis, and despite its commander's call for more troops, the UN Security Council failed to respond until it was too late. Although UNAMIR did establish a humanitarian protection zone and provided security for relief-supply depots and escorts for aid convoys, peacekeeping failed disastrously.

The UN's response to the crisis in Darfur, Sudan, has also proven problematic. When in 2003 thousands of people fled their villages to escape attacks from the government-based Arab militias (the Janjaweed), the UN system and NGOs responded with humanitarian aid, setting up refugee camps and providing emergency food and health care. But the Security Council issued only weak warnings to Sudan, despite evidence that Darfur was becoming a genocide, with over 300,000 killed and 2.7 million displaced. But both China and Russia opposed coercive measures against Sudan. Eventually, Sudan did accept a small monitoring force from the African Union, but that force did not have the authority to prevent the violence. Only in 2007 was a stronger UN-AU peacekeeping force approved, but that force has never reached its maximum size and is ill equipped. Meanwhile, the crisis has become more complex, with the number of different factions increasing. The United Nations, indeed the international community, failed to take definitive action.

ENFORCEMENT AND CHAPTER VII   Since the end of the Cold War, the Security Council has intervened in situations deemed threatening to international peace and security as authorized in Chapter VII of the UN Charter. That provision enables the Security Council to take measures (economic sanctions, direct military force) to prevent or deter threats to international peace or to counter acts of aggression. Previously, such actions had been invoked only twice, the UN preferring the more limited, traditional peacekeeping. The disarmament provisions overseen by the U.S. Special Commission for the Disarmament of Iraq and the International Atomic Energy Agency (IAEA), one of the United Nations' specialized agencies, and the economic sanctions against Iraq during the 1990s were enforcement actions under Chapter VII. Indeed, the 1990s were labeled the "sanctions decade" for the

A UN-African Union peacekeeping force in Darfur, Sudan, has proved ill equipped to end the violence that has killed hundreds of thousands and driven 2.7 million from their homes. Many Sudanese, including the children pictured above, have taken shelter in refugee camps.

numerous times targeted sanctions were imposed. But getting agreement on when to impose sanctions can be difficult. In 2008, the United States and the European Union sought targeted sanctions against the Mugabe regime in Zimbabwe for its systematic human rights abuses against its citizens. But Russia and China vetoed a draft in the Security Council, reiterating the principle of noninterference in the domestic affairs of states.

The 1991 Gulf War was an enforcement action under Chapter VII. The Security Council authorized members "to use all necessary means," a mandate that led to direct military action by the multinational coalition under U.S. command. In 2002, the United States went to the Security Council seeking Chapter VII enforcement against Iraq again, claiming that Iraq was in material breach of its obligations under previous UN resolutions. The Security Council was divided, with the United States and Great Britain supporting enforcement and France, Russia, and China opposing the action. When the stalemate solidified, the United States chose not to return to the Security Council to seek formal authorization for the use of force. Thus, the U.S.-led coalition in the 2003 Iraq War was not authorized by the United Nations, leading many to ponder whether the United Nations is still a relevant player in international politics.

POLICY DEBATE

Is the United Nations still a relevant actor in world politics in the twenty-first century?

Yes

- No other international organization is more legitimate than the UN because of its longevity and worldwide membership.
- The UN Security Council remains the premier forum where issues related to the maintenance of international peace and security are discussed and actions authorized.
- Both traditional UN peacekeeping and complex peace operations have successfully kept warring parties apart and enforced peace settlements in both intrastate and regional conflicts.
- The UN has organized, conducted, and monitored democratic elections in numerous states.
- The UN worked in the 2003 Iraq War. The UN weapons inspection and sanctions regime was vindicated on the issue of Iraq's weapons of mass destruction. The UN Security Council did not authorize the U.S. invasion of Iraq, making the war illegitimate in the eyes of many.
- The UN was critical in the decolonization effort and played an essential role in placing human rights onto the international agenda and shaming deviant states.
- UN agencies such as UNICEF, UNESCO, the Food and Agriculture Organization, and the World Health Organization have improved the lives of many through health, agricultural, and educational programs aimed at developing state capacity and conducting field operations.
- Many of the most pressing issues, from financial crises to global warming, are addressed in UN-related institutions, from the International Monetary Fund to the UN-convened meetings renegotiating the Kyoto Protocol.

No

- The UN is clearly unable to undertake any significant action without the political and financial support of the major powers.
- The UN has proven incapable of generating the type of consensus necessary for major action on divisive international issues, when the national interests of a major power are at stake, as with the 2003 Iraq War or the Darfur conflict.

(continued)

- The Security Council is an unrepresentative and hence illegitimate institution. Major donors such as Japan and Germany are not permanent members. Emerging states and developing countries from Latin America and Africa are underrepresented.
- The UN system's bureaucracy is inefficient and ineffective in its response to humanitarian disasters, whether in Rwanda, Sudan, the Indian Ocean tsunami, or Haiti. Resources and responsibility are spread over too many different competing agencies.
- The UN's counterproliferation machinery has been unable to halt Iran's and North Korea's pursuit of nuclear programs, making a mockery of UN resolutions.
- Democracies actually share more interests with other democracies. The creation of a "league of democracies" would allow these states to act on these interests without being blocked by autocracies that dominate the UN.

PEACEKEEPING AND ENFORCEMENT: SUCCESS OR FAILURE?   Scholarly studies using empirical data from multiple cases find that traditional peacekeeping has reduced the propensity of belligerents to fight in the future. The Cyprus peacekeeping mission averted overt hostilities between Greeks and Turks on the island. For eleven years, the Arab and Israeli states were kept apart, and India-Pakistan hostilities over Kashmir were contained at intermittent intervals, thanks in large part to traditional peacekeeping operations.

But success in traditional peacekeeping in interstate wars has not been matched by success in the more complex operations, notably in intrastate civil wars. In those cases, although the risk of war has been reduced by half, the risk of another war occurring within five years ranged from 23 to 43 percent.[6] When those complex operations involved verification of arms, monitoring, or election supervision, they were more successful. But in the most difficult conflicts, with a long history of violence and multiple belligerents, peacekeeping and peacebuilding have been less successful.

REFORM: SUCCESS AND STALEMATE Faced with escalating demands and saddled with structures that no longer reflect the power realities of the international system, the United Nations has been confronted with persistent calls for reform. Although many reforms have been undertaken, the challenges remain critical. Because amending the charter is difficult—requiring ratification of two-thirds of the members, including all five permanent members of the Security Council—most reforms have been undertaken without actually amending the charter.

To address management problems publicized in the 2004 oil-for-food scandal, when UN officials were accused of taking bribes and showing favoritism in awarding contracts in Iraq, new financial accountability mechanisms have been put in place and internal oversight has been established. To address newer issues, structures have been created or reorganized, including the High Commissioner for Human Rights in 1997 and the Counter-Terrorism Committee in 2001 to help countries become more effective in addressing terrorism. To manage peacekeeping operations more efficiently, the Department of Peacekeeping Operations has been expanded, military staff have been added from the troop-contributing countries, and strategic deployment stocks and rapid deployment teams organized. In 2006, a Peacebuilding Commission was formed to address postconflict recovery systematically. Its mandates included monitoring economic stabilization and building government capacity, a long-term project whose success is not guaranteed. UN economic development activities have become more coordinated with UN Houses in recipient countries, providing a focal point for activities. And a body formed in 2002 began the practice of bringing the heads of twenty-eight UN programs and agencies together, including the World Bank, the International Monetary Fund, and the World Trade Organization—a step that has been on the agenda for decades.[7]

In 2005, on the occasion of the United Nations' sixtieth birthday, one major reform emerged: Security Council reform. This is critical to the legitimacy of the Security Council's role in enforcement with the use of force. The five permanent members of the Council, the victors of World War II with their veto power over substantive issues, are an anachronism. Europe is overrepresented; China is the only developing country and the only Asian member; both Germany and Japan contribute more financially to the organization than the other four permanent members do. Virtually all agree that membership should be increased. But there agreement ends. What other countries should be admitted? Germany, Japan, and/or Italy? India, Pakistan, South Africa, and/or Nigeria from the developing world? Argentina or Brazil? Should the new members have the veto? Should the differentiation between permanent and nonpermanent membership be maintained? Contending proposals continue to be discussed and debated, but no agreement has been reached. After all, reform begins and ends with states.

A COMPLEX NETWORK OF INTERGOVERNMENTAL ORGANIZATIONS The central organs of the United Nations discussed above are only a small part of the UN system of organizations. Today, there are nineteen specialized agencies formally affiliated with the United Nations, each a reflection of functionalist thinking. That is, these organizations address specialized areas of activity that individual states themselves cannot manage alone due to the characteristics of the problems. Public health and disease do not respect national borders; neither do weather systems. Specialized expertise across states is needed to monitor such phenomena. Mail and telecommunications move across national borders; marine transport and airplanes fly between states; technical rules are needed to govern these areas. Given the importance of these functional activities, it is not surprising that many of the specialized UN agencies actually predate the United Nations itself. The International Telecommunications Union dates from 1865, the Universal Postal Service from 1874, and international sanitary conferences from the middle of the nineteenth century. Others, such as the International Civil Aviation Organization and the International Maritime Organization, date from immediately after World War II.

Other specialized UN agencies and UN programs perform operational activities dedicated to limited tasks, although those tasks may be much more controversial: delivering food to those in need (World Food Programme); settling refugees and internally displaced people (UN High Commissioner for Refugees); or establishing labor standards (International Labor Organization). Many of the tasks that these programs and agencies perform began under the auspices of the League of Nations following World War I. These organizations have separate charters, memberships, budgets, and secretariats. Although each reports directly or indirectly to the UN's Economic and Social Council, none can be instructed by it or by the General Assembly (see Table 7.6).

Included under the specialized agencies are the Bretton Woods institutions—the International Monetary Fund and the World Bank—examined in Chapter 9. In addition are numerous other intergovernmental organizations not affiliated with the United Nations, including the World Trade Organization and the Organization of the Petroleum Exporting Countries (both also examined in Chapter 9), as well as a plethora of regional and subregional organizations.

The European Union—Organizing Regionally

Regional organizations also play an increasingly visible role in international relations. But none has been as visible, as strong, or as copied as the European Union. The idea of a united Europe goes back centuries. Both Immanuel Kant and Jean-Jacques Rousseau presented plans on how to unite Europe.[8] After World War I, idealists dreamed that a united Europe could have forestalled the conflagration.

TABLE 7.6

Representative International and Regional Organizations

UN SPECIALIZED AGENCIES	INDEPENDENT ORGANIZATIONS
WORLD HEALTH ORGANIZATION	Organization of the Petroleum Exporting Countries
FOOD AND AGRICULTURE ORGANIZATION	World Trade Organization
INTERNATIONAL LABOR ORGANIZATION	Organisation of the Islamic Conference
INTERNATIONAL ATOMIC ENERGY AGENCY	North Atlantic Treaty Organization
WORLD BANK GROUP	
INTERNATIONAL MONETARY FUND	
REGIONAL ORGANIZATIONS	**SUBREGIONAL ORGANIZATIONS**
EUROPEAN UNION	Nordic Council
ORGANIZATION FOR SECURITY AND CO-OPERATION IN EUROPE	European Free Trade Association
AFRICAN UNION	Economic Community of West African States
ORGANIZATION OF AMERICAN STATES	Mercosur
ARAB LEAGUE	Gulf Cooperation Council

World War II only intensified these sentiments. Hence, after that war, vigorous debate ensued over the the future organization of Europe. On the one hand were federalists; drawing on the writings of Rousseau, they believed that because sovereign states instigated wars, peace could be attained only if states gave up their sovereignty and invested in a higher federal body. If states joined together with other states, each surrendering some pieces of sovereignty to a higher unit, the root cause of war, military competition among states, could eventually be eliminated. Advocates of federalism proposed the European Defense Community, which would have placed the military under community control, thus touching the core of national sovereignty.

On the other hand were the functionalists. Their principal proponent, Jean Monnet, believed that the weakened forces of nationalism could in the long run be undermined by the logic of economic integration. Beginning with the creation of the European Coal and Steel Community (the predecessor of the European Economic Community [EEC]), he proposed cooperative ventures in nonpolitical issue areas. According to the political theorist David Mitrany, these ventures would spill over eventually from the economic arena to issues of national security. The federalist European Defence Community was defeated by the French Parliament in 1954, and the functionalists' logic prevailed. No one at the time could have envisioned a union that in 2010 would bring together 493 million citizens in 27 countries, allowing each of them to travel freely with a burgundy EU passport, enjoying an economy of over \$14 trillion, and with many of them (13) using a common currency, the euro.

HISTORICAL EVOLUTION   The impetus for the creation of the European Union grew not only from wartime experience, but also from the threat that remained. Urged on by the United States, an economically strong Europe (made possible by the reduction of trade barriers) knew it would be better equipped to counter the threat of the Soviet Union if it integrated. Europe also understood that if the Germans were enmeshed in such agreements, they would pose less of a threat to other states. Of course, U.S.-based multinational corporations would also benefit from an expanded market. Thus, security threats, economic incentives, and a postwar vision all played a role in the drive of political elites for European integration.[9]

The European Coal and Steel Community, placing French and (West) German coal and steel production under a common "High Authority," was the first step toward realizing this idea. Although Germany was treated as an equal, its key economic sector supporting the arms industry was brought into a community with France, Italy, and the Benelux countries. This functionalist experiment was so successful in boosting coal and steel production that the member states agreed to expand cooperation under the European Atomic Energy Community and the European Economic Community. Thus the Treaties of Rome, signed in 1957, committed the six states to create a common market—removing restrictions on internal trade; imposing a common external tariff; reducing barriers to the movement of people, services, and capital; and establishing a common agricultural and transport policy. In 1968, two years ahead of schedule, most of these goals had been achieved.

New policy areas were gradually brought under the umbrella of the community, including health, safety, and consumer standards. As success in these areas waxed and waned, and economic stagnation hindered progress, action was taken. The first initiative was expanding the size of the community in the so-called widening process. The original six members were joined by three others in 1973. Five successive enlargements followed, the most recent in 2007, resulting in today's twenty-seven-state membership. The enlargements have quadrupled membership and increased the influence of the organization, as well as complicating its decision making.

TABLE 7.7

Significant Events in the Formation and Expansion of the European Union

YEAR	EVENT
1952	European Coal and Steel Community created by Belgium, France, Italy, Luxembourg, Netherlands, and West Germany.
1954	French National Assembly rejects proposal to form the European Defence Community.
1957	Treaties of Rome establish the European Economic Community (EEC) and the European Atomic Energy Community, comprising same six members.
1968	Customs union is completed; all internal customs, duties, and quotas are removed and common external tariff is established.
1973	EEC is joined by Denmark, Ireland, and the United Kingdom.
1975	Lomé Convention between the EEC and forty-six developing countries in Africa, the Caribbean, and the Pacific signed.
1979	High-level negotiations on European Monetary System are completed; first direct elections to the European Parliament.
1981	Greece joins the EEC; European political cooperation is extended.
1986	Signing of the Single European Act designed to ensure faster decisions; more attention to environmental and technological issues; list of measures compiled that need to be taken before achieving single market in 1992; Spain and Portugal join the EEC.
1990	West and East Germany reunited after fall of Berlin Wall; larger Germany maintains EEC membership.
1992	Maastricht Treaty completed, committing members to political union, including the establishment of a common foreign and defense policy, a single currency, and a regional central bank; name changed to European Union (EU); controversial referendums held in several countries.
1995	Austria, Finland, and Sweden join EU.
1997	Treaty of Amsterdam extends competence on Justice and Home Affairs, defines European citizenship.
1999	Common monetary policy and single currency (the euro) launched.
2002	Euro in circulation.
2004	Ten new members join; European Constitution negotiated.

TABLE 7.7

(continued)

YEAR	EVENT
2005	French and Dutch publics reject the proposed constitution; ongoing discussions.
2007	Bulgaria and Romania join EU; Lisbon Treaty proposed changes in institutions and decision making
2009	Lisbon Treaty approved

In 1986, the most important step was taken in deepening the integration process—the signing of the Single European Act (SEA), which established the goal of completing a single market by the end of 1992. This meant a complicated process of removing the remaining physical, fiscal, and technical barriers to trade; harmonizing national standards of health; varying levels of taxation; and eliminating the barriers to movement of peoples. New environmental and technological issues were also addressed. Three thousand specific measures were needed to complete the single market.

Even before that process was completed, the Maastricht Treaty was signed in 1992. The European Community became the **European Union (EU)**. Members committed themselves not only to an economic union, but also to a political one, including the establishment of common foreign and defense policies, a single currency, and a regional central bank. Five years later, in 1997, the Amsterdam Treaty was signed, making some changes to the previous treaties, including granting more power to the European Parliament but generally putting more emphasis on the rights of individuals, citizenship, justice, and home affairs.

The increased power of the EU has not been without its opponents. After the Maastricht Treaty, for example, the United Kingdom opted out of the monetary union and some social commitments. The Danish public rejected the treaty the first time, reversing itself a year later. The French electorate approved it by only a slim margin. These events signaled to European leaders that although the European public supports the idea of economic and political cooperation, it also fears a diminution of national sovereignty and is reluctant to surrender democratic rights by placing more power in the hands of bureaucrats and other nonelected elites.

The debate over the proposed European Constitution brought these issues to a head. Pushed forward by political leaders, the European Constitution was signed by the heads of state in 2004. Designed to bring together the many treaties and agreements it specifies the powers of the EU and the role of the EU institutions. However, in 2005, two states dealt a serious blow to the constitution, the Dutch

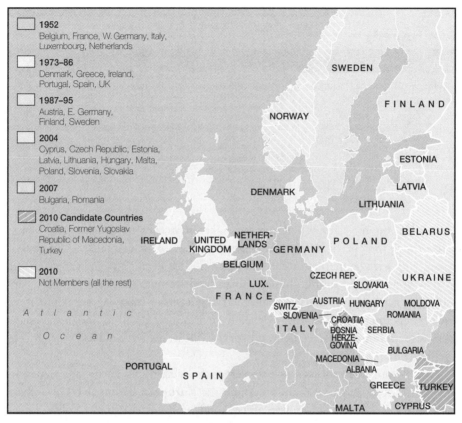

Expansion of European Union, 1952–2010

and French electorate rejecting the document in respective referendums. In 2007, the Treaty of Lisbon was signed, replacing the Constitution. This treaty is another attempt to enhance the efficacy of the EU by creating the offices of president of the European Council and a High Representative for Foreign Affairs for a more united policy, and increasing the use of qualified majority voting. The treaty also is aimed at improving the democratic legitimacy of the EU by increasing the authority of the European Parliament. With Irish and Czech Republic ratification, the treaty became law on December 1, 2009.

STRUCTURE   Table 7.8 provides the basic information about the EU's decision-making bodies, membership, voting, and responsibilities. Just as power has shifted among the UN organs, so, too, has power shifted in the EU. Initially, power resided in the European Commission, which is designed to represent the interests of the community as a whole. Although each state is entitled to one member, commission members are expected to be impartial and are not national representatives. Each

TABLE 7.8

Principal Institutions of the European Union

INSTITUTION	MEMBERSHIP AND VOTING	RESPONSIBILITIES
EUROPEAN COMMISSION	27 members, 4-year terms plus 23,000 support staff (Eurocrats)	Initiates proposals; guards treaties; executes policies
COUNCIL OF MINISTERS	Ministers of member states; unanimity or qualified majority voting depending on issue; one minister per state	Legislates; sets political objectives; coordinates; resolves differences
EUROPEAN PARLIAMENT	736 members, divided among members; elected every 5 years by citizens; organized around political parties	Legislates; approves budget; supervises executive
EUROPEAN COUNCIL	Heads of government; summit meetings twice yearly	Key body for EU initiatives
ECONOMIC AND SOCIAL COMMITTEE	344 members drawn from economic/social interest groups; represents employers, employees, others	Has consultative role; acts as platform for civil society; forwards opinions to other institutions
EUROPEAN COURT OF JUSTICE	Judges and advocates-general; appointed by states for 6-year terms	Adjudicates disputes over EU treaties; ensures uniform interpretation of EU laws; renders advisory opinions to states

is responsible for a particular policy area, known as a directorate-general, which, in turn, is divided into directorates that cover specific parts of that policy area. For much of its history, the EU Commission has played this engine role, with the Council of Ministers ratifying, modifying, or vetoing proposals, even though the Commission formally reports to the Council. Increasingly, the Council, with its weighted voting system, has assumed more power; some policy decisions in foreign and security affairs, immigration, and taxation even require unanimous support.

The increasing power of the European Parliament is also another change. Since the mid-1980s, it has gained a greater legislative and supervisory role. Because members are elected by universal suffrage, this body has an element of democratic accountability not found in the other institutions. The relatively low turnout in the 2009 parliamentary elections indicates that the legitimacy of the institutions remains a problem that the provisions of the Lisbon Treaty are intended to rectify.

So, too, has the power of the European Court of Justice (ECJ) expanded. The court's wide-ranging responsibilities for interpreting and enforcing EU law include ruling on the constitutionality of all EU law; interpreting treaties; providing advisory opinions to national courts; and settling disputes among member states, EU institutions, corporations, and individuals. Member states are obligated to uphold the law. If they fail to comply, the European Commission may undertake infringement proceedings that may include fines or imposition of sanctions. Virtually every member state has been brought before the court for failing to fulfill its obligations. The twenty-seven judges of the ECJ have heard over fifteen thousand cases and issued more than seventy-five hundred opinions covering such diverse topics as disputes over customs duties, tax discrimination, elimination of nontariff barriers, agricultural subsidies, environmental law, consumer safety issues, and mobility of labor. More than its founders ever envisioned, the ECJ plays a major institutional role in European regionalism and the new legal order that is embodied in EU law.

POLICIES AND PROBLEMS   The EU has moved progressively into more policy areas, from trade and agriculture (discussed in Chapter 9) to transport, competition, social policy, monetary policy, the environment, justice, and common foreign and security policy. Among the many controversial issues has been the failed effort to develop a common European foreign and security policy. The split between those states that supported the United States' Iraq policy (Great Britain and Spain) and those that opposed it (Germany and France) is suggestive. The difficulties in security policy have had repercussions in other arenas. The war against terrorism has brought into question key EU policies, including open borders versus the security threats resulting from the absence of border controls, and the commitment to human rights versus the increased call for limitations on immigration and on revising the rights of aliens. Thus, disputes over deepening continue to be vexing. Should current members continue to widen the range of cooperation? Should members try to reduce the tensions that develop when states differ over foreign policy?

Equally problematic are the issues surrounding membership. Should the EU continue to expand its membership by reaching out to the newly democratic states of Eastern Europe and the former Soviet Union, or to those in need, such as Iceland? How rapidly can these new members come to adhere to the eighty thousand pages of EU law and regulations currently in effect? How will the special concessions these countries won affect the functioning of the Union? Although the new members have been given extra time to phase in EU law, they also need to wait before receiving full benefits that range from agricultural subsidies to free movement of labor. Can Turkey, the first candidate state with a majority Muslim population, eventually meet the criteria for membership: stable democratic institutions, a functioning market, and a capacity to meet union obligations? Turkey has already made enormous improvements in its human rights record and minority protection, but its admission is still undecided. Will the EU governing institutions be able to change? So far, the debate over the European Constitution suggests that the answers will not be easy ones.

OTHER REGIONAL ORGANIZATIONS: THE OAS AND THE AU   For many years the critical question was whether other regions would follow the European Union model. Clearly the circumstances surrounding the development of the European Union were unlikely to be duplicated precisely. Although most Asian leaders strongly thought the European model inappropriate for that region, some subregional groups, such as the Economic Community of West African States and the Caribbean Community (CARICOM), saw the EU as a model. (We will examine the North American Free Trade Agreement in Chapter 9.)

Continent-wide regional organizations, such as the Organization of American States (OAS) and the African Union (AU), have followed a different path. At its establishment in 1948, the OAS adopted wide-ranging goals: political (now promotion of democracy), economic (enhancing development, preferential treatment in trade and finance), social (promotion of human rights), and military (collective defense against aggression from outside the region and peaceful settlement of disputes within). No other regional organization includes such a North/South split between a hegemonic member such as the United States (and Canada) on one hand and a "southern constituency" on the other. With that division, the OAS has adopted many of the foreign policy concerns of the hegemon: the defeat of communist/leftist factions during the Cold War and an emphasis on democracy promotion. In 1985, the OAS resolved to take action should an irregular interruption of democracy occur, and a member should be suspended if its government is overthrown by force. The OAS has acted against coups or countercoups nine times, including, for example, in Haiti (1991–94), Peru (1992), Paraguay (1996, 2000), and Venezuela (1992, 2002). It instituted sanctions against Haiti, and in 2009 suspended Honduras from membership after that country's coup. The overall record is mixed, however, constrained by a dearth of economic resources and political will. And although the EU has pursued its goal of creating an economic union, as covered in Chapter 9, the OAS has played a limited role in economic development of the region.

The African Union replaced the Organization of African Unity in 2002. The latter had been deliberately designed as a weak intergovernmental body at its founding in 1964. The newly independent countries at the time sought to protect their new sovereignty. They were in no mood to permit interference in domestic affairs, and they preferred sovereign equality of all states. Although the illegality of apartheid in South Africa remained a rallying cry of the OAU, members were largely silent on the major economic and development issues of the day. The newly reconstituted AU is an attempt to give African states an increased ability to respond to the issues of economic globalization and democratization affecting the continent. Thus, the AU is committed to good governance and democratic principles, suspending illegitimate governments and pledging to intervene in the affairs of members should genocide and crimes against humanity occur. Such promises are predicated on the belief that better governance is key to economic development and necessary for external development funds. Yet although the AU did suspend Mauritania from membership (2008), impose sanctions on Togo (2005), and reverse a coup in the Comoros Islands (2008), additional measures were not taken, nor has the AU acted in the Zimbabwe crisis, despite its own findings of major human rights abuses in 2007 and evidence of election fraud in 2008.

Following through on obligations and enforcement remains a problem not only for the OAS and the AU, but for most regional organizations, because funding is limited and commitment waxes and wanes. But each of the over 240 international government organizations seldom acts alone. Often they carry out their activities with the cooperation of other international or regional organizations and with nonstate actors, including nongovernmental organizations.

Nongovernmental Organizations

The 192 states are the major constituents in the international system and members of international governmental organizations such as those discussed above. But thousands of other nonstate actors are also part of the international system, though they are not sovereign and do not have the same kinds of power resources as states. They include nongovernmental organizations (NGOs), transnational networks, foundations, and multinational corporations. In this chapter, the emphasis is on NGOs. We will examine multinational corporations in Chapter 9.

NGOs are generally private, voluntary organizations whose members are individuals or associations that come together to achieve a common purpose, often oriented to a public good. They are incredibly diverse entities, ranging from entirely local and/or grassroots organizations to those organized nationally and transnationally. Some are entirely private—that is, their funding comes only from private sources. Others rely partially on government funds or aid in kind. Some are open to mass membership; others are closed-member groups or federations. These differences have led to an alphabet soup of acronyms specifying types of NGOs. These include GONGOs (government-organized NGOs), BINGOs (business and industry NGOs), DONGOs (donor-organized NGOs), and ONGOs (operational NGOs), to name a few.

The number of NGOs has grown dramatically, although estimates vary enormously. The *Yearbook of International Organizations* identifies about seventy-five hundred nongovernmental organizations that have an international dimension in terms of either their membership or their commitment to conducting activities in several states. Exclusively national NGOs may number upwards of 26,000. Grassroots local NGOs may number in the millions. Their numbers are rising exponentially. That growth can be explained by the global spread of democracy, which provides an opening for NGO inputs; by the explosion of UN-sponsored global conferences in the 1990s, where NGOs took on new tasks; and by the electronic communication revolution, which enable NGOs to communicate and network both with each other and with their constituencies, providing a more forceful voice in the international policy arena.

The Growth of NGO Power and Influence

Although NGOs are not new actors in international politics, they are growing in importance.[10] The antislavery campaign was one of the earliest NGO-initiated efforts at transnational organization to ban a morally unacceptable practice. Its genesis lay in societies established in the 1780s dedicated to the abolition of slavery in the United States, Britain, and France. The group was strong enough to force the British Parliament in 1807 to forbid the slave trade to British citizens. In 1815, at the Congress of Vienna and in the Treaty of Ghent, the international community again considered the abolition of the slave trade and reaffirmed that these practices were inhumane and unjust. Although NGOs took the first steps toward enforcing the principles, they were not strong enough to accomplish it. Successful enforcement did not come until almost a century later.

NGOs organizing on behalf of peace and noncoercive methods of dispute settlement also appeared during the 1800s, as did the International Committee of the Red Cross, which advocated for humanitarian treatment for wounded soldiers, and international labor unions fighting for better working conditions. During the first half of the twentieth century, these same groups were instrumental in lobbying for a "league of nations" and the International Labor Organization, and subsequently in supporting the establishment of the United Nations and the related agencies protecting different groups of people, including refugees (UN High Commissioner for Refugees) and women and children (UNICEF), among others.

During the 1970s, as the number of NGOs grew, networks and coalitions were formed among various groups, and by the 1990s these NGOs were able to mobilize the mass public effectively and influence international relations. A number of factors explain the remarkable resurgence of NGO activity and their increased power as actors in international politics. First, the issues seized on by NGOs have been increasingly viewed as interdependent, or transnational ones that states cannot solve alone and whose solutions require transnational and intergovernmental cooperation. Airline hijackings during the 1970s; acid rain pollution and ocean dumping during the 1970s and 1980s; and global warming, land mines, and the AIDS epidemic during the 1990s are examples of issues that require international action and that are "ripe" for NGO activity. Some have been increasingly viewed as human security issues, an argument many NGOs have promoted. Second, global conferences became a key venue for international activity beginning in the 1970s, each designed to address one of the transnational issues—the environment (1972, 1992), population (1974, 1984), women (1975, 1985, 1995), and food (1974, 1996, 2002). A pattern emerged when NGOs began to organize separate but parallel conferences on the same issues. This creates opportunities for NGO representatives not only to network with each other and form coalitions on specific issues but also to lobby governments and international bureaucrats. In some cases, those linkages between the governmental and nongovernmental conferees enhance the power of the latter. Third, the end of the Cold War and the expansion of democracy in the former communist world and developing countries have provided an unprecedented political opening for NGOs into parts of the world previously untouched by NGO activity. Finally, the communications revolution also partly explains the rise of NGOs. First the fax, then the Web and e-mail, have enabled NGOs to communicate with core constituencies, build coalitions with other like-minded groups, and generate mass support. They can disseminate information rapidly, recruit new members, launch publicity campaigns, and encourage individuals to participate in ways unavailable two decades before. NGOs have benefited from these changes and have been able to capitalize on them to increase their own power.

Functions and Roles of NGOs

NGOs perform a variety of functions and roles in international relations. They advocate specific policies and offer alternative channels of political participation, as Amnesty International has done through its letter-writing campaigns on behalf of victims of human rights violations. They mobilize mass publics, as Greenpeace did in saving the whales (through international laws limiting whaling) and in forcing the labeling of "green" (non–environmentally damaging) products in Europe and Canada. They distribute critical assistance in disaster relief and to refugees, as Médecins Sans Frontières (Doctors without Borders), World Catholic Relief, and Oxfam have done in Somalia, Yugoslavia, Rwanda, Sudan, and Haiti. They are the principal monitors of human rights norms and environmental regulations and provide warnings of violations, as Human Rights Watch has done in China, Latin America, and elsewhere.

NGOs are also the primary actors at the grassroots level in mobilizing individuals to act. For example, during the 1990 meeting to revise the 1987 Montreal Protocol on Substances That Deplete the Ozone Layer, NGOs criticized the UN

NGOs are influential in many areas of world politics. Greenpeace successfully mobilized support for international laws limiting whaling, and continues to press for a stricter ban on whaling. Here, Greenpeace activists confront a Japanese whaling ship.

Environment Program secretary-general, Mostafa Tolba, for not advocating more stringent regulations on ozone-destroying chemicals. Friends of the Earth International, Greenpeace International, and the Natural Resources Defense Council held press conferences and circulated brochures to the public, media, and officials complaining of the weak regulations. The precise strategy of each group varied. Friends of the Earth approached the matter analytically, whereas Greenpeace staged a drama to show the effects of environmental degradation. But the intent of each was the same—to focus citizen action on strengthening the Montreal Protocol. By publicizing inadequacies, NGOs force discussion both within states and among states in international forums.

Nowhere has the impact of NGOs been felt more strongly than at the 1992 UN Conference on the Environment and Development (UNCED) in Rio de Janeiro. NGOs played key roles in both the preparatory conferences and the Rio conference itself, adding representation and openness (or "transparency") to the process. They made statements from the floor; they drafted informational materials; they scrutinized working drafts of UN documents; they spoke up to support or oppose specific phrasing. The UNCED provided extensive opportunities for NGO networking. Among the more than four hundred accredited environmental organizations were not only traditional, large, well-financed NGOs, such as the

World Wildlife Fund, but also those working on specific issues and those with grassroots origins in developing countries, many of which were poorly financed and had had few previous transnational linkages.

The persistence of the NGOs paid off. Agenda 21, the official document produced by the conference, recognized the unique capabilities of NGOs and recommended their participation at all levels from policy formulation and decision making to implementation. What began as a parallel informal process of participation within the UN system evolved into a more formal role, which was replicated at the 1994 International Conference on Population and Development in Cairo and at the 1995 Fourth World Conference on Women in Beijing.

NGOs also play unique roles at the national level. In a few unusual cases, NGOs take the place of states, either performing services that an inept or corrupt government is not or stepping in for a failed state. Bangladesh hosts the largest NGO sector in the world, a response in part to that government's failure and the failure of the private for-profit sector to provide for the poor. Thus, NGOs have assumed responsibility in education, health, agriculture, and microcredit, originally all government functions. Other NGOs are working to change various countries' public institutions, the Muslim Brotherhood in Egypt being a salient example. This nonviolent group, dating back to 1928, has had a long, confrontational relationship with the Egyptian government and seeks first social justice and then the implementation of *sharia* (Islamic law).

Yet NGOs seldom work alone. The communications revolution has linked NGOs with each other, formally and informally. The Muslim Brotherhood, for example, maintains close connections with groups considered more militant, such as Hamas, and is active in several Middle Eastern countries and in Europe. Increasingly, NGOs are developing regional and global networks through linkages with other NGOs. These networks and coalitions create multilevel linkages among different organizations, each of which retain its separate organizational character and membership, but through the linkages enhance each other's power. These networks have learned from each other, just as constructivists would have predicted. Environmentalists and women's groups have studied human rights campaigns for guidance in building international norms. Environmentalists seeking protection of spaces for indigenous peoples also increasingly use the language of human rights.

We usually associate NGOs with humanitarian and environmental groups working for a greater social, economic, or political good, but NGOs may also be formed for malevolent purposes, the Mafia, international drug cartels, and even Al Qaeda being prominent examples. The Mafia, traditionally based in Italy but with networks in Russia, Eastern Europe, and the Americas, is engaged in numerous illegal business practices, including money laundering, tax evasion, and fraud. International drug cartels, many with origins in Colombia, function with suppliers in such far-reaching states as Peru, Venezuela, Afghanistan, and Myanmar, while maintaining links with middlemen in Nigeria, Mexico, and the Caribbean, in order to deliver illegal drugs to North America and Europe. Their illegal activity is calculated to be $400 billion annually, or 8 percent of world trade. What these NGOs share is a loose series of networks across national boundaries, moving illicit goods and services in international trade. Their leadership is dispersed and their targets ever changing, making their activities particularly difficult to contain.

Al Qaeda, too, is such an NGO—decentralized, dispersed, with individuals deeply committed to a cause, even at the price of death, and able and willing to take initiatives independent of a central authority. The organization has changed and expanded its goals over time, which has enabled it to recruit members willing to die for diverse causes. Osama bin Laden has forged broad links and alliances with various groups. Like all NGOs, Al Qaeda has benefited from new communications technologies, using the World Wide Web to collect information and train individuals, and e-mail to transfer funds and communicate messages, all virtually untrackable.[11] Opponents of Al Qaeda and these other NGOs are waging a different battle, a war on organized crime, a war on drugs, and a war against terror.

The Power of NGOs

What gives NGOs the ability to play such diverse roles in the international system? What are their sources of power? NGOs rely on soft power, meaning credible information, expertise, and the moral authority that attracts the attention and admiration of governments and the public. This means that NGOs have resources such as flexibility to move staff rapidly depending on need, independent donor bases, and links with grassroots groups that enable them to operate in different areas of the world. This very flexibility enables them to create networks to increase their power potential, banding together with other like-minded NGOs and forming coalitions to promote their respective agendas. The new communication technologies have facilitated this networking and coalition-building source of NGO power.

NGOs have distinct advantages over individuals, states, and intergovernmental organizations. They are usually politically independent from any sovereign state, so that they can make and execute international policy more rapidly and directly, and with less risk to national sensitivities, than IGOs can. They can participate at all levels, from policy formation and decision making to implementation, if they choose. Yet they can also influence state behavior by initiating formal, legally binding action; pressuring authorities to impose sanctions; carrying out independent investigations; and linking issues together in ways that force some measure of compliance. Thus, NGOs are versatile and increasingly powerful actors, especially if they are able to network with other NGOs.

NGOs: Views from the Former Soviet States

The formation and rise of NGOs in the newly independent states of the former Soviet Union can be traced back to the early 1990s, following the disintegration of the USSR. Newly formed, indigenous NGOs had only the experience of a few Soviet associations to draw on, and those associations had always been closely affiliated with the state. The new NGOs drew on financial support from sympathetic states abroad (the United States and members of the European Union) and from international NGOs eager to engage in activities in this newly democratizing region. Neither type of NGOs could depend on a strong domestic constituency for political or material support.

Following the disintegration of the Soviet Union, the Baltic states (Lithuania, Latvia, and Estonia) were a success story for civil society development in general and for NGOs specifically, at least from a Western perspective. NGOs in these countries enjoy widespread legitimacy and a strong financial base, due to expanded public and private resources. Those donating to NGOs are awarded tax advantages, resulting in not only more material resources but also broader public commitment to the NGOs' activities and national ownership of their goals and achievements. NGOs benefit from being operated mostly by professionals. In short, NGO strength and reach are rapidly approaching those of NGOs based in well-established Western democracies.

In the rest of the newly independent former Soviet states, however, the process of civil society formation and NGO development has been difficult. At first the international NGOs flocked to the region, eager to advance democracy, human rights, and social programs. But when these countries experienced a difficult transition from socialism to liberal economic systems and an uncertain legal environment, the indigenous NGOs were dependent on contributions from Western governments, overseas foundations, and international NGOs themselves. Leadership, likewise, was provided by these external donors. In some countries certain NGOs received support from their national governments, which immediately undermined their independence and neutrality.

Generally cautious about affiliating with these new actors, the population chose not to exercise leadership and did not play a role in supporting social activities. Nationals became the beneficiaries of NGO services without participating in shaping the policies.

In the first few years of the new millennium, a number of democratic revolutions swept through several formerly socialist states within a relatively short period of time: the Rose Revolution in Georgia in 2003, the Orange Revolution in Ukraine in 2004-5, and the Tulip Revolution in Kyrgyzstan in 2005. All of these "color" revolutions followed a similar pattern: the newly installed governments maintained a clear pro-American profile and enjoyed broad support from Washington (most notably Georgia and Ukraine); they indulged in sharply anti-Russian rhetoric. The photo on the next page shows Georgian opposition supporters celebrating the resignation of Eduard Shevardnadze, the Georgian president and former Soviet official. Very quickly, the suspicion of a foreign hand behind these revolutions, which arose through civil society associations, turned into a firm belief held by most government officials.

Several U.S.-based groups and organizations—such as the National Democratic Institute, the International Republican Institute, Freedom House, and the Open Society Institute—became closely identified with these revolutions. By providing financial support, training, and consultative

assistance to domestic opposition groups, they became known as "color revolutions exporters." In Kyrgyzstan, for example, it was believed that the photos of the former president Askar Akayev's mansion in a Kyrgyz newspaper were printed on a press financed by an American NGO or even the American government itself.

These events have led many of these governments to review their internal policies toward NGOs and impose strict governmental control over their operations. That decision affected all NGOs regardless of their sphere of activities and their level of political involvement. For example, Uzbekistan and Tajikistan mandate state registration and reregistration of all public associations in their territory. In the process, many "undesirable" NGOs are denied registration under various pretexts. The Russian Federal Security Service made official statements in the Russian Duma about NGOs serving as a cover for collecting sensitive information for foreign governments and exporting color revolutions. Thus, as the result of a 2006 law, Russia increasingly denies entry to individuals working for NGOs, closes NGO offices, conducts long audits, and challenges the organizations' tax-exempt status. Belarus, too, imposes strict procedures: registration of all technical assistance or humanitarian projects involving foreign funds and submission of detailed reports on their implementation to relevant ministries. As a result, the government exercises control over specific projects. Severe monetary penalties and revoked registration follow in cases of alleged improper use of funds

or for projects not approved by the government. Outright closure of NGO offices, confiscation of assets, frequent financial audits, increased control of NGO workers' movements, and denial of visas for NGO workers have become widespread examples of bureaucratic "red tape" in Russia, Turkmenistan, Belarus, and Uzbekistan. The governments want full control over the NGOs' sources of funding, finances, and activities.

In the Central Asian countries as well as Russia and Belarus, NGOs are now viewed by the governments with a good deal of suspicion and hostility. This is especially true of American-financed NGOs promoting democracy or human rights. They are seen as advocating regime change or reflecting U.S. government policy, rather than espousing an independent position. These states see such activities as encroachment on their sovereignty and contrary to the national interest of the sovereign state. With full implementation of these restrictions, each state has enhanced its capacity to control what occurs within its borders. These states ask, What right do the United States and its state-supported NGOs have to promote political and civil unrest within our borders? The governments of the region will not accept interference from the agents of what they regard as an imperialistic state that tortures people abroad and occupies foreign lands.

For Critical Analysis

Answer these questions on **wwnorton.com/studyspace**

1. *NGOs are not independent actors; they exist by consent of host states. Explain.*

2. *How can NGOs use soft power? What other kinds of power do they have at their disposal?*

3. *How might realists and radicals justify a state's opposition to foreign-financed NGOs?*

4. *To constructivists, NGOs may be the conduit for transmitting or socializing norms. How might they do so in the newly independent states of the former Soviet Union?*

The International Campaign to Ban Landmines (ICBL) is an outstanding example of the power of the network. Beginning in 1992, nine NGOs were eventually joined by more than a thousand other NGOs and local groups (such as the Landmine Survivors Network, Medico International, Vietnam Veterans of America Foundation, and Human Rights Watch) in over sixty countries. They used the electronic media to craft the message that landmines are a human rights issue and have devastating effects on innocent civilians. Not only was the issue framed to resonate with a large constituency, the leaders formed a network. What became known as the Ottawa Process was bolstered by the death in 1997 of Diana, Princess of Wales, one of its vocal supporters; coordinated by Jody Williams, a founder of the ICBL and winner of the 1997 Nobel Peace Prize for her efforts; and joined by Canada, whose foreign minister pushed the issue, hosted the conference, and provided financial support. The Convention to Ban Landmines was ratified in 1999.

The Limits of NGOs

NGOs often lack material forms of power. Except for some of the malevolent groups, they do not have military or police forces as governments do, and thus they cannot command obedience through physical means.

Most NGOs have very limited economic resources, because they do not collect taxes as states do. Thus the competition for funding is fierce; NGOs sharing the same concerns—for example, human rights organizations—often compete for the same donors. They have a continuous need to raise money, leading some NGOs to find new causes to widen their donor base. To expand their resources, NGOs increasingly rely on governments, an alternative that comes with its own set of limitations. If NGOs choose to accept state assistance, then their neutrality and legitimacy are potentially compromised. They may be forced continually to report "success" in order to renew their financing, even though success may be difficult to prove or even be an inaccurate description of reality. In short, NGOs are locked in a competitive scramble for resources.[12]

Do most NGOs succeed in accomplishing their goals? This is difficult to evaluate, because the NGO community is itself diverse; they have no single agenda, and NGOs often work at cross-purposes, just as states do. Groups can be found on almost any side of every issue, resulting in countervailing pressures. In a world that is increasingly viewed as democratic, are NGOs appropriate? To whom are NGOs accountable if their leaders are not elected? How do they maintain transparency when they have no publicly accountable mechanism? Do NGOs reflect only liberal values? Incomplete or unsatisfactory answers to these questions have led scholars to suggest that NGOs may be more like other actors and less altruistic than supposed—self-interested, self-aggrandizing, concerned with their own narrow agendas, hierarchical rather democratic, more worried about financial gains than achieving progressive social purposes. This suggestion has led some critics to refer to NGOs as "wild cards," and "benign parasites."[13] Some disturbing case studies have found that NGOs' actions have led to unintended and detrimental consequences. In refugee camps in Rwanda run by NGOs such as Doctors without Borders and the International Rescue Committee, the leaders of the genocide were actually being protected. When NGOs are active in war zones, are they becoming more like "force multipliers"?[14] The roles NGOs play and the legitimacy they may or may not have depend in part on how they answer critical questions of accountability and transparency. Whether accountable and transparent or not, NGOs increasingly work with states, IGOs, and regional organizations.

International Law

Since the beginning of the new millennium, international law has captured the headlines more than perhaps at any other time. In the aftermath of 9/11, the U.S. military actions in Afghanistan and Iraq, and mounting humanitarian crises, international treaties have become well-known documents: the Geneva Conventions (technically the Geneva Convention for Victims of War, 1949), the Convention Against Torture (the UN Convention Against Torture and Other Cruel, Inhuman or Degrading Treatment or Punishment, 1984, 1987), and the Genocide Convention (Convention on the Prevention and Punishment of Genocide, 1948). Debate has raged over the definitions of terms such as torture, genocide, terrorism, enemy combatants, enemy detainees, and rendition. NGOs such as the International Committee of the Red Cross and Human Rights Watch, once known to only a few, have attained international recognition. Thus, understanding the characteristics of international law and its limitations is all the more urgent.

International Law and Its Functions

International law consists of a body of both rules and norms regulating interactions among states, between states and IGOs, and in more limited cases among IGOs, states, and individuals. Laws serve several purposes: setting a body of expectations, providing order, protecting the status quo, and legitimating the use of force by a government to maintain order. Law provides a mechanism for settling disputes and protecting states from each other. It serves ethical and moral functions, aiming in most cases to be fair and equitable and delineating what is socially and culturally desirable. These norms demand obedience and compel behavior.

At the state level, law is hierarchical. Established structures exist for both making law (legislatures and executives) and enforcing law (executives and judiciaries). Individuals and groups within the state are bound by law. Because of a general consensus within the state on the particulars of law, compliance with the law is widespread. It is in the interest of everyone to maintain order and predictability. But if the law is violated, the state authorities can compel violators to judgment and use the instruments of state authority to punish wrongdoers.

In the international system, authoritative structures are absent. There is no international executive, no international legislature, and no judiciary with compulsory jurisdiction. So can there be international law, given the absence of a sovereign body with enforcement power and the inability to compel compliance with effective physical coercion? Legal scholar Christopher C. Joyner argues "yes": binding legal rules are created, states recognize their obligations, and resorting to force is not necessary for the international legal system to operate. After all, "international legal rules obtain their normative force not because any superior power or world government prescribes them but because they have been generally accepted by states as rules of conduct, with the expectation that states will follow suit."[15]

Liberals acknowledge that law in the international system is different from that in domestic systems. To them, international law not only exists, but it also has an effect in daily life. As the political scientist Louis Henkin explains,

> If one doubts the significance of this law, one need only imagine a world in which it were absent. . . . There would be no security of nations or stability of governments; territory and airspace would not be respected; vessels could navigate only at their constant peril; property—within or without any given territory—would be subject to arbitrary seizure; persons would have no protection of law or diplomacy; agreements would not be made or observed; diplomatic relations would end; international trade would cease; international organizations and arrangements would disappear.[16]

We turn now to an assessment of the ways in which international law is similar to and different from national law.

The Sources of International Law

International law, like domestic law, comes from a variety of sources (see Figure 7.1). Virtually all law emerges from custom. Either a hegemon or a group of states solves a problem in a particular way; these habits become ingrained as more states follow the same custom, and eventually the custom is codified into law. For example, Great Britain and later the United States were primarily responsible for developing

FIGURE 7.1 | Sources of International Law

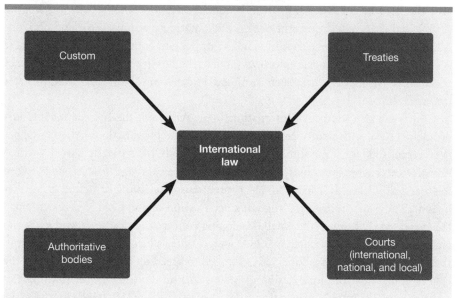

the law of the sea. As great seafaring powers, each state adopted practices—rights of passage through straits, methods of signaling other ships, conduct during war, and the like—that became the customary law of the sea and were eventually codified into treaties. The laws protecting diplomats and embassies likewise emerged from long-standing customs.

But customary law is limited. For one thing, it develops slowly; British naval custom evolved into the law of the sea over several hundred years. Sometimes customs become outmoded. For example, the 3-mile territorial extension from shore was established because that was the distance a cannonball could fly. Eventually law caught up with changes in technology, and states were granted a 12-mile extension of territory into the ocean. Furthermore, not all states participate in the making of customary law, let alone give assent to the customs that have become law through European-centered practices. And the fact that customary law is initially uncodified leads to ambiguity in interpretation.

International law also arose from treaties, the dominant source of law today. Treaties, explicitly written agreements among states, number more than twenty-five thousand since 1648 and cover all issues. When deciding cases, most judicial bodies look to treaty law first. Treaties are legally binding: only major changes in circumstances give states the right not to follow treaties they have ratified.

Authoritative bodies have also formulated and codified international law. Among these bodies is the UN International Law Commission, composed of prominent international jurists. That commission has codified much customary law: the Law of the Sea (1958), the Vienna Convention of the Law of Treaties (1969), and the Vienna Conventions on Diplomatic Relations (1961) and on Consular Relations (1963). The commission also drafts new conventions for which there is no customary law. For example, laws on product liability and on the succession of states and governments have been formulated in this way, then submitted to states for ratification.

Courts are also sources of international law. Although the International Court of Justice (ICJ), with its fifteen judges located in The Hague, the Netherlands, has been responsible for some significant decisions, the ICJ is basically a weak institution, for several reasons. First, the court actually hears very few cases; between 1946 and 2008, the ICJ has had 114 contentious cases brought before it and has issued 25 advisory opinions, although since the end of the Cold War its caseload has increased. Ever since the small developing country of Nicaragua won a judicial victory over the United States in 1984, such countries have shown greater trust in the court. Although procedures have changed to speed up the lengthy process, the court's noncompulsory jurisdiction provision still limits its caseload. Both parties must agree to the court's jurisdiction before a case is taken. This stands in stark contrast to domestic courts, which enjoy compulsory jurisdiction. Accused of a crime, you are compelled to judgment. No state is compelled to submit to the ICJ. Second, when cases are heard, they rarely deal with the major controversies of the day, such as the war in Vietnam, the invasion of Afghanistan, or the unraveling of the Soviet Union or of Yugoslavia, although Kosovo's status has been referred to the ICJ after its 2008 declaration of independence. Those controversies are generally political and outside of the court's reach, although interstate boundary disputes are major issues on the court's agenda. Third, only states may initiate proceedings; individuals and nongovernmental actors such as multinational corporations cannot. Hence, with such a limited caseload concerning few fundamental issues, the court could never be a major source of law. In contrast, the European Court of Justice of the European Union is a significant source of European law. It has a heavy caseload, covering virtually every topic of European integration.

National and even local courts are also sources of international law. Such courts have broad jurisdiction; they may hear cases occurring on their territory in which international law is invoked or cases involving their own citizens who live elsewhere, and they may hear any case to which the principle of universal jurisdiction applies. Under **universal jurisdiction,** states may claim jurisdiction if the conduct of a defendant is sufficiently heinous to violate the laws of all states. Several states claimed such jurisdiction as a result of the genocide in World War II and more recently for war crimes in Bosnia, Kosovo, and Rwanda. In the European Union, national and local courts are a vital source of law. A citizen of an EU country can ask a national court to invalidate any provision of domestic law found to be in conflict with provisions of the EU treaty. A citizen can also seek invalidation of a national law found to be in conflict with self-executing provisions of community directives issued by the EU's Council of Ministers. Thus, in the European system, national courts are both essential sources of European community law and enforcers of that law.

Enforcement of International Law

A key trend now clear in the new millennium has been the expansion of the international judiciary, motivated by the idea of individual responsibility for war crimes and crimes against humanity. This idea is not new. After World War II, the Nuremberg and Tokyo trials punished individuals for war crimes, but because these trials were the victors' punishment of the vanquished, they were not seen as precedents. Following the atrocities in Yugoslavia, Rwanda, and later East Timor, the United Nations established two ad hoc criminal tribunals, the International Criminal Tribunal for the Former Yugoslavia, in 1993, and the International Criminal Tribunal for Rwanda, in 1994. These tribunals, approved by the UN Security Council, have developed procedures to deal with the myriad issues involved in these cases, including jurisdiction, evidence, sentencing, and imprisonment. Among the accused on trial was the former Serbian president Slobodan Milošević until his death in 2006. Among those sentenced are a number of Rwandan officials, including the former prime minister, Jean Kambanda. Because of the need to establish procedures and the difficulty of finding those accused, the trials have been subject to criticism.

In light of the difficulties with the ad hoc tribunals, in 1998 and under UN auspices, states concluded the statute for the International Criminal Court (ICC), an innovative court having both compulsory jurisdiction and jurisdiction over individuals. Four types of crimes are covered: genocide (attacking a group of people and killing them because of race, ethnicity, or religion); crimes against humanity (murder, enslavement, forcible transfer of population, torture), war crimes, and crimes of aggression (undefined). No individuals (save those under eighteen years of age) are immune from jurisdiction, including heads of states and military leaders. The ICC functions as a court of last resort, hearing cases only when national courts are unwilling or unable to deal with prosecuting grave atrocities.

In 2003, the eighteen justices of the ICC were installed, and work began. Pending cases all concern crimes committed in African countries. With the exception of Darfur, most of the cases (for example, the Central African Republic, Democratic Republic of Congo, and Uganda) have attracted little international attention. Yet the ICC is controversial. Widely hailed by many, including a broad-based coalition of over one thousand NGOs, the court is seen as essential for establishing international law and enforcing individual accountability for actions

Radovan Karadžić (right) was indicted in 2008 for war crimes by the UN's International Criminal Tribunal for the former Yugoslavia (ICTY) and put on trial beginning in 2010. Karadžić is being tried for the killing of almost 8,000 Bosnian Muslim men and boys in Srebrenica in 1995. Since it was established in 1993, the ICTY court has completed proceedings for over 100 persons indicted.

taken during conflict. However, some states, including the United States, China, India, and Turkey, are critical. Specifically, the United States objects to provisions of the statute that might make U.S. military personnel or the U.S. president subject to ICC jurisdiction, believing that as a hegemon the United States has "exceptional" international responsibilities that should make its military and leaders immune from the ICC's jurisdiction. The United States objects more generally on the grounds that the ICC infringes on U.S. sovereignty. The controversy continues, while the ICC proceeds despite the United States' refusal to sign the treaty.[17]

With weak authoritative structures at the international level, such as the International Court of Justice and the International Criminal Court, why do most states obey international law most of the time? The liberal response is that states obey international law because it is right to do so. States want to do what is right and moral, and international law reflects what is right. To liberals, individual states benefit from doing what is right and moral, and all states benefit from living in an ordered world where there are general expectations about other states' behavior. States want to be looked on positively, according to liberal thinking. They want to be respected by world public opinion, and they fear being labeled as pariahs and losing face and prestige in the international system.

Should states choose not to obey international law, other members of the international system do have recourse. A number of the possibilities are self-help mechanisms that realists rely on:

- Issue diplomatic protests, particularly if the offense is a relatively minor one.
- Initiate reprisals, actions that are relatively short in duration and intended to right a previous wrong.
- Threaten to enforce economic boycotts or impose embargoes on both economic and military goods if trading partners are involved.
- Use military force, the ultimate self-help weapon.

But liberals contend, rightly in many cases, that self-help mechanisms of enforcement by one state alone are apt to be ineffective. A diplomatic protest from an enemy or a weak state is likely to be ignored, although a protest from a major ally or a hegemon may carry weight. Economic boycotts and sanctions by one state will be ineffective as long as the transgressor state has multiple trading partners. And war is both too costly and unlikely to lead to the desired outcome. In most cases, then, for the enforcement mechanism to be effective, several states have to participate. For enforcement to be most effective, all states have to join together in collective action against the violator of international norms and law. In the view of liberals, states find protection and solace in collective action and in collective security.

Realist Views of International Organization and Law

Realists are skeptical about international law, intergovernmental organizations, and nongovernmental organizations, though they do not completely discount their place. Recall that realists see anarchy in the international system, wherein each state is forced to act in its own self-interest and obliged to rely on self-help mechanisms. International law purportedly creates some order, as many realists acknowledge. But why do states choose to comply with these norms? The realist answer to this question is different from the response of the liberals. Realists contend that compliance occurs not because the norms are good and just in themselves but because it is in a state's self-interest to comply. States benefit from living in an ordered world, where there are some expectations about other states' behavior. A constant fear of infringement on territory and insecurity for their population is costly for states, in terms of both the economic cost of having to prepare for every possible contingency and the psychological cost of anxiety and fear. It is in the self-interest of most states to have their territory and airspace respected, to have their vessels free to navigate international waters, and to enjoy the secure procedures of diplomatic relations and international trade. Yet realists also know that states can opt out of following international law, and if the more powerful do so, other states can do little about it.

Realists are also skeptical about international organizations, both IGOs and NGOs, as independent actors. IGOs are controlled by states, and states often prefer weak organizations. For example, realists point to the failure of the council of the League of Nations to act when Japan invaded Manchuria in 1931 and its slow response to the Italian invasion of Ethiopia in 1935. These failures confirmed the fundamental weaknesses of the League and of its collective approach to punishing aggressors. Without the great powers to support the League's principles, especially its commitment to prevent war, the institution's power and legitimacy deteriorated. Realists likewise do not put much faith in the United Nations. They can legitimately point to the Cold War era, when the Security Council proved impotent in addressing the conflict between the United States and the Soviet Union. And the failure in 2003 of the United Nations to enforce Security Council resolutions against Iraq is another reminder of the organization's weakness and supposed irrelevance.

In the state-centric world of the realists, NGOs are generally not on the radar screen at all. After all, most NGOs exist at the pleasure of states; it is states that grant them legal authority, and it is states that can take away that authority. To realists, NGOs are not an independent actor.

Realists recognize that international law and international organizations have the potential to provide an alternative to self-help mechanisms. It may be in states' self-interest to utilize these institutions. Yet they do not. States are uncertain whether such institutions will function as intended. They have mistrust and skepticism about whether long-term gains can be achieved. Realists doubt that collective action is possible and believe states will refuse to rely on the collectivity for the protection of their individual national interests.

The Radical View of International Organization and Law

Radicals in the Marxist tradition are also very skeptical about international law, IGOs, and many NGOs, albeit for very different reasons from those of the realists. Radicals see contemporary international law and organization as the product of a specific time and historical process, emerging out of eighteenth-century economic liberalism and nineteenth-century political liberalism. Thus, international law primarily comes out of Western capitalist states and is designed to serve the interests of that constituency. International law is biased against the interests of socialist states, the weak, and the unrepresented.

Similarly, IGOs, most notably the League of Nations, the United Nations, and the United Nations' specialized agencies, were designed to support the interests of the powerful. According to radicals, those institutions have succeeded in sustaining the powerful elite against the powerless mass of weaker states. For example, international legal principles, such as the sanctity of national geographic boundaries, were developed during the colonial period to reinforce the claims of the powerful. Attempts to alter such boundaries are, according to international law, wrong, even though the boundaries themselves may be unfair or unjust. Radicals are quick to point out these injustices and support policies that overturn the traditional order. Thus, from their viewpoint, the actions by the United Nations following the Iraqi invasion of Kuwait in 1990, including a series of resolutions condemning Iraq and imposing sanctions on that country, were designed to support the

THEORY IN BRIEF

Contending Perspectives on International Organization and Law

	LIBERALISM/ NEOLIBERAL INSTITUTIONALISM	REALISM / NEOREALISM	RADICALISM/ DEPENDENCY THEORY	CONSTRUCTIVISM
INTERGOVERN- MENTAL ORGANI- ZATIONS	Important independent actors for collective action; neoliberals see as forums	Skeptical of their ability to engage in collective action	Serve interests of powerful states; biased against weak states and the unrepresented	Both IGOs and NGOs can be norm entrepreneurs and socialize actors which may change state behavior
NONGOVERN- MENTAL ORGANI- ZATIONS	Increasingly key actors that represent different interests and facilitate collective action	Not independent actors; power belongs to states; any NGO power is derived from states	Represent dominant economic interests; unlikely to effect major political or economic change	Both IGOs and NGOs may lead to dysfunctional behavior; but may also represent new ideas and norms
INTERNATIONAL LAW	Key source of order in the international system; states comply because law ensures order	Acknowledges that international law creates some order, but stresses that states comply only when it is in their self-interest; states prefer self-help	Skeptical because origins of law are in Western capitalist tradition; international law only reaffirms claims of the powerful	Law reflects changing norms, shapes state expectations and behavior

position of the West, most notably the interests of the hegemonic United States and its capitalist friends in the international petroleum industry. To radicals, the UN-imposed sanctions provide an excellent example of hegemonic interests injuring the marginalized—Iraqi men, women, and children striving to eke out meager livings. Radicals also view NATO's actions in Kosovo as another example of hegemonic power harming the poor and the unprotected.

To most radicals, the lack of representativeness and the lack of accountability of NGOs are key issues. Most radicals see the world of NGOs based in the North as dominated by members of the same elite that runs the state and international organizations. They see NGOs as falling under the exigencies of the capitalist economic system and as captive to the dominant interests of that system. According to radicals, only a few NGOs have been able to break out of this mold and develop networks enabling mass participation designed to change the fundamental rules of the game. After all, radicals desire major political and economic change in favor of an international order that distributes economic resources and political power more equitably. Contemporary international law and organizations are not the agents of such change.

The Constructivist View of International Organization and Law

Constructivists place critical importance on institutions and norms.[18] Both international governmental organizations and nongovernmental organizations can be norm entrepreneurs that socialize and teach states new norms. Those norms may change state preferences, which in turn may influence state behavior. Constructivists acknowledge that new international institutions have been developing at a rapid rate and are taking on more tasks. But, they warn, with such international authority, international institutions may become dysfunctional, serving the interests of international bureaucrats.

Law plays a key role in constructivist thinking, not because law establishes precise rules, but because it reflects changing norms. Thus, both adherents of customary international law and constructivists see the critical role such norms play in providing shared expectations about appropriate state behavior. Over time, those norms are internalized by states themselves, they change state preferences, and they shape behavior. A number of key norms are of particular interest to constructivists, for example, multilateralism, the practice of joining with others in making decisions. Occurring both outside and within formal organizations, participants learn the value of this norm. Through multilateral participation, states have also learned other norms, including the emerging prohibition against the use of nuclear weapons, the norm of humanitarian intervention, and the increasing attention to human rights norms. Yet just as these norms and ideas affect state behavior, states also participate in shaping them. All of these norms are discussed in coming chapters. Thus, with the steady expansion of international institutions and international law and influence, constructivists have an active research agenda.

In Sum: Do Intergovernmental Organizations, Nongovernmental Organizations, and International Law Make a Difference?

Realists remain skeptical about the utility of intergovernmental organizations, nongovernmental organizations, and international law. In the view of many realists (though not all), they are but reflections of state power and hence have no independent identity or role in international relations. Radicals, too, view international organizations and law with skepticism. Radicals see them as mere reflections of political and economic hegemony. In contrast, liberals and constructivists are convinced that IGOs, NGOs, and international law do matter in international politics, albeit with different emphases. To liberals, these organizations and international law do not replace states as the primary actors in international politics, although in a few cases they may be moving in that direction; but they do provide alternative venues, whether intergovernmental or private, for states themselves to engage in collective action and for individuals to join with other like-minded individuals in pursuit of their goals. They permit old issues to be seen in new ways, and they provide a venue for discussing new transnational issues and an arena for action. To constructivists, the emphasis is on how changing norms and institutions shape issues. We analyze the substantive issues in international relations in the next three chapters.

DISCUSSION QUESTIONS

1. Write a position paper listing priorities for a reform agenda to make the United Nations a more representative and more effective international organization.

2. A major earthquake has just devastated Sumatra. Do research on other natural disasters in Haiti, Kashmir, and Myanmar to determine which specific international governmental organizations and NGOs would respond. What would they do? What difficulties would they encounter?

3. Do international organizations, NGOs, and international law threaten state sovereignty, or do they not? Substantiate your position.

4. Find two recent newspaper articles that give examples of states complying with international law and two other articles about states that are failing to comply. What explains the difference between the two sets of cases?

KEY TERMS

collective good, p. 183
complex peacekeeping, p. 193
European Union (EU), p. 205
General Assembly, p. 191
Group of 77, p. 191
Group of 20, p. 191
human security, p. 189
intergovernmental organizations
   (IGOs), p. 181

international regimes, p. 186
nongovernmental organizations
   (NGOs), p. 181
peacebuilding, p. 193
Security Council, p. 190
traditional peacekeeping, p. 193
universal jurisdiction, p. 222

 Find chapter outlines, practice quizzes, flashcards, and other study and review materials for this chapter at wwnorton.com/studyspace.

08

War and Strife

- What makes security a preeminent value in international relations?
- How do the levels of analysis help us to explain the causes of war?
- Is interstate war becoming obsolete? Why?
- What are the key characteristics of asymmetric conflict?
- How is the terrorism of the last decade different from earlier forms of terrorism?
- When is a war just? How can we fight justly?
- How do realist and liberal approaches to managing insecurity differ?

AMONG THE MANY ISSUES engaging the actors in international relations, war is generally viewed as the oldest, the most prevalent, and in the long term, the most salient. Wars—in particular major wars—have been the focus of historians of international relations for centuries. Major works on war include Thucydides's *History of the Peloponnesian War* and Carl von Clausewitz's *On War*. World War I and its aftermath (the founding of the League of Nations) led American diplomatic historians and legal scholars to create a new discipline called international relations. Prominent scholars in this field have addressed many of the critical and vexing issues surrounding war—its causes, its conduct, its consequences, and its prevention. This attention to war and security is clearly warranted. Of all human values, security comes first; all other competing values—good government, economic development, human rights, a clean environment, quality health—presuppose a basic level of security. Consider the difficulties the United States has had in Iraq with reviving the Iraqi economy, establishing legal authority, and guaranteeing a new level of human rights. All these activities have proved problematic in the absence of basic security.

Yet history suggests that security has not always been attainable. Historians have recorded approximately 14,500 armed struggles over time, with about 3.5 billion people dying either as a direct or an indirect result. Since 1816, there have been between 224 and 559 international and intrastate wars, depending on how war is defined. After the horrific great wars of the twentieth century and a slight rise in the number of wars in the following decades, a new trend has emerged: the incidence of war has declined since 1991. Both the frequency and intensity of war dropped by one-half in the subsequent fifteen years. The number of battlefield deaths dropped by 80 percent.[1] Yet, war remains perhaps the most compelling issue in world politics, and international relations theorists continue to analyze why international and intrastate conflicts occur.

Theorists are also concerned with the possibility of *transcending* war as a means of settling conflicts of interest. Is war natural and hence inevitable? Or is it a deliberate practice that can be abandoned? The four theoretical traditions answer this question differently. For realists, war is a necessary condition of interstate politics: it can be managed but never eradicated. Classical realists, ranging from Thucydides to Machiavelli and Hobbes to Hans Morgenthau, argued that human nature mitigated against the possibility of transcending war. Neorealists have replaced the emphasis on human nature (either individual or specieswide) with an emphasis on structure, arguing that war will be a permanent feature of interstate politics so long as anarchy remains. This formulation at least hints at a possibility that war might be done away with, but it depends on an extremely unlikely distribution of power: a condition in which a single state gathers to itself the power to defeat all other states arrayed against it. Because this possibility is so remote, neorealists share the pessimism of classical realists: as a prominent feature of interstate politics, war can never be transcended. One key concept that attaches to realism is the prisoner's dilemma (see Chapter 3), a conflict of interest structured in such a way that rational actors choose to harm each other as a best strategy for avoiding the worst outcome. (The analogy is meant to suggest that depending on the structure of relations between actors, conflict may be an ideal strategy as opposed to cooperation.) Another key concept is the **security dilemma**, in which even actors with no hostile or aggressive intentions may be led by their own insecurity into a costly and risky arms race. As the political scientist John Herz described it, "Striving to attain security from attack, [states] are driven to acquire more and more power in order to escape the power of others. This, in turn, renders the others more insecure and compels them to prepare for the worst. Since none can ever feel entirely secure in such a world of competing units, power competition ensues, and the vicious circle of security and power accumulation is on."[2] The security dilemma, then, results in a permanent condition of tension and power conflicts among states even when none seek conquest and war.

For liberals, in contrast, the possibility of transcending war is real, though it will likely take generations to achieve. The core logic of the liberal position acknowledges the structural constraint of anarchy, but argues that states seeking power, including economic power, will be led by self-interest into successively deeper and broader cooperation with other states, punctuated at times by war, but leading over time toward competition by means other than war. One key concept associated with liberalism is the notion of **institutions** as enablers of economic and other forms of interaction between states. In this view, institutions reduce the costs of transactions and increase the costs and risks of cheating. Liberals also focus on the nature of a state's political system, arguing that, in contrast to the realist view, there are essentially "good" (liberal and open) and "bad" (authoritarian and closed) states. Over time the rewards that accrue to good states will create pressures and incentives on more and more bad states to become responsible partners in an interstate system. Finally, liberal theorists argue that a **democratic peace** provides powerful empirical support for their arguments, because it is virtually impossible to cite an example of two democratic states going to war against one another.

Radicals, including Marxists, share liberal optimism regarding the possibility of transcending war as a permanent feature of interstate politics. For Marxists, whose ideas have fallen into wide disrepute, war was expected to end when the "state" (as a form of political association) ended, as it must after the triumph of socialism worldwide. Marxists viewed the state as a form of political association that must necessarily support the repressive forces of capital at the expense of labor. But they also believed that this system of exploitation and repression created the very forces that would inevitably combine to destroy the state in a worker's revolution, leading to communism: a secular paradise in which the state had withered away (and with it war and poverty), replaced by a world of workers who shared the fruits of their labors with all, obviating scarcity and any need for a state. In Marxist theory, a key question was whether humans are inherently self-interested, which might mean that a system based on collective rather than individual interest could never exist. The Marxist response was that self-interest was not natural but was socially constructed—a kind of "false consciousness" that could be corrected by reeducation.

Constructivists argue along similar lines when they note that much of the world we perceive is socially constructed: objects have no necessary or inherent meaning. Instead, human beings bring meaning to objects. This is why, when constructivists analyze the security dilemma, they point to the simple mechanism of "friend or foe" to show that the acquisition of, say, fifty new long-range missiles by Great Britain has a dramatically different implication for U.S. security than does the acquisition of the identical missiles by North Korea or Iran. If the missiles had a fixed meaning, a fixed *threat* as suggested by realist theory, then Great Britain's missiles should alarm the United States just as much as North Korea's. Yet they don't. Constructivists then ask, Where else are the implications of material objects (capabilities) assumed rather than explained and compared? For constructivists then, war is not a necessary, natural, or inevitable feature of interstate politics. Instead, actors have been socialized to understand key features of interstate politics (for example, anarchy) as threatening. A clear implication follows: if human beings (and by extension, states) were socialized differently, the possibilities of either cooperation or nonviolent competition would be sufficient to reduce war to a historical footnote.

Over time, some mix of realism and liberalism has held sway as a theoretical guide to foreign policy in advanced industrial states. In general, the more a state feels threatened by physical conquest (e.g. contemporary Iran, Israel, Pakistan, North Korea, Georgia, and Poland), the more likely it is that some variation of realism will become a guide to that state's foreign policy. Where physical threats seem less intense (e.g. northern and western Europe), realism often plays a minor role compared with liberalism. This chapter focuses on each theoretical tradition's explanation of the causes of war and, by extension, each tradition's understanding of the requirements of peace.

The Causes of War

What causes war? An analysis of any war—Vietnam, Angola, Cambodia, World War II, or the Franco-Prussian War—would find a variety of reasons for the outbreak of violence. In *Man, the State, and War*, Kenneth Waltz posits three levels of analysis that are useful for explaining war in international politics. He argues that the international system is the primary framework of international relations.[3] But that framework exists all the time, so to explain why wars occur at some times but not others, we also need to consider the other levels of analysis.[4] Characteristics of individuals, both leaders and the masses, and the internal structure of states are some of the forces that operate within the limitations of the international system.

The Individual: Realist and Liberal Interpretations

Both the characteristics of individual leaders and the general attributes of people (discussed in Chapter 6) have been blamed for war. Some individual leaders are aggressive and bellicose; they use their leadership positions to further their causes. Thus, according to some realists and liberals, war occurs because of the personal characteristics of major leaders. It is impossible, however, to prove the general veracity of this position. Would past wars have occurred had different leaders—perhaps more pacifist ones—been in power? What about wars that nearly happened but didn't, due to the intervention of a charismatic leader? As we can see, the impact of individual leaders on war is difficult to generalize. We can identify some wars in which individuals played a crucial role, but overall, we can only speculate.

If it is not the innate character flaws of individuals that cause war, is it possible that leaders, like all individuals, are subject to misperceptions? According to liberals, misperceptions by leaders—seeing aggressiveness where it may not be intended, attributing the actions of one person to a group—can lead to the outbreak of war. Historians have typically given a key role to misperceptions. Several types of misperceptions may lead to war. One of the most common is exaggerating the hostility of the adversary, believing that it is more hostile than it may actually be or that it has greater military or economic capability than it actually has. This miscalculation may lead a state to respond, taking such actions as building up its own arms, which, in turn, may be viewed as hostile activities by its adversary. Misperceptions thus spiral, potentially leading to war. The events leading up to World War I are often viewed as a conflict spiral, caused by misperceived intentions and actions of the principal protagonists. But, again, we can only speculate.

If not those of leaders, perhaps characteristics of the masses lead to the outbreak of war. Some realist thinkers—Saint Augustine and Reinhold Niebuhr, for example—take this position. Augustine wrote that every act is an act of self-preservation on the part of individuals. For Niebuhr the link goes even deeper; the origin of war resides in the depths of the human psyche.[5] This approach is compatible with that of sociobiologists who study animal behavior. Virtually all species adopt aggressive behavior to ensure survival; it is biologically innate. Yet this view does not explain subtle differences among species; some animals do engage in cooperative behavior. Sociobiologists regard human beings as an infinitely more complex species than any animal species. If true, these presumptions lead to two possible alternative assessments, one pessimistic and the other optimistic. For pessimists, if war is the product of innate human characteristics or human nature, then there can be no reprieve; wars will inevitably occur all the time. For optimists, if war or aggression is innate, the only hope of eliminating war resides in trying to alter fundamental human nature.

Yet war does not, in fact, happen all the time; it is an *unusual* event, not the norm. Thus, characteristics inherent in all individuals cannot be the only cause of war. Nor can the explanation be that human nature has, indeed, fundamentally changed, because wars do occur. Most experiments aimed at changing mass human behavior have failed miserably, and there is no visible proof that basic attitudes have been altered.

Thus the individual level of analysis, though clearly implicated in some wars, is unlikely to stand as a good cause of war *in general*. Individuals, after all, are organized into societies and states.

State and Society: Liberal and Radical Explanations

A second level of analysis suggests that war occurs because of the internal structures of states. States vary in size, geography, ethnic homogeneity, and economic and political preferences. The question, then, is how do the characteristics of different states affect the possibility of war? Are some state structures more correlated with the propensity to go to war than others?

State and societal explanations are among the oldest. Plato, for example, posited that war is less likely where the population is cohesive and enjoys a moderate level of prosperity. Since the population would be able to thwart an attack, an enemy is likely to refrain from coercive activity. Many thinkers during the Enlightenment, including Immanuel Kant, believed that war was more likely in aristocratic states.

Drawing on the Kantian position, liberals posit that republican regimes (those with representative governments and separation of powers) are least likely to wage war; that is the basic position of the theory of the democratic peace introduced in Chapter 5. Democracies are pacific because democratic norms and culture inhibit their leaders from taking actions leading to war. Democratic leaders hear from multiple voices that tend to restrain decision makers, decrease the likelihood of misperceptions, and therefore lessen the chance of war. Such states provide outlets for individuals to voice opposing viewpoints, and structural mechanisms are in place for replacing warlike or aggressive rulers. To thrive in a democratic state, individuals learn the art of compromise. In the process, extreme behavior such as waging war is curbed. Democracies engage in war only periodically and then only if necessary to make their own democracies safe.

Other liberal tenets hold that some types of economic systems are more susceptible to war than others. Liberal states are also more likely to be capitalist states whose members enjoy relative wealth. Such societies feel no need to divert the attention of dissatisfied masses to an external conflict; the wealthy masses are largely satisfied with the status quo. Such conflicts as do arise can be limited to altering terms of trade, or by other concessions short of outright war. Furthermore, war interrupts trade, blocks profits, and causes inflation. Thus, liberal capitalist states are more likely to avoid war and to promote peace.

But not every theorist sees the liberal state as benign and peace loving. Indeed, radical theorists offer the most thorough critique of liberalism and its economic counterpart, capitalism. They argue that capitalist, liberal modes of production inevitably lead to competition between the two major social classes within the state—the bourgeoisie and the proletariat—for economic dominance and political leadership. This struggle leads to war, both internal and external, because the state, dominated by the entrenched bourgeoisie, is driven to accelerate the engine of capitalism at the expense of the proletariat and for the economic preservation of the bourgeoisie.

This view attributes conflict and war to the internal dynamics of capitalist economic systems, which stagnate and slowly collapse in the absence of external stimulation. Three different explanations have been offered for what happens to capitalist states and why they must turn outward. First, the British economist John A. Hobson claimed that the internal demand for goods will slow down in capitalist countries, leading to pressures for imperialist expansion to find external markets to sustain economic growth. Second, according to Lenin and other Marxists, the problem is not underdemand but declining rates of return on capital. Capitalist states expand outward to find new markets; expanding markets increase the rates of return on capital investment. Third, Lenin and many later-twentieth-century radicals point to the need for raw materials to sustain capitalist growth; external suppliers are needed to obtain such resources. So according to the radical view, capitalist states inevitably expand, but radical theorists disagree among themselves on precisely why expansion occurs.

Although radical interpretations help explain colonialism and imperialism, the link to war is more tenuous. One possible link is that capitalist states spend not only for consumer goods but also for the military, leading inevitably to arms races and eventually war. Another link points to leaders who resort to external conflict in order to avert domestic economic crises. Such a conflict is called a **diversionary war** and is likely to provide internal cohesion, at least in the short run. For example, considerable evidence supports the notion that the Argentinian military used the Falkland/Malvinas conflict in 1982 to rally the population around the flag and draw attention away from the country's economic contraction. Still another link suggests that the masses may push a ruling elite toward war. This view is clearly at odds with the liberal belief that the masses are basically peace loving. Adherents of this view point to the Spanish-American War of 1898 as an example where the public, supported or inflamed by the reports in the new mass print media, might have pushed reluctant leaders into aggressive action.

Those who argue that contests over the structure of states are a basic cause of war have identified another explanation for the outbreak of some wars. Numerous civil wars have been fought over which groups, ideologies, and leaders should control the government of the state. The United States' own Civil War (1861–65) between the North and the South; Russia's civil war (1917–19) between liberal and socialist forces; China's civil war (1927–49) between nationalist and communist forces; and the civil wars in Vietnam, Korea, the Sudan, and Chad—each pitting north against south—are stark illustrations. In many of these cases, the struggle among competing economic systems and among groups vying for scarce resources within a state illustrates further the proposition that internal state dynamics are responsible for the outbreak of war. The American Civil War was fought not only over slavery and which region should control policy, but also over Southerners' belief that the government inequitably and unfairly allocated economic resources. China's civil war pitted a wealthy landed elite supportive of the nationalist cause against an exploited peasantry struggling, often unsuccessfully, for survival. The intermittent Sudanese civil war pits an economically depressed south against a northern government that poured economic resources into the region of the capital. Yet in virtually every case, neither characteristics of the state nor state structures were solely responsible for the outbreak of war. State structure is embedded in the characteristics of the international system.

The International System: Realist and Radical Interpretations

If one key issue or argument distinguishes realists from their liberal and radical critics, it is that for realists, war is a natural, and hence inevitable and immutable, feature of interstate politics. War is as tragic and unpreventable as hurricanes and earthquakes. In advancing this argument, contemporary realists tend to focus on a single description of the international system as *anarchic*. Such an anarchic system is often compared with a "state of nature," after Hobbes's characterization. By extension, the international system is equivalent to a state of war, and Hobbes's description of that state perfectly characterizes the realist view. In his most famous book, *Leviathan*, Hobbes argued that whenever men live without a common power to keep them all in fear, they are in a condition of war: "every man against every man." War, Hobbes went on, was not the same thing as battle or constant fighting. Instead, it was any tract of time in which war was possible. Hobbes likened this situation to the relationship between climate and weather: it may not rain every day, but in some climates rain is much more common than in others. Essentially, Hobbes concluded that so long as a single strong man (or state) was not more powerful than all the others combined, human beings would be forced to live in a climate of war, not peace.[6]

According to realists, war breaks out *because nothing in the interstate system prevents it*. So long as there is anarchy, there will be war. War, in such a system, might even appear to be the best course of action that a given state can take. After all, states must protect themselves. A state's security is ensured only by its accumulating military and economic power. One state's accumulation makes other states less secure, according to the logic of the security dilemma.

An anarchic system may have few rules about how to decide among contending claims. One of the major categories of contested claims is territory. For thousands of years, the Jewish-Arab dispute has rested on competing territorial claims to Palestine; in the Horn of Africa, the territorial aspirations of the Somali people are disputed; and in the Andes, Ecuador and Peru have competing territorial claims. According to the international-system-level explanation, there are no authoritative and legitimized arbiters of such disputes over territorial claims. John Mearsheimer calls this the "911 problem—absence of central authority, to which a threatened state can turn for help."[7]

Neither is there an effective arbiter of competing claims on self-determination. Who decides whether the Chechen, Bosnian, or Quebecois claims for independence are legitimate? Who decides whether Kurdish claims against Turkey and Iraq are worthy of consideration? Without an internationally legitimized arbiter, authority is relegated to the states themselves, with the most powerful ones often becoming the decisive, interested arbiters.

In actuality, several realist variants attribute war to the anarchic nature of the international system. One system-level explanation for war, delineated in the work of Kenneth Organski, is power transition theory. To Organski and his intellectual heirs, not only the inequality of capabilities among states leads to war; *changes* in state capabilities lead to war. War occurs when a dissatisfied challenger state begins to attain the same level of capabilities as the hegemon. The challenger will launch a war to solidify its position. Power transition theorists find that war can be explained by a challenger approaching the power of the dominant hegemon, as illustrated in the Franco-Prussian War (1870–71), the Russo-Japanese War (1904–5), and the two world wars.[8]

A variant derived from power transition theory is that war is caused by the changing distribution of power among states that occurs because of uneven rates of economic development. George Modelski and William R. Thompson find regular cycles of power transition starting in 1494. They point one-hundred-year cycles between hegemonic wars, wars that fundamentally alter the structure of the international system. A hegemonic war creates a new hegemonic power; its power waxes and wanes, a struggle follows, and a new hegemon assumes dominance. The cycle begins again.[9]

To radicals also, the international system structure is responsible for war. Dominant capitalist states within the international system need to expand economically, waging war with developing regions over control of natural resources and labor markets, or with other capitalist states over control of developing regions. According to radicals, the dynamic of expansion inherent in the international capitalist system is the major cause of wars.

Realist and radical reliance on one level of explanation may be overly simplistic, however. In actuality, most wars are caused by interaction between various factors at different levels of analysis. Iraq's invasion of Kuwait in 1990 and the civil war in Georgia resulting from the breakup of the Soviet Union in 1991 provide examples of why wars occur. A list of these general causes is given in Table 8.1.

TABLE 8.1

Causes of War by Level of Analysis

LEVEL	CAUSE
INDIVIDUAL	Aggressive characteristics of leaders
	Misperceptions by leaders
	Attributes of masses (innate behavior or flawed character)
	Communications failure
STATE / SOCIETY	Liberal capitalist states, according to radicals
	Nonliberal / nondemocratic states, according to liberals
	Domestic politics, scapegoating
	Struggle between groups for economic resources
	Ethnonational challengers
INTERNATIONAL SYSTEM	Anarchy
	Lack of an arbiter
	Prominence of long cycles of war and peace
	Power transitions
	Aggressiveness of the international capitalist class

The Case of Iraq's Invasion of Kuwait

In August 1990, Iraq invaded and successfully annexed Kuwait. Between August and November of that year, the UN Security Council approved twelve successive resolutions in an effort to get Iraq to withdraw. January 15, 1991, was set as the deadline for Iraq's compliance, but Iraq did not comply. On January 16, 1991, a U.S.-led multinational coalition launched a war against Iraq with five hundred thousand members of land, sea, and air forces. Air attacks, followed by ground combat, pushed Iraq's troops out of Kuwait. Forty-two days later a cease-fire was accepted by both sides.

Why did Iraq invade Kuwait? Can we find the explanation by examining the personality characteristics of Saddam Hussein? Because he controlled the state as an authoritarian leader and because his advisers were unlikely to support differing views, the negative impact of Saddam's personal characteristics, including his basic insecurity and his ruthlessness, were not easily countered. Did he miscalculate or misinterpret the U.S. ambassador April Gillespie's prior statements supporting Iraqi intentions in the region? Did he miscalculate Saudi Arabia's response in permitting U.S. forces on Arab territory? These are individual-level explanations.

Or was Iraq just acting in its own national interest? Iraq had historic claims on the territory (and oil fields) of what is now Kuwait. During the nineteenth century, this land had been a part of the southern Iraqi province of Basra. Iraq believed that the land had been illegally seized during British occupation around World War I. Thus, no Iraqi government had ever legally recognized Kuwait as a separate state. Given this historical claim, was it not in the vital interest of Iraq to secure its rightful land on the Persian Gulf? The fact that Kuwait has approximately 9 percent of the world's known oil reserves strengthened the economic dimension of Iraq's national-interest justification. Was it not also in Iraq's national interest to guarantee more oil resources, since its national economic development demanded such enormous expenditures? After all, Iraq's 1980–88 war with Iran had reduced oil revenues, and Kuwait had refused to increase oil outflow within OPEC to make up for that decline in revenue. And, Iraq argued, Kuwait was pumping too much oil out of the fields near the territorial border. These explanations encompass the state level of analysis.

But not all authoritarian leaders choose to use military force against a tiny neighbor because of their own national interest. So why did Iraq invade? International-level explanations are also relevant. Perhaps Saddam calculated that his actions would not elicit a military response from the international community. The United Nations Security Council had rarely been able to muster a united front among the permanent five members. The council's repeated threats did not appear credible. Was not the international community preoccupied with other more important events, including the unraveling of the Soviet Union? Iraq also felt the Arab League would be unlikely to condemn actions by a fellow Arab state. These are possible explanations at the international level of analysis.

Why did the United States and its coalition partners respond with military force? Was this the first action of the New World Order announced by George H. W. Bush, in which the major powers, as well as many of the developing states, united against an aggressor state on behalf of a tiny, largely defenseless neighbor?[10] Or was the United States acting on behalf of its own national interest? Kuwait's oil resources (and also neighboring Saudi Arabia's) were crucial to the United States. These resources had to be kept under the control of friendly powers. In addition, the United States felt that Iraq must be ousted from Kuwait and punished for its aggressive action. Or did the U.S. stance simply obey the call of the international petroleum companies, whose power was threatened by Iraq's takeover of Kuwait? Clearly all three levels of analysis are critical for explaining the cause of war.

The Case of South Ossetia

Are the causes of interstate wars equally relevant for civil conflicts? The South Ossetia war of 2008 illustrates how explanations at the individual, state, and international levels are also useful for explaining key aspects of civil wars. This case also shows how what began as an intrastate war quickly became internationalized.

The 1991 collapse of the Soviet Union suddenly left its former republics in a condition of semi-anarchy because Moscow's power to enforce peace or distribute economic resources temporarily collapsed. Some of the successor states sought to maintain the status quo by acknowledging the Russian Federation as the de facto inheritor of the Soviet Union's role as regional hegemon. Other republics or regions designated as autonomous within the old USSR sought either to renegotiate their economic and political relations with the Russian Federation or declare outright political independence. The larger republics, such as Belorussia, Ukraine, and Georgia became independent and internationally recognized states, each with autonomous regions or ethnic minorities of their own.

In 1991, South Ossetia was an autonomous region of Georgia. After Georgia sought to strip the region of its autonomous status, South Ossetia attempted to break away and become an independent state. Georgia resisted, and the conflict quickly escalated to a war that cost the lives of as many as 2,000 people. South Ossetia's bid for independence was openly supported by the Russian Federation, which lent regional authorities arms, transport, intelligence, and air support. Atrocities occurred on both sides, prompting large transfers of refugees (23,000 ethnic Georgians and about 100,000 South Ossetians). In a 1992 agreement, Georgia was forced to accept South Ossetia as a semi-independent state on its northern flank, with over 1,000 Russian Federation "peacekeepers" permanently stationed there.

The cease-fire held until the 2003 ouster of Georgia's President Eduard Shevardnadze by Mikheil Saakashvili in the Rose Revolution. Saakashvili's promises included restoring Georgian pride and securing Georgia against future pressure from the "bully" (the Russian Federation) by seeking full membership in NATO. With U.S. aid, Saakashvili strengthened Georgia's military. In 2004, in a violation of the 1992 agreement, Georgia sent troops into South Ossetia to reassert control. Although those forces were rebuffed, Georgia's actions convinced Russia to support South Ossetia's demand for full independence. Georgia responded by offering South Ossetia greater autonomy *within* Georgia, but the South Ossetians refused, demanding to be recognized as an independent republic.

In 2008, matters reached a head when independent observers began to report an increase of Russian military equipment and personnel in South Ossetia. Russia claimed its troops were needed to protect ethnic Russians in South Ossetia from what it alleged was a threatening buildup of Georgian military forces along the border. That summer, both sides began escalating the transfer of troops and military hardware into the disputed region, ostensibly in support of large-scale military exercises.

In August 2008, the tension erupted into violence. Georgian forces began an assault on Russian and South Ossetian forces in the nominal capital, Tskhinvali. Despite some initial success, Georgian forces were routed. In a few days Russian Federation forces had not only pushed Georgian forces out of the disputed region, but advanced into undisputed territory in Georgia itself. Observers reported widespread abuses, particularly in areas occupied by Russian Federation forces,

In 2008, Russia increased its military presence in South Ossetia, where tensions with Georgia soon erupted into armed battle.

where ethnic Georgians were subjected to violent pogroms at the hands of angry South Ossetians. Strikingly, neither side's political leadership appeared to have full control of its troops on the ground. Russian and Georgian leaders would call a cease-fire, only to hear reports that fighting had either continued or intensified. After publicly stating that the war was over and agreeing to withdraw and leave Georgian territory they had illegally occupied, Russian leaders were embarrassed by reports that in fact, Russian troops had not moved at all, but were maintaining their positions in defiance of orders.

For the first time since the collapse of the USSR, Russian armed forces handily defeated an opponent in battle. South Ossetia benefited as well, becoming another de facto independent state in the Caucasus. Georgia was the big loser, and its defeat weakened it considerably. In addition, Russia's aggressive policies in the region called into question the utility of Georgian membership in NATO and the wisdom of accepting or encouraging further U.S. military aid. As of this writing, tensions between Russia and Georgia remain.

What caused this war? What insights might we draw from theories developed to explain interstate politics apply? At the most basic or human level of analysis, pride and election promises clearly contributed to the escalation of an ongoing conflict of interests to outright war. The accession of Saakashvili to the presidency marked a significant escalation of tensions. Without Russian assistance South Ossetia could never have defeated Georgia's military. For its part, Russia was still led by the newly elected prime minister Vladimir Putin, whose popularity as president had rested in large measure on his promise to use force and aggressive diplomacy to reestablish Russia's place as a preeminent great power in the international system. Putin's popularity in Russia had soared after his apparent defeat of separatist Chechens in 1999; it would have been uncharacteristic of his administration to hold back in South Ossetia. At the state level, neither Georgia nor the Russian Federation are exemplary democracies where civil liberties, enforcement of property rights, punishment of corruption, and popular sovereignty are concerned. Both Saakashvili and Putin have been cited as "dictatorial" by opposition leaders in their own countries and by more neutral observers abroad. In short, as states they are more like the authoritarian states many think are most likely to go to war with each other or with more truly democratic states. Most likely, regional and interstate politics played the greatest role in advancing the conflict to violence. Russia sought a confrontation to keep Georgia weak and divided, to enhance the reputations of Putin and Dmitry Medvedev (Russia's new president) as strong leaders, and to put the United States—Georgia's distant ally—on notice that Russia would not tolerate a U.S. "satellite" and full NATO member on its southern flank. Georgia may have hoped for U.S. diplomatic support and anticipated that fear of more active U.S. engagement might deter Russia from a more active military role in South Ossetia. However, Russia acted as a good realist state should, using measured but decisive violence to deter the creation of a more powerful state on its border. In addition, Russia's willingness to use force in Georgia might warn other bordering states that attempting to increase their power relative to Russia's would be met with direct intervention ranging from economic and diplomatic pressure on the low end to support of opposition parties or outright invasion.

Thus, each of the three levels of analysis helps us understand why war broke out in both Iraq in 1990 and the Caucasus in 2008. Kenneth Waltz was perhaps correct in his belief that the characteristics of the international system—a general state of anarchy, the lack of an accepted arbiter—provide the strongest overall general explanation, but to understand the particulars, we need to understand the interaction of all three levels of analysis.

Categorizing Wars

Once the decision has been made to go to war, decision makers are still faced with a variety of options on how to proceed. The nineteenth-century Prussian general Carl von Clausewitz describes the political nature of these decisions in his book, *On War*: "War is not merely a political act, but also a real political instrument, a continuation of political commerce, a carrying out of the same by other means."[11]

The most significant decisions are about what kind of war will be fought and what mix of weapons will be used.

International relations scholars have developed many classification schemes to categorize wars. At the broadest level, we distinguish between wars that take place between sovereign states (**interstate wars**), and wars that take place within states (**intrastate wars**). Beyond this, we divide wars into total and limited (based on their aims and the percentage of resources applied to these aims), and finally, the type of war fought, conventional or unconventional.

Interstate and Intrastate War

Since the advent of the state system in the years following the conclusion of the Thirty Years War (1618–48), the state, as a form of political association, has proven ideal at organizing and directing the resources necessary for waging war. As one famous social scientist put it, "War made the state and the state made war."[12]

As a result, wars between states have captured the lion's share of attention from international relations theorists and from scholars of war. This is true for two reasons. First, by definition, states have recognizable leaderships and locations. They have legal weight among other states. When we say "France," we understand we are speaking about a government that controls a specific territory that others recognize as France. So states make good subjects for analysis and comparison. Second, states have formal militaries—some tiny and not much more than police forces, others vast, and capable of projecting force across the surface of the globe and even into outer space. These militaries, and the state's capacity to marshal resources in support of them, make them very formidable adversaries. Thus interstate wars are often characterized by relatively rapid loss of life and destruction of property. By the end of World War II, states faced the prospect that interstate war might not only literally destroy them as such, but might, in a nuclear exchange, end all human life as we know it.

Yet over time, the number of interstate wars has declined. After World War II they dropped dramatically, to be replaced by intrastate war—violence whose origins lay within states, sometimes supported by neighboring or distant states—as the most common type of war. The First Indochina War (1946–54), the Greek civil war (1944–49), the Malayan Emergency (1948–60), and the Korean War (1950–53) were all examples of the new pattern.

Intrastate wars—civil wars—have decreased over time as well, but not nearly so precipitously as interstate wars. Intrastate wars include those between factions within a state over control of territory; establishment of a government for control of a "failed state" (Somalia or Liberia); ethnonationalist movements seeking greater autonomy or secession (Chechens in Russia, Tamils in Sri Lanka); or wars between ethnic, clan, or religious groups for control of the state (Colombia, Peru, Algeria, Rwanda). The American Civil War and the Russian Civil War are prime examples.

Although some civil wars remain contained within state boundaries, civil wars are increasingly international. The repercussions of civil wars are felt across borders, as refugees from civil conflicts flow into neighboring states and funds are transferred out of the country. States, groups, and individuals from outside the warring country become involved, funding particular groups, selling weapons to various factions, and giving diplomatic support to one group over another. Thus, few civil wars are really solely domestic; they are often international events.

Total and Limited War

Total wars tend to be armed conflicts involving massive loss of life and widespread destruction, usually with many participants, including multiple major powers. These wars are fought for many reasons: to conquer and occupy enemy territory or to take over the government and/or to control the economic resources of an opponent. Wars may also be fought over conflicts of ideas (communism versus capitalism; democracy versus authoritarianism) or religion (Catholic versus Protestant; Shiite versus Sunni Muslim; Hinduism versus Islam). To prevail militarily over opponents, decision makers utilize all available weapons of warfare and target both civilian and military sites. The Thirty Years' War (1618–48), the longest total war ever fought, involved numerous great powers (England, France, Habsburg Austria, the Netherlands, Spain, Sweden) and resulted in over 2 million battlefield deaths. The War of the Spanish Succession (1701–14) pitted most of the same powers against each other and ended in over 1 million deaths. At the beginning of the nineteenth century, the Napoleonic Wars (1799–1815) resulted in over 2.5 million deaths in battle. For much of the eighteenth and nineteenth centuries, wars between and among great powers were common.

World War I and World War II were critical turning points in making total war a policy option. The same great powers fought in both: Britain, France, Austria-Hungary [in World War II, Germany], Japan, Russia/the Soviet Union, and the United States. With industrialization, these wars involved most of the respective societies. The battlefield included not just combatants, but also the people making the armaments and growing the food. Casualties were horrific: most belligerents lost 4 to 5 percent of their prewar population in World War I, and double this in World War II.

Since the end of World War II, however, interstate wars, particularly large-scale wars between or among the great powers, have become less frequent; the number of countries participating in such wars has fallen; and the duration of such wars has shortened. These factors have led several political scientists to speculate on whether or not extremely costly total wars like World Wars I and II are events of the past.

From the perspective of the U.S.-led NATO forces, the war in Afghanistan has been a limited war in which these states have not committed their entire armed forces to the conflict. Nonetheless, for many Afghan citizens, the fighting has been devastating.

For example, John Mueller argues that such wars have become obsolete. Among the reasons he cites are the memory of the devastation of World War II, the postwar satisfaction of the great powers with the status quo, and the recognition that any war among the great powers, nuclear or not, could escalate to a level that would become too costly.[13] Robert Jervis has offered an explanation embedded in the notion of a security community that combines thinking drawn from the various theoretical perspectives. In the security community composed of the United States, Western Europe, and Japan, war is unthinkable. Realists explain the security community as arising from American hegemony. U.S. military spending is greater than the combined spending of the next eight countries, and the United States has no viable rivals. That dominance is magnified by the effect of nuclear weapons and by the continued recognition that an all-out, general war would be unwinnable and hence irrational, just as Mueller posits. The liberal explanation is based on the democratic peace argument. Not only are democracies unlikely to go to war with each other, but that effect also becomes magnified if they are economically interdependent and if they share membership in international organizations. And constructivists posit that the explanation rests not with material conditions (American hegemony or interdependency) but with individuals who are increasingly "socialized into attitudes, beliefs, and values that are conducive to peace."[14] As Jervis explains,

"The destructiveness of war, the benefits of peace, and the changes in values interact and reinforce each other."[15]

Both interstate and intrastate wars can be classified as either total or **limited wars**, depending on the objective and on the degree to which a given actor's resources are mobilized to achieve its objective. Thus, World War I began as a limited war for Austria-Hungary, which sought only to punish Serbia for supporting the assassination of Archduke Franz Ferdinand. Yet by the end of August 1914, what had begun as a series of limited wars had rapidly escalated into a total war, involving goals as ambitious as the complete conquest of adversaries (marked by their unconditional surrender) and using all national means available. In other cases, a war might be fought with less ambitious objectives or by mobilizing only a fraction of national resources.

The 1950 Korean War and the 1991 Gulf War are excellent examples of wars fought with less than total national resources and for limited goals. In the Korean War, U.S. and soon UN forces were mobilized to prevent the outright conquest of South Korea by the North. The original goal was to eject the North Koreans from the South and possibly to do enough damage to the North Korean state in the process to cause its communist government to collapse. After the stunning success of General Douglas MacArthur's Inchon operation, the North Korean military collapsed, retreating all the way to the frontier with the newly communist China. This opened the possibility of the unification of Korea under noncommunist rule—a much more ambitious goal. But once China intervened, the war threatened to expand to include the Soviet Union as well. The U.S. president, Harry S. Truman, and his advisors decided to settle for a disappointing return to the status quo of 1950. Although the United States possessed nuclear weapons and could have mobilized and deployed additional combat forces, the fear of escalation to another—perhaps nuclear—world war led to an armistice instead of an outright victory. In the Iraq case, after being routed from Kuwait by U.S. and British forces, Iraqi troops were pushed behind a line across which the victorious forces chose not to pass in 1991.

In limited wars, not all available armaments are unleashed. In these two cases, conventional weapons of warfare were used—tanks, foot soldiers, aircraft, and missiles. But despite their availability, nuclear weapons were not deployed. There is no better illustration of limited war than the long-standing Arab-Israeli disputes from 1973 onward, described in Chapter 2 and debated in Chapter 5. Israel has fought six interstate wars against its neighbors—Egypt, Syria, Jordan, and Lebanon—and struggled against three Palestinian uprisings in the West Bank and Gaza. Since the conclusion of the 1973 Yom Kippur War (limited from the Egyptian perspective, total from the Israeli), none of the opposing states have sought the complete destruction of their foes, and the conflict has blown "hot" and "cold." Both sides have employed some of the techniques described below. With the increased destructiveness of modern warfare, limited war has become the most common option for states contemplating violence against other states.

Whereas the number of interstate wars has declined precipitously, limited wars and particularly civil wars that are total in nature have not. In the century between 1816 and the end of World War I, there were about fifty civil wars. In the 1990s, this increased to about 195 civil wars. Although the number of civil wars has declined modestly from 2000–2010, two-thirds of all conflicts since World War II have been civil wars.

Civil wars share several characteristics. They often last a long time, even decades, with periods of fighting punctuated by periods of relative calm. Whereas the goals may seem relatively limited by the standards of major interstate wars—secession, group autonomy—the human costs are often high because in the context of the rivalry between incumbent governments and rebels, these stakes are often perceived to be total. Both combatants and civilians are killed and maimed; food supplies are interrupted; diseases spread as health systems suffer; money is diverted from constructive economic development to purchasing armaments; and generations of people grow up knowing only war.

The African continent provides examples of these total civil wars; most such conflicts are now concentrated there. Ethiopia's war with two of its regions (Ogaden and Eritrea) lasted decades, as did the civil war between the north and south in both Sudan and Chad. Liberia and Sierra Leone, likewise, have also been sites of civil conflict where various factions, guerrilla groups, paramilitary groups, and mercenaries fought for control. The Democratic Republic of Congo is another example of a civil war, but one that has become internationalized. In 1996 an internal rebellion broke out against the long-time dictator Mobutu Sese Seko. Very quickly it was supported by both Uganda and Rwanda, the latter interested in eliminating Hutu militias that had fled from Rwanda during the 1994 genocide. After Mobutu was ousted, a wider war erupted two years later. Powerful Congolese leaders and ethnic groups opposed the new leader, Laurent Kabila. They were supported by Rwanda and Uganda. Angola and Zimbabwe supported Kabila's government, as did Chad and Eritrea. In this conflict, now called "Africa's First World War," an estimated 5.4 million people have been killed between 1998 and 2009, despite the efforts of the UN's largest peacekeeping force.

In virtually all these cases, the civil wars have been intensified by the availability of small arms, the recruitment of child soldiers, and financing from illicit commodity trades (narcotics, diamonds, oil). In all these cases, too, human rights abuses and humanitarian crises have captured media attention but not the political commitment or financial resources of the international community.

The total civil war in the Democratic Republic of the Congo turned into an interstate war as neighboring states were drawn into the conflict after it began in 1996. Images of child solders and human rights abuses have captured international attention, but UN peacekeeping forces have been unable to end the fighting.

How Wars Are Fought

Conventional War

Throughout most of human history, wars were fought by people—almost invariably male—who were specially chosen, trained, and authorized to attack or defend against their counterparts in other political communities. In almost all societies, some groups are also considered off limits, at least where killing is concerned. The tools of war reflected this restriction. Weapons of choice have ranged from swords and shields to bows, guns, and cannons; to industrialized armies fielding infantry and riding in tanks; navies sailing in specialized ships; and air forces flying fixed-wing aircraft. Such weapons are utilized to defeat the enemy on the territorial battlefield. The key aspect of conventional *weapons* is that their destructive effects can be limited in space and time to those who are the legitimate targets of war. Conventional wars are won or lost when the warriors of one group, or their leaders, acknowledge defeat following a clash of arms.

The two world wars challenged the prevalence of conventional war in three ways. World War I saw the first large-scale use of chemical weapons on the battle-field. Near the French town of Ypres, in 1915, German forces unleashed 168 tons of chlorine gas against French positions. French troops suffered six thousand casualties in just a few minutes as prevailing winds carried the poisonous gas across the fields and into their trenches. But German forces were unable to exploit the 4-mile-wide gap in French lines that opened as a result. Many of their own troops had been wounded or killed in handling the gas or by moving through areas still affected. This attack proved the first of many by both sides in the war, but subsequent attacks exhibited a similar pattern. After the gas caused horrific casualties, it proved difficult to exploit the temporary advantages gained. In addition, the effects of the weapons had proved difficult to restrict to combat. Chemicals leached into the soil and water table, affecting combat troops, their supporting troops, and agriculture for months afterward. After the war, winners and losers signed a Geneva Protocol outlawing the use of chemical weapons in war.

World War II added two additional challenges to the prevalence of conventional weapons. First, the advent of strategic bombing led both to the possibility of indiscriminate damage on a large scale—that is, harm to noncombatants—and to a reexamination of who or what a "noncombatant" actually was. Prior to the war, the simple rule had been that civilians were to be protected from intentional harm. But the belligerents possessed large fleets of ships, armored vehicles, and planes, all of which demanded a constant supply of inputs. Were the civilians who made and supplied these great machines of war to be protected too? What about the farmers who fed the soldiers, airmen, and sailors? As the war intensified, the dividing line between those who were to be protected from deliberate harm and those who could be legitimately targeted broke down. By the war's end, both sides had taken to deliberately targeting civilians with massive air strikes. In March 1945, even before the atomic bombings of Hiroshima and Nagasaki in August, bombers from the U.S. Eighth Air Force had targeted Japan's capital, Tokyo, with incendiary bombs, killing over one hundred thousand Japanese in a single raid, most of them civilians. World War II also fast-forwarded the development of a nuclear weapon.

Weapons of Mass Destruction

The dropping of atomic bombs on Hiroshima and Nagasaki in 1945 did not have an immediate and dramatic impact on war-fighting capability. The destructiveness of the atomic bomb and its capacity to kill hundreds of thousands without discrimination had already been matched to some extent by conventional means. Many in the U.S. military, for example, considered atomic weapons to be simply more economical extensions of conventional bombs. But these first steps into the nuclear age—the first and last time nuclear weapons were deliberately used against human beings—had already hinted at a key problem of nuclear weapons: the long-lasting effects of radiation. During the Cold War, both the United States and the Soviet Union constructed bigger and more lethal weapons, developing more accurate delivery systems, ballistic missiles, and cruise missiles, each capable of reaching around the world and killing the earth's population many times over. Thermonuclear weapons led to the possibility that the destruction of a nuclear exchange—now multiplied hundreds of times over what had been dropped on Hiroshima—could not be restricted to the target only, but might rapidly escalate into an exchange that could extinguish life on earth, either by radiation from fallout, or by altering the climate in a "nuclear winter." This mutual assured destruction (or MAD) led the major antagonists to shelve plans to fight using nuclear weapons. Instead they fought through proxies using more conventional weapons, as discussed in Chapter 2.

The fact that nuclear weapons have never been employed in war except against Japan has led to a controversial debate about the effects of nuclear weapons on the decision to wage war. Has the very existence of nuclear weapons increased the probability that an all-out war will occur at some point? After all, a country with a nuclear advantage may be able to achieve all its objectives in short order. So are nuclear weapons a destabilizing influence in the long run? Or have they actually insured the peace, their very destructiveness making rational decision makers less likely to resort to their use? Can nuclear weapons then become a stabilizing force in the world? Scott Sagan and Kenneth Waltz debated these issues in the 1980s. They renewed the debate in the beginning of the twenty-first century after the traditional rivals India and Pakistan had each acquired nuclear capability. Waltz argues that "more may be better," that a slow proliferation of nuclear weapons means that states are enhancing their capability, making it more likely that potential enemies will refrain from action. Sagan disagrees, arguing that the proliferation of nuclear weapons is more likely to lead to a failure in deterrence or an accidental war.[16] This debate over the threat posed by the possession of nuclear weapons has gained a new salience as the technology to build nuclear weapons has proliferated. The tangled web in the case of the Pakistani official A. Q. Khan, who provided parts of nuclear technology, from Europe to Pakistan and then North Korea, has led many to question the stabilizing effect of proliferation.

Chemical and biological weapons, together with nuclear weapons, make up the more general category of **weapons of mass destruction (WMD)**. Chemical and biological weapons have existed for many more years than nuclear weapons have. Although surreptitious testing and use of such weapons have persisted, their lack of an efficient delivery system has not made them a weapon of choice. However, as with nuclear weapons, what has changed is the possibility that such weapons can find their way into the hands of rogue states or terrorists. The key factor that separates WMD from conventional weapons is that *by their very nature* their destructive effects cannot be limited in space and time. This is why they are sometimes also referred to as "indiscriminate" weapons.

The possibility that Saddam Hussein was developing WMD led to the 2003 U.S. invasion of Iraq. And the realization that Iran is developing uranium enrichment capacity and refuses to renounce a nuclear option has led to some of the most contentious political conflicts of the new millennium. Likewise, North Korea's tests of nuclear weapons since 2006 have raised serious concerns in the international community.

Unconventional Warfare

Unconventional warfare is as old as conventional warfare and is distinguished in general by a willingness to ignore conventions of war, whether by flouting restrictions on legitimate targets of violence or by refusing to accept the traditional outcomes of battles— say, the loss of a capital or capture of a national leader—as an indicator of defeat.

Roman legions were plagued by terrorists, bandits, and guerrillas in many of their successful campaigns, but unconventional warfare, though noteworthy, rarely proved decisive when conventional armies clashed. Rome's most common response to home-grown resistance was notoriously brutal: entire communities would be killed, buildings razed, and a few survivors sold as slaves. News of such brutality often convinced others that it was better to live under the Roman yoke than face torture or certain death in resistance to Rome's will.

Two major changes progressively moved unconventional war from an adjunct to conventional war to a prominent feature of war. First, the French Revolution unleashed the power of nationalism in support of large-scale military operations, enabling Napoleon Bonaparte's armies to make use of tactics the older professional militaries of Europe could not easily counteract. Nationalism inflamed common people to resist "foreign" aggression and occupation, even against the possibility of receiving bribes or under penalty of torture and death. Nationalism has proven a double-edged sword ever since. Although Napoleon's forces initially swept aside the old order, the source of his greatest defeats lay in nationalist-inspired resistance in Russia and Spain (Spanish resistance came to be called "small war" or, in Spanish, *guerrilla* **warfare**). But nationalist-inspired resistance was not by itself sufficient to make unconventional warfare effective against the power of states or incumbent governments. That took a strategic innovation that combined the ancient doctrine of principles of guerrilla warfare with explicit use of the power of nationalism.

That strategy was first called "revolutionary guerrilla war" by its chief innovator, Mao Zedong. It was specifically designed to counter a technologically advanced, and well-equipped industrial adversary by effectively reversing the conventional relationship between soldiers and civilians. In conventional war, soldiers risk their lives to protect civilians. In guerrilla warfare, civilians risk their lives to protect the guerrillas, who hide among them and who cannot easily be distinguished from ordinary civilians when not actually fighting.[17]

Going Nuclear: A View from Iran

In recent years, no decision has been so controversial as the decision to go nuclear. The debates over nuclear programs in India, Pakistan, North Korea, and Iran have centered on what this decision means, the reasons for this decision, and how it relates to international law. Iran, whose foreign policy aims at reestablishing the nation as a major regional power, defends its decision to go nuclear on several grounds.

At the United Nations General Assembly in 2005, the Iranian president, Mahmoud Ahmadinejad, stated it was his country's "inalienable right" to acquire nuclear technology. Indeed, under the terms of the Nuclear Nonproliferation Treaty (NPT), to which Iran is a party, states have the "inalienable right to develop research, production and use of nuclear energy for peaceful purposes without discrimination." This position is not unique to Ahmadinejad, who in 2009 won a controversial election to a second term as Iran's president after a campaign in which *all* the candidates endorsed that same position. According to the Iranian government, the country's significant deposits of petroleum and natural gas will one day be depleted, and it must be prepared to use alternative energy resources, including nuclear power. Thus research on a centrifuge to speed enrichment is necessary. The Iranian government regarded attempts by the United Nations to block Iran's efforts with limited economic sanctions in 2006 as part of an Anglo-American plot to keep Iran from economic development. That view did not change in 2009, when Mohamed ElBaradei, the director general of the International Atomic Energy Agency (IAEA), urged Iran to "substantively re-engage" with the agency over the issue of Iran's nuclear development. President Ahmadinejad responded in September 2009 by saying that as far as Iran is concerned, "the nuclear issue is over." But in October 2009 Iran agreed in principle to export almost all of its low-enriched uranium to Russia, where it could then be processed as fuel. This agreement opened the way for Iran both to continue its peaceful nuclear development and to reassure its neighbors and the international community that it is not building a bomb.

Some Iranian officials also point to legitimate security threats that might lead Iran to push for more than only the right to develop nuclear-fuel-production capabilities. Iran is located near its traditional enemies Israel, with a nuclear arsenal estimated to contain over two hundred weapons; and Iraq, which fought a decade-long war against Iran in the 1980s. Shiite Iran also has unstable relations with many of the Persian Gulf states, which have large, sometimes unhappy Shiite minorities. On the country's western border is Turkey, a NATO member and close American ally with economic and political ties with Israel. On Iran's eastern border is Sunni Pakistan, another nuclear power and ally of the United States.

The Iranian decision to maintain the option to make the leap to nuclear weaponry is also influenced by national pride and domestic politics, which have been propelled by actions of the United States. Most Iranians believe the United States has been the country's enemy since the 1950s, when the CIA engineered the overthrow of Iran's reforming nationalist prime minister Mohammed Mossadegh in 1953. Mossadegh was planning to nationalize Iran's petroleum facilities, which were owned by the British. After the coup that toppled Mossadegh, the United States and Britain

relied on the young shah of Iran, Mohammed Reza Pahlavi, who remained in power until 1979, as their favored ally. But the shah attempted to modernize Iran too quickly, first alienating and then violently suppressing Iran's clerics. Iranians remember his rule—buttressed by extensive use of secret police and torture—with considerable bitterness and consider U.S. support for the shah as further evidence of American disregard for the lives and freedoms of Iranians.

More evidence of U.S. ill intent is provided by the American reaction to Iran's efforts to reach out to the United States in sympathy over the terrorist attacks of 9/11. After the attacks, Iran's supreme ayatollah, Ali Khamenei, ordered suspension of the weekly "death to America" chant, which had been a regular part of religious services in Iran since the fall of the shah. In addition to this public display of sympathy, through diplomatic back channels Iranian diplomats offered to aid the United States in its coming fight with Afghanistan's Taliban by providing intelligence support. Both gestures were ignored. The preemptive U.S. attack against Iraq in 2003 reflected the American position that Iraq was part of an "axis of evil," a group in which the George W. Bush administration also included Iran and North Korea. The fact that Iran has long been considered a potential target by American war planners causes further anxiety. Iran's move to develop a nuclear weapons program could be a major deterrent to the United States, decreasing the likelihood that the United States will forcibly promote regime change in Iran, as it did in the cases of

Serbia in 1999, Afghanistan in 2001, and Iraq in 2003. None of these countries possess nuclear weapons. North Korea, another member of the "axis," does possess such weapons. To many Iranians, the lesson seems clear: those who oppose U.S. interests *and* possess a nuclear deterrent are much less likely to be subject to military attack.

The domestic population strongly supports Iran's nuclear program. Iranians wonder why *they* have come under such scrutiny and criticism for what they argue is a legal right under NPT. Israel, which already possesses *active nuclear weapons* and harshly represses a Palestinian minority, escapes such criticism and scrutiny. That double standard seems unjust not only to Iran, but also to many other states in the region. Iranians see their nuclear program as a symbol of the revival of Persian glory and a reflection of pride in the 1979 revolution. To supporters of that revolution, Iran represents the forces of good and the United States the forces of evil. Nuclear weapons are the power necessary to drive America out of the region, chasten what most Iranians consider a long history of Israeli arrogance, and secure a leadership position in the world for Iran.

For Critical Analysis

Answer these questions on wwnorton.com/studyspace

1. *Would Iran's acquisition of nuclear weapons make the region more or less stable?*

2. *Could the United States deter Iran should it acquire nuclear weapons? Could Iran deter the United States? How critical are Iran's intangible sources of power? Base your answers on the theory of deterrence.*

3. *How should Israel respond to Iran's nuclear development? What might be the consequences of a preemptive military attack on Iran by Israel?*

4. *Which international relations theory best explains Iran's position?*

Using revolutionary guerrilla warfare during the Chinese Civil War (1927–37, 1945–49) and in China's resistance to Japanese occupation during World War II (1937–45), Mao's Red Army was able to survive many setbacks. Eventually it defeated the well-armed and U.S.-supplied Nationalist armies of Jiang Jieshi (Chiang Kai-shek), whose forces fled to the island of Formosa, now Taiwan. This unexpected outcome left Mao with a vast storehouse of captured weapons and led to the spread of revolutionary guerrilla warfare as a template for other insurgents, particularly in Asia.

The second half of the twentieth century witnessed a string of unexpected defeats of the major advanced industrial powers, each of which lost wars against "weak" or "backward" adversaries. Britain granted independence to India. France was defeated in Indochina and Algeria; Portugal in Mozambique and Angola; the United States in Vietnam; the Soviet Union in Afghanistan; and Israel in Lebanon. In each case, well-equipped, industrialized militaries had sought to overcome smaller, nonindustrial adversaries and lost. Ominously, both the French experience in Algeria and the Soviet experience in Afghanistan added a new element to the mix: religion as a means of inspiring and aggregating resistance.

Today, this pattern of advanced industrial states pitted against either nonstate actors or relatively weak states has become commonplace. International relations theorists now refer to such contests as **asymmetric conflicts**.

Asymmetric conflict undercuts an important proposition of both conventional warfare and nuclear war: that conventional weapons and nuclear confrontations are more likely to occur among states with rough equality of military strength that utilize similar strategies and tactics. If one party is decidedly weaker, the proposition goes, fear of defeat makes it unlikely to resort to war. Asymmetric conflicts, in contrast, are conducted between parties of unequal strength. The weaker party seeks to neutralize its opponent's strengths, including its technological superiority, by exploiting that opponent's weaknesses.[18]

One such strategy—revolutionary guerrilla warfare—has already been discussed. But like any strategy, revolutionary guerrilla warfare itself has weaknesses. In two asymmetric conflicts following World War II, the strong actors—Britain during the Malayan Emergency (1948–60) and the United States in the Philippines (1952–53)—were able to devise a counterinsurgency strategy that effectively defeated revolutionary guerrilla wars. That strategy aimed not at insurgent armed forces (terrorists and guerrillas) or even their leaders, but instead focused on the real strength of successful guerrilla warfare: the people. As Mao recognized in his early writings, there are only two ways for incumbent governments to defeat a well-led, well-organized guerrilla resistance: either change the minds of the people (via a conciliation, or "hearts and minds," strategy) or destroy them utterly (a strategy one theorist calls "barbarism").[19] In either case, the social support of a guerrilla resistance is destroyed, and that resistance will collapse. But Mao was confident that his

"Western" and democratic adversaries were too arrogant in their own power to attempt to change minds and too squeamish in their ethical conduct to pursue a genocidal counterinsurgency. Yet in both Malaya and in the Philippines, incumbent governments, supported by Britain and the United States, sought to redress the grievances that had led many of the country's poor or disaffected either to active support of guerrillas or to political apathy. Since World War II, "hearts and minds" strategies have proven the most effective method of counterinsurgency on the ground, but they are costly in political terms because they take a long time to work and in most cases they demand large numbers of troops.

Yet guerrilla warfare is only one of several strategies that might be used to overcome a more materially powerful incumbent and its allies. Another is terrorism.

Terrorism

Techniques used in asymmetric conflicts may include terrorist attacks against an adversary's population, such as those that Al Qaeda carried out against U.S. embassies in Africa in 1998, against cities on U.S. soil in 2001, at the Madrid rail station in 2004, and in the London Underground and buses in 2005. **Terrorism** is a particular kind of asymmetric conflict that is increasingly perceived as a major international security threat.

According to Audrey Kurth-Cronin, terrorism involves four major elements:

1. It is political in nature or intent.
2. Perpetrators are nonstate actors.
3. Targets are noncombatant, such as political figures, bureaucrats, or innocent bystanders.
4. Terror attacks are unconventional and unpredictable.[20]

Like guerrilla warfare, terrorism has a long history. During Greek and Roman times, terrorist acts were often carried out by individuals against a ruler. During the Middle Ages, groups perpetuated violence against other groups. During the French Revolution, acts of terrorism were sponsored by the state itself. Organized state terrorism used against a state's own citizens reached its zenith in Nazi Germany and the Soviet Union under Joseph Stalin.

During the 1970s, terrorists began to hijack aircraft to project their message. In December 1973, Arab terrorists killed thirty-two people in Rome's airport during an attack on a U.S. aircraft. Hostages were taken in support of the hijackers' demand for the release of imprisoned Palestinians. In 1976, a French plane with mostly Israeli passengers was hijacked by a Middle Eastern organization and flown to Uganda, where the hijackers threatened to kill the hostages unless Arab prisoners in

In 2004, terrorists associated with Al Qaeda detonated bombs on commuter trains in Madrid, killing 191 people and wounding hundreds, if not thousands. Terrorism has a long history, but in the past decade attacks have become more lethal.

Israel were released. In the aftermath of a number of such high-profile cases, the international community responded by signing a series of international agreements designed to tighten airport security, sanction states that gave refuge to hijackers, and condemn state-supported terrorism. The 1979 International Convention against the Taking of Hostages is a prominent example of such an agreement.

Much recent terrorist activity has its roots in the Middle East—in the Palestinians' quest for self-determination and their own internal conflicts over strategy, in the hostility among various Islamic groups toward Western forces, and in the resurgence of Islamic fundamentalism. Among the groups with roots in the Middle East are Hamas, Hezbollah, and Palestine Islamic Jihad. Since September 11, 2001, Al Qaeda has been the most publicized of these groups. A shadowy network of Islamic fundamentalists from many countries, including some outside of the Middle East, Al Qaeda, led by Osama bin Laden, is motivated by the desire to install Islamic regimes in the Middle East, support Islamic insurgencies in Southeast Asia, and punish the United States for its support of Israel and for its tight linkages with corrupt regimes in the Middle East—regimes that allowed the stationing of non-Muslim combat forces on Saudi Arabian soil even after the defeat of Iraq in 1991.

But terrorism also has a long history in other parts of the world, reflecting diverse, often multiple, motivations. Some groups adhere to extreme religious positions, such as the Irish Republican Army, the protector of Northern Irish Catholics in their struggle against Protestant British rule. The Hindu-Muslim rivalry in India has led to numerous terrorist incidents. Other groups seek territorial separation or autonomy from a state. The Basque separatists (ETA) in Spain, the Tamil Tigers in Sri Lanka, Abu Sayyaf Group in the Philippines, and Chechen groups in Russia are all excellent examples.

Since the 1990s, terrorism has taken a new turn.[21] Terrorist acts have become more lethal, even as the groups responsible have become more dispersed. In the 1970s, about 17 percent of terrorist attacks killed someone, whereas in the 1990s, almost 25 percent of terrorist attacks resulted in deaths. Until 2000, the worst loss of life was in the 1985 bombing of an Air India flight, in which 329 people were killed. That changed dramatically on September 11, 2001, when over three thousand civilians died and $80 billion in economic losses were incurred. The choices of terrorist weapons have become more diverse. AK-47s, sarin gas, shoulder-fired missiles, anthrax, backpack explosives, and airplanes as missiles have all been used. The infrastructure that supports terrorism has also become more sophisticated. It is financed through money-laundering schemes and illegal criminal activities. Training camps attract not just young, single, and uneducated potential terrorists, but also older, better-educated individuals who are increasingly willing to commit suicide to accomplish their objectives. Terrorist groups have also made use of the Internet as a recruitment tool.

The groups practicing terrorism have become wider ranging, from nationalists and neo-Nazis to religious, left-wing, and right-wing militants (see Table 8.2). State-sponsored terrorism, the support of terrorist groups by states, is increasingly common. North Korea, Iran, Iraq, Syria, Libya, Sudan, and Cuba have all been singled out as state sponsors of terrorism. Terrorists are increasingly launching attacks in developing countries: Turkey, Morocco, Indonesia, India, Kenya, and Pakistan are all examples.

Preventing terrorist activity has become increasingly difficult, because most perpetrators have networks of supporters in the resident populations. Protecting populations from random acts of violence is an almost impossible task, given the availability of guns and bombs in the international marketplace and the necessity, at least in Western democratic states, of balancing civil and human rights with anti-terrorist legislation. Pressure on governments is very strong because people worry disproportionately about terrorism, even though it kills a relatively small number of people, and because they are likely to support violent responses that are often counter-productive. Despite better devices for detection, committed individuals or groups of terrorists are difficult to deter. Indeed, such individuals may become heroes in their community—one person's terrorist is another person's freedom fighter.

The international community has taken action against terrorists first by creating a framework of international rules dealing with terrorism, including twelve

TABLE 8.2

Selected Terrorist Organizations

GROUP	LOCATION	CHARACTERISTICS AND ATTACKS
AL QAEDA	Formerly in Afghanistan; now dispersed throughout Afghanistan, Pakistan, Iran, Indonesia	Formed by Osama bin Laden in the late 1980s among Arabs who fought the Soviets in Afghanistan; responsible for the bombings in Africa (1998), Yemen (2000), U.S. (2001), Spain (2004), Great Britain (2005), India (2006)
HAMAS (ISLAMIC RESISTANCE MOVEMENT)	Israel, West Bank, Gaza Strip	Its leader signed bin Laden's 1998 *fatwa* calling for attacks on U.S. interests; elected in 2006 as governing authority in Gaza
HEZBOLLAH (PARTY OF GOD)	Lebanon	Also known as Islamic Jihad; often directed by Iran and suspected in the bombing of the U.S. embassy and marine barracks in Beirut in 1983; dominates Lebanon politically; fights against Israel
PALESTINIAN ISLAMIC JIHAD	Israel, West Bank, Gaza Strip, Jordan, Lebanon, Syria	Committed to the creation of an Islamic Palestinian state; conducts suicide bombings against Israel and opposes Arab governments considered tainted by secularism
EUZKADI TA ASKATASUNA BASQUE FATHERLAND AND LIBERTY (ETA)	Spain, primarily autonomous regions in north	Separatists, involved in bombings, assassinations of government officials, violence against civilians; 2006 cease-fire, but broken later that year. In April 2009, the military leader of ETA, Jurdan Martitegi, was captured in France, but violence continues
COMMUNIST PARTY OF PHILIPPINES/ NEW PEOPLE'S ARMY (CPP/NPA)	Northern, rural Philippines cells in Manila and other metropolitan centers	Opposes U.S. military presence; NPA targets U.S. personnel in NPA areas
REVOLUTIONARY ARMED FORCES OF COLOMBIA (FARC)	Colombia, with some activities in neighboring Brazil, Venezuela, Panama	Marxist; bombings, murder, kidnapping, extortion, narcotrafficking against Colombian officials

conventions that address such issues as punishing hijackers and those who protect them; protecting airports, diplomats, and nuclear materials in transport; and blocking the flow of financial resources to global terrorist networks. Steps have also been taken by individual states to increase state security, such as the United States' controversial USA PATRIOT Act; to support counterintelligence activities; and to promote cooperation among national enforcement agencies in tracking and apprehending terrorists. States that have been seen as supporting terrorists, or as not taking effective enforcement measures, have been sanctioned by other states. Libya, Sudan, Afghanistan, Syria, Iran, and Iraq are prominent examples. But it is important to recall that even a state as powerful as the United States has had difficulty in "taking effective enforcement measures" against terrorists. Should we consider the United States a state supporter of terrorism because it hosted some of the terrorists who later attacked New York's World Trade Center and the Pentagon on September 11, 2001?

Piracy

A final form of unconventional challenge to states—it is not warfare per se—is piracy. Like guerrilla warfare and terrorism, piracy has a long history that highlights the dual nature of its participants' motives. When entirely in the pursuit of wealth, guerrilla warfare and terrorism are more aptly termed as banditry. Piracy has a similar history and character, being both the enterprising work of one or a group of organized criminals (piracy proper, a form of organized crime), and an adjunct to war with the full support of states (privateering).

Piracy has recently reemerged as a major security problem, in particular the coordinated attacks on shipping off the coast of the failed state of Somalia. Since the collapse of the government in 1992, Somali pirates have led a series of successful and highly lucrative attacks on international shipping passing through vital offshore waterways, including the Gulf of Aden. In 2008 these attacks became more frequent, leading to UN Security Council Resolution 1838, directing that UN-member naval forces be deployed to stop the piracy.

The Just War Tradition

When, if ever, is it just for states to go to war? Is war always an illegal and immoral act, or are there any conditions under which resorting to war is acceptable? What constitutes an appropriate justification—*jus ad bellum*—to enter into war? And what constitutes moral and ethical conduct—*jus in bello*—once the decision has been made to go to war? Normative political theorists draw our attention to the classical **just war tradition.** Although a Western and Christian doctrine dating from medieval times, just war theory draws on ancient Greek philosophy and precepts found in the Koran. As developed by Saint Augustine, Saint Thomas Aquinas, Hugo Grotius, and more recently the political philosopher Michael Walzer, just war theory asserts that several criteria can make the decision to enter a war a just one.[22] There must be a just cause (self-defense or the defense of others, or a massive violation of human rights) and a declaration of intent by a competent authority (which, since the formation of the United Nations, has been interpreted to mean the Security Council). The leaders need to have the correct intentions, desiring to end abuses and establish a just peace. They also need to have exhausted all other possibilities for ending the abuse, employing war as a last resort. Forces must be removed rapidly after the humanitarian objectives have been secured. Because states choose war for a variety of reasons, however, it may not always be easy to assess the justness of a particular cause or of particular intentions.

The just war tradition also addresses conduct in war. Combatants and noncombatants must be differentiated, with the latter protected from harm as much as possible. Violence must be proportionate to the ends to be achieved. Undue human suffering should be avoided at all costs. Particularly heinous weapons must not be employed. Because mustard gas caused especially cruel deaths during World War I, it was subsequently outlawed, thus providing the basis for future chemical and biological warfare conventions. Many of the extended norms of the just war tradition were codified in the four 1949 Geneva Conventions and two additional protocols concluded in 1977. These are designed to protect civilians, prisoners of war, and wounded soldiers, as well as to ban particular methods of war and certain weapons that cause unnecessary suffering.

Just war is an evolving practice. Key contemporary debates surround the question of how newer killing technologies—nuclear weapons, land mines, cluster munitions, fuel air explosives—affect our assessments of *jus in bello*. A key concern of just war theorists is the notion of noncombatant immunity, or defending noncombatant immunity from the argument that some technological advance, or something inherent in warfare, requires abandoning that ancient principle. The use of nuclear weapons has been viewed as a just war issue for two reasons. First, unlike with most conventional weapons, the destructive effects of nuclear weapons are impossible to restrict in time and space. Although as many as 110,000 Japanese were killed in the first few hours after the atomic bombings of Hiroshima and Nagasaki, the Japanese government estimates that total fatalities directly attributable to the bombings today exceed 250,000. Second, the destructive potential of contemporary thermonuclear weapons is simply unprecedented. No one can say for certain what the impact on the global ecosystem of even a limited exchange of such weapons might be. An all-out exchange, in which many such weapons were deliberately detonated, might end all life on the planet (save perhaps insect life), damage the atmosphere, or plunge the earth into an extended "nuclear winter."

Thus the proportionality of means and ends, which stands as a second pillar of just war theory, would be violated.

Other weapons have also come under fire under the "nondiscriminatory nature" theory of unjust war. Two of particular note include antipersonnel land mines and cluster munitions. Although land mines originally were viewed under a "reason of state" theory as legitimate weapons, the International Campaign to Ban Landmines (ICBL), as discussed in Chapter 7, has succeeded in shifting perceptions of these weapons by emphasizing—as with other weapons of mass destruction—the indiscriminate character of their capacity to harm. That approach and process has also been adopted by the Cluster Munitions Coalition, a coalition of 300 NGOs with the support of Norway and other countries. In 2008, the Convention on Cluster Munitions was signed, banning the use of weapons that harm innocents and providing assistance for clearance and victim assistance.

Although the destructive objects themselves—their mode of causing harm—have changed little over the years, we see growing pressure to restrict or eliminate their use in accord with just war principles, constructivists can rightly cite the power of norms and socialization to alter the behavior of both state and nonstate actors. The level of discussion in the general media on the question before and during the 2003 Iraq war suggests that the prohibitions are taken seriously and failure to follow them is increasingly met by criticism.

The Debate over Humanitarian Intervention

No issue emerging from the just war tradition has been more critical or controversial than the debate over **humanitarian intervention.** The just war tradition asserts that military intervention by states or the international community may be justified or even obligatory to alleviate massive violations of human rights. Yet that position directly contradicts a hallmark of the Westphalian tradition—respect for state sovereignty. Throughout history, military intervention on behalf of humanitarian causes was applied selectively: in the nineteenth century, Europeans used military force to protect Christians in Turkey and the Middle East, though they chose not to protect other religious groups. European nations did not intervene militarily to stop slavery, though they prohibited their own citizens from participating in the slave trade.[23]

Since the end of World War II, the notion has emerged that all human beings need protection—not just particular groups—and that states have an obligation to intervene, a **responsibility to protect (R2P).** This belief gained even greater prominence during the 1990s after humanitarian crises in Somalia and Rwanda. The idea is that in the case of massive violation of human rights and when domestic avenues for redress have been exhausted, and actions by other states might reasonably end the abuse, states have a responsibility to interfere in the domestic affairs of the state where the abuse is occurring. If one's own state does not provide such protection, then it is the obligation of others to protect and intervene as necessary. As two UN officials put it, this "marks the coming of age of the imperative of action in the face of human rights abuses, over the citadels of state sovereignty." But as the same two writers warn, military intervention can often be "devoid of legal sanction, selectively deployed and achieving only ambiguous ends."[24]

But questions remain: How massive do the violations of human rights have to be to justify intervention? Who decides when to respond to the abuses? Might some states use humanitarian intervention as a pretext for achieving other, less humanitarian goals? Do states have an obligation to intervene militarily in these humanitarian emergencies? How can some interventions be justified (Kosovo) whereas others were not (Rwanda)?

Given their colonial experiences, many Asian and African countries are skeptical about altruistic claims by Western countries. Other states, such as Russia and China, have insisted that for a claim of humanitarian intervention to be legitimate, it must be authorized by the UN Security Council. Thus, when Western states sought military intervention in Kosovo, Russia opposed the measure, and the Western powers turned to the North Atlantic Treaty Organization (NATO). The United States opposed increased use of the military to protect civilians in Rwanda in 1993–94 despite the genocide, having suffered humiliation in Somalia several years earlier. Thus, only a small military contingent from the African Union was originally mobilized for the Darfur region, despite 300,000 deaths and the culpability of the Sudanese government. In the Darfur case, other national interests were deemed more vital (China's access to Sudanese oil; Russia's export arms market; U.S. preoccupation with Iraq and the war on terrorism) than support for humanitarian intervention.

So although there is an emergent norm in support of humanitarian intervention, it is still the subject of debate. Because states will never intervene in all situations of humanitarian emergency, state sovereignty remains intact. But in the case of widely recognized gross violations and when military intervention does not conflict with other national interests, then humanitarian intervention is seen as a justified use of force.

Approaches to Managing Insecurity

Disparity in power between states, the inability to know the intentions of states and individuals, and the lack of an overarching international authority means that states are continually confronted by the need to manage their insecurity. The need to manage insecurity is made more urgent by the recent proliferation of military weapons and increases in military spending, enhancing the capacity of both

POLICY DEBATE

Can military intervention halt genocide?

Yes

- The Genocide Convention empowers states to act against a systematic attempt by one group to exterminate another on the basis of national, ethnic, racial, or religious affiliation. There is only one way to save the targeted individuals.
- Force is the only response fast enough to save lives once mass murders and rapes are under way.
- A forceful intervention warns others contemplating similar acts that they will be thwarted and punished should they attempt them, thus resulting in deterrence of genocide.
- The morale and reputation of armed forces who are risking their lives to halt genocide will be high, making them more effective.
- Military intervention, coupled with nonmilitary humanitarian aid, is the most effective way to stop the violence, alleviate suffering, and prepare the ground for long-term peace.

No

- States rarely believe that their interests are engaged in genocides beyond state borders. Therefore, states are generally unwilling to sacrifice the lives of their soldiers to prevent genocide.
- Most states cannot organize quickly enough to halt genocides, which often break out in distant corners of the world.
- It is costly to send armed forces long distances. Few states have the material resources to transport and supply troops far beyond their own borders.
- Militaries from developing countries, which are often closer, more interested, and better informed than militaries from distant developed countries, have neither adequate equipment nor training to halt genocide effectively.
- Nonmilitary aid to victims is the only practical response with potential long-term effectiveness.
- Military intervention into the affairs of another sovereign state may be interpreted as neocolonialism and should therefore be avoided at all costs.
- Because few who attempt genocide are rational actors, even a successful military intervention to halt genocide in one country will not deter others from attempting genocide in their own countries.

developed and developing states, as well as nonstate groups, to fight using nuclear, conventional, and small-arms weapons.

Four approaches to managing insecurity are well tested. Two of these approaches reflect realist thinking, requiring individual states themselves to maintain an adequate power potential. The other approaches reflect the liberal theoretical perspective and thus focus largely on multilateral responses by groups of states acting to coordinate their policies. Realists and liberals support different policy responses to arms proliferation, the resulting security dilemma, and managing insecurity more generally, as illustrated in Figure 8.1.

Realist Approaches: Balance of Power and Deterrence

Realist approaches to managing insecurity rely on balancing power, where *power* is broadly understood to mean the power to win wars. Although realism itself imagines inter- and intrastate warfare as enduring features of international politics, realists advance important arguments about how to increase the time between wars and how to reduce wars' destructiveness once they break out. The core logic of power balancing is simple: when power is unbalanced, stronger actors will be tempted to use their advantage to secure still more power. The greater the imbalance, the greater the temptation. This is because the costs and risks of war seem low in comparison to potential gains, thus making war a *rational* strategy. But when aggressive, insecure, or greedy actors face others with relatively equal power, they are likely to be deterred by the possibility that the costs of war will far exceed expected benefits. Realism's logic therefore explains much of what we observe in interstate politics. It can provide an effective guide to policies aimed at preserving a status quo short of war. However, realist security-management strategies depend crucially on the notion that adversaries share definitions of relevant costs and benefits and that they assign roughly equal values to both. When they don't, a realist strategy for security management can easily go awry, making warfare more rather than less likely and more rather than less destructive.

BALANCE OF POWER   In Chapter 4, we saw that a balance of power is a particular configuration of the international system. But theorists use the terms in other ways as well. So *balance of power* may refer to an equilibrium between any two parties, and *balancing power* may describe an approach to managing power and insecurity. The latter usage is relevant here.

Balance-of-power theorists posit that to manage insecurity, states make rational and calculated evaluations of the costs and benefits of particular policies that determine the state's role in a balance of power. Should we enlarge our power by seeking new allies? Is our enemy (or friend) altering the balance of power to our detriment? What can we do to make the balance of power shift in our favor? By either explicitly

FIGURE 8.1 | Approaches to Managing Insecurity

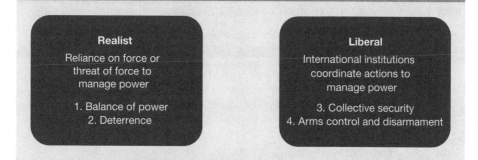

Realist

Reliance on force or
threat of force to
manage power

1. Balance of power
2. Deterrence

Liberal

International institutions
coordinate actions to
manage power

3. Collective security
4. Arms control and disarmament

or implicitly asking and responding to such questions, states minimize their insecurity by protecting their own interests. All states in the system are continually making choices to increase their own capabilities and to undermine the capabilities of others, thereby maintaining the balance of power. When that balance of power is jeopardized, insecurity leads states to pursue countervailing policies.[25]

Alliances are the most important institutional tool for enhancing one's own power and meeting the perceived power potential of one's opponent. If a state is threatening to achieve a dominant position, the threatened state will join with others against the threat. This is external balancing. Formal and institutionalized military alliances play a key role in maintaining a balance of power, as the NATO and Warsaw Pact alliances did in the post–World War II world. States may also engage in internal balancing, increasing their own military and economic capabilities to counter potential threatening enemies.

A balance of power operates at both international and regional levels. At the international level during the Cold War, for instance, a relative balance of power was maintained between the United States and the Soviet Union. If one of the superpowers augmented its power through the expansion of its alliances or through the acquisition of deadlier, more effective armaments, the other responded in kind. Absolute gains were not so critical as relative gains; no matter how much total power one state accrued, neither state could afford to fall behind the other. Gaining allies in the uncommitted areas of the Third World through foreign aid or military and diplomatic intervention was one way to ensure that power was balanced. Not maintaining the power balance was too risky a strategy; national survival was at stake.

Balances of power among states in specific geographic regions are also a way to manage insecurity. In South Asia, for example, a balance of power maintains a tense peace between India and Pakistan; a peace made more durable by the presence of nuclear weapons, according to realist thinking. In East Asia, Japan's alliance with the United States creates a balance of power with China. In the Middle East, the

Realists believe that balancing power is the most important way to manage insecurity. During the Cold War, the NATO and Warsaw Pact alliances maintained a balance of power. With the end of the Cold War, NATO has taken on new functions.

balance of power between Israel and its Arab neighbors continues. In some regions a complex set of other balances has developed: between the economically rich, oil-producing states of Saudi Arabia and the Persian Gulf and the economically poor states of the core Middle East; and between Islamic militants (Iran, Libya), moderates (Egypt, Tunisia), and conservatives (Saudi Arabia). With the breakup of the Soviet Union, the newly independent states of Central Asia are struggling for position within a newly emerging regional balance of power.

Realist theorists assert that the balance of power is the most important technique for managing insecurity. It is compatible with human nature and that of the state, which is to act to protect one's self-interest by maintaining one's power position relative to those of others. If a state seeks preponderance through military acquisitions or offensive actions, then war against that state is acceptable under the balance-of-power system. If all states act similarly, the balance can be preserved without war.

One major limitation of the balance-of-power approach, however, is its inability to manage security during periods of rapid change. A balance-of-power approach supports the status quo. When change occurs, or if the status quo comes to be perceived as unjust, how should other states respond? Rapid change occurred at the end of the Cold War, for example, with the dismemberment of the Soviet Union and the dissolution of the Warsaw Pact alliance. A balance-of-power strategy would have suggested that the United States also reduce its power potential, particularly its military capability, because the military of its rival had been impaired. Yet such a rational response is not only politically difficult to make, but also wrong in the view of offensive realists. Fear of a resurgence of power by the opponent, fear of a return to the old order, and pressure from domestic constituencies to maintain defense spending and employment all make dramatic changes in policy difficult to accommodate.

Balance of power is especially problematic during periods of transition. The end of the Cold War was such a transition, and it has dramatically affected the role of NATO, the major Western alliance formed after World War II to counter the threat posed by the Soviet Union. With the disintegration of the Soviet Union as a state and the end of communist leadership in it and neighboring states, some scholars predicted the imminent demise of NATO. What happened was not the organization's demise but its reconfiguration in terms of both the tasks it undertakes and the expansion of its membership.

With the bloody civil war in Yugoslavia and attendant refugee crises in Europe, NATO increasingly took on peacekeeping and stabilization roles in Bosnia. In 1999, NATO undertook its largest military operation since its creation in 1949: Operation Allied Force, the air war over Serbia. Without UN authorization, NATO forces conducted a seventy-eight-day air war against the Federal Republic of Yugoslavia in an attempt to halt attacks against ethnic Albanians in the Serbian province of Kosovo. The war resulted in a popular uprising and the attendant overthrow of the Serbian leadership, the extradition of the Serbian strongman Slobodan Milošević to the Hague War Crimes Tribunal, and the petition by Serbia to join NATO's Partnership for Peace program.

Since the "global war on terrorism" began in September 2001, NATO has sought to maintain its relevance in the new security environment.[26] NATO has enhanced its operational capabilities to keep up with technology, created a rapid reaction force to respond to crises, and streamlined its military command structure. It has employed forces "out of area"—outside Europe, in Afghanistan—and has practiced for operations in Africa. Its members have helped train the Iraqi military, although the organization has not joined in the U.S.-led coalition in Iraq.

NATO membership has also expanded as its tasks have diversified. In 1997, the first wave of new members, including Poland, Hungary, and the Czech Republic, were admitted. These new members were to be contributors to enhanced security in the region, not just the recipients of a security umbrella. It has proven more difficult than anticipated to convince these states to make necessary defense reforms, increase defense expenditures, and modernize equipment and training. Yet despite these problems, a second wave of members was admitted in 2004. They included Estonia, Latvia, Lithuania, Slovakia, Slovenia, Romania, and Bulgaria. Albania and Croatia formally joined in 2009, bringing the total NATO membership to twenty-eight, along with twenty-six Partnership for Peace member states and seven Mediterranean Dialogue states. This round of admissions was a reaction to the war on terrorism: a search by the United States and others for dependable allies where bases more proximate to the Middle East could be maintained at a cheaper cost. The newer NATO members could curry favor with the United States and did not have to make reforms to be admitted to the organization.

During most of the 1990s, Russia opposed NATO enlargement, alarmed at seeing its old allies coming under NATO auspices. Expansion of the alliance itself was viewed as a potential military threat. Yet in the aftermath of 9/11 and the newest expansion of membership, Russian opposition softened; especially once it realized that NATO's newest members were turning it into a kind of "toothless lion." And Russia still has military bases in Georgia, Ukraine, Moldova, Armenia, Tajikistan, and Kyrgyzstan.

To most member states, particularly the United States, expansion was seen as a natural consequence of winning the Cold War, establishing a new post–Cold War security order, and more recently, trying to respond to new security threats posed by terrorism. Some realists see NATO expansion as a means of achieving relative gains over Russia and further enhancing Western security. Many liberals view expansion as a means of strengthening democracy in former communist states and bringing institutional stability to areas threatened with crises, and as a way to use a security institution to facilitate membership in a much more important set of economic and diplomatic institutions, in particular the European Union. NATO has worked closely with Russia to convince it that NATO's expansion is not an offensive threat and has institutionalized dialogue with Russia on key NATO issues that pertain to Russia's own security. For constructivists, the issue of NATO expansion powerfully engages issues of national identity. For states formerly dominated by the Soviet Union, accession to NATO reflected their resentment over that domination. Russia opposed NATO expansion not only over security concerns, but also due to the implied insult. To a constructivist, then, the politics of NATO expansion highlight the nonmaterial bases of interstate relations between the successor states in the former Soviet Union and the former Warsaw Pact member states.

DETERRENCE: BALANCE OF POWER REVISITED The goal of deterrence, like that of the balance of power, is to prevent the outbreak of violence. Deterrence theory posits that violence such as war can be prevented by the credible *threat* of the use of force. In its 2002 National Security Strategy, the United States made the threat very explicit for those who may pursue global terrorism. The United States writes that it will defend "the United States, the American people, our interests at home and abroad by identifying and destroying the threat before it reaches our border. . . .

We will not hesitate to act alone, if necessary, to exercise our right of self-defense by acting preemptively against such terrorists, to prevent them from doing harm against our people and our country."[27]

Deterrence theory as initially developed is based on a number of key assumptions.[28] First and most important is the assumption of the rationality of decision makers. The theory assumes that rational decision makers want to avoid resorting to war in those situations in which the anticipated cost of aggression is greater than the gain expected. Second, the theory assumes that nuclear weapons pose an unacceptable level of destruction, and thus that decision makers will not initiate armed aggression against a nuclear state. Third, the theory assumes that alternatives to war are available to decision makers irrespective of the issue of contention. Thus, under deterrence, war will not occur and insecurity is reduced, as long as rational decision makers are in charge, the liklihood of net gain is sufficiently low, and other nonmilitary options are available.

For deterrence to work, then, states must build up their arsenals in order to present a credible threat. Information regarding the threat must be conveyed to the opponent. Thus, knowing that an aggressive action will be countered by a damaging reaction, the opponent will decide, according to deterrence theorists, not to resort to force and thereby destroy its own society.

As logical as deterrence sounds and as effective as it seemed during the Cold War—after all, there was no nuclear war between the superpowers—the very assumptions on which deterrence is based are frequently subject to challenge. Are all top decision makers rational? Might not one individual or a group of individuals risk destruction, deciding to launch a first strike? Might some states be willing to sacrifice a large number of people, as Germany's Adolf Hitler, Iran's Ayatollah Khomeini, and Iraq's Saddam Hussein were willing to do in the past? How do states convey to a potential adversary information about their own capability? Why not bluff or lie, to feel more secure? The Soviet Union tried this, attempting to place missiles in Cuba, and almost caused a nuclear confrontation with the United States. For states without nuclear weapons, or for nuclear-weapons states that are launching an attack against a nonnuclear state, the costs of war may be acceptable: their own society may not be threatened with destruction. In such cases, deterrence may fail.

The security environment makes deterrence even more problematic in the new millennium. First, the rise of terrorism conducted by nonstate actors

In Focus ◎

ASSUMPTIONS OF DETERRENCE THEORY

- Decision makers are rational.
- The threat of mutual destruction from warfare is great.
- Alternatives to war are available.

organized in horizontal networks appears to decrease the possibility that deterrence will work. Because nonstate actors do not hold territory, the threat to destroy such territory in a retalitory strike cannot be a potent deterrent. Flexible networks, spread over different geographic areas, rather than an organizational hierarchy located within a particular state, make eliminating those networks very difficult. The increasing willingness of some groups to use suicide terrorism to achieve their objectives has made the logic of deterrence appear particularly shaky. Deterrence depends on the calculation that rational actors will never deliberately act to invite costly reprisals, yet suicide terrorists are willing to sacrifice their own lives. Since loss of life has traditionally been thought of as the highest of all costs, suicide terrorism appears to render deterrence meaningless.[29]

Second, in the changed security environment, the United States is approaching nuclear primacy.[30] It may be possible for the United States to destroy the long-range nuclear arsenals of both Russia and China with a first strike because of improvements in U.S. nuclear capacity, including the ability to track submarines and mobile missiles, the declining capability of the Russian military, and the slow pace of China's modernization. In fact, China has no long-range bombers and no advance-warning system. So U.S. primacy may prevent other states from acting against America, but it may not restrain U.S. actions. Some states worry that the United States may be emboldened to make a preemptive nuclear strike.

Can realist approaches to managing insecurity be effective in the new security environment of the new millennium? Balance of power may not operate during periods of international system change. Deterrence cannot work against a preeminent hegemon unless the hegemon itself exercises self-restraint. Deterrence cannot be effective against terrorists who feel they have nothing to lose. What is the liberal alternative?

Liberal Approaches: Collective Security and Arms Control/Disarmament

Liberal approaches to managing insecurity call on the international community or international institutions to coordinate actions in order to reduce the likelihood and destructiveness of war, as well as other forms of harm (i.e. global economic collapse).

THE COLLECTIVE SECURITY IDEAL   Collective security is captured in the old adage "one for all and all for one." Based on the proposition that aggressive and unlawful use of force by any state against another must be stopped, collective security posits that such unlawful aggression will be met by united action: all (or many) other states will join together against the aggressor. Potential aggressors will know this fact ahead of time and thus will choose not to act.

Collective security makes a number of fundamental assumptions.[31] One assumption is that although wars can occur, they should be prevented, and they are prevented by restraint of military action. In other words, wars will not occur if all parties exercise restraint. Another assumption is that aggressors—no matter who they are, "friends or foes"—should be stopped. This assumption presumes that the aggressor can be identified easily by other members of the international community. (In some conflicts, it is difficult to differentiate between the aggressor and the victim.) Collective security also assumes moral clarity: the aggressor is morally wrong because all aggressors are morally wrong, and all those who are right must act in unison to meet the aggression. Finally, collective security assumes that aggressors know that the international community will act to punish an aggressor.

Of course, the underlying hope of collective-security proponents is compatible with the logic of deterrence (a realist strategy). If all countries know that aggression will be punished by the international community, then would-be aggressors will refrain from engaging in aggressive activity. Hence, states will be more secure in the belief that would-be aggressors will be deterred by the prospect of united action by the international community. But for collective security to work, the threat to take action must be credible, and there must be cohesion among all the potential enforcers.

Collective security does not always work. In the period between the two world wars, Japan invaded Manchuria, and Italy overran Ethiopia. In neither case did other states act as if it was in their collective interest to respond. Were Manchuria and Ethiopia really worth a war? In these instances, collective security did not work because of a lack of commitment on the part of other states and an unwillingness of the international community to act in concert. In the post–World War II era, collective security could not work because of fundamental differences in both state interests and ideologies. Agreement among the most powerful states was virtually impossible. And a collective-security response against one of the five permanent members of the UN Security Council—the United States, the Soviet Union, Great Britain, France, or China—was impossible due to the veto power that each held. Two major alliance systems—the North Atlantic Treaty Organization (NATO) and the Warsaw Pact—arrayed states into two separate camps. States dared not engage in action

In Focus ◎ ▇▇▇▇▇▇▇▇▇▇

ASSUMPTIONS OF COLLECTIVE SECURITY THEORY

- Wars are caused by aggressive states.
- Aggressors must be stopped.
- Aggressors are easily identified.
- Aggressors are always wrong.
- Aggressors know the international community will act against them.

against an ally or a foe, even if that state was an aggressor, for fear of embarking on another world war.

Collective security is also likely to be unworkable because of the problematic nature of its assumptions. Can the aggressor always be easily identified? Clearly not. In 1967 Israel launched an armed attack against Egypt: this was an act of aggression. The week before, however, Egypt had blocked Israeli access to the Red Sea. Clearly that, too, was an act of aggression. Twenty years earlier, the state of Israel had been carved out of Arab real estate. That, too, was an act of aggression. Many centuries before, Arabs had ousted Jews from the territory they inhabited, also an aggressive action. So who is the aggressor? Furthermore, even if an aggressor can be identified, is that party always morally wrong? Collective-security theorists argue, by definition, yes. Yet trying to right a previous wrong is not necessarily wrong; trying to make just a prior injustice is not always unjust. Like the balance of power, collective security in practice supports the status quo at a specific point in time.

ARMS CONTROL AND DISARMAMENT **Arms control** and general **disarmament** schemes have been the hope of many liberals over the years. The logic of this approach to security is straightforward: fewer weapons mean greater security. Regulating the upward spiral of arms proliferation (arms control) and reducing the amount of arms and the types of weapons employed (disarmament) reduces the costs of the security dilemma.

During the Cold War, many arms control agreements were negotiated to reduce the threat of nuclear war. For example, in the 1972 Treaty on the Limitation of Antiballistic Missile Systems (ABM treaty), both the United States and the Soviet Union agreed not to use a ballistic missile defense as a shield against a first strike by the other. The Strategic Arms Limitations Talks in 1972 and 1979 (SALT I and SALT II, respectively) put ceilings on the growth of both Soviet and U.S. strategic weapons. However, due to the Soviet invasion of Afghanistan in 1979, the second SALT treaty was never ratified by the U.S. Senate. The Treaty on the Nonproliferation of Nuclear Weapons (NPT) was negotiated in 1968 at the United Nations in response to the Cuban Missile Crisis.

Table 8.3 lists some of the important arms control agreements negotiated to date. Most of these treaties, whether bilateral or multilateral, call for individual states to reduce either the number or the type of armaments already deployed. A few are designed to halt the spread of particular weapons to states that do not yet have them; a few provide verification mechanisms to monitor whether the terms of the treaty are being met. Nevertheless, virtually all arms control treaties are fraught with difficulties.

The NPT illustrates both positive and negative effects of such treaties. The NPT spells out the rules of nuclear proliferation in force since 1970. In the treaty,

TABLE 8.3

Representative Arms Control Agreements since 1959

AGREEMENT	CURRENT NUMBER OF SIGNATORIES	PROVISIONS	YEAR FIRST SIGNED
ANTARCTIC TREATY	47 states	Prohibits all military activity in Antarctic area	1959
PARTIAL NUCLEAR TEST BAN TREATY	133 states	Prohibits nuclear explosions in the atmosphere, in outer space, and underwater	1963
OUTER SPACE TREATY	127 states	Prohibits all military activity in outer space, including on the moon and other celestial bodies	1967
TREATY OF TLATELOLCO	33 states	Prohibits nuclear weapons in Latin America	1967
NUCLEAR NONPRO-LIFERATION TREATY (NPT)	189 states	Prohibits acquisition of nuclear weapons by non-nuclear nations and commits nuclear states to negotiations for general and complete nuclear disarmament	1968
STRATEGIC ARMS LIMITATION TREATY (SALT)	U.S., USSR	Limits deployment of antiballistic missile systems to two sites in each country, reduced to one site by 1974 agreement	1972
SALT I: INTERIM OFFENSIVE ARMS AGREEMENT	U.S., USSR	Provides for freeze on aggregate number of fixed land-based ICBMs and SLBMs*	1972
BIOLOGICAL WEAPONS CONVENTION	175 states	States agree not to develop, produce, acquire biological agents or toxins as well as weapons or means of delivery	1975
SOUTH PACIFIC NUCLEAR-FREE ZONE TREATY	13 states	Bans testing, manufacture, acquisition, stationing of nuclear weapons in the South Pacific	1985
CONFIDENCE- AND SECURITY-BUILDING MEASURES AND DISARMAMENT IN EUROPE	54 states	Requires notification of military movements and maneuvers, observers, and inspection	1986

*ICBM = intercontinental ballistic missile; SLBM = submarine-launched ballistic missile.

TABLE 8.3

(continued)

AGREEMENT	CURRENT NUMBER OF SIGNATORIES	PROVISIONS	YEAR FIRST SIGNED
INTERMEDIATE-RANGE NUCLEAR FORCES TREATY	U.S., USSR	Eliminates all missiles with range between 500 and 5,500 kilometers	1987
CONVENTIONAL ARMED FORCES IN EUROPE (CFE) TREATY	30 states	Sets specific limits on NATO and former members of Warsaw Pact for tanks, other armored vehicles, artillery, combat helicopters, and aircraft	1990
STRATEGIC ARMS REDUCTION TREATY (START) I	U.S., USSR (now Russia, Belarus, Kazakhstan, Ukraine)	Reduces number of U.S. and former Soviet strategic nuclear warheads by approximately one-third; makes Russia, Belarus, Ukraine, and Kazakhstan responsible for carrying out former USSR treaty obligations	1991
START II	U.S., Russia	Reduces the number of deployed U.S. and Russian strategic nuclear warheads by the year 2003; bans multiple-warhead land-based missiles	1993
CHEMICAL WEAPONS CONVENTION (CWC)	178 states	Bans the use, production, development, and stockpiling of chemical weapons within ten to fifteen years of treaty's entry into force	1993
UN REGISTRATION OF CONVENTIONAL ARMS	97 states	Requires that states submit information on seven categories of major weapons exported or imported during prior year	1993
WASSENAAR ARRANGEMENT ON EXPORT CONTROLS FOR CONVENTIONAL ARMS AND DUAL-USE GOODS AND TECHNOLOGIES	40 states	Regulates transfer of dual-use technologies	1995
ASEAN NUCLEAR-WEAPON-FREE ZONE TREATY	10 states	Creates nuclear-free zone in Southeast Asia	1996

TABLE 8.3

(continued)

AGREEMENT	CURRENT NUMBER OF SIGNATORIES	PROVISIONS	YEAR FIRST SIGNED
AFRICAN NUCLEAR-WEAPON-FREE ZONE TREATY (TREATY OF PELINDABA)	45 states	Creates nuclear-free zone in Africa	1996
COMPREHENSIVE TEST BAN TREATY (CTBT)	176 states	Bans testing of nuclear weapons	1996
ANTI-PERSONNEL LANDMINES TREATY	149 states	Bans production and export of land mines	1999
INTER-AMERICAN CONVENTION ON TRANSPARENCY IN CONVENTIONAL WEAPONS ACQUISITIONS	34 states	Requires Organization of American States (OAS) members to report export and import of weapons	1999
TREATY BETWEEN U.S. AND RUSSIAN FEDERATION ON STRATEGIC OFFENSIVE REDUCTIONS (MOSCOW TREATY)	U.S., Russia	Limits operationally deployed strategic warheads to 1,700–2,200; no verification; no time limit	2003
CONVENTION ON CLUSTER MUNITIONS	106 states	Prohibits an explosive weapon which scatters submunitions	2008
STRATEGIC ARMS REDUCTION TREATY	U.S., Russian Federation	Obligates U.S. and Russia to reduce overall arsenals by 2017	2010

signatory countries without nuclear weapons agree not to acquire or develop them; states with nuclear weapons promise not to transfer the technology to nonnuclear states and to eventually dismantle their own. As with many of the arms control treaties, however, a number of key nuclear states and threshold non-nuclear states (those that probably have or could quickly assemble nuclear weapons) remain outside the treaty, including Cuba, India, Israel, and Pakistan. During the 1990s, three states that previously had nuclear weapons programs—South Africa, Brazil, and Argentina—dismantled their programs and became parties to the treaty, along with three other states—Belarus, Kazakhstan, and

Ukraine—that gave up nuclear weapons left on their territory after the dissolution of the Soviet Union. The International Atomic Energy Agency (IAEA), a UN-based agency established in 1957 to disseminate knowledge about nuclear energy and promote its peaceful uses, is the designated guardian of the treaty. The IAEA created a system of safeguards, including inspection teams that visit nuclear facilities and report on any movement of nuclear material, in an attempt to keep nuclear material from being diverted to nonpeaceful purposes and to ensure that states that signed the NPT are complying. Inspectors for the IAEA visited Iraqi sites after the 1991 Gulf War and North Korean sites in the mid-1990s. Their purpose in the first case was to verify that illegal materials in Iraq had been destroyed and in the second case to confirm that nuclear materials in North Korea were being used for nonmilitary purposes only. But the work of the IAEA has been constantly challenged. In 2009 Iran, which as a signatory to the NPT was obligated to report any facility actively enriching fissile material, was discovered to have an unreported facility in violation of its treaty obligations. In addition, signatories that already possess nuclear weapons are expected to reduce their stockpiles, but they have proven reluctant, in most cases, to do so very quickly.

The end of the Cold War and the dismemberment of the Soviet Union have resulted in major new arms control agreements, as Table 8.3 shows. More arms control agreements between the United States and Russia and its successor states are likely as the latter are forced by economic imperatives to reduce their military expenditures. Yet the logic of arms control agreements is not impeccable. Arms control does not eliminate the security dilemma. You can still feel insecure if your enemy has a bigger or better rock than you do. And as realists would argue, state policy toward such agreements is never assured. Verification is spotty and difficult to implement. That is one reason that the United States is not party to some of the treaties. For example, in 1994, the United States and North Korea signed the Agreed Framework. North Korea agreed to stop its nuclear weapons program in exchange for a U.S. package deal of energy supplies, light-water reactors, and security guarantees. The framework collapsed in 2002, when North Korea announced it was pulling out of the Nuclear Nonproliferation Treaty in response to U.S. decisions to halt shipments of fuel oil supporting North Korea's electric grid. On North Korea's restarting of the Yongbyon nuclear reactor, used to process weapons-grade nuclear material, the United States and Japan halted aid shipments.

In 2003, North Korea publicly admitted that it was engaged in a nuclear-weapons program and has subsequently tested both long- and short-range missiles, causing great consternation in the region and in the United States. Is North Korea using nuclear weapons to destabilize further an already volatile region? Or is North Korea bargaining for more aid in return for promising to halt its nuclear-weapons program? The agreement brokered in 2007 as a result of negotiations conducted among six parties—North Korea, China, Japan, the United States, South Korea, and Russia—directed that North Korea would close its main nuclear reactor in exchange for a package of fuel, food, and other aid. The agreement has proven highly unstable, however. In 2008, North Korea's leader, Kim Jong-Il, threatened to resume weapons development because the promised aid package was too small and had arrived too slowly. Later that year, further progress was stalled by rumors that Kim was near death. Kim reappeared in 2009, after which North Korea exploded a nuclear device underground, to widespread dismay and condemnation. Little progress has been made since that time. Threatening nuclear proliferation as a coercive measure to secure aid is an alarming new security twist.

Given how risky such a scheme would be, complete disarmament schemes as envisioned by utopian liberal thinkers are unlikely. Unilateral disarmament would place the disarmed state in a highly insecure position, and cheaters could be rewarded. But incremental disarmament—as outlined in the Chemical Weapons Convention (CWC), which bans the development, production, and stockpiling of chemical weapons—remains a possibility. However, the increasing sophistication and miniaturization of chemical and biological weapons makes them difficult to detect, so that it is hard to guarantee compliance. Liberals place their faith in international institutions such as the IAEA to monitor adherence to such limited disarmament schemes.

In Sum: A Changing View of International Security

Traditionally, international security has meant states' security and the defense of states' territorial integrity from external threats or attack by other states. This was because only states could master the technology of mass killing; as a result, interstate war proved the largest threat to life and property. Over time this definition has broadened to include intrastate conflicts as well. In both situations, conflicts arise not only over control of territory, but also over control of government and ideas. One problem is that although major interstate wars, such as the last century's two world wars, concentrate destruction in time, intrastate violence has resulted in just as much or even more destruction, spread out over fifty years. By some estimates, over 40 million human beings have lost their lives in so-called low-intensity conflicts in Africa, Asia, and Latin America since the end of World War II. Moreover, the advent of the container ship, extremely durable small arms, food-storage and water-purification technology, and improvements in communications technology have made it progressively less likely that the destruction caused by civil wars can be

Private security contractors, such as these Blackwell employees, were hired by the U.S. government to perform various tasks in the 2003 Iraq war and its aftermath. These tasks included protecting high-profile officials, transporting troops and materials, and engaging in occasional combat operations. The role of private contractors in international security raises numerous questions about lines of authority and responsibility.

contained within the states of their origins. Instead, they are more likely than ever to involve regional and international actors than at any time in world history. Typically, government officials, in democracies, acting in consultation with society, and the military have been responsible for national security and provide humanitarian intervention. This has been the major focus of our chapter.

But a new trend is occurring more and more: the outsourcing of security from governments to private security firms.[32] Companies with such deliberately obscure names as Executive Outcomes, Blackwater (now Xe), Eric, Sandline International, Alpha Force, BDM, COFRAS, and Southern Cross are new actors in security. These contracting private companies perform diverse tasks: servicing military airplanes and ships, providing food for armies, protecting high-profile officials, guarding and interrogating prisoners of war, training troops, and sometimes carrying out low-intensity military operations on behalf of a client. Their "soldier" employees—the mercenaries of the twenty-first century—come from all over the world, from the Ukraine to Fiji, Australia to Chile. Many are former government military personnel. They serve in locations from Sierra Leone to Sri Lanka and Bosnia to the Democratic Republic of Congo to Iraq and Afghanistan.

What are the problems—logistic, legal, and ethical—emerging from this trend? Are these people merely mercenaries acting out of pecuniary self-interest? Or are they pragmatically solving problems that the military could not otherwise solve? Do they save the military money through competitive bidding? Where do their loyalties lie? To what state or what ideology do they belong? What is their relationship with the organized military? Can they be held accountable for actions they take in war? In other words, does *jus in bello* also apply to these forces? Should they be employed by the international community for UN-mandated peacekeeping?

In the waning years of the twentieth century, another change occurred concerning who or what should be protected. Changing notions about what security is and who should be protected have been a key topic in constructivist discourse. Should only states be protected? Or should individuals be protected as well, not only from inter-state rivalries but from failures of their own government to protect life, property, and ideas? That states and the international community have the obligation, indeed the responsibility, to protect human beings, even if it means intervention in the affairs of another state, is the norm of humanitarian intervention.

But what should the individual be protected against? Should protection include more than that against the physical violence typically associated with interstate conflict, civil war, genocide, nuclear weapons, or terrorism discussed in this chapter? Or should the concept of security be broadened? In 2004, the UN High-level Panel on Threats, Challenges, and Change identified additional threats to what it labeled *human security*, a term that has increasingly been used since the early 1990s. Should individuals be protected from infectious diseases and environmental degradation? Should they be protected from the harmful effects of economic globalization or from poverty? It is to economic issues that we now turn.

DISCUSSION QUESTIONS

1. How can we identify an aggressor in international conflicts? Is such identification important? Why or why not?

2. Before World War II, European colonial powers had relatively little difficulty controlling their large overseas empires with few troops. After World War II this changed dramatically. What explains the change?

3. An American decision maker charged with U.S.-Afghanistan policy gets option papers from realists (an offensive realist and a defensive realist), a liberal,

a radical, and a constructivist. How would their respective recommendations differ?

4. The norm of nonproliferation, embodied in the Nuclear Nonproliferation Treaty, has been challenged by North Korea. Is Iran's nuclear development also a challenge to the NPT? Or is it within the treaty's bounds? What are the legal issues? The political issues?

KEY TERMS

arms control, p. 274

asymmetric conflict, p. 256

democratic peace, p. 233

disarmament, p. 274

diversionary war, p. 237

guerrilla warfare, p. 253

humanitarian intervention, p. 263

institutions, p. 233

interstate war, p. 245

intrastate wars, p. 245

just war tradition, p. 261

limited wars, p. 248

responsibility to protect (R2P), p. 263

security dilemma, p. 232

terrorism, p. 257

total war, p. 246

weapons of mass destruction (WMD), p. 252

Find chapter outlines, practice quizzes, flashcards, and other study and review materials for this chapter at wwnorton.com/studyspace.

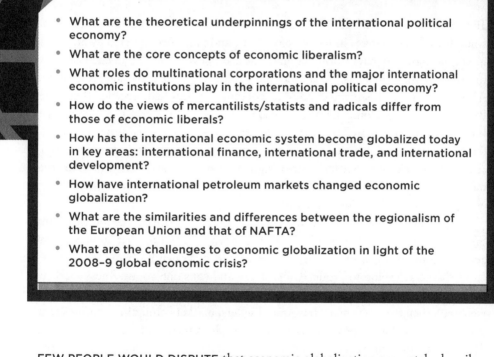

09

International Political Economy

- What are the theoretical underpinnings of the international political economy?
- What are the core concepts of economic liberalism?
- What roles do multinational corporations and the major international economic institutions play in the international political economy?
- How do the views of mercantilists/statists and radicals differ from those of economic liberals?
- How has the international economic system become globalized today in key areas: international finance, international trade, and international development?
- How have international petroleum markets changed economic globalization?
- What are the similarities and differences between the regionalism of the European Union and that of NAFTA?
- What are the challenges to economic globalization in light of the 2008-9 global economic crisis?

FEW PEOPLE WOULD DISPUTE that economic globalization accurately describes the international political economy of 2010. As Chapter 1 reminds us, our clothes, food, and consumer products are produced around the world, often in several different countries; our financial and religious institutions as well as our coffee shops and NGOs enjoy an international market. At the individual level, we interact daily in the real world with people from many countries, whether in the classroom or the workplace. We are linked in the "virtual" world by the new technologies of cell phones, faxes, and the Internet. As Thomas Friedman describes in *The Lexus and the Olive Tree*, globalization is the "inexorable integration of markets, nation-states and technologies to a degree never witnessed before in a way that is enabling individuals, corporations and nation-states to reach around the world further, faster, deeper and cheaper than ever before."[1] But economic liberalization and new technologies stimulate not only the increasing flows of capital and trade, but also the decreasing territorialization of economic life both at the global and regional level. But the international political economy was not always as globalized as it is today. Over time, how has the international economy changed? What ideas propelled these changes? How does the globalized economy of today function?

The Evolution of the International Economy: Clashing Ideas and Practices

The era from the late Middle Ages through the end of the eighteenth century saw a number of key changes in technology, ideas, and practices. Spurred by advances in ship design and navigation systems, the European explorers opened up new frontiers in the Americas, Asia, and the Middle East to trade and commerce. Although Greek, Phoenician, and Mesopotamian traders had preceded them, the British East India Company, the Hudson's Bay Company, and the Dutch East India Company facilitated trade in goods (and people, slaves) and provided capital for investments in the agriculture of the new lands, transporting cotton, tobacco, and sugar to Europe. Settlers increasingly moved to these lands, linked to the motherland by economics, politics, and culture, a nascent transnational class pursuing individual economic interests.

Writing during this time was the eighteenth-century British economist Adam Smith. As we noted in Chapter 2, Smith began with the notion that human beings act in rational ways to maximize their self-interest. When individuals act rationally, markets develop to produce, distribute, and consume goods. These markets enable individuals to carry out the necessary transactions to improve their own welfare. When there are many buyers and sellers, market competition ensures that prices will be as low as possible. Low prices result in increased consumer welfare. Thus, in maximizing economic welfare and stimulating individual (and therefore collective) economic growth, markets epitomize economic efficiency. Those markets need to be virtually free from government interference; only through a free flow of commerce will efficient allocation of resources occur. That is the rationale underpinnning the theory of economic liberalism.

Yet the policies of many European governments at the time reflected an alternative view, **mercantilism** (also called **statism**). The goal of a mercantilist government was to build economic wealth as an instrument of state power. Drawing on the views of the Frenchman Jean-Baptiste Colbert (1619–83), an adviser to Louis XIV, states needed to accumulate gold and silver to guarantee power. A strong central government was needed for efficient tax collection and maximization of exports, all geared to guaranteeing military prowess. Statist governments encouraged exports over imports, and industrialization over agriculture, protected domestic

THEORY IN BRIEF

The Statist Perspective on the International Political Economy

VIEW OF HUMAN NATURE	Humans are aggressive; conflictual tendencies
RELATIONSHIP AMONG INDIVIDUALS, SOCIETY, STATE, MARKET	Goal is to increase state power, achieved by regulating economic life; economics is subordinate to state interests
RELATIONSHIP BETWEEN DOMESTIC AND INTERNATIONAL SOCIETY	International economy is conflictual; insecurity of anarchy breeds competition; state defends itself

production against competition from imports, and intervened in trade to promote employment. The United States' first secretary of the treasury, Alexander Hamilton (1757–1804), advocated policies to protect the growth of the new nation's manufacturers. In his "Report on Manufactures" to Congress in 1791, he supported protectionist policies and investment in inventions. Mercantilist policies included high tariffs and discouraged foreign investment in the name of achieving national self-sufficiency. Those practices led the economic historian Jeffrey Williamson to refer to this period as "anti-Global Mercantilist Restriction." This restriction was true even though there had been a boom in world trade and the share of trade in the world GDP increased markedly.[2]

From the beginning of the nineteenth century to World War I, the expansion of colonialism and the Industrial Revolution occurred as the result of other major technological improvements in transoceanic communications, transportation, and manufacturing processes. The European states needed the raw materials found in the colonies, so international trade expanded, as did international investment; capital moved from Europe to the Americas in search of higher profits. Often those economic links were followed by political and cultural domination. Britain, in particular, was the center of the Industrial Revolution, the major trading state and source of international capital, as well as political and cultural hegemony, contested only by France. It facilitated trade by lowering its own tariffs and opening its markets; it policed the sea to provide safer transit; it encouraged investment abroad. It is no wonder that this period has been labeled the "Pax Britannica," when the hegemonic power of Great Britain, under the guise of economic liberalism, expanded so that "the sun never set on the British empire." Indeed, in the view of **hegemonic stability theorists,** a hegemon is needed to provide services in such an open liberalized economy, services that no other state can provide. Such collective goods (security, capital, common currency) facilitate the working of the international economic system and benefit the hegemon at the same time.[3]

The excesses of that period gave rise to another economic perspective, **radicalism**, drawing on the body of Marxist and neo-Marxist writings. Having seen the harsh living conditions of the working class during nineteenth-century industrialization and imperialist expansion, and cognizant of the economic chasm between the developed and the developing worlds during the twentieth century, radicals blame the capitalist system under liberalism. Although the interpretations vary, the core beliefs found in Marxist and neo-Marxist writings is that society is basically conflictual. Conflict emerges from the competition among groups of individuals, namely the owners of wealth and the workers, for scarce resources. The state tends to support the owners of the means of production. Finally, the owners of capital are determined to expand and accumulate resources at the expense of the working class and those in the developing world. As Marx himself argued, it is the constantly expanding markets of capitalism that lead to crises; dangerous speculation by those holders of capital only exacerbates these crises. Radical states may choose not to participate in the international political economy.

The most recent phase of the internationalization of the economy began at the end of World War II. That phase was a direct response to the interwar period, when the worldwide depression of the 1930s saw a major decline in trade and investment, made worse by "beggar thy neighbor" policies. States enacted policies to protect themselves from the effects of the crisis. Those protectionist measures only hurt others. Britain was forced to end its support of a common monetary unit, gold. With the uncertainty and instability, investment contracted, and trade declined even further. At the end of the war, the goal was to promote openness of trade and stimulate international capital flows while establishing a stable exchange rate system. That is the underpinning of economic globalization.

THEORY IN BRIEF

The Radical / Marxist Perspective on the International Political Economy

VIEW OF HUMAN NATURE	Naturally cooperative as individuals; conflictual in groups
RELATIONSHIP AMONG INDIVIDUALS, SOCIETY, STATE, MARKET	Competition among groups, particularly between owners of wealth and laborers; conflictual and exploitative
RELATIONSHIP BETWEEN DOMESTIC AND INTERNATIONAL SOCIETY	Conflictual relationships because of inherent expansion of capitalism; seeks radical change in international economic system

How can we study these developments? Most international political economists have adopted a rational choice perspective. That perspective is based on the assumption that individuals are rational actors; participants in economic life have preferences that are fixed and known. The study of international political economy, then, is the study of how states make strategic choices that best promote their interests. It is grounded in liberal economic theory, as introduced in Chapter 3. Contesting the rational choice perspective are social constructivists, who acknowledge that policies are affected by historical and societal factors. Neither individual nor state preferences are assumed. Rather, there is a contestation over beliefs and ideologies.

This chapter introduces liberal economic theory and the role that multinational corporations (MNCs) and international institutions play. We then turn to an explanation of how the international economy functions in this globalized era in terms of major issues of international finance, trade, and development, and the emergence of economic regionalization. Finally, we examine the challenges to economic globalization both in the past and in light of the 2008–9 global economic crisis.

The Basis of the Contemporary International Economy

Key Concepts in Liberal Economic Theory

Liberal economics is based on the recognition that states differ in their resource endowments: land, labor, and capital. Under these conditions, worldwide wealth is maximized if states engage in international trade. The British economist David Ricardo (1772–1823) developed a theory that states should engage in international trade according to their **comparative advantage.** That is, states should produce and export those products which they can produce most efficiently, relative to other states. Because each state differs in its ability to produce specific products—because of differences in the natural-resource base, labor force characteristics, and land values—each state should produce and export that which it can produce relatively most efficiently and import goods that other states can produce more efficiently. Thus, gains from trade are maximized for states, but individual actors can be hurt, necessitating government intervention to ensure that all people gain.

Consider the production of cars and trucks in the United States and Canada. The United States can produce both cars and trucks using fewer workers than Canada, making production less expensive in the United States. Under the principle of *absolute* advantage, the United States would manufacture both cars and trucks and export both to Canada. However, under *comparative* advantage, each country should specialize; the United States should produce the car, for which it has a relative advantage in production, and Canada, the truck. By trading cars for trucks, each country gains by specialization. Each state minimizes its opportunity cost. Each gives up something to get something else. The United States gives up the production of trucks for more car production; Canada gives up the production of cars in favor of more truck production. Each gains by shifting resources to manufacturing more of the commodity it produces more efficiently and by trading for the other commodity. Both countries can consume more than if they remained in isolation, consuming only what they produced domestically. Liberal economics posits that under comparative advantage, production is oriented toward an international market. Efficiency in production is increased, and worldwide wealth maximized.

In liberal economic thinking, national currencies, like goods and services, should be bought and sold in a free market system. In such a system of *floating exchange rates,* the market—individuals and governments buying and selling currencies—determines the actual value of one currency compared with other currencies. Just as for a tangible good, there is a supply and demand for each national currency, and the prices of each currency adjust continually in response to market supply and demand. According to liberal thinking, floating exchange rates will result in market equilibrium, in which supply equals demand.

The Role of Multinational Corporations

Multinational corporations (MNCs) play a key role as engines of economic growth. To many economic liberals, MNCs are the vanguard of the liberal order. They are the "embodiment par excellence of the liberal ideal of an interdependent world economy. [They have] taken the integration of national economies beyond trade and money to the internationalization of production. For the first time in history, production, marketing, and investment are being organized on a global scale rather than in terms

THEORY IN BRIEF

Contending Perspectives on the International Political Economy

	STATISM	ECONOMIC LIBERALISM	RADICALISM / MARXISM
VIEW OF HUMAN NATURE	Humans are aggressive; conflictual tendencies	Individuals act in rational ways to maximize their self-interest	Naturally cooperative as individuals; conflictual in groups
RELATIONSHIP AMONG INDIVIDUALS, SOCIETY, STATE, MARKET	Goal is to increase state power, achieved by regulating economic life; economics is subordinate to state interests	When individuals act rationally, markets are created to produce, distribute, and consume goods; markets function best when free of government interference	Competition among groups, particularly between owners of wealth and laborers; conflictual and exploitative
RELATIONSHIP BETWEEN DOMESTIC AND INTERNATIONAL SOCIETY	International economy conflictual; insecurity of anarchy breeds competition; state defends itself	International wealth is maximized with free exchange of goods and services; on the basis of comparative advantage, international economy gains	Conflictual relationships because of inherent expansion of capitalism; seeks radical change in international economic system

of isolated national economies."[4] To liberals, MNCs are a positive development: economic improvement is made through the most efficient mechanism. MNCs invest in capital stock worldwide, they move money to the most efficient markets, and they finance projects that industrialize and improve agricultural output. MNCs are the transmission belt for capital, ideas, and economic growth. In the liberal idea, MNCs prefer to act independently of states; the market itself will regulate their behavior.

MNCs take many different forms and engage in many different activities:

- direct importing and exporting
- making significant investments in a foreign country
- buying and selling licenses in foreign markets
- engaging in contract manufacturing—permitting a local manufacturer in a foreign country to produce their products
- opening manufacturing facilities or assembly operations in foreign countries

MNCs may open manufacturing plants in foreign countries—like this Toyota factory in China—for a variety of reasons. Sometimes they are seeking lower labor and production costs or less stringent regulations; sometimes their goal is easier access to local markets.

Whatever the specific form that their business takes, all MNCs choose to participate in international markets for a variety of reasons. They seek to avoid tariff and import barriers, as many U.S. firms did in the 1960s when they established manufacturing facilities in Europe to circumvent the external barriers of the newly established European Economic Community. They may seek to reduce transportation costs by moving facilities closer to consumer markets. Some MNCs are able to obtain incentives such as tax advantages or labor concessions from host governments; these incentives can cut production costs and increase profitability. Others go abroad in order to meet the competition and the customers, capitalize on cheaper labor markets (e.g., U.S. firms operating in Mexico or Romania), or obtain the services of foreign technical personnel (e.g., computer firms in India). Note that these reasons are based in economics, but rationales based on the political policies of the host state may also play a role. MNCs may move abroad to circumvent tough governmental regulations at home, such as banking rules, currency restrictions, or environmental regulations. In the process, MNCs become not only economic organizations but also political ones, potentially influencing the policies of both home and host governments.

Some liberal economists go further than extolling the economic benefits of liberalism or the virtues of MNCs. They see a positive relationship between the international liberal economy and war and peace. We saw one aspect of this view in our discussion of the democratic peace in Chapter 5. Norman Angell, recipient of the 1933 Nobel Peace Prize, argued in favor of stimulating free trade among liberal capitalist states, in the belief that enhanced trade would be in the economic self-interest of all states. But more than that, Angell argued that national differences would vanish with the formation of an international market. Interdependence would lead to economic well-being and eventually to world peace; war would become an anachronism.[5] Although not all liberals agree with this formulation, economic liberalism does suggest specific economic policies (open markets, free trade, free flow of goods and services). Liberals also posit that government's role should be as limited as possible, merely protecting property rights and providing a functioning legal system. Under this formulation, liberals view international competition as healthy and desirable, with the potential to lead to more peaceful interactions.

Roles of the International Economic Institutions

At the end of World War II, policy makers established a set of intergovernmental organizations to support economic liberalism. The so-called Bretton Woods institutions—the World Bank, the International Monetary Fund (IMF), and to a lesser extent the General Agreement on Tariffs and Trade (GATT), now the World Trade Organization (WTO)—have all played and continue to play key roles in the expansion of economic liberalism (see Figure 9.1).

The **World Bank** was designed initially to facilitate reconstruction in post–World War II Europe, hence its formal name: the International Bank for Reconstruction and Development. During the 1950s, the World Bank shifted its primary emphasis from reconstruction to development. It generates capital funds from member-state contributions and from borrowing in international financial markets. Like that of all banks, its purpose is to loan these funds, with interest, and in the case of the World Bank, to loan them to states for their economic development projects. Its lending is designed not to replace private capital but to facilitate the use of private capital. Over the years, a high proportion of the World Bank's funding has been used for infrastructure projects, including hydroelectric dams, basic transportation needs such as bridges and highways, and agribusiness ventures.

The **International Monetary Fund (IMF)** was designed to promote monetary cooperation and to provide stability in exchange rates. Originally, the fund established a system of fixed exchange rates and, with the United States, guaranteed currency convertibility. From the 1940s to the 1970s, the United States guaranteed the stability of this system by fixing the value of the dollar against gold at $35 an ounce. In 1972, however, this system collapsed when the United States announced that it would no longer guarantee a system of fixed exchange rates. This decision

FIGURE 9.1 | **The International Economic Institutions**

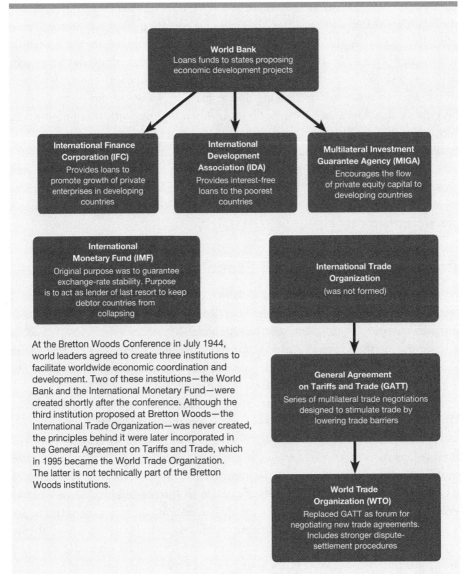

At the Bretton Woods Conference in July 1944, world leaders agreed to create three institutions to facilitate worldwide economic coordination and development. Two of these institutions—the World Bank and the International Monetary Fund—were created shortly after the conference. Although the third institution proposed at Bretton Woods—the International Trade Organization—was never created, the principles behind it were later incorporated in the General Agreement on Tariffs and Trade, which in 1995 became the World Trade Organization. The latter is not technically part of the Bretton Woods institutions.

was revised in 1976 when the International Monetary Fund formalized the system of floating exchange rates, a policy more consistent with economic liberalism. At that time, monetary cooperation became the responsibility of the **Group of 7 (G7),** composed of the United States, Japan, Germany, Great Britain, France, Italy, and Canada. The IMF was to provide short-term loans for member states confronted by temporary balance-of-payments difficulties.

The third part of the liberal economic order was the **General Agreement on Tariffs and Trade (GATT)**. This treaty enshrined important liberal principles:

- Support of trade liberalization, because trade is the engine for growth and economic development
- Nondiscrimination in trade (i.e., **most-favored-nation (MFN) principle**), whereby states agree to give the same treatment to all other GATT members as they give to their best (most-favored) trading partner
- Preferential access in developed markets to products from the South in order to stimulate economic development in the South
- Support for "national treatment" of foreign enterprises (that is, treating them as domestic firms)

Procedures have put these principles into practice. The GATT established a continual process of multilateral negotiations among those countries sharing major interests in the issue at hand (major producers and consumers of a product, for example); the agreements reached in these negotiations were then expanded to all GATT participants. Individual states could claim exemptions (called *safeguards*) to accommodate any domestic or balance-of-payments difficulties that might occur because of the resulting trade agreements.

How the Globalized Economy Works Today

For twenty years after the end of World War II, economic growth occurred much as liberal economic theory predicted. Growth rates in the developed and the developing world averaged over 4 percent. Trade volume increased over sevenfold. There was a dramatic reduction in poverty rates worldwide. But the reality has not always followed the theory.

International Finance

Capital movements played a key role in the earlier phases of the development of the international political economy as they do today. International capital traditionally moves in two ways: **direct foreign investment** includes the building of factories and investing in the facilities for extraction of natural resources. **Portfolio investment** includes investing in another country's stocks or bonds, either short or long term, without taking direct control of those investments.

The MNCs play a major role in that movement of capital. Before World War II, most MNCs were in manufacturing (General Motors, Ford, Toyota, Sony, Siemens, Nestlé, Bayer). Today, there are over sixty thousand MNCs, with more than eight hundred thousand subsidiaries, employing over 90 million people. The top one thousand produce 80 percent of the world's industrial output. Out of the largest one hundred companies, more than ninety are based in the United States, Europe, or Japan, as well as a handful of Asian and Latin American states, including China, Malaysia, Hong Kong, South Korea, Singapore, Brazil, and Mexico. Together they produce 25 percent of the world's wealth. Those MNCs provide both foreign direct investment (Toyota and Honda investments in U.S.-based auto plants) and portfolio investments, as shown by the emergence of MNCs in international financial services: Citigroup, ICI, Bank of America, Deutsche Bank, and Fuji Bank.

Indeed, between the 1960s and the 1980s, private international capital provided essential lending to the successful Asian "tigers," including Taiwan and South Korea, although private capital alone cannot explain their success. The infusion of private investment in particular emerging economies—China, Brazil, Argentina, Chile, South Korea, Mexico, Singapore, Turkey, and Thailand—has been substantial. Capital has played a major role in their economic success. Yet the very volatility of private capital flows makes them unreliable for sustained development in some parts of the world.

Critics from all perspectives realize that some states have more difficulty attracting private investment than others. For example, even now, Africa receives only 8 percent of private capital, and most of that still goes to South Africa. The World Bank has expanded its mission by providing capital to developing countries. In fact, separate institutions within the World Bank were established for that purpose. The International Finance Corporation (IFC) and the International Development Association (IDA) were created in 1956 and 1960, respectively, for that purpose. The IDA provides capital to the poorest countries, usually in the form of interest-free loans. Repayment schedules of fifty years theoretically allow the developing countries time to reach economic takeoff and sustain growth. Funds for the IDA need to be continually replenished by major donor countries. The IFC provides loans to promote the growth of private enterprises in developing countries. In 1988, the Multilateral Investment Guarantee Agency (MIGA) was added to the World Bank group. This agency meets its goal—augmenting the flow of private equity capital to developing countries—by insuring investments against losses. Such losses may result from expropriation, government currency restrictions, or civil war or ethnic conflict. Even with these changes, since the mid-1980s, the flows from both multilateral institutions (the World Bank institutions, regional development banks) and official bilateral donors (the United States, Germany, Japan) have declined as a percentage of total capital flows ($100 billion in 2006), whereas private capital flows from MNCs and other private sources have expanded ($600 billion in 2006).

Beginning in the 1980s, international financial flows accelerated through several other mechanisms. Exchange rates were no longer fixed, so traders in currency exchange markets and in MNCs could capitalize on buying and selling currencies, often in very short periods of time, facilitated by increasing technological sophisti-cation of communications. By the beginning of the new millennium, such currency transactions averaged over $3 trillion a day. Markets developed new financial instruments, such as **derivatives** (options against the future in a variety of asset classes, including loans and mortgages). These instruments were packaged and sold around the world, spreading risk and accelerating the flow of capital. New economic actors, **sovereign wealth funds**, formed in capital-surplus countries such as China and in the major petroleum exporters such as Kuwait, the United Arab Emirates, Norway, Russia, and Canada. Those wealth funds have been able to move capital quickly across national boundaries, taking advantage of currency differentials and buying and selling new financial instruments. Finally, economic liberalization has led to the emergence of **offshore financial centers**, such as the Cayman Islands, Bermuda, and the British Virgin Islands. These jurisdictions have low taxation and little or no regulation. Individuals, companies, and states can move capital in and out rapidly via electronic transfers, making up to 12 million transfers daily.

The Asian financial crisis of the 1990s illustrates the possible outcomes of the globalization of finance. Beginning in Thailand in 1997, in a relatively short period of time, 2 percent of gross domestic product fled that country. Within weeks, the crisis spread to Indonesia, Malaysia, and the Philippines, and beyond. Many countries were unable to adjust to the rapid withdrawal of capital. Exchange rates plummeted to 50 percent of precrisis values, stock markets fell 80 percent, and real GDP dropped 4 to 8 percent. Individuals lost their jobs as companies went bankrupt or were forced to restructure. Millions of people were forced into poverty. In Southeast Asian countries such as South Korea and Taiwan, and spreading to Brazil and Russia, economies that had previously depended on external trade expe-rienced an unparalleled sense of economic vulnerability. Fueled by instantaneous communication, global financial markets capable of moving $1.3 trillion daily, and the power of MNCs, traders, and financial entrepreneurs, economic globalization quickly displayed its pitfalls. The largely unregulated market had melted down, and states and individuals appeared helpless.

The IMF responded to the social and political upheaval with large, controversial bailout packages to three of the affected countries (Thailand, $17 billion; Indonesia, $36 billion; and South Korea, $58 billion); lengthy sets of conditions that each country was supposed to follow; and monitoring devices to ensure compliance. Governments had to agree to carry out extensive structural reforms that would transform their economies from semimercantilist to more market-oriented ones. In South Korea, for example, the government lifted restrictions on capital movements and foreign ownership, permitted companies to lay off workers, and adopted measures to restructure the country's financial institutions. Budget cuts eliminated more social services and pushed more families below the poverty line, leading to a backlash against governments and the IMF. Yet following two years of economic stress and the wounded credibility of the IMF, none of the countries involved retreated from globalization or the international financial markets, and all resumed a path of strong economic growth. Critics of the IMF response focus on the so-called **moral hazard** problem: states were rescued from the consequences of their reckless behavior, providing little incentive for them to change that behavior.

International Trade

The goal of economic liberal thinking was to create an international free trade system. Yet just as happened during the interwar period, governments often have policy objectives other than economic efficiency. They want to protect home industries from competition to mitigate the effects of economic adjustment on individuals or groups such as laborers in a certain industry or producers of a specific agricultural crop. They may protect domestic capacity for national security reasons, even if that policy may not be economically efficient.

The goal of the post–World War II GATT was to promote international trade by lowering trade barriers. That work was carried out over the course of eight negotiating rounds, with each round progressively cutting tariffs, giving better treatment to the developing countries, and addressing new problems (subsidies and countervailing duties). For example, in the Kennedy Round between 1963 and 1967, tariff cuts averaged 35 percent on $40 billion of trade among sixty-two countries. In the following Tokyo Round (1973–79), 102 states negotiated tariff cuts, again amounting to more than 35 percent for $100 billion of trade. In addition, more favorable arrangements were negotiated for developing countries. Overall, between 1946 and the mid-1990s, tariffs were reduced from an average of 40 percent to 5 percent on imported goods for the major trading countries.

The final round, called the Uruguay Round, began in 1986. The Uruguay Round covered new items such as services (insurance), intellectual property rights (copyrights, patents, trademarks), and for the first time, agriculture. Previously, agriculture was seen as too contentious an issue, complicated by both U.S. agricultural subsidies and the European Union's protectionist Common Agricultural Policy (CAP). Agreement was reached to begin to phase out agricultural subsidies. In late 1994, the most comprehensive trade agreement in history was finally reached, a four-hundred-page document covering everything from paper clips to computer chips. Tariffs on manufactured goods were cut by an average of 37 percent among members. The developing countries that participated in these tariff cuts—the liberalizers—enjoyed a full percentage point per year boost in growth compared with the nonliberalizers.[6]

In 1995, GATT became a formal institution, renaming itself the **World Trade Organization (WTO).** The WTO incorporated the general areas of GATT's jurisdiction, as well as expanded jurisdiction in services and intellectual property.

Regular ministerial meetings give WTO a political prominence that GATT lacked. Representing states that conduct over 90 percent of the world's trade, the WTO has the task of implementing the Uruguay Round, serving as a forum for trade negotiations, and providing a venue for trade review, dispute settlement, and enforcement.

Two important procedures were initiated in WTO. First is the Trade Policy Review Mechanism (TPRM), which conducts periodic surveillance of the trade practices of member states. Under this procedure there is a forum where states can question each other about trade practices. Second is the Dispute Settlement Body, designed as an authoritative panel to hear and settle trade disputes. With the authority to impose sanctions against violators, this body is more powerful than previous economic dispute-resolution arrangements.

Getting global participation in WTO has proved a painstaking task. China's accession to the WTO in 2001, after fifteen years of negotiations, illustrates the problems. During the initial negotiations, China revised its laws to permit foreign ventures in previously restricted areas, leading to a significant inflow of foreign investment in telecommunications, tourism, and banking. China's membership requires its continual dismantling of barriers to trade, including opening up insurance markets to foreign companies and reducing tariffs on foreign auto-mobiles. These changes also require China to translate WTO rules into domestic legislation and clarify current laws inconsistent with WTO rules. Teams of Chinese trade officials were sent to local areas to enforce compliance; special courts were established to hear WTO-related disputes. The WTO is thus facilitating China's transition to an open-market economy, although the country still has a long way to go: compliance is best in the agricultural sector but lags on intellectual property rights issues. But to disentangle the government from the economy is a difficult task. Vietnam, which joined the WTO in 2007, is undergoing some of the same reforms.

Trade liberalization, the major goal of the WTO, remains controversial. The Doha Round, launched in 2001, illustrates the difficulties. After seven years, the talks reached an impasse between the U.S. and the EU on one hand and the Group of 20 (G20) emerging countries, such as India, Brazil, and China, on the other. The main sticking point has been the liberalization of agricultural markets. Neither the United States nor the EU was willing to reduce farm subsidies significantly, which would have made agricultural products from developing countries more competitive in international markets. India and China, in particular, sought if not an end to farm subsidies, then special safeguard mechanisms for their own poor farmers to ensure food security. No compromise was achieved on that technical issue, and the talks collapsed. More generally, the Doha Round failed over the perception of fairness in trade. Already dissatisfied with new rules that opened competition in investment and government procurement, the developing countries sought more advantages

The WTO's efforts to liberalize trade are controversial. WTO meetings are often accompanied by protests, like this 2009 protest in India, as farmers from developing countries and others hurt by WTO policies express their concerns about policies that seem to favor rich countries.

in the politically sensitive areas of agriculture and other labor-intensive sectors. Low-level negotiations have continued, but the 2009 economic slowdown makes protection of domestic markets economically and politically advantageous and multilateral agreement more difficult to achieve. Will such developed countries as the United State and the members of the EU, traditionally strong supporters of the WTO, continue to support the organization? What will be the impact of Doha's failure on trade on the development agenda? So far, as one commentator on the Doha process noted, "Affixing the label 'development'. . . may have warmed a few hearts, but it has not filled any bellies."[7]

International Development

The Doha Round of trade negotiations brought out some of the differences between the developed North and the developing South. It is not only geography that matters. The North basks in relative wealth, with high consumption habits, high levels of education and health services, and social welfare nets. Parts of the South lie mired in relative poverty, struggling to meet basic caloric needs, with poor educational and health services and no welfare nets to meet the needs of the poorest of the poor. In 2007, the high-income countries of the Organisation for Economic Co-operation and Development (OECD) reached a GDP per capita of $32,647, whereas the least-developed (in sub-Saharan Africa) had $2,031. If we view other indicators such as the Human Development Index (HDI; see Table 9.1), the differences across a variety of indicators including health and education are even

TABLE 9.1 ▰▰▰▰▰▰▰▰▰▰▰▰▰▰▰▰▰▰▰▰▰▰▰▰▰▰▰

Human Development Index, 2007

	LIFE EXPECTANCY AT BIRTH (IN YEARS), 2007	ADULT LITERACY RATE (% AGED 15 AND ABOVE), 1999–2007	COMBINED GROSS ENROLLMENT RATIO IN EDUCATION (%), 2007	REAL GDP PER CAPITA (PPP* US$), 2007	HUMAN DEVELOPMENT INDEX VALUE, 2007†
ARAB STATES	68.5	71.2	66.2	8,202	0.719
CENTRAL AND EASTERN EUROPE AND THE CIS	69.7	97.6	79.5	12,185	0.821
EAST ASIA AND THE PACIFIC	72.2	92.7	69.3	5,733	0.770
LATIN AMERICA AND THE CARIBBEAN	73.4	91.2	83.4	10,077	0.821
SOUTH ASIA	64.1	64.2	58.0	2,905	0.612
SUB-SAHARAN AFRICA	51.5	62.9	53.5	2,031	0.514
ORGANISATION FOR ECONOMIC CO-OPERATION AND DEVELOP- MENT (OECD)	79.0	—	89.1	32,647	0.932
EUROPEAN UNION (EU27)	79.0	—	91.0	29,956	0.937
GULF COOPERA- TION COUNCIL (GCC)	74.0	86.8	77.0	30,415	0.868

* PPP is purchasing power parity. It is a way to compare levels of economic data cross-nationally free of price and exchange-rate distortions.

† The HDI has three components: life expectancy at birth; educational attainment, comprising adult literacy, with two-thirds weight, and a combined primary, secondary, and tertiary enrollment ratio, with one-third weight; and income. The HDI value for each country indicates how far that country has to go to attain certain defined goals: an average life span of 85 years, access to education for all, and a decent level of income. The closer a country's HDI is to 1.0, the closer it is to attaining those goals.

Source: UN Development Programme (UNDP), *Human Development Report 2009* (New York: UN Development Programme, 2009), http//hdr.undp.org/en/reports/global/hdr2009/ (accessed 2/2/10).

more pronounced. Caused by many factors—colonialism, earlier industrialization of Europe, geography, poor government policies, unaccountable governments—this is the development gap, or development trap.[8]

Proponents of economic liberalism point to the progress made in closing that development gap. Average per capita incomes in developing countries have doubled over a fifty-year period, the gross national products (GNPs) of some economies have grown by more than 500 percent, and the same countries enjoy an increasing share of exports. However, detractors of economic liberalism, including many radicals and some working within the UN development community, point to a different set of indicators. They contend that the gap between rich and poor is actually increasing. The share of world income held by the richest 20 percent is 86 percent, whereas the share of the poorest 20 percent has declined over the years to 1.1 percent of world income. All agree that the gap between rich and poor needs to be narrowed by supporting economic growth and development.

In liberal economic theory, trade liberalization based on comparative advantage is viewed as a key engine of economic growth. Less clear is whether economic growth at the aggregate level will lead to economic improvement in the lives of individuals. Ideas about how development occurs have evolved from the work of state policy makers, and officials within the UN system and within such institutions as the World Bank. In the constructivist perspective, there has been a conflict over different economic ideas and development norms.

Although the World Bank has remained largely committed to liberal economic policy, there has been some debate over the appropriate approach.[9] During the 1950s and 1960s, the bank, like other development institutions and major donors such as the United States, adopted a strategy for development that emphasized the critical role of large infrastructure projects such as dams, electric power, and telecommunications. In the 1970s, realizing that not all groups were benefiting from such investments, the bank began to fund projects in health, education, and housing, designed to improve the economic life of the poor. During the 1980s, the bank shifted toward reliance on private-sector participation to meet the task of restructuring economies and reconstructing states torn apart by ethnic conflict. In the 1990s, **sustainable development,** an approach to economic development that incorporates concern for renewable resources and the environment, became part of the bank's rhetoric, although that rhetoric did not always translate into its practices.

Of these various changes, the bank's support of private-sector participation in reconstruction and development has been the most profound. When areas of the economy are privatized, the government's fiscal burden is reduced, and state spending in education and health can then increase. This approach to economic growth has become known as the **Washington Consensus,** a version of liberal economic ideology. Its adherents hold that only with certain economic policies—including privatization, liberalization of trade and foreign direct investment, government

FIGURE 9.2 | IMF Structural Adjustment Programs

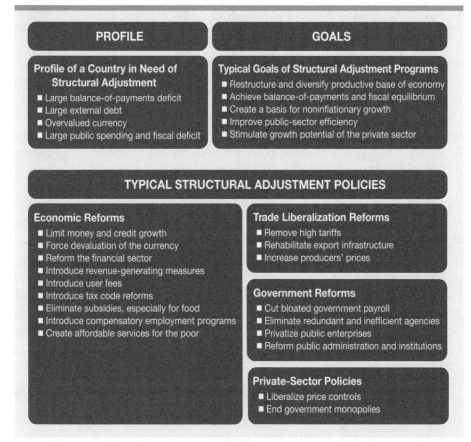

deregulation in favor of open competition, and broad tax reform—will development occur. The bank and its sister institution, the International Monetary Fund, are leaders in advocating these policies.

Although the IMF was not originally charged with development, very quickly, it realized that many countries' seemingly temporary balance-of-payments problems were actually long-term structural problems that prevented those countries from developing and that the IMF's short-term loans could not address. Thus, during the early 1980s, the IMF began to provide longer-term loans if states adopted **structural adjustment programs** consistent with the Washington Consensus. If a state adopted those policies, the IMF gave its stamp of approval, leading other multilateral lenders as well as bilateral and international private banks to lend as well (see Figure 9.2).

During the 1990s, it became apparent that even under structural adjustment, some countries could not get out from under the weight of debt and begin to develop. That debt had been escalating; developing countries owed $2.2 trillion in 2000; twenty years earlier it had been $577 billion. There was also mounting pressure for adopting a more systematic approach to debt. Buoyed by Jubilee 2000, a social movement that promoted changes in the name of social justice and supported by radicals who thought debt doomed states to permanent under-development, a major policy shift occurred, sponsored by the IMF, the World Bank, and the G7 economic powers. The Heavily Indebted Poor Countries (HIPC) Initiative was a historic one, for never before had foreign national debt been canceled or substantially rescheduled. While implementation of the plan and its attendant conditions has been slow and controversial, by 2008, fourteen states had all of their debt canceled.

Uganda was one beneficiary, with the cancelation of $126 million in debt. The Ugandan president, Yoweri Museveni, invited both local and international NGOs to play a role in developing debt-reduction strategies beginning in the 1990s. His government, working with NGOs through the Uganda Debt Network, implemented sound macroeconomic policies and poverty reduction strategies by slowly decreasing public expenditures. That network also initiated a number of consensus-building activities to campaign for debt relief, including the Jubilee 2000 campaign, and established a Public Information Center to provide electronic and audiovisual information to both the NGOs and the public. A Poverty Eradication Action Plan made major poverty issues top priorities and allotted appropriate resources for school construction, feeder roads, and water systems, developed by local communities during the consultative process. Debt relief proved to be part of the answer for some countries.

Until the beginning of the 1990s, the Soviet Union and its allies were not members of the Bretton Woods institutions. However, the demise of the Soviet Union, and with it the transition to capitalism in Russia and other former communist states, gave the IMF another role. The IMF played an active role, giving $27 billion in assistance to help Russia and the other former communist countries make the transition to market economies. The goal was to make that adjustment an orderly one. IMF credits have helped to replenish state reserves, keeping those countries out of major debt. The results have been mixed, with the most advanced economies able to achieve success, liberalizing foreign trade and keeping inflation down.

With the IMF initiating such programs, the distinction between the IMF and the World Bank has become blurred. A broad consensus has emerged among virtually all states on the viability of market-oriented economic policies and political pluralism as the foundation for sustainable economic development. The South cannot develop in the same way that Great Britain, the United States, Germany, and other industrialized nations did. Scarce natural resources cannot be exploited as in the past; sustainability means that growth can be ensured for future generations. There must be more emphasis on human development—education and health. The targets of development—the people—should have a say in how funds are allocated.

NGOs play a critical role in this new approach, organized at the grassroots level to carry out locally based projects. NGOs such as World Catholic Relief, Oxfam, and Doctors without Borders not only deliver food and medical assistance during emergencies but also distribute seeds, drill wells, and plan local-level projects that they hope will bring economic development. NGOs can also be an alternative channel for finance to individuals and small groups, often neglected by the national or international banks. One particularly effective effort has been the Grameen Bank in Bangladesh. Created in 1983 by an academic turned banker, Muhammad Yunus (who won the Nobel Prize in 2006), the bank provides average loans of $100, although many loans can be as small as $20.

The Grameen Bank has been a tremendous success. It now has more than two thousand branches, each run as a franchise by staff trained in established branches. Branches borrow money from headquarters at 12 percent interest and lend money at 20 percent, providing the franchisees considerable opportunity for profit. The bank has made loans to more than 7.5 million borrowers, moving over one-half of those above the poverty line. Its loan recovery rate is 97 percent! The effects are more than economic: in families that have received loans, more children attend school, nutrition levels are higher, and child mortality is lower.[10] The microfinance model, rooted in the economic empowerment of women, has been duplicated in more than 450 microfinance institutions. Such institutions increasingly work with others, the private sector or public partnerships.

Yet the important question is, with economic globalization, are benefits being distributed fairly? Is the development gap being closed both between countries and within particular countries? The UN has undertaken the tasks of setting the goals of sustainable development and monitoring its progress. In 2001, the UN-sponsored Millennium Summit set forth eight goals known as the Millennium Development Goals (MDGs). These goals are designed to reduce poverty by 2015 and promote sustainable human development in direct response to globalization. Each substantive goal (poverty reduction, better education, improved health, environmental sustainability, and global partnerships) has specific targets, time frames, and performance indicators, along with an implementation plan (see Figure 9.3).[11]

Substantial progress toward achieving these goals has been made. The total number of those living in extreme poverty in the developing world was slightly more than 25 percent in 2005; in 1990, that figure was 50 percent. That still translates to about one-quarter of the world's population living on less than $1.25 a day. Enrollments in primary education are up to 88 percent in 2007, increasing 5 percent since 2000. The biggest increases were in sub-Saharan Africa and South

FIGURE 9.3 | The Millennium Development Goals

Goal 1: Eradicate extreme poverty and hunger

Halve proportion of people living on less than $1.50 a day and proportion that suffer from chronic hunger.

Goal 2: Achieve universal primary education

Ensure that all children complete full course of primary education.

Goal 3: Promote gender equality and empower women

Eliminate gender disparity in primary, secondary, and tertiary education.

Goal 4: Reduce child mortality

Reduce the mortality rate of children younger than five years by two-thirds.

Goal 5: Improve maternal health

Reduce by 75 percent the maternal mortality rate by 2015.

Goal 6: Combat HIV/AIDS, malaria, and other diseases

Reverse the spread of HIV/AIDS. Slow spread of malaria and other diseases.

Goal 7: Ensure environmental sustainability

Halve the proportion of people without sustainable access to safe drinking water and basic sanitation.

Goal 8: Develop a Global Partnership for Development

Address special needs of least-developed countries, including more generous development assistance.

Asia (15 and 11 percent increases, respectively). Even considering the growth in population, child mortality has declined, dropping from 12.6 million in 1990 to about 8.8 million eight years later. The Asian and Pacific countries have been generally on track to meet the development goals. In these two regions, accounting for about one-half of the world's population, access to drinking water, hunger reduction, and access to sanitation are all improving, thanks to the progress in China and India. Yet the repercussions of the global economic crisis, explained below, suggest possible negative economic growth, diminished resources, and reduction in trade and aid for the developing world. Most notable, hunger in the developing world appears to be on the rise, with children bearing the cost. As unemployment escalates, meeting gender-equality goals appears less likely, because women are often in insecure positions. In light of these changes, the critics of economic liberalism have found a stronger voice.

Critics of International Economic Liberalism

The triumph of economic liberalism in the twenty-first century has not been without its critics. These include both traditional critics of the theory of economic liberalism and critics of particular policies, most notably of the international financial institutions.

As they did in the seventeenth and eighteenth centuries, old-style mercantilists, with their interpretation of statism, argue that economic policy should be subservient to the state and its interests; for them, politics determines economics. This mercantilist thinking dominated explanations of the economic success of Japan as well as that of the newly industrializing countries of East Asia during the 1960s and 1970s, as discussed above. Those states used their power to harness industrial growth. Consistent with mercantilist and statist logic, they singled out certain industries for special tax advantages; they promote exports over imports and encourage education and technological innovations to make their respective economies more competitive internationally. Those governments could then harness MNCs in the state's interest. Setting national economic and political objectives above international economic and political objectives, statists see MNCs as economic actors to be controlled. They suggest imposing national controls on MNCs, including denying market entry to some of them; using taxing powers to control repatriation of profits; and imposing currency controls. Mercantilists, like realists, believe that the international system is dominated by competition among states for power. States will take any action necessary to survive, protecting their self-interests.

Radical theorists have also been critical of the liberal economic path, just as they were in the nineteenth century. Development has not occurred, and for dependency theorists particularly, multinational corporations are the culprit; they exploit the resources of the poor; they perpetuate the dominance of the North and the dependency of the South. So whereas economic liberals value the interdependencies that MNCs create, radicals see them as instruments of dependency, exploitation, and even imperialism. Decisions made in the economic and financial centers of the world—Tokyo, Berlin, New York, Seoul—create an inherently unequal and unfair international economic system. That system must significantly be altered. Because developing states cannot adequately control multinational corporations, and because many of the leaders of these states have been co-opted by those very MNCs, radicals have sought international regulations in many forums. These views undergirded much of the thinking and the agenda of the developing countries in the 1960s and 1970s. The New International Economic Order (NIEO) is one manifestation of such thinking. The Group of 77 sought changes in major areas of international economic relations: adjustment in the terms of trade by stabilizing the prices of commodities the less-developed countries (LDCs) exported, greater authority over natural resources and foreign investment, more favorable arrangements for technology transfer, relief for debt, and restructuring of the international financial institutions. Most of those policies were not reformed, but the debt and restructuring proposals remain prominent on the agenda for the twenty-first century, a remnant of the theoretical split between economic liberalism and radicalism over the international political economy.

Not all the critics are radicals. Reformers both outside and within the international financial institutions question both governance and specific policies.[12] In terms of governance, reformers propose altering the weighted voting system used by the IMF and the World Bank in favor of greater representation for the emerging economies. In the current system, the major donors are guaranteed voting power commensurate with their contributions. The largest share holders in each institution—the United States, the European Union states, Japan, and Canada— hold about 60 percent of the total votes. Reformists believe a more representative voting structure might lead to the promotion of different policies. Further, hiring a more diverse group of bureaucrats, instead of the current predominance of economists trained in Western developed countries, might bring new, innovative solutions to development dilemmas.

Other reformers are critical of specific policies; here the critics differ. On the one hand, some argue that both the IMF and the World Bank have strayed too far from their liberal economic foundations, taking on too many different tasks (trying to promote an environmental agenda or gender equality) and deviating from actions promoting market liberalization. In fact, some maintain that aid and loans themselves should be allocated by competition, creating a liberal market for aid funds. Radical political economists also blame the international economic institutions, particularly the World Bank and the IMF, for perpetuating economic inequality by promoting the interests of private international capital. In his aptly titled book *Imperial Nature,* Michael Goldman suggests that both the bank and the multinational corporations are merely profit seekers.[13] Development dollars distributed by the bank bring economic returns only to the North, to the rich, developed countries whose firms provide the services for the dams and power plants. Other bank policies that have been rigidly developed without considering local conditions and local knowledge end up disproportionately affecting the disadvantaged sectors of population: the unskilled, women, and the weak.

The World Trade Organization has also become a lightning rod for domestic groups from many countries. They feel that the WTO, a symbol of economic globalization, is usurping local decisions and degrading the welfare of individuals. NGOs are some of the major critics of WTO activities. Some of them oppose the idea that the WTO has the power to make regulations and settle disputes in high-handed ways that intrude on or jeopardize national sovereignty. Still others fear that promotion of unregulated free trade undermines the application of labor and environmental standards; they believe that the WTO sets economic liberalization above other social values. We will examine these views in the section on the antiglobalization movement, discussed later in the chapter.

The Key Role of Petroleum Markets

No international economic issue and no single commodity is more connected to economic globalization than petroleum. Ever since World War II, the industrialized countries have relied on crude oil as their fuel for economic development and growth. For many years, the United States was both the largest producer and largest exporter of oil. The other developed countries, including Japan and Europe, had few domestic sources, making them dependent on cheap Middle Eastern petroleum. Most developing oil-producing countries with low levels of industrialization had excess capacity and thus were eager to sell. This fundamental interdependency between producers and consumers, between developing countries and industrialized countries, has changed. World demand for oil has escalated. Since 2000, 84 percent of that increase has come from the emerging markets, including India and China. And despite intense exploration for new oil fields, supplies of conventional oil and natural gas remain limited. Those supplies are unevenly distributed around the world, making these commodities key items in international commerce, valuable sources of earnings for producer states, and key ingredients of state power, as explained in Chapter 5. The fact that over 60 percent of the world's oil reserves are located in the Middle East—25 percent in Saudi Arabia, 11 percent in Iraq, and 9 percent in both the United Arab Emirates and Iran—makes that region politically powerful.

Several other key changes have made petroleum crucial to understanding economic globalization in the twenty-first century. The Western oil giants known as the Seven Sisters—Exxon, Mobil (now Exxon-Mobil), Texaco, Shell, Standard Oil of California, British Petroleum, and Gulf—controlled the production of oil and hence the supply from the 1930s to the late 1950s. But it was the very actions of these MNCs that caused the oil-exporting countries to seize the initiative. In 1959 and 1960, the multinational oil companies acted in unison, but without consulting the oil-exporting countries, to reduce average crude prices from 5 to 7 percent to compensate for the world glut in oil. In response to that action, the Arab producer states and Venezuela met for the first time in 1960 to restore prices to former levels and develop plans to unify policies. The Organization of the Petroleum Exporting Countries (OPEC) was born.

During the 1960s, OPEC consolidated its power. States such as Libya and Algeria won significant concessions from the oil companies and thus increased their revenue from oil exports. Iraq and Iran joined, and in 1968 the producers in the Gulf region formed their own subgroup, the Organization of Arab Petroleum Exporting Countries (OAPEC). Nigeria and Indonesia became more active participants as their oil production increased. The balance in power shifted from the multinational oil companies, which still possessed the necessary technology and technical skills, to the oil-exporting states themselves and their state-owned companies. Today OPEC's twelve members produce about 40 percent of the world's oil. But the number of oil producers has expanded to include Norway, Mexico, Angola, Azerbaijan, and Russia. These states, sharing 60 percent of the world's production, are not members. Although neither OPEC nor any one producer no longer has the power to control the international oil market, a significant realignment of power has occurred.

The structure of the international oil market has also changed as the result of a number of shocks, each demonstrating the repercussions of economic globalization and its political ramifications. In 1974, the Arab members of OPEC began an embargo to withhold oil from states supporting Israel, causing a significant increase in oil prices (and hence revenues) and substantial economic disruption in both the United States and the Netherlands, both of which were embargoed. Inspired by OPEC's success, Southern producers of other primary commodities joined the bandwagon, forming cartels in copper, tin, cocoa, coffee, and bananas. Although these other cartels met with little success, OPEC members enjoyed the economic benefits of their political actions. This first shock brought home to the American policy makers and the public the issues of natural resource interdependence and potential vulnerability. Americans were forced to cut back on driving in order to conserve fuel, were relegated to inconvenient lines at the pump, and had to pay much higher prices for that privilege.

Another shock occurred at the end of the 1970s following the seizure of power by Islamic fundamentalists in oil-rich Iran. Although Iran's output accounted for less than 20 percent of OPEC exports, oil prices escalated dramatically in the face of the shortage and the possibility that oil could once again be a political weapon. Panic set in, as import bills for petroleum increased three- to fourfold. The outbreak of the Iran-Iraq war in 1980 only exacerbated the situation, destabilizing oil markets further, with a 10 percent drop in world production. The 1991 Gulf War resulted in a short-term doubling of oil prices. Iraq's invasion and occupation of Kuwait cut both Iraqi and Kuwaiti production. When Iraq burned Kuwait's oil fields in its hasty retreat, production was cut even more. As in earlier crises, markets also feared that oil production in Saudi Arabia would be affected or transportation routes blocked, neither of which actually occurred. The panic that spread throughout both the international petroleum and international financial markets clearly confirms the economic interdependence characteristic of globalization.

Whereas these shocks emanated from threats to supply principally in the Middle East, the two most recent shocks emanated from demand. Since 2000, demand for oil has grown by 7 million barrels a day, 2 million barrels of which are destined for China and to a lesser extent, India. This demand has led both countries to seek new sources of oil to compensate for supply shortfalls in Venezuela and Iraq. That has led to a rush by the oil companies to find new sources of petroleum; China and India are eager to find reliable new suppliers in Africa, Central Asia, or the Middle East, putting themselves in competition with the United States and Europe.[14] Prices of oil rose to a high of $145 a barrel in mid-2008, resulting in serious repercussions for food prices and fuelling worldwide inflation. Yet just as rapidly, demand for oil fell with the onset of the global economic crisis of 2008–9. Oil prices plunged as low as $33 a barrel in the same year. That crisis is explained at the end of this chapter. Add to the 2008–9 crisis the recognition that global warming is caused by the burning of fossil fuels and it becomes clear that the international petroleum markets are in midst of a major transition. Producers and consumers are scrambling for alternative energy sources to slow the process of global warming and reduce their dependence on the oil-exporting states.

These changes in international petroleum market dynamics have had political implications. Oil-dependent states vying for contracts have changed or modified their political allegiances to improve their chance for a reliable oil supply. For example, after 1974, Japan not only adopted a domestic policy to lessen its dependence on foreign supplies but has also tilted toward support of the Arab political position in the Middle East in hopes of securing supply routes. In the wake of the the latest oil shock, China has refused to censure Sudan (the third largest producer in Africa) for its policies in Darfur for fear of losing new oil concessions. Some observers have argued that U.S. intervention in Iraq in 2003 can be partly explained by its desire to ensure steady oil supplies from that state and region.

Oil-producing states have enjoyed a massive increase in oil revenue. Many have formed sovereign wealth funds, investing billions of dollars in the international financial system. States with such wealth have the power to pursue domestic policies that are largely immune to international influences. For example, the so-called petrostates such as Russia, Kazakhstan, Nigeria, and even Saudi Arabia have been able to continue repressive antidemocratic domestic practices, knowing that criticism will be muted and consuming states unlikely to initiate sanctions to force destabilizing domestic changes. These same states can use oil as a strategic weapon, as Russia did in early 2006 when it cut natural-gas supplies to Ukraine after the latter refused to agree to price increases. The supply was restored only after Ukraine was forced to make concessions. Part of Russia's strategy was to use its oil and natural resources as a wedge to renew its claim to superpower status. Similarly, Venezuela used its petrodollars to pay off Argentina's loans to the IMF to lessen that country's dependence on the U.S.-supported institution. This posture led two commentators to suggest "an emerging 'axis of oil' that is acting as a counterweight to American hegemony on a widening range of issues."[15]

Natural resources like oil can generate enormous wealth for states, but that wealth may not benefit all members of society. Oil pipelines are often targeted by groups who are dissatisfied with the government or foreign oil companies, as in this photo from Nigeria, where a rebel militia was suspected of using dynamite to damage a shell pipeline.

Even international institutions have found it more difficult to exercise their influence in getting the oil-producing states to comply with international agreements. When petroleum was discovered in Chad, the World Bank provided partial funding to build a pipeline that would deliver the product to port, with the proviso that the country use its 40 percent in government revenue to improve the life of its 9 million poor citizens. Chad was to be the new model for how oil could be used as an engine of development in Africa. But that experiment has proved short lived: the oil-empowered government elites have broken their promises.

Finally, as oil has become more valuable, it has become a target for groups (both indigenous or international) trying to disrupt established governments by blowing up pipelines and interrupting supply. Nigerian pipelines, for example, are continually compromised by the actions of people in the Delta region who feel that their development needs are not being met. Similarly, the Iraqi pipelines are the object of attacks by terrorists who hope to undermine further that country's economic recovery and general stability. Al Qaeda and its affiliates have tried to attack Saudi facilities. No wonder the new pipelines across the Caucasus Mountains are in growing need of military protection, as ethnic groups and terrorists find that these lifelines have become new areas of state vulnerability. Indeed, the entire oil-supply market chain is vulnerable, another unintended consequence of globalization.

With economic globalization, an integrated market has emerged, linking key producer and consumer states not only with multinational companies but also with international investors and financial markets. After all, although petroleum is traded as a physical commodity, it is also traded as a financial asset—not only by oil traders but by others seeking high returns on capital—pension funds, money managers, hedge fund managers, and university endowments. Thus, the rise and fall of oil prices have a domino effect throughout the international financial system. Shifts in the distribution of power among these primary players have led to the emergence of petroleum not just as an ordinary traded commodity but also as a political weapon, with implications for the economic, political, and even strategic decisions that states, international organizations, and even subnational and transnational groups make.

Economic Globalization and Regionalism

Although economic globalization has emerged as the defining characteristic of the international political economy, regionalism has also been growing. Especially since the 1990s, more regional economic arrangements have been negotiated, and those already operational have been strengthened. What is the relationship between globalization and regionalism? Is this regionalism another step toward increased, enhanced globalization? When state barriers are removed in favor of regional markets and economies expand, will globalization be broadened? In other words, are the regional blocs trade-creating devices an extension of economic liberalism? Or is trade actually being diverted from one state or region to another? If regional blocs are trade-diverting devices, then regionalism is an extension of mercantilism. Is regionalism, then, a stumbling block to globalization? There is no doubt that the establishment of the European Union (discussed in Chapter 7) and the accompanying economic integration have had a major impact on the international political economy and have become as models for other regions.

European Economic Integration

European economic integration was predicated on the notion that a larger market, along with the free movement of goods and services, would permit economies of scale and specialization to stimulate growth; opportunities for investment would be enhanced; and competition and innovation stimulated, all goals compatible with liberal economics, albeit at the regional rather than the international level. The European Union has proven successful in achieving some of these objectives, creating a single market and developing a monetary union. Yet to achieve these objectives, the EU has also relied on protectionist measures, and in doing so, may have only diverted trade from one group to another.

European economic growth had been sluggish since the mid-1970s, when the United States and Japan were increasingly competitive. To stimulate Europe's growth and hence its international competitiveness, the Single European Act of 1987 accelerated the integration process, setting the goal of achieving a single market by 1992. That involved removing physical, fiscal, and technical barriers to trade and harmonizing national standards by adopting over three hundred community directives. Some parts of the goal were quickly achieved, for example, the elimination of customs barriers. Other areas have proved more problematic, notably the movement of persons. Although most countries eliminated passport controls and adopted similar visa rules, recognition of education and professional qualifications has also proven a thorny issue. Abolishing technical barriers to trade has been difficult because of differing health and safety standards, but the process is ongoing, as is the effort to break state monopolies and eliminate state aids to specific sectors.

The overall results have been positive, with the growth of all types of economic transactions across state borders, deepening integration among the national economies of the twenty-seven member states. Exports of goods and services are over one-third of the GDP for the average EU member. Over 70 percent of total trade in goods is conducted with other EU members. Not only is trade integrated but also capital flows; cross-border mergers and acquisitions have accelerated. The broad consensus is that European integration has resulted in greater trade creation and has also had a positive welfare effect on member and nonmember states.[16]

The EU is more than a regional trading area or a single market. During the discussions for the single market, the outlines of a monetary union were also negotiated. With monetary stability and a single currency, the union would grow and prosper even more. The European Monetary Union, set forth in the Maastricht Treaty in 1991, called for the establishment of a single currency, the euro, and a common monetary policy. The euro became the unit of exchange for businesses in 1998 and for consumers in 2002. Members that have agreed to these provisions—and not all have—no longer can use exchange rates and interest rates as instruments of economic policy. Whether the creation of the monetary union has stimulated the integration process further is subject to much debate. Yet most observers agree that the euro has facilitated business transactions and eliminated the uncertainty caused by fluctuations in exchange rates. Thus, through both a single market and a common monetary policy, the EU can voice a unified position in global economic affairs, although it does not always do so. These events have been an example for other parts of the world to follow, as explained below.

The European Union very early recognized, just as international trade negotiators did, that agriculture was different. Agricultural prices dramatically fluctuate with weather and disease, so there has long been a strong incentive to moderate the price fluctuations caused by supply volatility. Foodstuffs are viewed as vital for national security; in emergencies, no state wants its population to depend on others for food. In many countries, the well-organized farm sector enjoys disproportionate political power. For all these reasons, the EU adopted the Common Agricultural Policy (CAP). Contrary to free-trade ideology, the EU purchases surplus crops from farmers at guaranteed prices, then either stores it, anticipating higher prices, or donates it to food aid programs, absorbing the losses. Farmers are subsidized to the tune of over $45 billion annually, requiring a significant portion of the EU budget, although changes adopted in 2008 overhaul the subsidy programs and reduce payments to larger farmers. The CAP has proved to be one of the most controversial policies of the EU. Not only has it been a major issue for states seeking membership and wanting their share of the agricultural budget, but it is also a critical issue in multilateral negotiations, because nonmembers pay more for EU agricultural products.

Aside from the CAP, have the EU's policies contributed to economic globalization or proved an impediment? Most economists agree that the openness of the European markets has not only benefited Europeans but has also become increasingly compatible with the goals of the multilateral global system. Indeed, the EU has developed a web of preferential agreements with its neighbors (Mediterranean area) and with former colonies with shared histories (African countries), as well as with other regional trade agreements, including the North American Free Trade Agreement and Mercosur in Latin America. These actions enhance the EU as a global economic power giving it strong leverage against U.S. economic hegemony.[17]

One response by other states to the economic power and success of the European Union has been to establish their own regional trading blocs or negotiate preferential trade agreements that give their members more favorable access than states outside the bloc have. There has been in fact an explosion of such preferential arrangements, which now number almost four hundred. Among the largest and most successful are the Asia-Pacific Economic Cooperation (APEC), founded in 1989; and the ASEAN Free Trade Area (AFTA), established in 1992. APEC's twenty-one members, including Australia, Canada, Japan, Mexico, and the United States, seek economic cooperation as a counterweight to "Fortress Europe." AFTA's goal is to attract foreign investment to the region, taking advantage of economies of scale. But are conditions in Europe—similarity of economic, political, and social systems; a history of post–World War II cooperation; and the development of nascent community political institutions—also present in other parts of the world?

The North American Free Trade Agreement

The free trade area negotiated by the United States, Canada, and Mexico in 1994 differs substantially from the European Union and other regional schemes. It comprises one dominant economy and two dependent ones: Mexico's and Canada's combined economic strength is one-tenth that of the United States. The driving force behind NAFTA is not political elites but multinational corporations (MNCs) that seek larger market shares than their Japanese and European competition has. The phasing out of many restrictions on foreign investment and most tariff and nontariff barriers has allowed MNCs to shift production to low-wage labor centers in Mexico and to gain economically by creating bigger companies through mergers and acquisitions.

The social, political, and security dimensions we saw in the European Union are absent from NAFTA. Cooperation in trade and investment is not intended to lead to the free movement of labor, as championed by the European Union. The goal is quite the opposite; the United States expects that Mexican workers will *not* seek employment in the United States, because economic development in Mexico will provide ample employment opportunities. And economic cooperation does not mean political integration in NAFTA. As public questioning of the Maastricht Treaty suggests, even Europe may not be ready for this final step in regional integration. With NAFTA, economic integration is to remain just that—confined to specific economic sectors.

The North American Free Trade Agreement supports the phased elimination over ten years of tariff and nontariff barriers. In 2008, the final provisions of NAFTA were implemented, with the elimination of the last remaining trade restrictions on agricultural commodities that the United States exports to Mexico (corn, dry beans, and so on) and Mexican exports to the United States (sugar, certain horticultural products). With the completion of the free trade area and the dismantling of both trade and investment barriers, trade among the three partners was projected to increase. That clearly has happened, with trade in goods and services tripling from $341 billion in 1993 to more than $1 trillion in 2007. Foreign direct investment among the three has increased tenfold, making NAFTA the largest free trade area in the world.[18] Since 2005, the rate of growth in trade has slowed, however, largely because of the growth of trade with China and the latter's admission to the WTO in 2001.

Other provisions of NAFTA deal with property rights of companies making investments in the three countries and with protection of some domestic producers, notably the Mexican oil and gas industry and the U.S. shipping industry. NAFTA's sanitary and phytosanitary measures are designed to protect people and animals from health risks, although such protective measures may not be imposed for economic reasons alone. NAFTA's flexible standards permit national and local

NAFTA benefitted the American, Canadian, and Mexican economies in general but created hardships for certain groups. In 2008, these Mexican farmers protested against the removal of import tariffs on farm goods from the United States, claiming that cheaper U.S. goods would drive them out of business.

governments to impose stricter standards. Export subsidies are eventually to be eliminated, though they are permitted in the Mexican market. There are also incentives for buying within the region. Committees have been established to monitor and promote these various provisions.

Yet the economic controversies generated by NAFTA continue to be profound, illustrating that the state is not a unitary actor. Labor unions in the United States estimate that hundreds of thousands of workers have lost their jobs to Mexico and that over one-third of those individuals will never receive comparable wages again. Environmental groups in the United States fear free trade with Mexico comes at the expense of the environment, with firms in the United States relocating to Mexico to skirt domestic environmental regulations. They point to the degraded environment of the border regions between the two countries. Canadian labor contends that manufacturing in that country is fast becoming a lost art and that the country is becoming too dependent on exports of natural resources. Others fear that Canadian sovereignty is threatened. With economic decisions taken out of the country, its national identity is in jeopardy. Mexican supporters point to the fact that Mexican exports have increased to more than double those of the rest of Latin America combined, and that labor productivity has increased by 50 percent. Yet radical economists point to the slide in real manufacturing wages between 1994 and 2001, with lower-skilled jobs moving to China. Thus, for them, NAFTA is yet another example of U.S. expansionism and exploitation of the Mexican workforce.

The NAFTA case suggests that, as with other regional integration schemes, there will be winners and losers. In NAFTA, agriculture and manufacturing in general may well be the winners. Agricultural markets are better integrated, and consumers enjoy lower prices with virtually all tariffs eliminated. Both Canada and Mexico are now large markets for U.S. agricultural exports. The share of Canadian exports absorbed by the United States has doubled, and agricultural exports from Mexico have almost tripled. Tariffs on manufactured goods have been almost entirely eliminated. U.S.-Canadian trade has grown by 120 percent, and trade between the United States and Mexico has increased 300 percent since NAFTA. But some manufacturers and some groups of individuals have also been losers, with American jobs exported to lower-cost locations. Some Mexican workers are the losers, laboring in environmentally unsafe conditions or losing their jobs to still cheaper production facilities in China. So both radicals and statists have ample evidence to support their analyses.

Just as the EU's success has led to more liberalized agreements with other regions, so, too, has NAFTA's success led to subregional trade agreements. These developments have motivated the United States itself to pursue other bilateral free trade agreements or regional agreements beyond NAFTA. Thus, regionalism may well be a stepping stone to increased economic globalization, though the end of the story has yet to be told.

Emerging Challenges to Economic Globalization

During the waning years of the twentieth century, beliefs about economic theory converged. The principles of economic liberalism proved more effective at raising the standard of living for people worldwide, as the success of both China and Russia suggest. The radical alternatives that were created to foster economic development did not prove viable, even though statist alternatives have remained attractive to some states. This convergence, however, has not meant the absence of conflict over issues in the international political economy.

Economic globalization resulting from the triumph of economic liberalism has been confronted with a number of challenges. Some of those have developed at the local level. In 1994, an army of peasant guerrillas seized towns in the southern Mexican state of Chiapas to protest against an economic and political system that they viewed as biased against them. The date of the protest coincided with the beginning of NAFTA. Feeling that economic decisions were beyond their control, the peasants protested against the structures of the international market, the state, and economic globalization. This rebellion alerted the world to the challenges of globalization. Although NAFTA was designed to promote regional prosperity through trade liberalization, subgroups felt threatened. They were able to tell their side of the story, ironically enough, through the Internet, one of the byproducts of the globalization they opposed.

Some of those challenges, such as the Asian financial crisis, diffused regionally. Shocks in one state were magnified across state borders. Solutions implemented by the international financial institutions in one country proved counterproductive in others. Some groups within the affected countries became the losers, marginalized by structural adjustment programs that did not, they believed, respond appropriately to local conditions. That view reinforced a position already widely espoused by many developing countries—that these institutions were captive to the interests of the developed world.

A wider antiglobalization movement has grown in response to these challenges, often converging at annual meetings of the World Trade Organization and, to a lesser extent, at World Bank and IMF meetings, as well as meetings of the G7/G8.[19] The demonstrators largely shut down the 1999 WTO ministerial meetings in Seattle—and have been buoyed by success in other venues. Although many of these groups had their own agendas—jobs, environment, better labor conditions, local energy—they found unity in wanting more local control and participation in economic governance. These antiglobalizers have also been stimulated by other unanticipated repercussions resulting from the openness of economic markets.

One particularly contentious issue is the movement of labor. At the outset, the EU had adopted the goal of free movement of goods, services, *and* labor. Though the last has not been achieved, the Schengen Accord adopted in 1985 allowed the free movement of nationals from member states who no longer need passports and visas. Individuals from non-EU states have found that once they arrive in an EU country by whatever means, they can move more easily among countries. This has resulted in a flood of illegal aliens seeking better-paying jobs in EU countries as well as to a new market in human trafficking, including women and children for the sex trade. Some of those arriving may even be terrorists who seek to conduct illegal activities against a receiving country. In NAFTA, too, the porousness of the U.S.-Mexican border has fueled antiglobalist sentiments.

The antiglobalizers have been supported by those calling attention to the clandestine side of globalization: the rise of illicit markets.[20] This can include the illegal movement of commodities such as arms or even money to evade tariffs, trade restrictions, and sanctions. Or it can mean the illegal movement of banned commodities such as drugs, human organs, endangered species, or even protected intellectual property. These transnational crimes pose a challenge to the viability of states, as explained in Chapter 5. Thus, states and international organizations seeking the fruits of economic globalization are pitted against market forces that have given rise to undesirable outcomes. No challenge to economic globalization has been greater than the global economic crisis of 2008–9.

Case Study: The Global Economic Crisis

International crises have been a recurrent feature of the global economic system, for example, the Mexican debt crisis (beginning in 1982), the Asian financial crisis (1997–99), the booms and busts of petroleum markets, and market panics. Although Marx saw such crises as a fatal weakness of the capital system, economic liberal theory predicts that the market will regain its equilibrium and the booms and busts will not bring down the global system. Indeed, reforms were undertaken after many of the historic crises to ensure that the underlying conditions would not recur. For example, after the depression of the 1930s, the banking system was reformed. When new states were formed, global financial standards in accounting, bank regulations, and ratings agencies, among others, were developed to improve information and transparency. Yet most of those efforts were aimed at improving financial transparency in emerging markets, using standards adopted from the United States and Great Britain.

What had been neglected was ensuring transparency for the *developed* countries, mainly the United States. The 1980s and 1990s saw an explosion of unregulated (and little understood), highly leveraged financial instruments, including oil futures and derivatives markets. U.S.-based financial institutions and governmental units at all levels were participating in those markets. Excess credit against insufficient equity prevailed across a number of sectors—in the housing market, the financial sector, and consumer credit markets. That spending spree was accompanied by the importation of cheap goods from China, causing an unsustainable trade imbalance with China and with the oil-exporting countries. By 2007, however, it was clear the U.S. economy itself was exhibiting fundamental structural weaknesses, although few policy makers were ready to take action. First to feel the impact was the subprime mortgage market. With financial companies and international banks carrying unsustainable debt, defaults rose, and there were no assets to back up those loans. Credit became more difficult to acquire. Private investment to build factories and produce goods dried up.

What began as a financial crisis centered in the United States rapidly became a global economic crisis. The U.S.-based financial instruments that had spawned the excess lending had been sold abroad to investors ranging from local communities in Norway to banks in Europe and East Asia and investors in Japan and China. What safer place to invest in than the United States! That proved not to be the case. Financial institutions were unable to meet their obligations. Credit became almost impossible to get in the United States and Europe. Businesses cut expenditures and workforces. Consumer demand plummeted. States such as China, South Korea, and Japan, dependent on exports to the United States and Europe, saw their markets shrink and export earnings fall, forcing companies to curb production further. Oil prices dropped by 69 percent between July and December 2008, severely affecting such oil-exporting countries as Russia, Angola, and Venezuela. In emerging markets (especially eastern Europe and states of the former Soviet Union) dependent on private foreign investment, investment plummeted; in 2008 it was less than one-half than that of a year earlier. In late 2008, Iceland became the first state victim when its banking system collapsed and the government declared bankruptcy. European depositors in Icelandic banks in Europe lost their savings.

The Baltic states, the Ukraine, and Eastern European economies virtually collapsed. As international trade declined, world shipping plummeted, with ships languishing in the ports of Singapore and Hong Kong. The speed and depth of the collapse in global financial and international trade markets surprised even the experts.

Initial responses to the financial crisis were mostly unilateral. Both the United States and various EU member governments took unprecedented steps, bailing out banks and insurance companies to get credit markets functioning again and stimulate investor confidence. The United States, many EU governments, Japan, and China each responded with substantial economic stimulus packages to get their respective economies moving again. Some coordinated actions were taken among central bankers. The U.S. Federal Reserve, the European Central Bank, and the Bank of England engaged in currency swaps. The crisis rippled outward to developing countries that faced the prospect of sharply reduced or negative growth and the erosion of gains from globalization-driven growth. The African view from specific countries is instructive (see Global Perspectives box).

The IMF initially responded to the crisis by making available almost $250 billion for credit lines. Iceland became the first Western country to borrow from the IMF since 1976. Substantial loans have also been made to Ukraine, Hungary, and Pakistan. The Spring 2009 meetings of the G20 produced agreement on an added $750 billion for the IMF (including $250 billion in so-called special drawing rights) and more flexible credit lines. The IMF also created the Short-Term Liquidity Facility for emerging-market countries with temporary liquidity problems. It reorganized the Exogenous Shocks Facility, designed to help low-income states by providing assistance more rapidly and streamlining conditions. But the fact was that the IMF's capacity had already been weakened by those preferring market solutions over greater regulation and those wanting to abolish the Bretton Woods system itself.

Critics differ over whether the global financial system needs "a scalpel or a hatchet."[21] Some are reformist, whereas others demand a Bretton Woods II. Reforms within the IMF itself include giving China a more substantial role in the organization, both through a revision of the quota system and having China recycle its $2 trillion in foreign-currency savings through the IMF to stabilize markets and promote development. In that way, the IMF could actively manage currency reserves and have control over emergency assets. Other reforms focus on IMF surveillance functions of both the global economy and national economies, including risk assessment and analysis of exchange rates and external stability risks.[22] Yet improving surveillance capabilities does not necessarily give the IMF the authority and power to convince key states to change policies.

Although the IMF has reemerged as a major player in the immediate crisis, proposals for reform include strengthening other parts of the global financial

The Global Economic Crisis of 2008:
A View from African States

The 2008–9 global economic crisis is a critical test for African states. With its still-low levels of development, minor presence in international markets, strong bank supervision, declining debt, and still relatively small share of foreign direct investment, Africa's trends lag behind other regions. In the recent crisis, African states have encountered several problems particular to their region—as well as some possible advantages.

Africa's economies have shown positive developments. Growth in real GDP averaged 4.1 percent between 1997 and 2002, and since 2003 has averaged over 6 percent. Even on a per capita basis, the growth rate has climbed to over 4 percent, with the continent's GDP per capita having increased to $2,031 in 2007. Private capital investments amounted to $53 billion, a fourfold increase from 2000 to 2006, thanks in part to unprecedented Chinese and Indian economic activity. Under several multilateral debt-relief initiatives, fourteen African countries with a per capita income of less than $380 a year had effectively erased their debt by 2008.

As the 2008–9 financial crisis worsened, the links between the developed and developing worlds became more obvious. Problems particular to Africa include increased prices for imports and reduced demand for exports. Particular states illustrate these problems.

Malawi was not initially subjected to the worst of the financial crisis. Its underdeveloped banking sector and lack of exposure to complex and risky financial instruments limited the immediate negative impact of the crisis. In 2009, however, Malawi saw a reduction in foreign aid of nearly 25 percent from Great Britain. Reduced demand in developed countries affects Malawi's earnings from its major exports, tea, sugar, and tobacco. In addition, with increased unemployment in the developed world, Malawi will likely see a reduction in remittances from Malawians working abroad, which currently comprise 4 to 6 percent of GDP. Within the country, there are fears that the currency, the kwacha, is overvalued. There are calls for a currency devaluation, which would aid the export sector and help Malawi accumulate foreign exchange, but so far President Bingu wa Mutharika has resisted calls for devaluation. With reduced demand for commodities and reduced capital inflows, Malawi is feeling the aftershocks of the financial crisis.

Burkina Faso, one of the poorest African countries, is sub-Saharan Africa's largest producer of cotton. More than 15 percent of the population is employed directly by the cotton sector, with many others benefiting indirectly. The slacking off of worldwide demand for cotton, however, has the potential to harm many sectors of the Burkinabe economy. Cotton producers (like those pictured to the right) have been largely shielded from depressed cotton prices due to the government's price controls, but if prices continue to fall, the support fund may not be able to compensate producers fully, and banks may become overexposed, causing credit markets to freeze and imperiling future production. The government is experimenting with genetically modified cotton to increase yields as a hedge against future instability. However, many factors remain out of Burkina Faso's control, such as international prices, global demand, and liquidity in the international financial sector.

Ghana's outlook is more promising as a world leader in cocoa and gold exports. In 2007 the country discovered a potentially large petroleum field off its coast. The prediction is that Ghana may earn $1 billion annually from oil alone. With a newly elected democratic government, Ghana is in a better position to weather the crisis.

In 2009, President John Atta Mills highlighted three problems Ghana faces due to the financial crisis. One is a weakening in export markets. Fluctuating world demand for cocoa means unpredictable prices for Ghanaian farmers and consequently, more pressure on the government to stabilize prices. Second, although oil in the Gulf of Guinea is accelerating investment, with international credit markets tight and oil demand and oil prices down, that investment, too, may slow down. Third is a reduction in remittances from Ghanaian citizens employed abroad; in 2007 those remittances, at $1.6 billion, totaled more than foreign aid to the country. Rising unemployment is likely to result in a decline in remittances. With sound policies that bring Ghana's deficit under control, increased international capital, and steady revenue from natural resources, the country may emerge relatively undamaged from the financial crisis.

Until the financial crisis of 2008, South Africa had been experiencing more than 5 percent in annual growth since 2004. Such growth reflected high commodity prices, increased domestic household consumption, and sound macroeconomic policies. As the continent's largest economy, South Africa has a well-developed, well-regulated financial sector that allowed borrowing in the local currency. With the onset of the financial crisis, however, South Africa's shortcomings have become apparent. The nation's extremely high unemployment and inequality gaps exacerbate social tensions. High violent-crime rates and the HIV/AIDS epidemic make the country more vulnerable to shocks in the global system. In addition, underperforming sectors in agriculture, mining, and manufacturing have slowed South Africa's economy. Declines in these sectors, along with higher international prices for imported food and energy commodities, have increased South Africa's trade and current account deficits.

South Africa has experienced the same problems that have beset developed European and North American countries: a rapid decline in home prices and vehicle sales and a drop in consumer expenditures. As the largest economy on the continent and the one most tied to international markets, South Africa is most directly linked to recovery in places beyond Africa.

For Critical Analysis

Answer these questions on wwnorton.com/studyspace

1. *What advantages might African countries have in being less integrated into the global economy?*

2. *Explain the African position from the viewpoint of a radical theorist.*

3. *Why do African governments try to shield individual producers and consumers from the effects of international markets?*

4. *The African states most integrated with the global economy have the highest standards of living. How does this support a liberal economic view?*

architecture, both intergovernmental and quasi-private regulatory arrangements. Others have called for a reorganization of the G7, inviting China to join the club. That would reinvigorate the G7 and provide more legitimacy to bodies such as the Financial Stability Forum to develop oversight of the newer financial instruments.

One institution that has emerged as a major player is the G20. From its beginning in 1999 as an informal group of finance ministers and central bank officials, the G20 (and its heads of state from such states as Argentina, Australia, Brazil, China, Germany, and Indonesia) has become increasingly vocal. But the G20 may be too big and hence too unwieldy for macroeconomic policy coordination. States also recognize that reform must be coordinated by quasi-private governance arrangements such as the bond- and credit-rating agencies. These agencies have generally depended on voluntary codes and standards, but had too cozy a relationship with the agencies being evaluated, leading to poor supervision.

The need for reforms is urgent, because the global economic crisis is having extensive impacts on other international and regional economic institutions and states. The failure of the Doha Round had already raised questions about the WTO's future, but the economic downturn has now raised the specter of trade protectionism as states retreat into "beggar-thy-neighbor" policies. The economic crisis is threatening the EU's internal market, economic union, and unity. Non-euro countries have requested massive bailouts from euro-denominated countries, which are better able to weather the crisis, although Greece proved an exception in 2010. With the G20 playing a larger role many groups and changing coalitions will emerge, holding diverse views. China in particular is emerging as a bigger player in reshaping the world economy.

The crisis has also weakened the bargaining power of MNCs, particularly banks, some manufacturing companies, and insurance companies, resulting in calls for better corporate governance and transparency. Although some governments, such as that of the United States, were strengthened by the crisis, others found themselves under intense political pressure, as mass demonstrations in Iceland, the Baltic states, and Greece showed. People still turn first to their own governments for help and solutions, because few understand the complexities of the global economy and its institutions. The real question is, What will the crisis mean for economic globalization? Does it portend the end of economic globalization as now practiced? Or can economic globalization be made more effective, fair, and sustainable?

Mercantilists and statists might not be surprised by the return to the state-level policies protecting their own citizens. Radicals may see the crisis as a critical juncture when greater regulation and major reforms will provide a more just system. Social constructivists regard the contestation over the ideas about the economy as an ever evolving process. Economic liberals believe that the system can be preserved merely with modest reforms, giving more transparency to market transactions.

POLICY DEBATE

Does the global financial crisis mean that the era of economic globalization has ended?

Yes

- The origin of the crisis in the U.S. subprime mortgage market shows the dangers of the Anglo-Saxon (U.S., British) model of financial openness and minimal regulation.
- Large-scale nationalizations and quasi nationalizations of important industries such as banking and automobile manufacture are taking place across the industrialized world, threatening the role of private capital and private-sector-led economic growth.
- Both trade and financial flows have fallen precipitously. To protect its domestic economy, states are relying on higher tariffs and other protectionist measures (restricting contracts to national companies).
- The international institutions that have led economic globalization (the IMF, the G7, the World Bank, and the WTO) have shown that they have neither the tools nor financial resources to deal with the crisis.
- The economies that have been the least adversely affected by the downturn are those, such as India and China, that have intentionally isolated their financial markets.
- Developing countries are experiencing the dangers of being too closely integrated into the global economic system.

No

- The vast majority of WTO member countries have not restricted trade in ways that are inconsistent with international trade rules, with the exception of restrictions on wheat and rice during the 2008–9 food scare.
- The major growing economies of 2009—China, India, and Indonesia—remain dependent on international trade and thus remain committed to the current global trade system.
- No country has pulled out of the European Monetary System to take control of its own monetary policy, even though member states have major disagreements over approach and a wide divergence of the impacts within Europe.
- State and international policy makers have absorbed the major lesson of the Great Depression of the 1930s: trade protectionism and exchange-rate mechanisms designed to export unemployment are ineffective in the long run. They will not repeat that mistake.
- Developing countries continue to try to gain access to international markets, and some nonmembers are still seeking membership in the WTO.

They point to the promising economic recovery in 2010 as evidence that an equilibrium can reemerge.

None of the prominent theories dispute the evolution of globalization, although they disagree about its implications. But globalization is not just a characteristic of the international political economy. It is also reflected in the transnational issues discussed in the next chapter—health, the environment, and human rights.

DISCUSSION QUESTIONS

1. You are a citizen in rural Mexico. In what ways does the international political economy *directly* affect you?

2. You are an adviser to the emir of an oil-rich Gulf state. Outline to the emir the multiple ways that his state is tied to the global economy. Suggest how these ties give the emir power.

3. Liberals, statists, and radicals see multinational corporations in different ways. What are those differences?

4. Explain to a French student, a recent voter in the election for the European Parliament, how the objectives of NAFTA differ from those of the European Union.

KEY TERMS

comparative advantage, p. 287
derivatives, p. 295
direct foreign investment, p. 293
General Agreement on Tariffs and
   Trade (GATT), p. 293
Group of 7 (G7), p. 292
hegemonic stability theorists, p. 285
International Monetary Fund
   (IMF), p. 291
mercantilism, p. 284
moral hazard, p. 296
most-favored-nation (MFN)
   principle, p. 293

offshore financial centers, p. 295
portfolio investment, p. 293
radicalism, p. 286
sovereign wealth funds, p. 295
statism, p. 284
structural adjustment programs, p. 301
sustainable development, p. 300
Washington Consensus, p. 300
World Bank, p. 291
World Trade Organization
   (WTO), p. 296

 Find chapter outlines, practice quizzes, flashcards, and other study and review materials for this chapter at wwnorton.com/studyspace.

10

Transnational Issues

- What are the critical characteristics of transnational issues?
- What characteristics make communicable diseases a particularly difficult transnational issue?
- How do the concepts of collective goods and sustainability help us think about environmental issues?
- Which environmental issues may lead to international conflict?
- What are the different generations of human rights?
- How can international human rights standards be enforced?
- How have contending theories of international relations been modified or changed to accommodate transnational issues?

IN THE UNITED STATES, April 26, 1956 is not much remembered or celebrated, but it should be. What happened on this day would prove to be every bit as revolutionary as July 4, 1776; and every bit as consequential as December 7, 1941 or September 11, 2001. On this day Malcom McLean, a U.S. trucking entrepreneur, shipped a load of trucks from Newark, New Jersey, to Houston, Texas. What was remarkable about McLean's shipment was that his trucks would be transported aboard a converted World War II tanker ship in sealed, locked, and *standardized* containers. On being unloaded at port, the containers could simply be transferred unopened to waiting freight trucks and then sent on to their final destination. McLean did not invent what we now think of as "containerization" (which has gone through a number of important refinements since then), but he was the first to use it in the way that has become standard today.[1] Today, over 90 percent of the world's nonbulk cargo (bulk cargo includes wheat, ore, liquefied natural gas, and petroleum) is transported in container ships, the largest of which can carry as many as 15,000 containers. Each container can be unloaded and then reloaded onto waiting train or cargo-truck platforms without being opened.

The revolutionary consequences of the advent and spread of containerization, as was true of the advent of the railroad in the nineteenth century, were not obvious at first. But within a few decades the process of moving cargo from one place in the world to another had become relatively inexpensive. By the 1980s, the advent and miniaturization of computers would reduce the costs of shipping goods worldwide still further. The implications were staggering. Before World War II, nonbulk cargo had been transported in relatively small ships in nonstandard containers. A great deal of time and expense went into transporting cargo to ports and loading ships on the outbound side, then unloading them and transferring them to train or cargo truck on the inbound side. As these costs dropped, it became cheaper for manufacturers in advanced-industrial states to hire foreign labor to manufacture parts or entire products and ship them to consumer markets than to continue to pay relatively higher wages and benefits to domestic laborers to produce the same goods. By the 1980s, businesses in many advanced industrial countries began to see the huge profit potential in exporting production and assembly abroad. Costly domestic labor and environmental regulations—which depressed profits—could be sidestepped, and the destructive environmental byproducts of heavy manufacturing could be effectively exported to the producing countries. As we will see later in this chapter, the severe harm to air and water quality resulting in large part from this ongoing process of exporting production to the developing world could not be restricted to the producing countries. However, from a business perspective this harm made good sense, because instead of individual firms' having to bear the costs of compromised air and water quality (experienced as a tax on profits), the costs of a compromised environment would be diffused worldwide. The harmful effects might also be less concentrated in consuming countries, where many of these firms have their headquarters.

Perhaps more alarming, the container's very nature—sealed and opaque—makes it an ideal vehicle for smuggling, thus facilitating the inexpensive transfer of everything from human beings (immigrants, terrorists, women and children for sexual slavery) to exotic pets, contraband animal parts or plants, narcotics, and one day even possibly a nuclear device. Human cargo is dangerous not only because some of those "shipped" by containerization may intend harm once they arrive in their ports of destination, but because humans can spread communicable diseases.

But the container ship is only one example of a process that has effectively made the world smaller, often in ways that were not anticipated. (The Internet is another.) States are interconnected and interdependent to a degree never previously experienced. This "shrinking" of the world presents both tantalizing new opportunities and grave new risks. Economic globalization, discussed in the previous chapter, is but one illustration. In this chapter, we introduce four additional and representative transnational issues: communicable diseases, the environment, human rights, and transnational crime. For these issues, we highlight interconnectedness, the interaction among various international actors, and the impacts of these changes on core concepts and on the study of international relations. This provides a framework from which to explore the many other transnational issues that will affect all our lives in the years ahead.

In the twenty-first century, more different kinds of actors than ever participate in international politics: the state, ethnonational challengers, multinational corporations, intergovernmental organizations, nongovernmental organizations, transnational movements and networks, and individuals. The transition from states' being the main actors in international relations to the growing importance of nonstate actors portends a significant power shift. These new actors address a great variety of issues that are substantively and geographically interlinked from the local to the global level. The changes wrought by the global communications and technology revolutions diminish the determinacy of geography and undermine the primacy of territorial states. Distance and time are compressed; important issues can be communicated virtually instantaneously around the globe and to even the most remote villages of the developing world. The ability of state leaders to manage this flow of information has diminished. One aspect of the sovereignty of the state, namely internal control over its citizens, has eroded.

As a result of these changes, transnational issues demand further discussion. These issues are not new. Interest at the local and state level in health, the environment, human rights, and crime has been expressed for generations. These issues touch the quality of people's lives directly and are closely connected to war and strife and political economy. What is new is that there are now *global* identities, interests, and actions involved. How can we think conceptually about transnational issues? How do these issues intersect with the traditional ones of sovereignty, security and economics? Who are the various actors with interests? How would a realist, a liberal, a radical, or a constructivist approach these transnational issues?

Health and Communicable Disease— Protecting Life in the Global Commons

Public health and communicable disease are ancient issues that have never respected national boundaries. Around 1330, the bubonic plague began in China, transmitted from rodents and fleas to humans. Moving rapidly from China to Western Asia and then to Europe, by 1352 the plague had killed one-third of Europe's population,

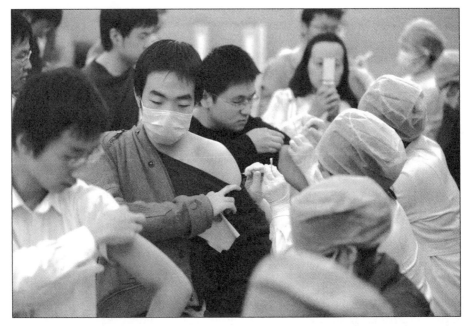

In 2009, outbreaks of the H1N1 virus—known as the "swine flu"—in several countries raised fears of a global epidemic. Here, Chinese students line up to receive a vaccine against the virus.

or 25 million people. The epidemic, like others before and after, followed trade routes. During the age of discovery, Europeans carried smallpox, measles, and yellow fever to the distant shores of the Americas, decimating the indigenous populations. Expanding trade and travel in the nineteenth century within Europe and between Europe and Africa accelerated the spread of deadly diseases such as cholera and malaria, leading to the first International Sanitary Conference in 1851. Between 1851 and 1903, a series of eleven International Sanitary Conferences developed procedures to prevent the spread of contagious and infectious diseases, establishing conditions of quarantine. As economic conditions improved and medical facilities expanded, the prevalence of diseases such as cholera, plague, yellow fever, and, much later, polio declined in the developed world.

Other diseases continued to ravage the developing world, some of them posing a transnational threat. The World Health Organization (the WHO), founded as one of the specialized UN agencies in 1948, tackled two of the most deadly with its 1955 malaria eradication program and its 1965 smallpox campaign. Malaria eradication proved successful in the United States, the Soviet Union, Europe, and a few developing countries, using a combination of the insecticide DDT and new antimalarial drugs. Yet in the developing world, the program failed to curb the disease, as the number of cases of malaria soared in Burma (Myanmar), Bangladesh, Pakistan, India, and much of Africa, where it is still prevalent. Efforts in malaria eradication continue, focusing today on low-cost mosquito netting to protect sleeping children, the most vulnerable victims. In contrast, the smallpox campaign was a stunning success. When the campaign began, there were an estimated 10 to 15 million smallpox cases a year, including 2 million deaths and 10 million disfigurements in the developing world. The last reported case of smallpox occurred in 1977.

Buoyed by the success of smallpox eradication, the WHO has tackled polio. In 1988, when the campaign began, this disease was estimated to paralyze 350,000 children a year. Using an effective and inexpensive vaccine and working with state officials, the WHO has immunized most of the world's population, leading to a 99 percent reduction in cases. Since 2003, however, polio resurged when religious authorities in northern Nigeria halted vaccinations. Cases have developed in Nigeria, Namibia, India, and Somalia.

After the widely hailed eradication of certain transmissible diseases, the international community was caught unawares by the new realities spawned by globalization. Economic and social globalization has had a dramatic effect on the vulnerability of individuals and communities to disease through migration and refugees, air and truck transport, trade, and troop movements. Twenty-first-century mobility has posed major problems for containing outbreaks of newly discovered diseases such as the Ebola virus, hantavirus, SARS (severe acute respiratory syndrome), avian (bird) flu, and HIV/AIDS, as well as for preventing the transmission of older diseases such as cholera, dengue fever, and typhoid. In 2007 WHO regulations were revised to address global health emergencies in a more effective, better-coordinated manner. States committed to notifying the WHO within twenty-four hours of an impending health threat. The WHO would also be able to use nongovernmental resources, such as press reports and the Internet, to report an emergent threat.

These resources and revised reporting standards have come into play most recently with the outbreak of H1N1 (swine) flu in 2009, called a flu pandemic by the WHO. In 1918 a substrain of the H1N1 virus (the "Spanish" flu), killed 50 to 100 million people worldwide. The WHO is committed to preventing another catastrophe and is armed with better tools for communicating crucial information to at-risk publics than ever before in world history. But the same tools that enable the WHO to develop preventive measures and quarantine standards also work against it. The costs of communications of all sorts continue to drop. As they do, more and more human beings will be brought into contact in ways that both benefit the world at large and place it at unprecedented risk.

HIV/AIDS as a Transnational Issue

Of all these diseases, the history of HIV/AIDS is perhaps the most illustrative of the challenges facing the world's peoples in the twenty first century. HIV/AIDS is the quintessential transnational issue. Originally transmitted from animals to humans

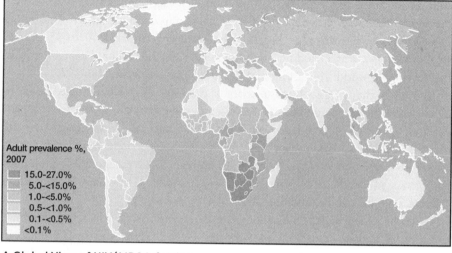

A Global View of HIV/AIDS Infection

Source: UNAIDS, 2008 Report on the Global AIDS Epidemic, Annex I.

in central Africa, it then spread from person to person through the exchange of bodily fluids. Then it was carried by those infected to others around the globe as people traveled among states, all long before any symptoms appeared. HIV/AIDS rapidly became a major health and humanitarian problem, with over 3.1 million deaths annually (an estimated 25 million deaths over the past twenty-five years) and an estimated 33 million people living with the disease. By 2007 the number of AIDS-related deaths had declined to 2 million, but sixty-seven percent of those infected live in sub-Saharan Africa. HIV/AIDS is also an economic issue, disproportionately affecting those in their primary productive years, between fifteen and forty five. As teachers, workers, military personnel, and civil servants are infected, economic development is stymied, and the viability of the military as an institution threatened. It is also a social issue, as families are torn apart and children are orphaned and left to fend for themselves. These children are often then forced to turn to prostitution or join the military in order to survive.

HIV/AIDS is a human rights and ethical issue, as well as a security issue. As the independent International Crisis Group has noted:

> HIV/AIDS can be so pervasive that it destroys the very fibre of what constitutes a nation: individuals, families and communities; economic and political institutions; military and police forces. It is likely then to have broader security consequences. . . . [2]

In 2000 the UN Security Council identified HIV/AIDS as a threat to global security, the first time that a health issue has been so recognized. One of the

UN's Millennium Development Goals is to halt and reverse the spread of HIV/AIDS.

Many different actors have responded to the HIV/AIDS problem, but individual states are key. Some states and leaders seized on the issue very rapidly, launching major public-relations campaigns to inform their populations of risky practices leading to transmission of the virus, distributing condoms, and now facilitating the distribution of life-extending drugs. Uganda, Botswana, and Brazil are examples of states that took initiatives very early. Each has seen the results of its national program as rates of infection have declined. Other states have been very slow to acknowledge the problem, including South Africa, India, and China. Consistent with a state-centric view of international relations, states are critical actors; without their willingness to act and respond openly, programs initiated by the international community cannot penetrate national borders.

Intergovernmental organizations took the leadership role at the early stages. For example, the WHO took steps to help states create national HIV/AIDS programs beginning in 1986. Subsequently, the WHO set standards for specific levels of care and recommendations for drug treatments, adding antiretroviral drugs to its essential drug list in 2002. Following the WHO's initiative, in 1996, the Joint United Nations Programme on HIV/AIDS (UNAIDS) was created, which coordinates cooperative projects among numerous UN agencies, including the WHO, the UN Development Program, and UNICEF. UNAIDS is also designed to promote joint programs with the World Bank, NGOs, corporations, and national governments. Dissatisfaction with UN leadership led to the Global Fund to Fight AIDS, Tuberculosis, and Malaria, an independent institution that uses local expertise and local ownership of issues to advance its cause. By 2009, the fund administered $11.4 billion through 550 individual programs.

Many NGOs have been actively involved in the issue, including Médecins sans Frontières (Doctors without Borders), CARE (Cooperative for Assistance and Relief Everywhere), the International Council of AIDS Service Organizations, and the Global Network of People Living with HIV/AIDS, as well as scores of local NGOs. Some work at the grassroots level, treating victims, and helping families and communities survive. Others train health-care workers in HIV/AIDS care, so that those workers can then spread out around the world to administer that care.

With the development of antiretrovirals to extend the lives of people living with HIV/AIDS, the multinational pharmaceutical companies have become major actors, albeit controversial ones. These drugs became available for treatment in the developed countries in the mid-1990s, but in the developing world, the cost of the drugs—between $10,000 and $15,000 per person annually—made that alternative essentially unavailable. But beginning in 1998, Brazilian and Indian drug companies began manufacturing generics, reducing the cost of the treatment to less than $500 per person annually. This activity was controversial because the World Trade Organization's intellectual-property protection rules prohibit internationally traded generics that violate patent restrictions. Brazil took its case to UN human rights bodies and to the international media, arguing that patients have a human right to treatment. NGOs have led the public campaigns in both developed and developing countries, charging that pharmaceutical companies essentially withhold treatment from patients because of the prices they demand, dooming those people to certain death. On one side of the issue are groups committed to lowering drug prices in order to provide treatment to a larger number of those infected. On the other are those who simply find the cost too prohibitive in any case and who believe that the available funding should therefore be targeted at changing the behavior of those not yet infected. A compromise of sorts has been reached, with the pharmaceutical companies lowering prices for the developing world and the international community raising funds for a variety of prevention strategies, including antiretroviral treatment. Successful use of antiretrovirals explains why the number of people living with HIV/AIDS has increased even as the number of fatalities has stabilized.

The major research institutes—the U.S. Centers for Disease Control and Prevention and National Institutes of Health and France's Pasteur Institute—conduct research and aid in global surveillance activities. Many of these activities are supported by private foundations, for example, the Wellcome Trust of Great Britain and the Rockefeller Foundation, neither often thought of as actors in international issues.

No organization has been more influential in global health than the Bill and Melinda Gates Foundation. Since its establishment in 2000, it has devoted considerable resources to global health initiatives, including combating HIV/AIDS. It supports basic research on prevention as well as national programs in India and Botswana. The 2006 decision by the U.S. businessman Warren Buffet to sign over his wealth to the foundation means that the organization will have assets of over $60 billion. With global health and American education as its two priorities, the foundation directs an unprecedented stream of new revenue toward supporting global health programs.

Individuals such as Bill and Melinda Gates and Bono have used their wealth, prestige, and bully pulpit in the fight against HIV/AIDS. But there are many others. President Yoweri Museveni of Uganda has played a major role in developing his country's response as has Peter Mugyenyi, a Ugandan infectious-disease expert known for his defiant action in administering cheaper HIV/AIDS drugs. In South Africa, it is Zackie Achmat, chairperson of the Treatment Action Campaign; in China, Dr. Wan Yanhai, founder of the Beijing Aizhi (AIDS) Action Project. As in other areas of international life, individuals made a difference.

As with other technical issues in international politics, another new group of actors has become increasingly important not only for HIV/AIDS and other health-related issues, but also critical in international environmental politics as well—transnational communities of experts, or **epistemic communities.** Such groups are composed of experts and technical specialists from international organizations, nongovernmental organizations, and state and substate agencies. Besides sharing a set of beliefs, these communities share expertise, notions of validity and a set of practices organized around solving a particular problem.[3] Members of epistemic communities can influence the behavior of both states and international organizations and have done so on the issue of HIV/AIDS.

Beyond HIV/AIDS

HIV/AIDS is not the only health issue affecting the global community. Other recent maladies have developed that infect animals and individuals. Among the most dreaded are the Ebola virus, mad cow disease, and avian flu, which not only wipe out animals but also can infect humans. Another is SARS (sudden acute respiratory syndrome), which caused worldwide panic in 2003. In each case, the movement of people from the countryside to urban areas, from one urban area to another, and then across national boundaries spreads the disease rapidly to places well beyond its origins. As a result of SARS and the threat of avian flu, new procedures were instituted, both short-term measures (such as a medical strike force ready in six hours) and long-term ones (such as training nationals and forming regional reporting networks).

Yet health issues include more than the transmission of infectious diseases. Like all transnational issues, health issues are broader. They involve regulations to ensure the quality of pharmaceuticals and to control what many consider to be unhealthy behaviors. Although the former is not generally controversial, the latter is. For example, in the early 1970s, health-care workers recognized that bottle-fed babies were dying at higher rates than breast-fed babies because of the use of diluted formula or impure water. Infant Feeding Action Coalition, (INFACT), an NGO, organized boycotts against Nestlé, a major infant formula producer, to push the company to change its marketing strategies. Along with NGOs, the WHO and UNICEF developed a controversial code of conduct regulating the marketing of infant formula. An even more politicized item is on the WHO agenda: tobacco. After years of debate, the WHO's Framework Convention on Tobacco Control came into effect, although its enforcement in the coming years will pit the large, profitable MNCs and states dependent on tax revenue from tobacco companies against health officials and professionals.

Increasingly, health is becoming recognized as a development issue. The economic development gap and the quality of individual lives cannot change without improvements in health conditions. That is why three of the Millennium Development Goals discussed in Chapter 9 are related to improving health, including reducing child mortality and improving maternal health. The fact that during the 1980s the World Bank became the largest multilateral financier of health programs in developing countries confirms the health-development connection. The bank uses a sector approach, funding programs to increase the capacity of national and local health facilities. Even more than a development issue, health more generally is seen in some circles as a human rights issue, just as Brazil argued with respect to access to antiretrovirals. Health is a transnational issue affecting politics, economics, society, and individuals.

A Theoretical Take

Health is an example of a quintessential functionalist issue (see Chapter 7). Virtually everyone agrees that prevention of disease is critical and that good health is desired by all. High levels of consensus are found on the need to prevent the spread of infectious diseases and to rely on technical experts (namely, highly regarded and well-trained medical personnel) to carry out the task. Given these two functionalist criteria, it is not surprising that one of the first historical areas of international cooperation was health. On this issue, liberals, realists, and radicals can all find common ground.

Another feature that all would agree on is the importance of the transnational communities of experts, often a natural outgrowth of functionalist cooperation. These medical experts, found in both public and private institutions and making up an epistemic community, have been key actors providing research and policy advice.

Where liberals, realists, and radicals may disagree is on the correct *approach* to addressing health issues. Liberals, particularly those emerging from an international society perspective, are more likely to focus on international responsibility for dealing with health issues and be willing to utilize all groups possible, including local, substate, state, international, and nongovernmental organizations when appropriate. Realists are more likely to stress individual state responsibility and to acknowledge the importance of health issues when state security is threatened. Radicals see health as yet another issue that illustrates the economic differential between the wealthy, developed world and the poor, developing world. They may be quicker to point to health inequities exacerbated by exploitative working and living conditions. They would be quick to join in the condemnation of multinational companies that are more concerned with bottom-line profits than with social and humane objectives. Radicals would see the reluctance of MNCs to provide HIV/AIDS antiretrovirals at favorable prices as a confirmation of their viewpoint. Yet health is not the only transnational issue.

The Environment—Protecting the Global Commons

Like health, the environment directly affects the quality of our individual and collective lives, as well as the political and economic choices we make. A contemporary perspective on the environment confirms that multiple issues of population, natural resources, energy, and pollution are integrally related. Trends in one of these issue areas affect trends in each of the others. Policy decisions made to address one issue have impacts on each of the others.

Conceptual Perspectives

Two conceptual perspectives help us think about the suite of environmental issues. These perspectives are not contending approaches; rather, they augment each other. First is the notion of collective goods (see Chapter 7). Collective goods help us conceptualize how to achieve shared benefits that depend on overcoming conflicting interests. How can individual herders in the commons be made not to pursue their own self-interest (increasing grazing on the commons) in the interests of preserving the commons for the collectivity? How can individual contributors to air pollution or ocean pollution be made to realize that their acts jeopardize the very collective goods they are utilizing (the air and the ocean)? Collective goods theory provides the explanation for environmental problems, as well as some ideas on how to address these problems.

The second conceptual perspective is sustainability, or sustainable development, as introduced in Chapter 9. How can growth and well-being be achieved simultaneously with environmental protection? Can the policy be implemented without using up the precious capital of the earth? How can development proceed and the earth and its resources be maintained? Employing the criterion of sustainability forces us to think about policies to promote changes that neither damage the environment nor use up finite resources, so that future generations will benefit.

Over time, principles and norms have evolved in customary international law concerning the environment. One core principle is the *no-significant-harm principle*, meaning a state cannot initiate policies that cause significant environmental damages to another state. Another is the *good neighbor principle* of cooperation. Beyond these are "soft law principles," often expressed in conferences, declarations, or resolutions, which although currently nonbinding, often informally describe acceptable norms of behavior. These include the *polluter pays principle*, the *precautionary principle* (action should be taken on the basis of scientific warning and before there is irreversible harm), and the *preventive action principle* (states should take action in their own jurisdictions). New emerging principles include sustainable development and intergenerational equity, both linking economics and the environment to future generations.

International treaties and agreements on numerous environmental issues have also been ratified. As one scholar put it, "the clearest evidence for the ecological trend in world politics is the astonishing array of recent treaties on a host of environmental problems."[4] These include the protection of natural resources such as endangered species of wild fauna and flora, tropical timber, natural waterways and lakes, migratory species of wild animals, and biological diversity in general, as well as protection against polluting in marine environments, on land, and in the air. Each of these treaties sets standards for state behavior, and some provide monitoring mechanisms. In doing so, they are very controversial, because they affect core political, economic, and human rights interests.

By studying three key environmental topics—population, natural resources, and pollution—we can see these conflicting interests. Although each topic may be treated separately, and often is, they are all three integrally related, and each has global implications.

Population Issues

Recognition of the potential population problem occurred centuries ago. In 1798, Thomas Malthus posited a key relationship. If population grows unchecked, it will increase at a geometric rate (1, 2, 4, 8, . . .), whereas food resources will increase at an arithmetic rate (1, 2, 3, 4, . . .). Very quickly, he postulated, population increases will outstrip food production. This scenario is referred to as the **Malthusian dilemma.** Although Malthus did not think productivity would keep up with population growth rates, he did acknowledge wars, famine, or moral restraint as ways to check excessive population.[5] Three centuries later, *The Limits to Growth*, an independent report issued by the Club of Rome in 1972, systematically investigated trends in population, agricultural production, natural resource utilization, and industrial production and pollution and the intricate feedback loops that link these trends. Its conclusion was pessimistic: the earth would reach natural limits to growth within a relatively short period of time.[6]

Neither Malthus nor the Club of Rome proved to be correct (see Figure 10.1). Malthus did not foresee the technological changes that would lead to much higher rates of food production, nor did he predict the **demographic transition**—that population growth rates would not proceed unchecked. Although improvements in economic development would lead at first to lower death rates and hence to a greater population increase, over time as the lives of individuals improved and women became more educated, birth rates would dramatically drop. As people moved to urban areas, birth rates declined. Likewise, the Club of Rome's predictions proved too pessimistic, as technological change stretched resources beyond

FIGURE 10.1 | **World Population Growth, 1750–2150 (projected)**

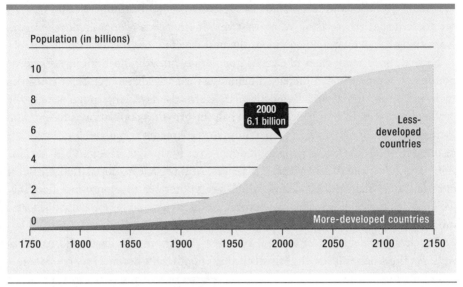

Population (in billions)

2000
6.1 billion

Less-developed countries

More-developed countries

1750   1800   1850   1900   1950   2000   2050   2100   2150

SOURCE: United Nations, World Population Prospects. The 2008 Revision, medium variant (2009).

the limits predicted in its 1972 report. The advent of safe, reliable birth-control technologies also led to a decline in birth rates.

Although Malthus and the Club of Rome missed some key trends, their prediction that population growth rates would increase dramatically has proved correct. Global population growth rates peaked in 1970, but that is not the whole story.

Three key observations make these population growth rates all the more disturbing. First, the population increase is not uniformly distributed. The developing world has much higher population growth rates than the developed world. Fertility rates in the developing world have averaged 3.4 children per woman, while in the developed world fertility has declined to 1.6 children per woman as a result of the demographic transition. Thus, there is a significant demographic divide between the rich North, with low population growth rates, and the poor South, with high population growth rates; 98 percent of the growth in the world population is occurring in the developing countries. In addition, a long tradition of favoring male over female children in India and China has led to an oversupply of males in these two states. By 2020 the estimated number of surplus males aged fifteen to thirty-four in these two countries will reach 57 million. These divides have politically sensitive consequences, as those in the South, laboring under the burden of the population explosion, attempt to meet the economic consumption standards of the North.

Realists see two threats emerging that could destabilize the balance of power. First, states with burgeoning populations and insufficient food might seek to expand their territory or acquire food by means of war. Second, surplus males who might otherwise turn to crime or destabilize the state from within might be channeled into state militaries and "expended" in aggressive wars.[7] Both liberals and radicals see these disparities as confirming that the South needs economic development. Narrowing the demographic divide is the best way to close the development gap.

Second, both rapid rates of overall population growth and high levels of economic development mean increased demands for natural resources. For countries such as China, India, and Bangladesh that already have large populations, the problem is severe. In Bangladesh and Nepal, the growing population is forced onto increasingly marginal land. In Nepal, human settlements at higher elevations have resulted in deforestation, as people cut down trees for fuel, resulting in hillside erosion, landslides, and other "natural" disasters. In Bangladesh, population pressures have led to settlements on deltas, which are vulnerable to monsoonal flooding, which strips topsoil, decreases agricultural productivity, and periodically dislocates millions of individuals.

Accelerating demand for natural resources occurs in the developed world as well. As the smaller (even slightly declining) population becomes more economically affluent, it increasingly demands more energy and resources to support its higher standards of living. People clamor for more living space, larger houses, and more highways, creating more demand for energy and resources.

Third, high population growth rates lead to numerous ethical dilemmas for state and international policy makers. How can population growth rates be curbed without infringing on individual rights to procreate? How can cultural barriers to birth control or to the value of female children be overcome? How can the developed countries promote lower birth rates in the developing world without sounding like supporters of eugenics? Can policies be developed that both improve the standard of living for those already born and guarantee equally high standards and improvements for future generations?

Population becomes a classic collective goods problem. It is eminently rational for a couple in the developing world to have more children: children provide valuable labor and often earn money in the wage economy, contributing to family well-being. Children are the social safety net for families in societies where no governmental programs exist. But what is economically rational for the couple is not economically sustainable for the collectivity. The amount of land in the commons shrinks on a per capita basis, and the overall quality of the resource declines. What is economically rational for a family is not environmentally sustainable. Over time, the finite resources of the commons have a decreasing capacity to support the population.

What actions can be taken with respect to population to alleviate or mitigate these dilemmas? The biologist Garrett Hardin's solution, using coercion to prohibit procreation, is politically untenable and pragmatically difficult, as China has discovered with its one-child policy. Relying on group pressure to force individual changes in behavior is also unlikely to work in the populous states.[8] Leaving coercion aside, even if individuals may desire smaller families, family-planning methods may be unavailable to them. It is estimated that 120 million couples in the developing world want access to such methods but do not have access to them due to high costs or unavailability. Without access to family-planning methods, birth rates will continue to rise, states may be forced to impose coercive restrictions, and abortion rates will rise. What is clear about the population problem is that it is an international one with effects on the whole globe. Decisions affect not just states with high rates of population growth but their neighbors, as people on overcrowded land contend for scarce resources and seek a better life in other countries through migration or turn to violence to get more desirable space.

States are not the only actors affected: this issue involves individuals, couples, and communities, along with their deepest-held religious and humanistic values. It also involves the nongovernmental community, those groups such as Population Connection or the Population Council that are in the business of trying to change public attitudes about population and procreation, as well as the Catholic Church and fundamentalist Islamic sects that oppose artificial restrictions on the size of families. It involves intergovernmental organizations such as the World Bank, charged with promoting sustainable development and yet hamstrung by the wishes of some member states to refrain from directly addressing the population issue. Perhaps most important, the population issue intersects inextricably with other environmental issues. Populations put demands on land use for enhanced agricultural productivity; they need natural resources and energy resources. Thus, ironically, population may well be the pivotal global environmental issue, but it may also be the one that states and other international actors can do the least about.

Natural Resource Issues

The belief in the infinite supply of natural resources was a logical one throughout much of human history, as peoples migrated to uninhabited or only sparsely inhabited lands. Trading for natural resources became a necessary activity once people recognized that those resources were never uniformly distributed. The belief in the infinite supply of key economic resources was dramatically challenged by radical Marxist thinkers. According to Lenin, one of the reasons for imperialism was the inevitable quest for sources of raw materials. Capitalist states depended on overseas markets and resources, precisely because resources are unevenly distributed.

In Chapter 9, we explored how one natural resource—oil—is one of the major issues in the contemporary global economy. But just as population pressures and increased per capita consumption has put a squeeze on energy markets, so, too, has water become a transnational issue.

Fresh water is necessary for all forms of life—human, animal, and plant. Only 3 percent of the earth's water is fresh (one-third lower than in 1970), at the same time that demand is increasing. Agriculture accounts for about two-thirds of the use of water, industry about one-quarter, and human consumption slightly less than one-tenth. It is estimated that by 2025, two-thirds of the world's people will live in countries facing moderate or severe water-shortage problems. Although most freshwater issues are national problems, increasingly such problems have an international dimension.

Several examples illustrate the international controversies and repercussions. American use of the Colorado River for irrigation has not only reduced the flow of that river but also diminished the quality of the water that ends up in Mexico, the downstream user. By the time the river crosses the border, the flow is a trickle and is highly saline, driving Mexican agricultural users out of business. U.S. plans to divert a border canal so that it sends water to thirsty San Diego led one newspaper to headline "Border Fight Focus on Water, Not Immigration."[9] Similarly, Israel's control of scarce water on the West Bank has resulted in rationing in neighboring regions. Hence, the World Bank predicts that in the twenty-first century, water could be the major political issue not only between Israel and Jordan, but also between Turkey and Syria and between India and Bangladesh.

The story is much the same in Central Asia, where two upstream countries with relatively poor land, Tajikistan and Kyrgyzstan, are the water source for areas downstream with good land. Under the old system in the Soviet Union, water was freely available for downstream users. Now, conflict has arisen because water systems are in decay and no new system for water allocation has been developed. Water is scarce in China's northern cities, so the country has embarked on a huge plan to rechannel water from the Yangtze basin via three 1,000-mile channels, at an estimated cost of $58 billion. That is more than twice the cost of China's other major water project, the Three Gorges Dam, the largest construction project ever. Three Gorges is designed to create hydropower. Yet both projects come at an enormous financial cost, diverting money from other sources, and are accompanied by detrimental environmental side effects.

Pollution

As pressures on the commons mount, the quality of geographic space diminishes. In the 1950s and 1960s, several events dramatically publicized the deteriorating quality of the commons. The oceanographer Jacques Cousteau warned of the degradation of the ocean, a warning confirmed by the 1967 Torrey Canyon oil spill off the coast of England. Rachel Carson's 1962 book *Silent Spring* warned of the impact of chemicals on the environment.[10] The natural world is being degraded by human activity associated with agricultural and industrial practices. Economic development in agriculture and industry has **negative externalities**—costly unintended consequences—for everyone, as well as positive ones.

Although many negative externalities may be local, others have national and international implications. Take the case of energy. To meet the rising demand for oil, the United States and China have turned to the oil sands of Alberta, Canada. In times of high oil prices, it becomes economically profitable to convert those sands into oil for use as gasoline. MNCs have heavily invested in the operation. Deleterious environmental externalities are, however, becoming evident. The extractive process requires a massive withdrawal of water, disturbing the fish populations and adversely affecting water quality. The tailing ponds containing extraction residues have proliferated, imperiling wildlife. Forests are cut—the same forests that provide carbon sinks to slow down global warming.

Halfway around the world, China's thirst for energy has led to increased coal usage. Coal-burning power plants emit soot, toxic chemicals, and gases, which, with weather inversions, create air pollution over not only China and neighboring Korea and Japan, but also over the west coast of the United States. These sulfur dioxide emissions carry known health risks—respiratory and heart disease and certain kinds of cancer. China is now taking critical initiatives to replace polluting plants, with some success in improving air quality.

Nothing affects our globe more than the pollution issues of the twenty-first century: ozone depletion and global warming. Both issues have characteristics in common. Both concern pollution in spaces that belong to no one state. Both result from negative externalities associated with rising levels of economic development. Both pit groups of states against each other. Both have been the subjects of highly contested international negotiations.

Thrust onto the international agenda in 1975, ozone depletion illustrates a relative success story with a reversal of the depletion of the ozone layer. States recognized this environmental problem, caused by the emission of chlorofluorocarbons before it grew to crisis proportions and reacted with increasingly strong measures. Both the developed and the developing worlds became involved, with the latter receiving financial aid from the former to finance the change in technology. Substitutes were developed, and MNCS eventually supported the prohibition of chlorofluorocarbons.

The issue of global climate change, or greenhouse warming, has proved more complicated. On the one hand, the scientific facts are indisputable. The preponderance of greenhouse gas emissions comes from the burning of fossil fuels in the industrialized countries of the North. But sources are also found in the developing countries, most notably from deforestation of the tropics caused by agriculture and the timber industry, and from the rising use of fossil fuels in China and India (see Figure 10.2).

The Environment: A View from Indonesia

Increasing economic growth and raising the standard of living of a population can come at the expense of other values, including a commitment to environmental sustainability and improving the quality of people's lives. Indonesia is experiencing firsthand this trade-off between development and environmental quality.

Agricultural production, forestry, and mining are all key sectors in the economy of Indonesia, an archipelago nation of 6,000 islands and 237 million people. Each of these activities is important to the country's economic development. Palm oil, timber, and mineral production all employ people and earn precious foreign exchange. Poor people in Indonesia struggle to find suitable land for agricultural production, often squatting on floodplains and building up the sides of steep mountains or flocking to cities whose infrastructure is old and incapable of handling the influx. The Indonesian government has limited funds for development, and as foreign-owned companies push for bigger profits, state decision makers find it difficult to enforce existing laws.

Indonesia acknowledges that deforestation is a major problem. Prized hardwood trees have been cut or burned deliberately by the MNCs and local operators to speed the clearing process. Natural-growth forests are being replaced by monoculture timber plantations and agricultural crops. Between 2000 and 2005, 1.45 million hectares a year were deforested, second only to deforestation in Brazil. The government estimates that about 10 percent of forestry exports are illegal, but other estimates suggest about 75 percent of the $1.6 billion worth of forest products the EU imported from Indonesia in 2008 came from illegally cut timber tied to multinational corporations. The government says laws against illegal loggers have improved, especially since 1997. But the government also acknowledges continuing problems. Deforestation erodes the soil;

crops are incapable of regeneration; animal species are lost and biodiversity threatened. Deforestation through burning led to massive forest fires in 1987, 1994, 1997–98, and 2005–6. They also resulted in a cloud of haze over Indonesia, especially over the island of Sumatra, that led to poor air quality and respiratory illnesses. Furthermore, in the long term, deforestation leads to an increase in greenhouse gas emissions and contributes to global warming. Its islands vulnerable to rising seas, floods, and landslides, Indonesia now has a strong national interest in slowing down deforestation and thus reducing its greenhouse emissions.

The Indonesian government is also cognizant of the economic needs of its poorest population. People's livelihoods depend on existing old-growth forests from which they harvest nontimber forest products. Some people in the highlands use traditional swidden agriculture. They live in stationary villages, and their fields are rotated through slash-and-burn techniques, then left fallow for the forest to regenerate. But the government also realizes that pressures from population growth, the economic interests of the timber industry, and pressures from national parks and environmental ministries have resulted in a policy making swidden agriculture illegal. Such traditional techniques are seen as a threat to the integrity of the forest for both logging and for protection of nature and biodiversity. Urban Indonesians and those who traditionally farmed at lower elevations also see this less-intensive agricultural technique as "lazy" or "uncivilized." Thus, communities that depend on the forest continually clash with national

such as the building of resorts, requires the use of valuable land resources and may displace people who previously lived in these areas. Though the tourism industry may provide a source of income for people who live in and around the resorts. Questions arise as to whether these new activities can provide the same income-generation possibilities as logging, mining, or other uses of natural resources.

Indonesia's environmental dilemmas, deforestation, and contribution to greenhouse gases have international ramifications. The infamous 1997–98 haze was not confined to the island of Sumatra but spread to neighboring states. In late 2005 and 2006, the haze returned, and the wind spread some of it to neighboring Malaysia.

Indonesian-based umbrella NGOs, such as the Indonesian Network for Forest Conservation and the Indonesian Environmental Network, publicize abuses and institute legal proceedings, frequently teaming with international NGOs such as the World Wide Fund for Nature to establish more sustainable environmental initiatives. The environmental cause may benefit from the effects of recent disasters, such as the 2004 tsunami and flooding in Jakarta in 2007, which may have been worsened by both environmental degradation and poor government economic decisions.

It is in Indonesia's national interest to act responsibly to promote economic development, curb environmental abuses, and especially help alleviate global warming.

authorities over its use. Decentralization of control, urged in part to respect the wishes of forest-dependent communities and advocated by multilateral institutions such as the World Bank, has created new loci of corruption as local governments fight businesses and each other regarding how to best use forest resources.

Mining is also a significant industry in Indonesia. Gold, copper, and coal are mined by several MNCs throughout Indonesia and are viewed by government officials as a vital part of the country's economic development. To extract the highest profits, mining companies often disregard environmental protocols, resulting in polluted water, air, and topsoil. In 2004, Indonesia sued the Newmont Mining Corporation, a U.S.-based gold producer, for emitting toxic mercury vapors into the air. In 2006, the company paid Indonesia $30 million in a settlement to compensate for the pollution.

Before the global financial crisis, tourism was a growing industry in Indonesia and another key to economic development. Tourists bring with them valuable foreign exchange, and the tension surrounding tourism highlights the general debate between the environment and development. Many tourists come to see areas of nature in Indonesia. However, development to accommodate tourists,

For Critical Analysis

Answer these questions on wwnorton.com/studyspace

1. *What conflicting choices does the Indonesian government face?*

2. *How are Indonesia's environmental dilemmas also transnational problems?*

3. *Are Indonesia's problems a tragedy of the commons? How?*

4. *Which, if either, of Garrett Hardin's solutions to a tragedy of the commons is likely to gain political support in the United States?*

FIGURE 10.2 | **Per Capita CO$_2$ Emissions for Select Major Emitters, 2007 and 2030 (Projected)**

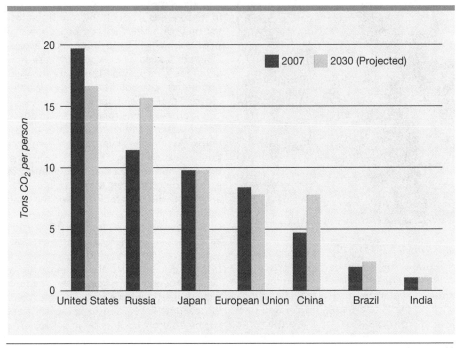

Sources & Notes: This chart is adapted from a previously published version in *Leveling the Carbon Playing Field: International Competition and U.S. Climate Policy Design.* Current–U.S. Energy Information Administration, 2009. Projected–EIA, Annual Energy Outlook 2009. World Carbon Dioxide Emissions and Population by Region, Reference Case. DOE/EIA.

The 2006 report issued by the U.S. National Academy of Sciences concluded that average temperatures in the Northern Hemisphere heated up 1 degree during the last century, much of that during the last two decades. The 2007 findings of the UN's Intergovernmental Panel on Climate Change found that human activity is more than 90 percent likely to be responsible. The two greenhouse gases blamed for retaining heat in the atmosphere—carbon dioxide and methane—have experienced sharp spikes after 12,000 years of relative consistency. The scientific community has found the evidence compelling. As illustrated in the 2006 documentary film *An Inconvenient Truth,* sea levels are rising, glaciers are melting, hurricanes are strengthening as the oceans warm, and weather patterns are becoming more severe, producing more droughts and more flooding.

Although scientists increasingly agree on the problem, politicians and economists have not agreed on the solution. This is not surprising, given the competing interests of various parties. Industrialized countries seek continued high levels of growth fueled by oil and natural gas, and the South wants to become industrialized and enjoy the North's consumer lifestyle, both made possible by oil and gas. So the parties disagree on whether voluntary restraints or market-related responses will be sufficient for both to reach their development objectives and reduce greenhouse emissions. Or are authoritative regulations needed? If regulation is needed, what authority should be invoked—international, state level, subnational, or even local?

The Kyoto Protocol of 1997 amended a weak 1992 UN framework. It provided for stabilizing the concentration of greenhouse gases and delineated international goals for reducing emissions by 2010. Under the protocol, developed countries (including the United States, Europe, and Japan) were to reduce their overall greenhouse gas emissions by at least 5 percent below 1990 levels by 2010; Japan committed to 6 percent, the United States to 7 percent, and the European Union to 8 percent. In neither the Kyoto Protocol nor the earlier agreement were developing countries included in the emission limitation requirement.

The protocol, which expires in 2012, was intended to provide flexible mechanisms designed to make reaching the emission targets more cost efficient. First, trading of international emission shares is permitted. This allows countries that achieve deeper reductions than their targets to trade their surplus shares to other countries. Second, credits can be earned from carbon sinks. Since forests absorb the carbon dioxide from the air as they grow and help slow the buildup of the gas in the atmosphere, states can offset the emissions they produce by gaining credits for planting forests. There is debate, however, over whether sinks can be used to meet all or only part of the emission-reduction required. Third, joint implementation permits countries to cooperate in projects for emission reductions and allows each to receive part of the credit. Each mechanism is a highly complex scientific technique designed to reduce emissions, yet each comes with economic costs that are often difficult, if not impossible, to estimate.

The Kyoto Protocol came into force in 2005, ratified by 156 states—but not the United States. The George W. Bush administration argued that the economic costs of moving away from a fossil-fuel–based economy would be too high, and an unacceptable number of jobs would be lost. The developed Northern countries would be forced to comply with restrictions, whereas the rapidly developing economies like India and China would have fewer restrictions, giving them an unfair economic advantage. From an ideological perspective, the Bush administration opposed international regulations on the issue. Instead, the president argued that markets—higher prices leading to decreased consumption, and a way to trade emission quotas—would be the best way to bring about the necessary changes.

Both European states and Japan signed the protocol and have made efforts to reduce emissions. Negotiations for a replacement treaty continue. All agree that commitment by the United States and China is vital.

In 2009, the new U.S. president, Barack Obama, attended a follow-up to Kyoto (as of 2009, 187 states have signed and ratified the protocol) in Copenhagen, Denmark. Although the president acknowledged for the first time that the United States is responsible for more carbon emission than any other state save China, and pledged to do more to curb emissions, the Copenhagen Accord of 2009 contained little in the way of specific guarantees, and left most environmentalists (and many small developing countries) angry and unsatisfied. Yet the 2008–9 global economic crisis makes a stronger treaty less likely.

Whether or not states decide to act to reduce emissions, global warming will continue to be a high-priority agenda item in the twenty-first century.

Environmental NGOs in Action

NGOs have played a vital role in environmental issues since the 1960s. Although the number of environmental NGOs has grown, as has the number of NGOs generally, their interests are diverse. On the issue of population, the Population Connection advocates population limitations, whereas the Catholic Church opposes artificial birth control. On the issue of natural resources, the Nature Conservancy and the Rainforest Action Network lobby for land protection. The Earth Island Institute and the Global Climate Coalition, the latter an industry-sponsored group opposed to limitations on greenhouse emissions, are concerned with pollution issues.

NGOs perform a number of key functions in environmental affairs. First, they are generalized international critics, often using the media to publicize their dissatisfaction and to get environmental issues onto international and state agendas. For example, Greenpeace's indictment of Brazil's unsustainable cutting of mahogany trees led that country to stop all mahogany exports until forestry practices could be improved. Second, NGOs may function through intergovernmental organizations, working to change the organization from within. For example, NGOs transformed the International Whaling Commission from a body that limited whaling through quotas into one that banned whale hunting altogether. Third, NGOs can aid in monitoring and enforcing environmental regulations, either by pointing out problems or by actually carrying out on-site inspections. For example, TRAFFIC, the wildlife-trade-monitoring program of the World Wildlife Fund and the International Union for the Conservation of Nature (IUCN), is authorized to conduct inspections under the Convention on International Trade in Endangered Species of Wild Fauna and Flora (CITES). Fourth, NGOs may function as part of transnational communities of experts, serving with counterparts in intergovernmental organizations and state agencies to try to change practices and procedures on an issue. One such epistemic community formed around the Mediterranean Action Plan of the UN Environmental Program. Experts gathered to discuss ways to improve the sea's water quality, data were shared, and monitoring programs were established. These same individuals also became active in domestic bargaining processes, fostering learning among government elites. Finally, and perhaps most important, NGOs can attempt to influence state environmental policy directly, providing information about policy options, sometimes initiating legal proceedings, and lobbying directly through a state's legislature or bureaucracy. For, despite the increased roles for NGOs, it is still states that have primary responsibility for taking action.

A Theoretical Take

What has made many environmental issues so politically controversial at the international level is that states have tended to divide along the developed/developing—North/South—economic axis, although some developed states have been more accommodating than others. To the developed world, many environmental issues stem from the population explosion, a developing world problem. In this view, the developing world's population growth rates must decline; then pressure on scarce natural resources will decrease, and the negative externality of pollution will diminish. Those in the developed world who have enjoyed the benefits of economic growth and industrialization may now be willing to pay the additional costs for a safe and healthy environment.

States of the developing South perceive the environmental issue differently. These states correctly point to the fact that many environmental problems—including the overutilization of natural resources and the pollution issues of ozone depletion and greenhouse gas emissions—are the result of the excesses of the industrialized world. By exploiting the environment, by misusing the commons, the developed countries were able to achieve high levels of economic development. Putting restrictions on developing countries, not allowing them to exploit their natural resources or restricting their utilization of vital fossil fuels, may impede their development. Thus, since the developed states have been responsible for most of the environmental excesses, it is they who should pay for the cleanup.

The challenge in addressing any transnational issue is to negotiate a middle ground that reflects the fact that both sides are, in fact, correct. High population growth rates are a problem in the South—one that will not be alleviated until higher levels of economic development are achieved. Overutilization of natural resources is primarily a problem of the North. Powerful economic interests in the North are continually reminding us that changes in resource utilization may lead to a lower standard of living. Pollution is a byproduct of both, which in the South tends to be in the form of land- and water-resource utilization because of excessive population, whereas in the North it stems from the byproducts and negative externalities of industrialization. Thus, more than the other transnational issues, the environmental issue involves trade-offs with economic interests. Economic security is more likely to lead to environmental security.

Realists, liberals, and radicals do not have the same degree of concern for environmental issues, although each group has modified its perspectives in response to external changes. Realists' principal emphasis has been on state security, although in some quarters that has recently expanded to include human security. Either type of security requires a strong population base, near self-sufficiency in food, and a dependable supply of natural resources. Making the costs of natural resources or the costs of pollution abatement too high diminishes the ability of a state to make independent decisions. Thus realists fit environmental issues into the theoretical concepts of the state, power, sovereignty, and the balance of power.

Radicals, likewise, are concerned with the economic costs of the environmental problem. Radicals are apt to see the costs borne disproportionately by those in the South and by the poorer groups in the developed North. Neither of these burdens is acceptable to most radicals, although a few ecoradicals define sustainability at the level of community.

Both realists and radicals clearly recognize that controversies over natural resources and resource scarcity can lead to violence and even war. The political scientist Thomas Homer-Dixon has proposed one model that directly links the environment to conflict.[11] Figure 10.3 shows these hypothesized relationships. Although not all scholars would agree with the lines of causation, they are intellectually provocative and a source of concern for policy makers.

In contrast, liberals have typically seen the environmental issue as appropriate to the international agenda for the twenty-first century. Their broadened view of security, coupled with the credence they give to the notion of an interdependent international system—perhaps even one so interconnected as to be called an international society—make environmental issues ripe for international action. Because liberal theory can accommodate a greater variety of different international actors, including nongovernmental actors from global civil society, they see environmental and human rights issues as legitimate, if not key, international issues of the twenty-first century. Unlike realists and radicals, who fear dependency on other countries because it may diminish state power and therefore limit state action, liberals welcome interdependency and have faith in the technological ingenuity of individuals to be able to solve many of the natural resource dilemmas.

Constructivists, too, are comfortable with environmental issues as an arena for international action because environmental issues bring out salient discourse on environmentalism and sustainability. Constructivists are interested in how political and scientific elites define the problem and how that definition changes over time as new ideas become rooted in their belief sets. Constructivists also realize that environmental issues challenge the core concepts of sovereignty. One of the major

FIGURE 10.3 | Some Sources and Consequences of Environmental Scarcity

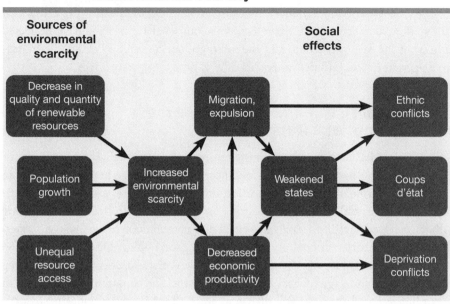

Source: Thomas F. Homer-Dixon, "Environmental Scarcities and Violent Conflict: Evidence and Cases," *International Security* 19:1 (Summer 1994): 31. Reprinted with permission.

intellectual tasks for constructivists has been to uncover the roots and practices of sovereignty.[12]

Human Rights—Protecting Human Dignity

The issue of human rights—the treatment of individuals and groups of individuals—has a longer historical genesis than environmental issues, but its global dimension is of more recent vintage. Prior to 1945, relations between a state and the individuals within the state were largely that state's concern. The state had absolute sovereignty and supreme legal authority over these individuals. Gradually five exceptions developed. In 1815 the major European powers began to negotiate a treaty, finally concluded in 1890, that recognized the obligation of states to abolish the slave trade. But not until 1926 did the international community abolish the practice of slavery. During the nineteenth century, individuals became entitled to medical treatment by belligerent states during war. In the twentieth century, legal aliens became entitled to minimum civil rights within a state. Laborers achieved some protection under the International Labor Organization, and specific minorities from the vanquished states of World War I were granted nominal international rights by the League of Nations. But the protection of individuals for all other purposes remained solely a state responsibility.[13]

Like the issue of population, the issue of human rights addresses core values that are sources of fundamental disagreements about what rights should be protected and what the role of the state and the international community should be in protecting such rights. Different theorists offer contrasting perspectives.

Conceptualizing Human Rights and the Development of a Regime

Political theorists have long been in the business of conceptualizing human rights. Three different generations of rights have been articulated. The first group of human rights to be formulated (**first-generation human rights**) was rights that an individual possesses and that the state cannot usurp. John Locke (1632–1704), among others, asserted that individuals are equal and autonomous beings whose natural rights predate both national and international law. Public authority is designed to secure these rights, which are detailed in key historic documents beginning with the English Magna Carta in 1215, the French Declaration of the Rights of Man in 1789, and the U.S. Bill of Rights in the 1791 Constitution. These documents listed rights of the individual that the government could not take away. For example, no individual should be "deprived of life, liberty, or property, without due process of law." Political and civil rights dominate first-generation rights: the right to free speech, free assembly, free press, and freedom of religion. Since these are rights that the government cannot take away, they are referred to as negative rights. To some theorists and to many U.S. pundits, these are the only recognized human rights. First-generation rights are squarely within the liberal tradition and are widely accepted by realists. Even Karl Marx regarded some civil rights as good, though not the emphasis on property rights.

Second-generation human rights were articulated in large part by the disciples of Marx and other radical socialist thinkers. Marx's concern was for the welfare of industrialized labor. He believed that the duty of states is to advance the well-being of their citizens; the right of citizens is to benefit from these socioeconomic advances. This view emphasizes minimum material rights that the state must provide to individuals in its responsibility to provide for their social welfare. Thus, individuals have the right to education, health care, social security, and housing; although the amount guaranteed is unspecified. These are referred to as positive rights. Without guarantees of those economic and social rights, Marx argued, political and civil rights are largely meaningless. The Soviet Union and other socialist states in the Cold War Eastern bloc considered economic and social rights to be either just as important, or more important, than political and civil rights; as do many social-welfare states of Europe today.

Third-generation human rights, a product of late-twentieth-century thinking, specify rights for groups. Groups that have rights include ethnic or indigenous minorities within a polity or designated special groups such as women, children, or the disabled. Some theorists have even added group rights to the list of individual human rights: the right to a safe environment, the right to peace and human security, the right to live in a democracy.

Drawing on long religious and philosophical traditions and the three generations of human rights, in 1948 the UN General Assembly approved the Universal Declaration of Human Rights, a statement of human rights aspirations. This document identified thirty principles incorporating both political and economic rights. These principles were eventually codified in two documents, the International Covenant on Economic, Social, and Cultural Rights and the International Covenant on Civil and Political Rights, approved in 1966 and ratified in 1976. They are together known as the International Bill of Human Rights. These rights have been expanded to include special conventions for women and refugees and to address various kinds of discrimination.

These wide-ranging human rights standards and the variety of actors involved in laying out the principles have led many scholars to conclude that there is an international regime of human rights. The term *regime* refers to agreed-on rules, norms, and procedures that emerge from high levels of cooperation—beyond the willingness to negotiate internationally and to coordinate policy outcomes on a periodic basis. The notion of a regime suggests that states develop principles about how to address certain problems. Over time, these principles solidify into accepted rules. Such rules and principles may be explicit—as indeed some international law is when it is codified—or they may be implicit. Regimes are "principles, norms, rules, and decision-making procedures around which actors' expectations converge in a given issue area."[14] Whether or not the principles are formalized in an organization or an international treaty, regimes guide state actions. The human rights regime, like other regimes, comprises a web of organizations—global and regional, general purpose and specialized, governmental and nongovernmental—that are engaged in activities related to issue areas relevant to the regime. These include not only UN instruments (such as the Human Rights Council, the Commission on the Status of Women, and the Office of the High Commissioner for Human Rights), but also the special monitoring committees established under the major international human rights treaties on political and civil rights, social and economic rights, rights of the child, the protection of indigenous peoples, and protection against racial discrimination. Regional groups have also set standards and developed monitoring and adjudicating bodies, most notably the European Commission of Human Rights and the European Court of Human Rights.

Of the disagreements and controversies within the human rights regime, two have proven to be enduring sources of controversy and discussion. First, can human rights principles survive threats to national security? Second, are different conceptions of human rights and the specific protected rights really universally applicable or not?

Nowhere is the potential clash between human rights and national security more focused than the issue of torture. What means may states, fearing imminent attack or grave harm, use in questioning those they believe have knowledge of the attack? If states restrain themselves and avoid torture in interrogations, some of their citizens may die as a result. Which then is the greater harm—violation of the human rights of those detained, or the very lives of innocent citizens? In 2009, the former U.S. vice president Dick Cheney argued publicly that political leaders had a greater responsibility to the security of the nation and its citizens, and that the use of "enhanced interrogation methods" on terrorism suspects "saved lives." Others responded by questioning whether much less violent methods might not have achieved the same results. Still others, including the U.S. senator John McCain, a Vietnam veteran who had been tortured by his North Vietnamese captors during the Vietnam War, argued that regardless of the effectiveness of these methods as an interrogation technique, Americans should not use them because they are wrong and because they violate what it means to *be* an American.

A second important controversy is whether a set of rights exists that can or should be **universal rights**. Clearly, some states give priority to one generation of rights over others. Pundits from different regions of the world have argued for **cultural relativism**, the idea that rights are culturally determined, and hence that different rights are relevant in different cultural settings. A group of Asian writers, including some in China, Indonesia, Malaysia, Singapore, and Vietnam, have made the argument that *global human rights* is a misnomer; human rights are culturally relative. In their view, when regional population and land pressures are severe, advocating the rights of the individual over the welfare of the community as a whole is unsound and potentially dangerous. First- and second-generation rights of the individual may conflict with the collective rights of groups. Asian cultures traditionally give primacy to the latter over the former.[15] Others disagree. The final document of the Vienna World Conference on Human Rights in 1993 asserts, "All human rights are universal, indivisible and interdependent and related." But the practice of human rights remains controversial.

The Human Rights Regime in Action

Over the last fifty years states, intergovernmental organizations, and nongovernmental organizations have helped to set and clarify human rights standards and norms, as elucidated above. States traditionally have argued that this is primarily the sovereign prerogative of the state, limited only by a state's own constitution. The United States made this argument during the civil rights era of the 1950s and 1960s. Discrimination against African Americans was a U.S. problem to be handled by federal authorities. The People's Republic of China has been one of the more vocal supporters of this point of view, disdainful of any interference in its domestic rights policies, including its treatment of national minorities, prisoners, and political dissidents.

During the twentieth century, with mass communication and the spread of information about how countries were treating their populations, a contending position emerged. That position was based on the realization that how a government treats its own citizens can affect the larger global community. Mistreatment of individuals and minorities can inflame ethnic tensions, causing unrest across national borders. Mistreatment of individuals in one country debases humans everywhere, threatening to undermine the essence of humanity worldwide. The Holocaust, the German Nazi genocide against Jews, gypsies, homosexuals, the disabled, and countless other minorities, brought this issue to the attention of the international community with unprecedented starkness. Nongovernmental groups participating in the UN founding conference in San Francisco pushed for the inclusion of human rights in the new organization's agenda. They argued that the international community, namely but not exclusively, should assume responsibility for the promotion and encouragement of global human rights standards.

What can the international community actually do? What can the United Nations and other intergovernmental organizations do when they are themselves composed of the very sovereign states that threaten individual rights? The UN's activities and the activities of other international organizations concerned with human rights have been confined to several areas.[16] First, the United Nations has been involved in the setting of the international human rights standards articulated in many treaties, prohibiting race and gender discrimination, protecting refugees and children, and constraining the actions of combatants during war.

Second, international and regional organizations have worked to monitor state behavior, establishing procedures for complaints about state practices, compiling reports from interested and neutral observers about state behavior, and investigating alleged violations. Monitoring has generally focused on political rights associated with democracy or on civil rights, rather than on second-generation rights.

NGOs can supplement the activities of intergovernmental organizations, and they have been particularly useful in monitoring activities. Amnesty International, founded in 1961, has become perhaps the most effective human rights monitor. Amnesty International was particularly involved in efforts to end the abuse of human rights in Uruguay and Paraguay, issuing reports of abuses, sending observers to trials, and lobbying governments. It was instrumental in bringing international attention to abductions and disappearances during the Argentinian military dictatorship in the early 1980s. Relying on accurate research and modest member contributions and utilizing publicity, Amnesty International has been able to

NGOs like Amnesty International have been instrumental in bringing human rights abuses to international attention. Here, Amnesty activists protest the treatment of Aung San Suu Kyi, the opposition leader, by the ruling junta in Burma (Myanmar).

capitalize on its reputation as an impartial, highly professional, politically neutral organization. Although it originally emphasized the protection of individual political prisoners, the organization has broadened its agenda to include systematic patterns of abuses of economic and social rights.

Third, the United Nations has taken measures to promote human rights by assuring fair elections with neutral monitors and providing a focal point for global human rights activity in the person of the High Commissioner for Human Rights. For example, since 1992, the United Nations has provided electoral assistance—election monitors and technical assistance—to many countries, including Afghanistan and Iraq. It has actually conducted elections in Namibia, Nicaragua, Cambodia, Eritrea, and Liberia, among other states.

Fourth, states and the international community are the primary enforcers of international human rights. States have always been the major enforcers of human rights and remain so. States can use their legal systems under the principle of universal jurisdiction, as when Spain tried to extradite the former dictator of Chile, General Augusto Pinochet, from Britain to Spain for trial for abuses against Spanish citizens. Although Spain's attempt failed, Pinochet was ultimately returned to Chile, but he died before he was to stand trial. States more commonly employ coercive measures such as sanctions or embargoes. Following China's crackdown on dissidents and the Tiananmen Square massacre in June 1989, the United States instituted an arms embargo against China and canceled new foreign aid; it was joined by Japan and members of the European Union. Some estimate that the coercive action may have cost China over $11 billion in bilateral aid over a four-year period.

States may also find that positive incentives or engagement may be a better approach to changing the human rights practices of another state. Engagement rests on the idea that because states have multiple interests—economic, security, diplomatic, and human rights—linking another issue to human rights may be a way of getting a state to change the former. For example, a state may be granted trade concessions if human rights abuses decline. Linking may work because of the notion that better economic relations and a more open economic system can create domestic pressure for more political freedom, including less offensive human rights practices. In the China case, after coercive measures failed to result in major changes, states and the international community turned to engagement. They believed that if China moved toward a more open economic system, then its human rights record would improve. At this point, engagement has not brought the anticipated results, although China's human rights abuses have become much more publicized because the regime is less able to hide its behavior.

UN enforcement is also an option. In the case of apartheid—legalized racial discrimination against the majority black population in South Africa and a comparable policy in Southern Rhodesia (now Zimbabwe)—under UN authority the international community instituted economic embargoes, seeking to punish those responsible for violating human rights standards and hoping to cause a change in those states' aberrant behavior. Although the embargo weakened the minority regimes, the states did not immediately change their human rights policy, nor were their governments immediately ousted from power. In a few cases, enforcement action may involve the use of military force. In the case of the humanitarian emergency in northern Iraq after the 1991 Gulf War, as well as in reaction to emergencies in Somalia, Bosnia, and Rwanda, the UN Security Council explicitly linked human rights violations to security threats and undertook enforcement action without the consent of the states concerned. Yet instances where the United Nations can intervene are few. Many states are suspicious of strengthening the United Nations' power to intervene in what many still regard as their domestic jurisdiction.

All of these approaches to human rights enforcement are fraught with difficulties. A state's signature on a treaty is no guarantee of its willingness or ability to observe the treaty's provisions. Monitoring state compliance through self-reporting systems presumes a willingness to comply and to be transparent. Taking direct action by imposing economic embargoes may not achieve the announced objective—change in human rights policy—and may actually be harmful to those very individuals whom the embargoes are trying to help. It has been reported that the international community's economic sanctions against Iraq after the first Gulf War resulted in a lower standard of living for the population and an imposition of real economic hardship on the masses, while the targeted elites remained unaffected. The sanctions did not have the intended effect of securing the elimination of Iraq's weapons of mass destruction.[17]

Even NATO's bombing of Kosovo and Serbia in 1999, designed to stop Serbian atrocities against the Albanian Kosovars and punish the Milošević regime, resulted in unintended Kosovar casualties and increased hardship for all the people while the regime went unpunished, at least in the short run. International and national action on behalf of human rights objectives remains a very tricky business. Use of power, whether hard or soft power, does not always produce the intended result.

Although the enforcement of human rights standards by the international community is clearly the exception rather than the norm, important precedents were established in the late twentieth century. Some kinds of international action are acceptable, though such actions are not always taken. But the international community may be closer now to saying it has a responsibility, even an obligation, to protect individuals, part of the norm of humanitarian intervention explained in Chapter 8. Most theorists and policy makers agree that genocide should elicit a concerted international response. In the aftermath of the Holocaust, the Convention against Genocide was negotiated. It elucidated clear principles that systematic killing of a group on the basis of race, gender, or ethnicity is prohibited under international law and norms. States have acted to stop genocide, for example, as when a NATO-backed coalition organized to stop the ethnic "cleansing" of Serbs in Kosovo, although NATO never used the word *genocide* to describe what was happening. One million Bangladeshis and 2 million Cambodians were killed in the 1970s; in the 1990s, over 800,000 Rwandans were killed while the world sat back and watched. In the latter case, neither the United Nations nor the United States ever used the word *genocide*, worrying that admitting it was genocide would obligate an international response. Instead, at the outset it was framed as an "ordinary" ethnic conflict; in retrospect, it was clearly anything but ordinary. In the case of Darfur, the word *genocide* was used by the U.S. government and human rights groups such as the Aegis Trust, but the international response remained underwhelming, illustrating the difficulty of building the political will to use armed forces to halt genocide, as debated in Chapter 8.

Advocates of each of the three theoretical perspectives might argue for different responses by states. Realists would generally focus on a state's national interest in the situation. According to realists, if genocide committed by one state jeopardizes another state's national interest, including intrusion on its core values, then it should act, although few states are likely to act alone. As the former U.S. national security adviser Henry Kissinger has warned, a wise realist policy maker would not be moved by sentiment alone or by personal welfare, but by the calculation of the national interest.[18] But the definition of that national interest may be broad, based on historical tradition or domestic values.

Liberals and radicals would be more likely to advise state intervention in response not only to genocide but also to less dramatic abuses. Liberals' emphasis on individual welfare and on the malleability of the state makes such intrusions into the actions of other states less offensive to them. Like realists, they may prefer nongovernmental actors to take the initiative, but they generally see it as a state's duty to intercede in blatant cases of human rights abuse. Likewise, radicals have few qualms about states' taking such actions. For them, however, the real culprit is an unfair economic system, namely, the international capitalist system, and so in their view the target is much more diffuse.

Other Human Rights Actors

Like global health and environmental issues, human rights issues involve a multiplicity of actors, not only state actors and international organizations. NGOs have also been particularly vocal and sometimes very effective in the area of human rights. Of the over 250 human rights organizations having interests that cross national borders, a core group has been the most vocal and attracted the most attention. It includes Amnesty International (as mentioned above), the International Committee of the Red Cross, Human Rights Watch, and the International Commission of Jurists. These organizations have played a key role in publicizing the issues, including abuses; in putting pressure on states (both offenders and enforcers); and in lobbying international organizations capable of taking concerted action. The groups have often formed coalitions, leading to advocacy networks and social movements.[19] The work of human rights NGOs, like that of environmental NGOs, has become more effective with the use of the Internet and the World Wide Web. NGOs can disseminate information quickly and to maximum effect. In constructivist terms, they can aid in the spread of ideas.

Women's Rights as Human Rights: The Globalization of Women's Rights

An examination of how women's rights has moved from the national to the international agenda illustrates many of the principles and problems we have just delineated. Women's rights, like other human rights issues, touch directly on cultural values and norms, yet like other human rights issues, they have gradually become a transnational issue.[20] As a UN poster prepared for the Vienna Conference in 1993 headlined, Women's Rights Are Human Rights. This has not always been the case in the eyes of the world.

EVOLVING POLITICAL AND ECONOMIC RIGHTS   Women first took up the call for political participation within national jurisdictions, demanding political and civil rights in the form of women's suffrage. Although British and U.S. women won that right in 1918 and 1920, respectively, women in many parts of the world had to wait until World War II (France, 1944) and after (Greece, 1952; Switzerland, 1971; Jordan, 1974; El Salvador, 1991; and Kuwait, 2006). In some Middle Eastern countries, women still do not have the vote, or else it is limited to local elections. Thus, although the efforts of Eleanor Roosevelt and her Latin American colleagues led to the inclusion of gender in the Universal Declaration of Human Rights (1949), at the time, gender discrimination was not yet globally seen as a human rights issue. In the immediate aftermath of the declaration, the priority of the United Nations and its Commission on the Status of Women was getting states to grant women the right to vote, hold office, and enjoy legal rights, part of first-generation human rights. Specifically, this led to the drafting of the Conventions on the Political Rights of Women in 1952, the Nationality of Married Women in 1957, and the Consent to Marriage in 1962. These actions helped to set the standard for assessing women's political rights. More than a decade later, the 1979 Convention on the Elimination of All Forms of Discrimination Against Women (**CEDAW**) further articulated these standards, positing not only that discrimination against women in political and public life is illegal, but so is trafficking in women and prostitution. Yet the treaty has no system for monitoring or enforcing such rights.

During the 1960s and 1970s, more attention was paid to second-generation human rights—economic and social rights—for women. The network of NGOs and IGOs charged with economic development had believed for many years that all individuals, including women, could participate and benefit equally from the economic development process. Yet, as they began to examine statistics on economic and social issues relevant to women, which were recorded beginning in the 1940s, they found that not to be the case. Esther Boserup's landmark book, *Women's Role in Economic Development,* recorded the finding that as technology improves, men benefit, but women become increasingly marginalized economically. Women would need special attention if they were to become participants in and beneficiaries of development.[21]

The result was the women in development (WID) movement, a transnational movement concerned with the failure of development to make an impact on the lives of the poor and with systematic discrimination against women. These issues developed and expanded over the life of four successive UN-sponsored world conferences on women. These conferences, with growing governmental and nongovernmental representation, mobilized women in interlocking networks, enabling them to set a critical economic agenda affecting women, including equal pay remuneration for male and female workers, minimum standards of social security, maternity protection, and nondiscrimination in the workplace. The delegates went further, however, arguing for special programs targeted to benefit women, since economic development was not working for them. The UN system responded by establishing programs to train and mobilize women in the development process and to give financial assistance to projects run by women. Virtually all the UN specialized agencies, including the World Bank, initiated programs for women's economic enhancement. Today the WID agenda is well integrated into most international assistance programs.

FROM POLITICAL AND ECONOMIC RIGHTS TO HUMAN RIGHTS   By the 1990s, the discussion of women's rights was clearly viewed as one of human rights. This shift was solidified at the 1993 Vienna Conference on Human Rights. As the Vienna Declaration asserted, "The human rights of women and of the girl-child are an inalienable, integral and indivisible part of universal human rights. . . . The human rights of women should form an integral part of the United Nations human rights activities, including the promotion of all human rights instruments relating to women."[22] The declaration included not only human rights protection in the public sphere (first- and second-generation human rights) but also protection against abuses in the private sphere, notably gender-based violence against women. The latter includes violence against women in the family and domestic life; gendered division of labor in the workplace, including work in the informal sector and sex work; and violence against women in war, particularly rape and torture. In short, violence against women and other abuses in all arenas were identified as breaches of both human rights and humanitarian norms. Their elimination was to be pursued through national and international action.

Three examples illustrate the widespread and often controversial problem of violence against women. The systematic usurpation of women's rights and accompanying violence was an issue in Taliban-run Afghanistan. When the Taliban seized power in 1996, all women's rights were revoked in both the public and private spheres. Women were not permitted to hold jobs or attend school. They were required to wear the *burqa*, a full-body veil, and submit to the authority of male family members. Violations of the rules resulted in assaults and sometimes death. A secret group, the Revolutionary Association of the Women of Afghanistan (RAWA), in a coalition with the U.S.-based Feminist Majority Foundation and over 180 human rights groups, launched a campaign in the international media that focused on the plight of Afghani women. As riveting as the issues were, it took the "war against terrorism" and the U.S. military to oust the Taliban and restore Afghani women some rights in the public sphere.

Rape is another example of violence against women. The rape of 2,000 Kuwaiti women by Iraqi soldiers during the 1991 Gulf War, of 60,000 Bosnian women in 1993 by Serb forces, of 250,000 women in the Burundi-Rwanda ethnic conflicts of 1993–94, and over 200,000 in the Democratic Republic of Congo, illustrate this unique form of violence against women. At the Nuremberg and Tokyo war trials, rape was not brought up as a war crime, even though states employed it systematically during World War II as an instrument of war. During the 1990s, rape as a systematic state policy became increasingly viewed as a human rights issue when NGOs urged the ad hoc international criminal tribunals for Yugoslavia and Rwanda to consider the crime of rape. At the ad hoc tribunal for Rwanda, the Rwandan politician Jean-Paul Akayesu was accused of gang rape and genocide. In a controversial 1998 decision, the judges issued the unprecedented ruling that rape constitutes not only a crime against humanity but also genocide. The precedent has been established, and now, thanks to NGO pressure, the statute for the International Criminal Court includes rape, sexual slavery, and forced prostitution among crimes against humanity, when such actions are part of a widespread and systematic attack against a civilian population.

Rape is not just a wartime issue. In South Asia and the Middle East, the problem is particularly acute even during peacetime. In some places, raping women may be seen as an acceptable act of revenge against a prior wrong. The raped women, being dishonored, may subsequently be killed. In other polities, rape may be difficult to prove, as in Pakistan when a woman herself may be convicted of adultery unless four male witnesses corroborate her rape story. Thus, although the act is illegal in virtually every jurisdiction, state authorities in certain countries rarely choose to prosecute. Increasingly, human rights NGOs such as Human Rights Watch or Amnesty International bring these cases to the attention of a horrified international community, and public pressure is brought to bear. But given different cultural norms, private-sphere activities are much easier to hide and more resistant to change.

Different feminist groups have placed different priorities on various types of human rights protection. Liberal feminists have found solace in granting women political and civil human rights, providing them the opportunity to secure privileges that were once exclusively male prerogatives. Socialist feminists point to the economic forces that have disadvantaged women and seek economic changes. In their view, as women become economically empowered, they will be able to alter patriarchal gender relations. More radical feminists highlight the distinctiveness of women and seek protection from all forms of gendered violence in both the public and private spheres.

Although the legal stage has been set by the protection provided in various human rights treaties under the auspices of international organizations, the mainstay of enforcement will continue to be at the state level. It is states, prodded by the normative requirements of international treaties and lobbied by prominent individuals and human rights networks, that undertake domestic reform. And it is states that, unilaterally or multilaterally, undertake punitive action against other, offending states.

Transnational Crime

Trafficking in women and children is another form of violence against women. But whereas the aim of many of those who deliberately seek to deprive human beings of their lives and dignity is political in nature (or genocidal), another segment of harm comes from the profit motive and is therefore essentially criminal. The practice of "**sex trafficking**," as it is commonly called, has ancient roots, but it became much more serious and widespread following the collapse of the Warsaw Pact and the Soviet Union in 1991. At that time, thousands of young women from Eastern Europe and the former Soviet Union, seeking opportunity in the West, became victims of highly organized and profitable transnational criminal networks that specialized in "delivering" them to clients. The profits were large, and led the criminal organizations involved to new investments in better communications technologies and methods, better targeting strategies, and better concealment and protection from law-enforcement authorities.

Human trafficking is prohibited under the CEDAW convention, but government corruption, lax border controls, pressures to keep labor costs low, poverty that drives women and families to seek any kind of employment, and the high profitability of the sex trade are driving forces. Although the number of women and children forced into bonded sweatshop labor and domestic servitude will never be known, estimates for those trafficked for the sex trade vary from between 600,000 to 1.75 million women and children (girls and boys) annually. This problem is especially vexing, because unlike with rape where consent is not given, desperate women may choose to be trafficked for economic reasons. Speaking through several treaties—the Convention on the Rights of the Child, the Convention on Suppression of International Trafficking, and the Convention on the Abolition of Slavery, Slave Trade and Institutions and Practices Similar to Slavery—the international community has declared this practice illegal. Although the standards have been set, monitoring and enforcement remain complicated.

Another form of transnational crime has recaptured international attention since the end of the Cold War: narcotrafficking. Narcotrafficking—the transportation of large quantities of narcotics such as heroin or cocaine across state borders—has always been a problem. But by the early 1970s, it had become severe enough in the United States that President Richard Nixon declared a "war on drugs" as U.S. domestic policy. Nixon reasoned that because the toll of lives lost to drug abuse—then disproportionately affecting poor and urban people—was akin to casualties of war, those who produced, refined, transported, and delivered these drugs to U.S. customers were essentially attacking the United States. The other advantage of declaring a war on drugs was that "war" implies a shared undertaking that mobilizes all sectors of society to victory. It also implied that the best way to resolve the crisis and reduce the harm caused by drug abuse was to target drug dealers and other elements of the narcotics production and delivery supply chain in what was essentially a supply-side strategy to cut off the supply of drugs to potential customers. But the real problem and the real reason that such a "war" can never be won has to do with the combination of demand for drugs (which varies, often with economic upsurges and downturns), and the ever-dwindling costs of transport, epitomized in our earlier discussion of the impact of the container ship. In short, even if demand drops, if the costs of supplying the drug drop still further, a point is soon reached at which the market clears. Not even the destruction of major tracts of land where opium poppies or coca plants are grown can bring victory closer, because again, the costs of shipping large quantities of product long distances are so low that cultivation destroyed in one region can quickly be replaced by new sources elsewhere. Because drug profits often get recycled into the purchase of arms, intelligence, and bribes for use by terrorist organizations, the harm of narcotrafficking is not restricted to violent and property crime, broken families, and shattered lives. It also takes the form of organized attacks against ordinary people all around the world in the form of transnational terrorism (see Chapter 8).

The Impact of Transnational Issues

Perhaps the most crucial point to observe about transnational issues is that they have advanced from tertiary and moral issues to primary and vital interests as an unexpected consequence of advances in communications technology, in particular, the container ship and the cell phone. Before World War II, developed states might have viewed more active economic, health infrastructure, and human rights interventions as morally desirable but either risky or unnecessary for reasons of state. Since the late 1970s, however, transnational issues such as organized crime (drug and sex trafficking), terrorism, pandemics, famine, natural disasters such as typhoons, floods, and droughts, civil war, and refugees stemming from all these have tended to affect the developed world more directly. Thus, it is fair to say that transnational issues have *become* issues because morality-based arguments for intervention to redress damages have increasingly transitioned into interest-based arguments for undertaking the same interventions. Transnational issues have effects on four major areas of international relations theory and practice.

First, the interconnectedness of the plethora of subissues within health, environmental, and human rights issues affects international bargaining. When states choose to go to the bargaining table, a multiplicity of issues is often at stake. Many issues are fungible; states are willing to make trade-offs between issues to achieve a desired result. For example, in the aftermath of the 1973 oil embargo and in the face of supply shortages, the United States was willing to negotiate with Mexico on cleaning up the Colorado River. The United States built a desalination plant at the

POLICY DEBATE

Has the global war on terror made human rights issues obsolete?

Yes:

- During a war, the right to security is paramount. A key right in President Franklin Roosevelt's famous "Four Freedoms" speech from 1941 is freedom from fear.
- Terrorists who indiscriminately attack innocent men, women, and children lose their right to be treated according to accepted political and civil rights standards.
- Laws of war and humanitarian law apply only to individuals acting in the name of the state. So nonstate terrorists enjoy no universal human rights protections.
- Terrorists have no respect for the human rights of their targets. So the targets have no responsibility to treat them any better.

No:

- Not respecting the political and civil rights of terrorists dehumanizes everyone, placing both the terrorist and the target on equal footing.
- The rise of terrorism underlines the importance of economic and social rights; it is often the absence of economic rights that gives rise to terrorists.
- Not respecting the rights of terrorists will only create more angry individuals willing to use force.
- If the rights of suspected terrorists are abrogated, then the cycle of violence and hatred will likely continue into the future, while each side responds to the wrongs of the other.
- Respect of human rights is the foundation of a democracy, so if the ultimate goal is to create a democratic state, then respect for human rights must be a priority.

U.S.-Mexican border and helped Mexican residents reclaim land in the Mexicali Valley for agriculture. To win an ally in the supply of petroleum resources, the United States made this major concession and also accepted responsibility for past legal violations.

Other issues, however, are less fungible, particularly if key concerns of national security are at stake. The United States was unwilling to compromise by signing the Mine Ban Treaty because of the security imperative to preserve the heavily mined border between North and South Korea. Supporters of the treaty framed the argument in human rights terms: innocent individuals, including vulnerable women and children, are being killed or maimed by such weapons, which must be eliminated. Yet in this case, the United States decided not to sign the treaty because of Korean security. Although some states, eager for U.S. participation, were willing to make concessions, others, afraid that the treaty would be weakened by too many exceptions, were not. Bargaining is a much more complicated process in the age of transnational issues.

Second, these transnational issues themselves may be the source of conflict, just as the Marxists predicted in the nineteenth century. The need to protect the petroleum supply was the primary motivation for the West's involvement in the 1991 Gulf War. Jared Diamond's book *Collapse: How Societies Choose to Fail or Succeed* documents how the struggle for scarce resources led to the collapse of empires in the past and to state failure in Rwanda and Burundi, resulting in the abrogation of human rights. The relationship between environmental and resource issues and conflict is a complex one.[23]

Issues of resource depletion and degradation, usually worsened by population increase and pressure on resources, are likely to result in conflicts when some groups try to capture use of the scarce resource. For example, Israeli authorities control access to scarce water on the West Bank of the Jordan River, exacerbating the conflict between the Israelis and the Palestinians. Israel permits its own settlers greater access to the resource and restricts access to the Palestinians. In the Gaza Strip, where population is growing 4.6 percent annually, resources have been depleted, intensifying the conflict with Israel.

Nonrenewable resources such as oil lead to particularly violent conflicts, because such resources are vital; there are few viable substitutes. Changes in the distribution of these resources may lead to a shift in the balance of power, creating an instability that leads to war, just as realists fear. In contrast, issues such as ozone depletion or global warming are not particularly conducive to violent interstate conflict. In both cases, the commons and responsibility for its management are diffuse. Future generations will feel the effects.

Third, these transnational issues pose direct challenges to state sovereignty, setting off a major debate about the nature of sovereignty. In Chapter 2, we traced the roots of sovereignty in the Westphalian revolution. The notion developed that states enjoy internal autonomy and cannot be subjected to external authority. That norm—noninterference in the domestic affairs of other states—was embedded in the UN Charter. Yet the rise of nonstate actors—multinational corporations, nongovernmental organizations, and supranational organizations such as the European Union—and the forces of globalization, whether economic, cultural, or political, undermine Westphalian notions of state sovereignty. Communicable diseases, the

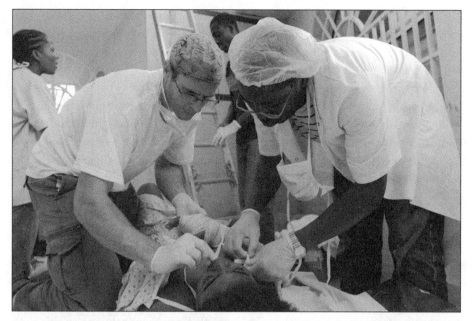

In an interconnected world, traditional notions of state sovereignty may come into conflict with the efforts of other international actors. For example, following the devastating earthquake in Haiti in 2010, some outside medical teams who sought to medevac critically injured victims to the U.S. for treatment ran afoul of the barely-functioning Haitian government, who insisted they wait for formal government approval.

environment, human rights, and transnational crime were traditionally sovereign state concerns, and interference by outside actors was unacceptable. After World War II, those norms began to change, a process that continues today. The problems raised by transnational terrorism, for example, imply a multinational response: by transnational terrorism's very nature, single states, no matter how powerful, cannot solve the problem on their own. This is one of the main reasons that discussion has turned to a power shift, an erosion of state authority and the severe weakening of state power overall. Issues that once were the exclusive hallmark of state sovereignty are increasingly susceptible to scrutiny and intervention by global actors.

Part of the problem is that in many areas of the world, particularly since the end of the Cold War, states themselves have become weak or have even failed. These so-called failing or failed states then become sites for transnational crime, terrorist organizations, and disease, all of which may be exported at relatively low cost to neighboring states and even around the world. Consider the fate of Zimbabwe under Robert Mugabe's heavy hand. In 2008 Zimbabwe's collapsed health care infrastructure was unable to prevent or control the outbreak of a cholera epidemic. The disease soon spread to affect (and infect) the citizens of neighboring states.

Yet traditions of sovereignty mitigate against interventions aimed at restoring a state to full functionality. Who is to judge whether an intervention will simply restore a state or become a kind of twenty-first-century neocolonialism, as debated in Chapter 8?

How then should we reconceptualize sovereignty? How has sovereignty been transformed? Mainstream theories in the realist and liberal traditions tend to talk of an erosion of sovereignty. Constructivists go further, probing how sovereignty is and always has been a contested concept. There have always been some issues where state control and authority are secure and others where authority is shared or even undermined. After all, sovereignty is a socially constructed institution that varies across time and place. Transnational issues such as health, the environment, and human rights permit us to examine in depth long-standing but varying practices of sovereignty. These issues give rise to new forms of authority and new forms of governance, stimulating us to reorient our views of sovereignty.[24]

Fourth, transnational issues pose critical problems for international relations scholars and for the theoretical frameworks introduced at the beginning of this textbook. Adherents of each framework have been forced to rethink key assumptions and values, as well as the discourse of their theoretical perspective, to accommodate transnational issues.

The very core propositions of realist theory—the primacy of the state, the clear separation between domestic and international politics, and the emphasis on state security—are made problematic by transnational issues. Issues of health and disease, the environment, human rights, drug and human trafficking, transnational terror and international crime are problems that no one state can effectively address alone. These issues have broken down the divide between the international and the domestic. They may threaten state security but may have no traditional military solution, even for a great power or superpower.

Responding to transnational issues, realists have generally adopted a more nuanced argument consonant with realist precepts. Although most realists admit that other actors have gained power relative to the state, they contend that state primacy is not in jeopardy. Competitive centers of power at the local, transnational, or international level do not necessarily or automatically lead to the erosion or elimination of state power. Most important, the fundamentals of state security are no less important in this age of globalization than they were in the past. What has changed is that the security discourse has been broadened to encompass human security. For humans to be secure, not only must state security be ensured, but economic security, environmental security, human rights security, and health and well-being must be secured as well. One form of security does not replace another; each augments the rest. Thus, although transnational issues have forced realists to add qualifications to their theory, they have thereby preserved it and enhanced its theoretical usefulness.

Transnational issues can be more easily integrated into the liberal theoretical picture. After all, at the outset liberals asserted the importance of individuals and the possibility of both cooperative and conflictual interests. They introduced the notion that many other issues may be as important as security. They see power as a multidimensional concept. Later versions of liberal thinking, such as

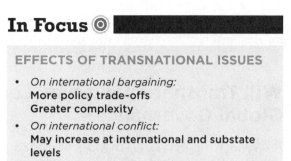

In Focus

EFFECTS OF TRANSNATIONAL ISSUES

- *On international bargaining:*
  More policy trade-offs
  Greater complexity
- *On international conflict:*
  May increase at international and substate levels
- *On state sovereignty:*
  Traditional notion challenged
  Need for reconceptualization
- *On study of international relations:*
  Core assumptions of theories jeopardized
  Theories modified and broadened

neoliberal institutionalism, recognized the need for international institutions to facilitate state interactions, to ensure transparency, and to add new issues to the international agenda. Though not denying the importance of state security, they quickly embraced the notion of other forms of security compatible with health, environmental, and human rights issues.

Radicals have never been comfortable with the primacy of the state and the international system that the dominant coalition of states created. For them, a shift in power away from the state and that international system is a desired transition. With their pronounced emphasis on economics over security, radicals may be able to accommodate such transnational issues as communicable diseases, the environment, human rights, and transnational crime. However, a prominent radical interpretation of both communicable disease and the environment is that economic deprivation and perceived relative economic deprivation are the root causes of disparities in health care and environmental degradation. Human rights violations, according to radical thought, are caused by elites and privileged groups trying to maintain their edge over the less fortunate.

Constructivists have presented a different approach for tapping into transnational issues. They have alerted us to the nuances of the changing discourse embedded in discussions of health, the environment, and human rights. They have illustrated how both material factors and ideas shape debates over these issues. They have called attention to the importance of norms in influencing and changing individual and state behavior. More directly than other theorists, constructivists have begun to explore the variable impacts of these issues on the traditional concepts of the state, national identity, and sovereignty. Yet though sometimes pathbreaking and often suggestive, constructivism itself remains under construction.

As all transnational issues assume greater salience in the twenty-first century, all international relations theories will need modification and reformulation.

Will Transnational Issues Lead to Global Governance?

Recognition of transnational issues and their effects has led some scholars and pundits to conclude that governance processes need to be conceptualized differently than they have been in the past. The processes of interaction among the various actors in international politics are now more frequent and intense, ranging from conventional ad hoc cooperation and formal organizational collaboration to nongovernmental and network collaboration and even virtual communal interaction on the Internet. These changes have led some to think that global governance has various components. **Global governance** implies that through various structures and processes, actors can coordinate interests and needs even in the absence of a unifying political authority.

Yet for global governance to come together, for the international relations puzzle to be whole and complete, there must be a global civil society. The political scientist Ronnie Lipschutz describes the essential component of global civil society:

> While global civil society must interact with states, the code of global civil society denies the primacy of states or their sovereign rights. This civil society is 'global' not only because of those connections that cross national boundaries and operate within the 'global, nonterritorial region,' but also as a result of a growing element of global consciousness in the way the members of global civil society act.[25]

Some liberals would find this a desirable direction in which to be moving—a goal to be attained—whereas many fear that global governance might undermine democratic values: as the focus of governance moves farther from individuals, democracy becomes more problematic.

Skeptics of global governance do not believe that anything approaching it, however defined, is possible or desirable. For realists, there can never be global governance in anarchy; outcomes are determined by relative power positions rather than by law or other regulatory devices, however decentralized and diffuse those devices might be. For Kenneth Waltz, the quintessential neorealist, the anarchic structure of the international system is the core dynamic. For other realists, such as Hans Morgenthau, there is space for both international law and international organization. His textbook includes chapters on both, but each is relatively insignificant in the face of power politics and the national interest. Few realists would talk in global governance terms. Radicals are also uncomfortable with global governance discourse. Rather than seeing global governance as a multiple-actor, multiple-process, decentralized framework, radicals fear domination by hegemons that would structure global governance processes to their own advantage. Skepticism about the possibility of global governance does not diminish the fact that there may be a need for it in the age of globalization.

In Sum: Changing You

In these ten chapters, we have explored the historical development of international relations, from the development of the state system to notions of an international system and community and global governance. We have introduced different theories—realism, liberalism, radicalism, and constructivism—that help us organize our perspectives about the role of the international system, the state, the individual, and intergovernmental and nongovernmental organizations in international relations. From these perspectives, we have examined the major issues of the day and analyzed how these issues affect interstate bargaining, conflict, sovereignty, and even the study of international politics.

A citizenry able to articulate these arguments is better able to explain the whys and hows of events that affect our lives. A citizen who can understand these events is better able to make and support informed policy choices. In the transnational era of the twenty-first century, as economic, political, social, and environmental forces both above the state and within the state assume greater saliency, the role of individuals becomes all the more demanding—and all the more important.

DISCUSSION QUESTIONS

1. Before World War II, crises and disasters in distant parts of the world stayed there. This is no longer the case today. What are two important implications of this new reality?

2. International cooperation on health has traditionally been viewed as a functionalist issue, but increasingly the issue has been politicized. What has changed? With what effect? Cite specific examples.

3. When and how should states intervene in the affairs of other states with poor human rights records? What threshold of violations has to be crossed first? Who decides when it has been crossed?

4. Global warming is a problem of the global commons, but not all environmental problems are. How should different environmental issues be approached?

5. Select two news accounts that address the trade-off between economic development and environmental sustainability. Can these two objectives be harmonized in the twenty-first century?

KEY TERMS

CEDAW, p. 358
cultural relativism, p. 352
demographic transition, p. 336
epistemic communities, p. 333
externalities, p. 341
first-generation human rights, p. 350
global governance, p. 368

Malthusian dilemma, p. 336
negative externalities, p. 341
second-generation human rights, p. 350
sex trafficking, p. 361
third-generation human rights, p. 351
universal rights, p. 352

 Find chapter outlines, practice quizzes, flashcards, and other study and review materials for this chapter at wwnorton.com/studyspace.

NOTES

Chapter 1

1. Stephen M. Walt, "International Relations: One World, Many Theories," *Foreign Policy* 110 (Spring 1988): 30.

2. Thucydides, *History of the Peloponnesian War,* trans. Rex Warner, rev. ed. (Harmondsworth: Penguin, 1972).

3. See Jeffrey Record and W. Andrew Terrill, "Iraq and Vietnam: Differences, Similarities, and Insights" (Carlisle, PA.: Strategic Studies Institute, U.S. Army War College, 2004), www.strategicstudiesinstitute.army.mil/pubs/display.cfm?pubID=377 (accessed 12/15/09). For more on the use of historical analogies, see Yuen Foong Khong, *Analogies at War: Korea, Munich, Dien Bien Phu, and the Vietnam Decision of 1965* (Princeton, N.J.: Princeton University Press, 1992).

4. Plato, *The Republic*, trans. Desmond Lee (Harmondsworth: Penguin, 1955).

5. Aristotle, *The Politics,* ed. Trevor J. Saunders, trans. T. A. Sinclair (Harmondsworth: Penguin, 1981).

6. Thomas Hobbes, *Leviathan*, ed. C. B. Macpherson (Harmondsworth: Penguin, 1968).

7. Jean-Jacques Rousseau, "Discoures on the Origin and Foundations of Inequality among Men," in *Basic Political Writings of Jean-Jacques Rousseau,* ed. and trans. Donald A Cress (Indianapolis, IN: Hackett Publishing, 1987).

8. Jean-Jacques Rousseau, "On the Social Contract," Book 2, Ch. 1, in *Basic Political Writings of Jean-Jacques Rousseau*, p. 153.

9. Rousseau, "Social Contract," Book 1, Ch. 6, p. 148.

10. See Immanuel Kant, *Idea for a Universal History from a Cosmopolitan Point of View* (1784) and *Perpetual Peace: A Philosophical Sketch* (1795), both reprinted in *Kant Selections,* ed. Lewis White Beck (New York: Macmillan Co., 1988).

11. J. David Singer and Melvin Small, *The Wages of War, 1816–1965: A Statistical Handbook* (New York: Wiley, 1972).

12. Cynthia Weber, *Simulating Sovereignty: Intervention, the State, and Symbolic Interchange* (Cambridge: Cambridge University Press, 1994).

13. Christine Sylvester, "Emphatic Cooperation: A Feminist Method for IR," *Millennium: Journal of International Studies* 23:2 (1994): 315–34.

14. Peter J. Katzenstein, ed., *The Culture of National Security: Norms and Identity in World Politics* (New York: Columbia University Press, 1996).

Chapter 2

1. Dante, *De Monarchia,* in *The Portable Dante,* ed. Paolo Milano (New York: Penguin, 1977).

2. Niccolò Machiavelli, *The Prince,* ed. and trans. Peter Bondanella and Mark Musa (New York: Oxford University Press, 1998); Machiavelli, *The Discourses on Livy,* trans. Julia Conway Bondanella and Peter Bondonella (New York: Oxford University Press, 2003).

3. Jean Bodin, *Six Books on the Commonwealth,* trans. M. J. Tooley (Oxford: Basil Blackwell, 1967), p. 25.

4. Bodin, *Commonwealth,* p. 28.

5. Bodin, *Commonwealth,* p. 28.

6. Adam Smith, *An Inquiry into the Nature and Causes of the Wealth of Nations* (New York: Modern Library, 1937).

7. John Locke, *Two Treatises on Government* (Cambridge: Cambridge University Press, 1960).

8. Hilaire Belloc, as quoted in John Ellis, *A Social History of the Machine Gun* (New York: Random House, 1975), p. 18.

9. Quoted in A. C. Walworth, *Woodrow Wilson* (Baltimore, MD: Penguin, 1969), p. 148.

10. E. H. Carr, *The Twenty Years' Crisis, 1919–1939: An Introduction to the Study of International Relations* (New York: Harper Torchbooks, 1939, rep. 1964), p. 224.

11. George F. Kennan ["X"], "The Sources of Soviet Conduct," *Foreign Affairs 25* (July 1947): 566–82.

12. Quoted in Charles W. Kegley, Jr. and Eugene R. Wittkopf, *World Politics: Trend and Transformation,* 5th ed. (New York: St. Martin's, 1995), p. 94.

13. Joseph Stalin, "Reply to Comrades," *Pravda,* August 2, 1950.

14. George F. Kennan, "The United States and the Soviet Union, 1917–1976," *Foreign Affairs* 54 (July 1976): 683–84.

15. John Lewis Gaddis, "The Long Peace: Elements of Stability in the Postwar International System," *International Security* 10:4 (Spring 1986): 92–142.

16. Kenneth N. Waltz, *Theory of International Politics* (Reading, MA: Addison-Wesley, 1979), p. 173.

17. Mikhail Gorbachev, "Reality and Guarantees for a Secure World," as reported in Foreign Broadcast Information Service, *Daily Report, Soviet Union,* September 17, 1987, p. 25.

Chapter 3

1. Kenneth N. Waltz, *Man, the State, and War* (New York: Columbia University Press, 1954); and J. David Singer, "The Levels of Analysis Problem,"

in *International Politics and Foreign Policy*, ed. James N. Rosenau, rev. ed. (New York: Free Press, 1961), pp. 20–29.

2. Thucydides, *History of the Peloponnesian War*.

3. Augustine, *Confessions* and *City of God*, in *Great Books of the Western World*, ed. Robert Maynard Hutchins, vol. 18 (Chicago: Encyclopedia Britannica, 1952, 1986).

4. Niccolò Machiavelli, *The Prince and the Discourses* (New York: Random House, 1940).

5. Thomas Hobbes, *Leviathan*, ed. C. B. Macpherson (Harmondsworth: Penguin, 1968), p. 13.

6. Hans J. Morgenthau, *Politics among Nations: The Struggle for Power and Peace*, 5th ed., rev. (New York: Knopf, 1978).

7. John J. Mearsheimer, *The Tragedy of Great Power Politics* (New York: Norton, 2001), pp. 19–22.

8. Kenneth N. Waltz, *Theory of International Politics* (Reading, MA: Addison-Wesley, 1979).

9. Kenneth N. Waltz, "Realist Thought and Neorealist Theory," in *Controversies in International Relations Theory: Realism and the Neoliberal Challenge*, ed. Charles W. Kegley, Jr. (New York: St. Martin's, 1995) pp. 67–82.

10. Waltz, *Theory of International Politics*, p. 105.

11. John J. Mearsheimer, "The False Promise of International Institutions," *International Security* 19:3 (Winter 1994–95): 5–49.

12. Robert Gilpin, *War and Change in World Politics* (Cambridge: Cambridge University Press, 1981), p. 29.

13. Gilpin, *War and Change*, p. 210.

14. Ann Tickner, "Hans Morgenthau's Principles of Political Realism: A Feminist Reformulation," *Millennium: Journal of International Studies* 17:3 (1988): 429–40.

15. Montesquieu, *The Spirit of the Laws*, vol. 36, ed. David Wallace Carrithers (Berkeley: University of California Press, 1971), p. 23.

16. Immanuel Kant, *Perpetual Peace*, ed. Lewis White Beck (New York: Macmillan, 1957).

17. Robert Axelrod and Robert O. Keohane, "Achieving Cooperation under Anarchy: Strategies and Institutions," in *Cooperation under Anarchy*, ed. Kenneth Oye (Princeton, N.J.: Princeton University Press, 1986) pp. 226–54.

18. Robert O. Keohane and Joseph Nye, *Power and Interdependence*, 3rd ed. (New York: Longman, 2001); Robert O. Keohane and Joseph Nye, "Transnational Relations and World Politics," *International Organization* 25:3 (Summer 1971): 329–50, 721–48.

19. Francis Fukuyama, "The End of History?" *National Interest* 16 (Summer 1989): 4.

20. John Mueller, *Retreat from Doomsday: The Obsolescence of Major War* (New York: Basic Books, 1989).

21. Karl Marx, *Capital: A Critique of Political Economy*, trans. Ben Fowkes (New York: Random House, 1977).

22. John A. Hobson, *Imperialism: A Study*, ed. Philip Siegelman (Ann Arbor: University of Michigan Press, 1965).

23. Tony Smith, "The Underdevelopment of the Development Literature: The Case of Dependency Theory," *World Politics* 31:2 (January 1979): 247–88.

24. Stephen M. Walt, "International Relations: One World, Many Theories," *Foreign Policy* 110 (Spring 1998): 29–46.

25. Ted Hopf, "The Promise of Constructivism in International Relations Theory," *International Security* 23:1 (Summer 1989): 172.

26. Alexander Wendt, "Anarchy Is What States Make of It: The Social Construction of Power Politics," *International Organization* 46:2 (Spring 1992): 396. For a more complete analysis, see Wendt, *Social Theory of International Politics* (Cambridge: Cambridge University Press, 1999).

27. Wendt, "Anarchy Is What States Make of It."

28. John J. Mearsheimer and Stephen M. Walt, "An Unnecessary War," *Foreign Policy* 134 (January–February 2003): 50–59.

Chapter 4

1. See especially Morton Kaplan, *System and Process in International Politics* (New York: Krieger, 1976).

2. Kenneth N. Waltz, "International Structure, National Force, and the Balance of World Power," *Journal of International Affairs* 21:2 (1967): 229.

3. John J. Mearsheimer, "Back to the Future: Instability after the Cold War," *International Security* 15:1 (Summer 1990): 52.

4. Paul M. Kennedy, *The Rise and Fall of the Great Powers: Economic Change and Military Conflict from 1500 to 2000* (New York: Random House, 1987).

5. Robert O. Keohane, *After Hegemony: Cooperation and Discord in the World Political Economy* (Princeton, N.J.: Princeton University Press, 1984).

6. J. David Singer and Melvin Small, "Alliance Aggregation and the Onset of War," in *Quantitative International Politics*, ed. J. David Singer (New York: Free Press, 1968), pp. 246–86.

7. Michael C. Webb and Stephen D. Krasner, "Hegemonic Stability Theory: An Empirical Assessment," *Review of International Studies* 15 (1989): 183–98.

8. Robert Gilpin, *War and Change in World Politics* (Cambridge: Cambridge University Press, 1981).

9. Robert O. Keohane and Joseph S. Nye, *Power and Interdependence*, 3rd ed. (New York: Longman, 2001).

10. Hedley Bull and Adam Watson, eds., *The Expansion of International Society* (Oxford: Oxford University Press, 1984).

11. Martha Finnemore, *The Purpose of Intervention: Changing Beliefs about the Use of Force* (Ithaca, N.Y.: Cornell University Press, 2003), p. 94.

12. Finnemore, *Intervention*, 95.

13. Samuel Huntington, *The Clash of Civilizations: The Remaking of the World Order* (New York: Simon & Schuster, 1996).

Chapter 5

1. James N. Rosenau, *Turbulence in World Politics: A Theory of Change and Continuity* (Princeton, N.J.: Princeton University Press, 1990), pp. 117–18.

2. Minxin Pei, "The Paradoxes of American Nationalism," *Foreign Policy* 134 (May–June 2003): 31–37.

3. See Martha Finnemore, *National Interests in International Society* (Ithaca, N.Y.: Cornell University Press, 1996), chap. 1.

4. Stephen D. Krasner, *Defending the National Interest: Raw Materials Investments and U.S. Foreign Policy* (Princeton, N.J.: Princeton University Press, 1978).

5. Alfred T. Mahan, *The Influence of Seapower upon History 1660–1783* (Boston: Little, Brown, 1897).

6. Halford Mackinder, "The Geographical Pivot of History," *Geographical Journal* 23 (April 1904): 434.

7. Joseph S. Nye, Jr., *Soft Power: The Means to Success in World Politics* (New York: Public Affairs, 2004).

8. Andrew Mack, "Why Big Nations Lose Small Wars: The Politics of Asymmetric Conflict," *World Politics* 27:2 (January 1975): 175–200.

9. Robert D. Putnam, "Diplomacy and Domestic Politics: The Logic of Two-Level Games," *International Organization* 42:3 (Summer 1988): 427–69.

10. Putnam, "Two-Level Games," 434.

11. Raymond Cohen, *Negotiating across Cultures: Communication Obstacles in International Diplomacy*, 2nd ed. (Washington, D.C.: U.S. Institute of Peace, 1997).

12. Karen A. Mingst and Craig P. Warkentin, "What Difference Does Culture Make in Multilateral Negotiations?" *Global Governance* 2:2 (May 1996): 169–88.

13. David A. Baldwin, *Economic Statecraft* (Princeton, N.J.: Princeton University Press, 1985).

14. David Cortright and George A. Lopez, *The Sanctions Decade: Assessing UN Strategies in the 1990s* (Boulder, CO.: Lynne Rienner, 2000); Cortright and Lopez, *Sanctions and the Search for Security* (Boulder, CO.: Lynne Rienner, 2002).

15. Thomas C. Schelling, *Arms and Influence* (New Haven, CT: Yale University Press, 1966).

16. Immanuel Kant, *Perpetual Peace: A Philosophical Sketch* (1795), reprinted in *Kant Selections,* ed. Lewis White Beck (New York: Macmillan, 1988).

17. See, for example, William J. Dixon, "Democracy and the Peaceful Settlement of International Conflict," *American Political Science Review* 88 (1994): 14–32; and Joe D. Hagan, "Domestic Political Systems and War Proneness," *Mershon International Studies Review* 38:2 (October 1994): 183–207.

18. Norman M. Naimark, *The Russians in Germany: A History of the Soviet Zone of Occupation, 1945–1949* (Cambridge, MA.: Harvard University Press, 1995).

19. Jessica Matthews, "Power Shift," *Foreign Affairs* 76:1 (January–February 1997): 50.

20. Matthews, "Power Shift," 50–51.

21. See Moises Naim, *Illicit: How Smugglers, Traffickers, and Copycats Are Hijacking the Global Economy* (New York: Doubleday, 2005).

22. Jessica Stern, *Terror in the Name of God: Why Religious Militants Kill* (New York: HarperCollins, 2003), pp. 9–31.

23. Samuel P. Huntington, *The Clash of Civilizations and the Remaking of World Order* (New York: Simon & Schuster, 1996).

24. Jack Snyder, *From Voting to Violence: Democratization and Nationalist Conflict* (New York: Norton, 2000).

Chapter 6

1. Robert G. Herman, "Identity, Norms, and National Security: The Soviet Foreign Policy Revolution and the End of the Cold War," in *The Culture of National Security: Norms and Identity in World Politics,* ed. P. J. Katzenstein (New York: Columbia University Press, 1996), pp. 271–316.

2. Hans J. Morgenthau, *Politics among Nations: The Struggle for Power and Peace,* brief ed., ed. Kenneth W. Thompson (New York: McGraw-Hill, 1993), p. 5.

3. Margaret G. Hermann, "Explaining Foreign Policy Behavior Using the Personal Characteristics of Political Leaders," *International Studies Quarterly* 24:1 (March 1980): 7–46.

4. Stephen Benedict Dyson, "Personality and Foreign Policy: Tony Blair's Iraq Decisions," *Foreign Policy Analysis* 2:3 (July 2006): 289.

5. Betty Glad, "Personality, Political, and Group Process Variables in Foreign Policy Decision Making: Jimmy Carter's Handling of the Iranian Hostage Crisis," *International Political Science Review* 10 (1989): 58.

6. Betty Glad, "Why Tyrants Go Too Far: Malignant Narcissism and Absolute Power," *Political Psychology* 23:1 (2002): 6.

7. Jerold Post, quoted in Peter Carlson, "The Son Also Rises," *Washington Post National Weekly Edition,* May 26–June 1, 2003, pp. 10–11.

8. Ole Holsti, "The Belief System and National Images: A Case Study," *Journal of Conflict Resolution* 6 (1962): 244–52.

9. Harvey Starr, *Henry Kissinger: Perceptions of International Politics* (Lexington, KY.: University Press of Kentucky, 1984); and Stephen Walker, "The Interface between Beliefs and Behavior: Henry Kissinger's Operational Code and the Vietnam War," *Journal of Conflict Resolution* 21:1 (March 1977): 129–68.

10. Irving L. Janis, *Victims of Groupthink: A Psychological Study of Foreign-Policy Decisions and Fiascoes* (Boston: Houghton Mifflin, 1972), p. 9.

11. Herbert Simon, "A Behavioral Model of Rational Choice," in *Models of Man: Social and Rational* (New York: John Wiley, 1957).

12. Robert Jervis, "Hypotheses on Misperception," *World Politics* 20:3 (April 1968): 454–79.

13. Anne-Marie Slaughter, "Mercy Killings," *Foreign Policy* 134 (May–June 2003): 72–73.

14. David Makovsky, *Making Peace with the PLO: The Rabin Government's Road to the Oslo Accord* (Boulder, CO.: Westview, 1996).

15. For excellent case studies of South Africa and Tajikistan dialogues, see Harold Saunders, *Politics is about Relationships* (New York: Palgrave, 2005).

16. Cynthia H. Enloe, *Bananas, Beaches, and Bases: Making Feminist Sense of International Politics* (Berkeley: University of California Press, 1990).

17. Pamela Johnston Conover, Karen A. Mingst, and Lee Sigelman, "Mirror Images in Americans' Perceptions of Nations and Leaders during the Iranian Hostage Crisis," *Journal of Peace Research* 17:4 (1980): 325–37.

18. Swanee Hunt and Cristina Posa, "Women Waging Peace," *Foreign Policy* 124 (March–June 2001): 38–47.

19. Johanna McGeary, "The End of Milošević," *Time,* October 16, 2000, p. 60.

Chapter 7

1. Joseph M. Grieco, "Anarchy and the Limits of Cooperation: A Realist Critique of the Newest Liberal Institutionalism," in *Neorealism and Neoliberalism: The Contemporary Debate*, ed. David A. Baldwin (New York: Columbia University Press, 1993), p. 117.

2. David Mitrany, *A Working Peace System* (London: Royal Institute of International Affairs, 1946), p. 40.

3. Garrett Hardin, "The Tragedy of the Commons," *Science* 162 (December 13, 1968): 1243–48. See also Mancur Olson, Jr., *The Logic of Collective Action: Public Goods and the Theory of Groups* (New York: Schocken, 1968).

4. Margaret P. Karns and Karen A. Mingst, "The United States and Multilateral Institutions: A Framework," in *The United States and Multilateral Institutions: Patterns of Changing Instrumentality and Influence,* ed. Margaret P. Karns and Karen A. Mingst (Boston: Unwin Hyman, 1990), pp. 1–24.

5. See Karen A. Mingst and Margaret P. Karns, *The United Nations in the 21st Century,* 3rd ed. (Boulder, CO.: Westview, 2007).

6. See, for example, Virginia Page Fortna, "Does Peacekeeping Keep Peace? International Intervention and the Duration of Peace after Civil War," *International Studies Quarterly* 28:2 (June 2004): 269–92; Paul Collier et al., *Breaking the Conflict Trap: Civil War and Development Policy* (Washington, D.C.: World Bank and Oxford University Press, 2003); and Andrew Mack, "Global Patterns of Political Violence" (Working Paper, International Peace Academy, New York, March 2007).

7. United Nations, *A More Secure World: Our Shared Responsibility*, Report of the Secretary-General's High-level Panel on Threats, Challenges and Change (New York: UN, 2004), www.un.org/secureworld/(accessed 1/28/10).

8. Immanuel Kant, "Idea for a Universal History from a Cosmopolitan Point of View" (1784), reprinted in *Kant Selections,* ed. Lewis White Beck (New York: Macmillan, 1988); and Jeans-Jacques Rousseau, "State of War," "Summary," and "Critique of Abbé Saint-Pierre's Project for Perpetual Peace," in *Reading Rousseau in the Nuclear Age,* trans. and ed. Grace G. Roosevelt (Philadelphia, PA: Temple University Press, 1990), pp. 185–229.

9. This section draws on Margaret P. Karns and Karen A. Mingst, *International Organizations: The Politics and Processes of Global Governance,* 2nd ed. (Boulder, CO.: Lynne Rienner, 2010), chap. 5.

10. This section on NGOs draws on Karns and Mingst, *International Organizations,* 2nd ed., chap. 6.

11. Jessica Stern, "The Protean Enemy," *Foreign Affairs* 82:4 (July–August 2003): 27–40.

12. See Alexander Cooley and James Ron, "The NGO Scramble: Organizational Insecurity and the Political Economy of Transnational Action," *International Security* 27:1 (Summer 2002): 5–39.

13. See, for example, William DeMars, *NGOs and Transnational Networks: Wild Cards in World Politics* (London: Pluto, 2005); Volker Heins, *Nongovernmental Organizations in International Society: Struggles over Recognition* (New York: Palgrave Macmillan, 2008).

14. Fiona Terry, *Condemned to Repeat? The Paradox of Humanitarian Action* (Ithaca, NY: Cornell University Press, 2002); and Sarah Kenyon Lischer, "Military Intervention and the Humanitarian 'Force Multiplier,'" *Global Governance* 13:1 (January–March 2007): 99–118.

15. Christopher C. Joyner, *International Law in the 21st Century: Rules for Global Governance* (Lanham, MD.: Rowman & Littlefield, 2005), p. 6.

16. Louis Henkin, *How Nations Behave: Law and Foreign Policy*, 2nd ed. (New York: Columbia University Press, 1979), p. 22.

17. See Bartram S. Brown, "Unilateralism, Multilateralism, and the International Criminal Court," in *Multilateralism and U.S. Foreign Policy: Ambivalent Engagement,* eds. Stewart Patrick and Shepard Forman (Boulder, CO.: Lynne Rienner, 2002), pp. 323–44; and Henry A. Kissinger, "The Pitfalls of Universal Jurisdiction," *Foreign Affairs* 80:4 (July–August 2001): 86–97.

18. For pathbreaking theoretical and empirical work, see Martha Finnemore, *National Interests in International Society* (Ithaca, NY: Cornell University Press, 1996) and Finnemore, *The Purpose of Intervention: Changing Beliefs about the Use of Force* (Ithaca, NY: Cornell University Press, 2003); Michael Barnett and Martha Finnemore, *Rules for the World: International Organizations in Global Politics* (Ithaca, NY: Cornell University Press, 2004); and Margaret E. Keck and Kathryn Sikkink, *Activists beyond Borders: Advocacy Networks in International Politics* (Ithaca, NY: Cornell University Press, 1998).

Chapter 8

1. Data on war frequency and number of deaths can be found in several, sometimes divergent, sources. These include Quincy Wright, *A Study of War,* rev. ed., 2 vols. (Chicago: University of Chicago Press, 1942, 1965); J. David Singer and Melvin Small, *The Wages of War, 1816–1965: Statistical Handbook* (New York: Wiley, 1972); Jack S. Levy, *War in the Modern Great Power System, 1495–1975* (Lexington, KY: University Press of Kentucky, 1983); Ruth Leger Sivard, *World Military and Social Expenditures, 1996* (Washington, D.C.: World Priorities, 1996); and Human Security Group, "The Human Security Report 2005," www.humansecurityreport.info/index.php?option=content&task=view&id=28&Itemid=63 (accessed 2/1/10).

2. John Herz, "Idealist Internationalism and the Security Dilemma," *World Politics* 2:2 (January 1950): 157–80.

3. Kenneth N. Waltz, *Man, the State, and War: A Theoretical Analysis* (New York: Columbia University Press, 1954).

4. For a more comprehensive approach, see Jack S. Levy, "The Causes of War: A Review of Theories and Evidence," in *Behavior, Society and Nuclear War,* ed. Philip E. Tetlock et al. (New York: Oxford University Press, 1989), 1: 209–333.

5. Augustine, *Confessions* and *The City of God*, in *Great Books of the Western World*, vol. 18, ed. Robert Maynard Hutchins (Chicago: Encyclopedia Britannica, 1952, 1986); and Reinhold Niebuhr, *The Children of Light and Children of Darkness* (New York: Scribner, 1945).

6. Thomas Hobbes, *Leviathan*, rev. student ed. (New York: Cambridge University Press, 1996), pp. 88–89.

7. John J. Mearsheimer, *The Tragedy of Great Power Politics* (New York: Norton, 2001), 32.

8. A. F. K. Organski, *World Politics* (New York: Knopf, 1958), chap. 12; and Organski and Jacek Kugler, *The War Ledger* (Chicago: University of Chicago Press, 1980).

9. George Modelski and William R. Thompson, "Long Cycles and Global War," in *Handbook of War Studies,* ed. Manus I. Midlarsky (Boston: Unwin Hyman, 1989).

10. George H. W. Bush, Address to the Nation Announcing Allied Military Action in the Persian Gulf, January 16, 1991, http://bushlibrary.tamu. edu/resecarch/public_papers.php?id=2625&year=1991&month=01; Bush, Address Before a Joint Session of the Congress on the Cessation of the Persian Gulf Conflict, March 6, 1991, http://bushlibrary.tamu. edu/research/public_papers.php?id=2767&year=1991&month=3 (accessed 3/11/10).

11. Carl von Clausewitz, *On War,* ed. Anatol Rapoport (Middlesex: Penguin Books, 1968), p. 119.

12. Charles Tilly, "Reflections on the History of European State-Making," in *The Making of National States in Western Europe* (Princeton, NJ: Princeton University Press, 1975), p. 42.

13. John Mueller, "The Essential Irrelevance of Nuclear Weapons: Stability in the Postwar World," *International Security* 13:2 (Fall 1988): 55–79, and Mueller, *Retreat from Doomsday: The Obsolescence of Major War* (New York: Basic Books, 1989). See also Gregg Easterbrook, "The End of War?" *New Republic* (May 30, 2005): 18–21.

14. Robert Jervis, "Theories of War in an Era of Leading Power Peace," *American Political Science Review* 96:1 (March 2002): 11.

15. Jervis, "Theories of War," 9.

16. Scott D. Sagan and Kenneth N. Waltz, *The Spread of Nuclear Weapons: A Debate Renewed* (New York: Norton, 2003).

17. Michael Walzer, *Just and Unjust Wars* (New York: Basic Books, 1992), p. 185.

18. Andrew Mack, "Why Big Nations Lose Small Wars: The Politics of Asymmetric Conflict," *World Politics* 27:2 (January 1975): 175–200.

19. Ivan Arreguín-Toft, *How the Weak Win Wars: A Theory of Asymmetric Conflict* (New York: Cambridge University Press, 2005).

20. Audrey Kurth Cronin, "Behind the Curve: Globalization and International Terrorism," *International Security* 27:3 (winter 2002/3): 33.

21. See, for example, Dan Caldwell and Robert E. Williams Jr., *Seeking Security in an Insecure World* (Lanham, MD.: Rowman & Littlefield, 2006); and Walter Enders and Todd Sandler, "Distribution of Transnational Terrorism among Countries by Income Classes and Geography after 9/11," *International Studies Quarterly* 50:2 (June 2006): 367–68.

22. For contemporary views, see Michael Walzer, *Just and Unjust Wars*, 4th ed. (New York: Basic Books, 2006).

23. Martha Finnemore, *The Purpose of Intervention: Changing Beliefs about the Use of Force* (Ithaca, NY: Cornell University Press, 2003), pp. 52–84.

24. Shashi Tharoor and Sam Daws, "Humanitarian Intervention: Getting Past the Reefs," *World Policy Journal* 18:2 (Summer 2001): 23.

25. Hans J. Morgenthau, *Politics among Nations: The Struggle for Power and Peace*, 4th ed. (New York: Knopf, 1967), pp. 161–215.

26. Zoltan Barany, "NATO's Post–Cold War Metamorphosis: From Sixteen to Twenty-Six and Counting," *International Studies Review* 8:1 (March 2006): 165–78.

27. George W. Bush, "The National Security Strategy of the United States of America," September 17, 2002, http://georgewbush-whitehouse.archives.gov/nsc/nss/2002/index.html (accessed 2/1/10).

28. See Glenn Snyder, *Deterrence and Defense* (Princeton, NJ: Princeton University Press, 1961); and Alexander L. George and Richard Smoke, *Deterrence in American Foreign Policy: Theory and Practice* (New York: Columbia University Press, 1974).

29. For a good analysis of suicide terrorism, see Robert A. Pape, "The Strategic Logic of Suicide Terrorism," *American Political Science Review* 97:3 (August 2003): 343–61. On the discounted power of credible threats to kill as a challenge to deterrence, see Ivan Arreguín-Toft, "Unconventional Deterrence: How the Weak Deter the Strong," in *Complex Deterrence: Strategy in the Global Age*, ed. T. V. Paul, Patrick Morgan, and James Wirtz (Chicago: University of Chicago Press, 2009), pp. 204–21.

30. Keir A. Lieber and Daryl G. Press, "The Rise of U.S. Nuclear Primacy," *Foreign Affairs* 85:2 (March/April 2006): 42–54.

31. For a complete treatment, see Inis Claude, *Power and International Relations* (New York: Random House, 1962), pp. 94–204.

32. Deborah Avant, *The Market for Force: The Consequences of Privatizing Security* (New York: Cambridge University Press, 2005).

Chapter 9

1. Thomas L. Friedman, *The Lexus and the Olive Tree: Understanding Globalization* (New York: Farrar, Straus and Giroux, 1999), p. 257.

2. Jeffrey G. Williamson, "Globalization, Income Distribution and History," in *Inequality and Economic Integration*, ed. Francesco Farina and Ernesto Savaglio (New York: Routledge, 2006), pp. 9–31.

3. Charles P. Kindleberger, "International Public Goods without International Government," *American Economic Review* 76 (March 1986): 1–13.

4. Robert Gilpin, "Three Models of the Future," *International Organization* 29:1 (Winter 1975): 39.

5. Sir Norman Angell, *The Great Illusion* (New York: Putnam, 1933).

6. Antoni Estadadeordal and Alan Taylor, "Is the Washington Consensus Dead? Growth, Openness, and the Great Liberalization, 1970s–2000s." (Cambridge: NBER Working Paper 14264, August 2008).

7. David S. J. Christy, "Round and Round We Go," *World Policy Journal* 25:2 (Summer 2008): 24.

8. Paul Collier, *The Bottom Billion: Why the Poorest Countries Are Failing and What Can Be Done about It* (New York: Oxford University Press, 2007).

9. Michelle Miller-Adams, *The World Bank: New Agendas in a Changing World* (London: Routledge, 1999); and Ngaire Woods, *The Globalizers: The IMF, the World Bank and Their Borrowers* (Ithaca, NY: Cornell University Press, 2006).

10. Muhammad Yunus, quoted in Judy Mann, "An Economic Bridge Out of Poverty: Grameen Bank in Bangladesh Loans Money to Poor Women Who Want to Start Business," *Washington Post*, October 14, 1994, E3. See also Muhammad Yunus, *Banker to the Poor: Micro-Lending and the Battle Against World Poverty* (New York: Public Affairs, 2003).

11. For progress reports broken down by goal and by region, see the United Nations Web site, www.un.org/millenniumgoals/ (accessed 2/4/10). See also United Nations, *Human Development Report 2009*, http://hdr.undp.org/en/reports/global/hdr2009/ (accessed 2/4/10).

12. William Easterly, *The White Man's Burden: Why the West's Efforts to Aid the Rest Have Done So Much Ill and So Little Good* (New York: Penguin, 2006); and Joseph E. Stiglitz, *Globalization and Its Discontents* (New York: Norton, 2002).

13. See Michael Goldman, *Imperial Nature: The World Bank and Struggles for Social Justice in the Age of Globalization* (New Haven, CT.: Yale University Press, 2005).

14. See Daniel Yergin, "Ensuring Energy Security," *Foreign Affairs* 85:2 (March/April 2006): 69–82; and Richard G. Lugar, "The New Energy Realists," *National Interest* 84 (Summer 2006): 30–33.

15. Flynt Leverett and Pierre Noel, "The New Axis of Oil," *National Interest* 84 (Summer 2006): 62.

16. Loukas Tsoukalis, "Managing Interdependence: The EU in the World Economy," in *International Relations and the European Union*, ed. Christopher Hill and Michael Smith (Oxford: Oxford University Press, 2005), pp. 232–36.

17. Sophie Meunier and Kalypso Nicolaïdis, "The European Union as a Trade Power," in *International Relations and the European Union*, ed. Christopher Hill and Michael Smith (Oxford: Oxford University Press, 2005), pp. 264–65.

18. Robert Pastor, "The Future of North America: Replacing a Bad Neighbor Policy," *Foreign Policy* 87:4 (July–August 2008): 85.

19. See Susan Ariel Aaronson, *Taking Trade to the Streets: The Lost History of Public Efforts to Shape Globalization* (Ann Arbor: University of Michigan Press, 2001); and Robin Broad, *Global Backlash: Citizen Initiatives for a Just World Economy* (Lanham, MD.: Rowman & Littlefield, 2002).

20. Moises Naim, *Illicit: How Smugglers, Traffickers, and Copycats Are Hijacking the Global Economy* (New York: Doubleday, 2005).

21. Roger Altman, "The Great Crash, 2008: A Geopolitical Setback for the West," *Foreign Affairs* 88:1 (January/February 2009): 13.

22. See, for example, Barry Eichengreen, "Bad Credit History," *Current History* (January 2009): 14–19; and Harry James, "The Making of a Mess: Who Broke Global Finance, and Who Should Pay for It?" *Foreign Affairs* 88:1 (January-February 2009): 162–68.

Chapter 10

1. See Marc Levinson, *The Box: How the Shipping Container Made the World Smaller and the World Economy Bigger* (Princeton, NJ: Princeton University Press, 2006).

2. International Crisis Group, "HIV/AIDS as a Security Issue," June 19, 2001, www.crisisgroup.org/home/index.cfm?l=1&id=1831 (accessed 2/6/10).

3. Peter M. Haas, "Introduction: Epistemic Communities and International Policy Coordination," *International Organization* 46:1 (Winter 1992): 3.

4. Karen T. Litfin, "Constructing Environmental Security and Ecological Interdependency," *Global Governance* 5:3 (July–September 1999): 367.

5. Thomas Malthus, *An Essay on the Principle of Population: Text, Sources, and Background Criticism*, ed. Philip Appleman (New York: Norton, 1976).

6. Donella H. Meadows et al., *The Limits to Growth* (New York: Signet, 1972).

7. Andrea Den Boer and Valerie M. Hudson, "A Surplus of Men, a Deficit of Peace: Security and Sex Ratios in Asia's Largest States," *International Security* 26:4 (Spring 2002): 5–38.

8. Garrett Hardin, "The Tragedy of the Commons," *Science* 162 (December 13, 1968): 1243–48.

9. Randal C. Archibold, "Border Fight Focuses on Water, Not Immigration," *New York Times* (July 7, 2006), p. 1.

10. Rachel Carson, *Silent Spring* (Boston: Houghton Mifflin, 1962). See also Jacques Yves Cousteau with Frederick Dames, *The Silent World* (New York: Harper & Row, 1953); and Cousteau with James Dugan, *The Living Sea* (New York: Harper & Row, 1963).

11. Thomas F. Homer-Dixon, "Environmental Scarcities and Violent Conflict: Evidence and Cases," *International Security* 19:1 (Summer 1994): 5–40.

12. See Karen T. Litfin, *Ozone Discourses: Science and Politics in Global Environmental Cooperation* (New York: Columbia University Press, 1994).

13. For excellent overviews, see Jack Donnelly, *International Human Rights*, 3rd ed. (Boulder, CO.; Westview, 2006); and David P. Forsythe, *Human Rights in International Relations*, 2nd ed. (Cambridge: Cambridge University Press, 2006).

14. Stephen D. Krasner, "Structural Causes and Regime Consequences: Regimes as Intervening Variables," *International Organization* 36:2 (Spring 1982): 186.

15. See Joanne R. Bauer and Daniel A. Bell, eds., *The East Asian Challenge for Human Rights* (Cambridge: Cambridge University Press, 1999); and Amartya Sen, "Universal Truths: Human Rights and the Westernizing Illusion," *Harvard International Review* 20:3 (Summer 1998): 40–43.

16. Karen A. Mingst and Margaret P. Karns, *The United Nations in the 21st Century*, 3rd ed. (Boulder, CO.: Westview, 2007), chap. 6.

17. David Cortright and George A. Lopez, *The Sanctions Decade: Assessing UN Strategies in the 1990s* (Boulder, CO.: Lynne Rienner, 2000).

18. Henry Kissinger, *Diplomacy* (New York: Simon & Schuster, 1994).

19. See Margaret E. Keck and Kathryn Sikkink, *Activists Beyond Borders: Advocacy Networks in International Networks* (Ithaca, NY: Cornell University Press, 1998); and Charles Tilly, *Social Movements, 1768–2004* (Boulder, CO.: Paradigm, 2004).

20. V. Spike Peterson and Anne Sisson Runyan, *Global Gender Issues in the New Millennium*, 3rd ed. (Boulder, CO.: Westview, 2009).

21. Esther Boserup et al., *Woman's Role in Economic Development*, with new introduction by Nazneen Kanji (London: Earthscan Publications Ltd., 2007).

22. United Nations World Conference on Human Rights, Vienna Declaration and Programme of Action, July 12, 1993, Article 18, www.unhchr.ch/huridocda/huridoca.nsf/(symbol)/A.CONF.157.23.En?OpenDocument (accessed 2/6/10).

23. Jared Diamond, *Collapse: How Societies Choose to Fail or Succeed* (New York: Penguin, 2005).

24. See Stephen D. Krasner, *Sovereignty: Organized Hypocrisy* (Princeton, NJ: Princeton University Press, 1999); and Karen T. Litfin, ed., *The Greening of Sovereignty in World Politics* (Cambridge, MA.: MIT Press, 1998).

25. Ronnie Lipschutz, "Reconstructing World Politics: The Emergence of Global Civil Society," *Millennium: Journal of International Studies* 21:3 (1992): 398–99.

GLOSSARY

anarchy   the absence of governmental authority (7)

arms control   restrictions on the research, manufacture, or deployment of weapons systems and certain types of troops (274)

asymmetric warfare   war between political actors of unequal strength, in which the weaker party tries to neutralize its opponent's strength by exploiting the opponent's weaknesses (256)

balance of power   any system in which actors (e.g. states) enjoy relatively equal power, such that no single state or coalition of states is able to dominate other actors in the system (33)

behavioralism   an approach to the study of social science and international relations that posits that individuals and units like states act in regularized ways; leads to a belief that behaviors can be described, explained, and predicted (9)

belief system   the organized and integrated perceptions of individuals in a society, including foreign-policy decision makers, often based on past history, that guide them to select certain policies over others (164)

bipolarity   an international system in which there are two great powers or blocs of roughly equal strength or weight (63)

bureaucratic politics   the model of foreign-policy decision making that posits that national decisions are the outcomes of bargaining among bureaucratic groups having competing interests; decisions reflect the relative strength of the individual bureaucratic players or of the organizations they represent (140)

capitalism   the economic system in which the ownership of the means of production is in private hands; the system operates according to market forces whereby capital and labor move freely; according to radicals, an exploitative relationship between the owners of production and the workers (45)

CEDAW   convention for the elimination of all forms of discrimination against women; adopted by the UN General Assembly in 1979, came into force in September 1981; the United States remains the only developed state which has not ratified the convention (358)

cognitive consistency the tendency of individuals to accept information that is compatible with what has previously been accepted, often by ignoring inconsistent information; linked to the desire of individuals to be consistent in their attitudes (165)

Cold War the era in international relations between the end of World War II and 1990, distinguished by ideological, economic, political, and military rivalry between the Soviet Union and the United States (43)

collective good public goods that are available to all regardless of individual contribution—e.g., the air, the oceans, or Antarctica— but that no one owns or is individually responsible for; with collective goods, decisions by one group or state have effects on other groups or states (183)

collective security the concept that aggression against a state should be defeated collectively because aggression against one state is aggression against all; basis of League of Nations and United Nations (78)

colonialism the 15th–20th century practice of founding, maintaining, and expanding colonies abroad. Colonialism, now universally delegitimized, was marked by two main motivations: (1) showing indigenous peoples how best to live (a "civilizing mission"); and (2) exploiting indigenous people and their territory for labor and material resources in order to increase the power of the colonial authority (30)

comparative advantage the ability of a country to make and export a good relatively more efficiently than other countries; the basis for the liberal economic principle that countries benefit from free trade among nations (287)

compellence the use of threats to coerce another into taking an action it otherwise would not take (134)

complex peacekeeping multidimensional operations using military and civilian personnel, often including traditional peacekeeping and nation-building activities; more dangerous because not all parties have consented and because force is usually used (193)

constructivism an alternative international relations theory that hypothesizes how ideas, norms, and institutions shape state identity and interests (84)

containment a foreign policy designed to prevent the expansion of an adversary by blocking its opportunities to expand, by supporting weaker states through foreign aid programs, and by the use of coercive force only to oppose an active attempt by an adversary to physically expand; the major U.S. policy toward the Soviet Union during the Cold War era (44)

cultural relativism the belief that human rights, ethics, and morality are determined by cultures and history and therefore are not universally the same (352)

democratic peace theory supported by empirical evidence that democratic states do not fight wars against each other, but do fight wars against authoritarian states (136, 233)

demographic transition the situation in which increasing levels of economic development lead to falling death rates, followed by falling birth rates (336)

dependency theorists individuals whose ideas are derived from radicalism, and explain poverty and underdevelopment in developing countries based on their historical dependence on and domination by rich countries (83)

derivatives financial instruments often derived from an asset (mortgages, loans, foreign exchange, interest rates) which parties agree to exchange over time; way of buying and selling risk in international financial markets (295)

détente the easing of tense relations; in the context of this volume, détente refers to the relaxation and reappraisal of threat assessments by political rivals, for example, the United States and Soviet Union during the later years of the Cold War (55)

deterrence the policy of maintaining a large military force and arsenal to discourage any potential aggressor from taking action; states commit themselves to punish an aggressor state (56)

diplomacy the practice of states trying to influence the behavior of other states by bargaining, negotiating, taking specific noncoercive actions or refraining from such actions, or appealing to the foreign public for support of a position (129)

direct foreign investment investing in another state, usually by multinational corporations, by establishing a manufacturing facility or developing an extractive industry (293)

disarmament the policy of eliminating a state's offensive weaponry; may occur for all classes of weapons or for specified weapons only; the logic of the policy is that fewer weapons leads to greater security (274)

diversionary war the theory that leaders start conflicts to divert attention from domestic problems (237)

domino effect a metaphor that posits that the loss of influence over one state to an adversary will necessarily lead to a subsequent loss of control over neighboring states, just as dominos fall one after another; used by the United States as a justification to support South Vietnam, fearing that if that country became communist, neighboring countries would also fall under communist influence (53)

epistemic communities transnational communities of experts and technical specialists who share a set of beliefs and a way to approach problems (333)

ethnonational movements the participation in organized political activity of self-conscious communities sharing an ethnic affiliation; some movements seek autonomy within an organized state; others desire separation and the formation of a new state; still others want to join with a different state (150)

European Union (EU) a union of twenty-seven European states, formerly the European Economic Community; designed originally during the 1950s for economic integration, but since expanded into a closer political and economic union (205)

evoked set the tendency to look for details in a contemporary situation that are similar to information previously obtained (166)

externalities in economics, unintended side effects that can have positive or negative consequences (341)

first-generation human rights political or civil rights of citizens that prevent governmental authority from interfering with private individuals or civil society (negative rights) (350)

first-strike capability the ability to launch a nuclear attack capable of completely preventing a retaliatory strike (135)

General Assembly one of the major organs of the United Nations; generally addresses issues other than those of peace and security; each member state has one vote; operates with six functional committees composed of all member states (191)

General Agreement on Tariffs and Trade (GATT) founded by treaty in 1947 as the Bretton Woods institution responsible for negotiating a liberal international trade regime that included the principles of nondiscrimination in trade and most-favored-nation status; re-formed as the World Trade Organization in 1995 (293)

global governance   structures and processes that enable actors to coordinate interdependent needs and interests in the absence of a unifying political authority (368)

globalization   the process of increasing integration of the world in terms of economics, politics, communications, social relations, and culture; increasingly undermines traditional state sovereignty (144)

Group of 7 (G7)   group of the traditional economic powers (U.S., Great Britain, France, Japan, Germany, Italy, Canada) who meet annually to address economic problems; when Russia joins, the G-8 discussions turn to political issues (292)

Group of 77   a coalition of about 125 developing countries that press for reforms in economic relations between developing and developed countries; also referred to as the South (191)

Group of 20   group of finance ministers and heads of central banks (recently heads of state) of major economic powers, including China, Russia, Australia, Argentina, Brazil, Indonesia, Mexico, South Africa, South Korea, Turkey, as well as representatives from the G-7; meets periodically to discuss economic issues (191)

groupthink   the tendency for small groups to form a consensus and resist criticism of a core position, often disregarding contradictory information in the process; group may ostracize members holding a different position (167)

guerrilla warfare   the use of irregular armed forces to undermine the will of an incumbent government (or its foreign support) by selectively attacking the government's vulnerable points or personnel over a prolonged period of time; guerrillas hide among the people they aim to represent, and as such tend to place ordinary citizens at great risk; guerrillas require both social support (or at a minimum, social apathy) and sanctuary (either a remote base in a rugged environment or a weakly defended international border) in order to survive, and by surviving, to win (253)

hegemon   a dominant state that has a preponderance of power; often establishes and enforces the rules and norms in the international system (33)

hegemonic stability theorists those who support the theory that a dominant state is needed to support an integrated world economy; the hegemon is willing to bear the costs of maintaining the system (285)

humanitarian intervention actions by states, international organizations, or the international community in general, to intervene, usually with coercive force, to alleviate human suffering without necessarily obtaining consent of the state (263)

human security a concept of security broadened to include the protection of individuals from systematic violence, environmental degradation, and health disasters; the concept gained ground after the Cold War due to the inability or unwillingness of states (see also "responsibility to protect") to adequately protect their own citizens (189)

hypotheses tentative statements about causal relationships put forward to explore and test its logical and usually its empirical consequences (67)

imperialism the policy and practice of extending the domination of one state over another through territorial conquest or economic domination; in radicalism, the final stage of expansion of the capitalist system (30)

institutions processes and structures of social order around which relatively stable individual and group expectations and identities converge; for example, in most places the contemporary institution of marriage is a simultaneously social, political, and economic one (233)

intergovernmental organizations (IGOs) international agencies or bodies established by states and controlled by member states that deal with areas of common interests (181)

International Monetary Fund (IMF) the Bretton Woods institution originally charged with helping states deal with temporary balance-of-payments problems; now plays a broader role in assisting debtor developing states by offering loans to those who institute specific policies, or structural adjustment programs (291)

international regimes the rules, norms, and procedures that are developed by states and international organizations out of their common concerns and are used to organize common activities (186)

international relations the study of the interactions among various actors (states, international organizations, nongovernmental organizations, and subnational entities like bureaucracies, local governments, and individuals) that participate in international politics (3)

international society   the states and substate actors in the international system and the institutions and norms that regulate their interaction; implies that these actors communicate, sharing common interests and a common identity; identified with British school of political theory (103)

intrastate wars   organized and deliberate violence within a state which results in at least one thousand battle-related deaths per year; civil wars are by far the most common form of intrastate war, but some terrorist attacks within states have exceeded the one-thousand deaths threshold, and might therefore be counted as wars (245)

interstate war   organized violence between internationally-recognized states which results in at least one thousand deaths from combat in a calendar year; since 1900, wars between states have been responsible for the greatest concentration of deaths in a relatively short period of time in world history—for example, World War II resulted in from fifty to seventy million casualties from 1939 to 1945 (245)

irredentism   the demands of ethnonationalist groups to take political control of territory historically or ethnically related to them by separating from their parent state or taking territory from other states (119)

Islamic fundamentalism   believers within Islam who offer a critique of secular states and seek to change states and individual behaviors to conform to a strict reading of Islamic texts (147)

just war tradition   the idea that wars must be judged according to two categories of justice: (1) *jus ad bellum*, or the justness of war itself; and (2) *jus in bello*, or the justness of each actor's conduct in war (261)

League of Nations   the international organization formed at the conclusion of World War I for the purpose of preventing another war; based on collective security (38)

legitimacy   the moral and legal right to rule, which is based on law, custom, heredity, or the consent of the governed (24)

levels of analysis analytical framework based on the ideas that events in international relations can be explained by looking at individuals, states, or the international system and that causes at each level can be separated from causes at other levels (68)

liberalism the theoretical perspective based on the assumption of the innate goodness of the individual and the value of political institutions in promoting social progress (76)

limited wars armed conflicts usually between states in which belligerents acknowledge limits on both the resources applied to an armed conflict, and on the political objectives sought by means of war (namely, some objective less than the total defeat of the adversary or its unconditional surrender) (248)

Malthusian dilemma the situation that population growth rates will increase faster than agricultural productivity, leading to food shortages; named after Thomas Malthus (336)

mercantilism economic theory that international commerce should increase a state's wealth, especially gold; state power is inhanced by a favorable balance of trade (284)

mirror images the tendency of individuals and groups to see in one's opponent the opposite characteristics as those seen in one's self (166)

moral hazard problem when states or individuals are not made to pay the consequences of reckless behavior; they have little incentive to change that behavior (296)

most-favored-nation principle (MFN) principle in international trade agreements when states promise to give another state the same treatment in trade as the first state gives to its most-favored trading partner (293)

multinational corporations (MNCs) private enterprises with production facilities, sales, or activities in several states (83)

multipolar an international system in which there are several states or great powers of roughly equal strength or weight (63)

nation a group of people sharing a common language, history, or culture (25, 116)

national interest the interest of the state, most basically the protection of territory and sovereignty; in realist thinking, the interest is a unitary one defined in terms of the pursuit of power; in liberal thinking, there are many national interests; in radical thinking, it is the interest of a ruling elite (70)

nationalism   devotion and allegiance to the nation and the shared characteristics of its peoples; used to motivate people to patriotic acts, sometimes leading a group to seek dominance over another group (24)

nation-state   the entity formed when people sharing the same historical, cultural, or linguistic roots form their own state with borders, a government, and international recognition; trend began with French and American Revolutions (117)

negative externalities   economies term for costly (harmful) un-intended consequences of exchange, in political terms, a negative externality of a failed government might be refugees; in counter-insurgency, a negative externality for an incumbent government fighting insurgents might be increased terrorist group recruitment as a result of deliberately or inadvertenly harming noncombatants in disputed areas (341)

neoliberal institutionalism   a reinterpretation of liberalism that posits that even in an anarchic international system, states will cooperate because of their continuous interactions with each other and because it is in their self-interest to do so; institutions provide the framework for cooperative interactions (78)

neorealism   a reinterpretation of realism that posits that the structure of the international system is the most important level to study; states behave the way they do because of the structure of the international system; includes the belief that general laws can be found to explain events (73)

New International Economic Order (NIEO)   a list of demands by the Group of 77 to reform economic relations between the North and the South, that is, between the developed countries and the developing countries (105)

niche diplomacy   approach of some states to concentrate diplomatic efforts in a few areas of activity to increase power, often in human security issues (132)

nongovernmental organizations (NGOs)   private associations of individuals or groups that engage in political, economic, or social activities usually across national borders (137, 181)

normative   relating to ethical rules; in foreign policy and inter-national affairs, standards suggesting what a policy should be (9)

North the developed countries, mostly in the Northern Hemisphere, including the countries of North America, the European countries, and Japan (104)

North Atlantic Treaty Organization (NATO) military and political alliance between Western European states and the United States established in 1948 for the purpose of defending Europe from aggression by the Soviet Union and its allies; post–Cold War expansion to Eastern Europe (49)

offshore financial centers states or jurisdictions with few regulations on banking and financial transactions, often with low taxation; used by individuals and international banks to transfer funds (295)

organizational politics the foreign-policy decision making model that posits that national decisions are the products of subnational governmental organizations and units; the standard operating procedures and processes of the organizations largely determine the policy; major changes in policy are unlikely (139)

peacebuilding post-conflict political and economic activities designed to preserve and strengthen peace settlements, includes civil administration, elections, and economic development activities (193)

portfolio investment private investment in another state by purchasing stocks on bonds, without taking direct control of the investments (293)

power the ability to influence others and also to control outcomes so as to produce results that would not have occurred naturally (124)

power potential a measure of the power an entity like a state could have, derived from a consideration of both its tangible and its intangible resources; states may not always be able to transfer their power potential into actual power (124)

prisoner's dilemma a theoretical game in which rational players (states or individuals) choose options that lead to outcomes (payoffs) such that all players are worse off than under a different set of choices (78)

public diplomacy use of certain diplomatic methods to create a favorable image of the state or its people in the eyes of other states and their publics; methods include, for example, goodwill tours, cultural and student exchanges, and media presentations (131)

radicalism a social theory, formulated by Karl Marx and modified by other theorists, that posits that class conflict between owners and workers will cause the eventual demise of capitalism; offers a critique of capitalism (81, 286)

rational actor in realist thinking, an individual or state that uses logical reasoning to select a policy; that is, it has a defined goal to achieve, considers a full range of alternative strategies, and selects the policy that best achieves the goal (71)

realism a theory of international relations that emphasizes states' interest in accumulating power to ensure security in an anarchic world; based on the notion that individuals are power seeking and that states act in pursuit of their own national interest defined in terms of power (70)

regimes rules, norms, procedures around which the expectations of actors (state or international) converge in a specific issue area

responsibility to protect (R2P) emerging norm that the international community should help individuals suffering at the hands of their own state or others (263)

sanctions economic, diplomatic, and even coercive military force for enforcing an international policy or another state's policy; sanctions can be positive (offering an incentive to a state) or negative (punishing a state) (132)

satisfice in decision making theory, the tendency of states and their leaders to settle for the minimally acceptable solution, not the best possible outcome, in order to reach a consensus and formulate a policy (141)

second-generation human rights social and economic rights that states are obligated to provide their citizenry, including the rights to medical care, jobs, and housing (positive rights) (350)

second-strike capability in the age of nuclear weapons, the ability of a state to respond and hurt an adversary after a first strike has been launched against that state by the adversary; ensures that both sides will suffer an unacceptable level of damage (135)

security dilemma the situation in which one state improves its military capabilities, especially its defenses, and those improvements are seen by other states as threats; each state in an anarchic international system tries to increase its own level of protection leading to insecurity in others, often leading to an arms race (232)

Security Council one of the major organs of the United Nations charged with the responsibility for peace and security issues; includes five permanent members with veto power and ten nonpermanent members chosen from the General Assembly (190)

sex trafficking highly coercive and profitable organized criminal activity which forces mainly young women (but also young boys and some older women) to exchange sex for cash; distinguished by treatment of humans as disposable objects, and by interstate exchange (transport systematically isolates trafficked individuals from their language, culture, friends, and family; thus increasing their vulnerability) (361)

smart sanctions limited sanctions targeted to hurt or support specific groups; used to avoid the humanitarian costs of general sanctions (134)

socialism an economic and social system that relies on intensive government intervention or public ownership of the means of production in order to distribute wealth among the population more equitably; in radical theory, the stage between capitalism and communism (45)

soft power ability to change a target's behavior based on the legitimacy of one's ideas or policies, rather than on material power (economic or military) (128)

South the developing countries of Africa, Latin America, and southern Asia (104)

sovereignty the authority of the state, based on recognition by other states and by nonstate actors, to govern matters within its own borders that affect its people, economy, security, and form of government (21)

sovereign wealth funds state-controlled investment companies that manage large foreign exchange reserves; located in China or in petroleum-exporting countries (Norway, the Gulf states, Saudi Arabia) (295)

state an organized political unit that has a geographic territory, a stable population, and a government to which the population owes allegiance and that is legally recognized by other states (116)

statism modern version of mercantilism; use of state power to achieve economic and social goals (284)

stratification the uneven distribution of resources among different groups of individuals and states (104)

structural adjustment programs IMF policies and recommendations aimed to guide states out of balance-of-payment difficulties and economic crises (301)

summits talks and meetings among the highest-level government officials from different countries; designed to promote good relations and provide a forum to discuss issues and conclude formal negotiations (55)

superpowers highest-power states as distinguished from other great powers; term coined during the Cold War to refer to the United States and the Soviet Union (44)

sustainable development an approach to economic development that tries to reconcile current economic growth and environmental protection with the needs of future generations (300)

system a group of units or parts united by some form of regular interaction, in which a change in one unit causes changes in the others; these interactions occur in regularized ways (93)

terrorism the use of organized political violence by non-state actors against noncombatants in order to cause fear as a means to achieve a political or religious objective; a form of asymmetric warfare (257)

theory generalized statements about political, social, or economic activities that seek to describe and explain those activities; used in many cases as a basis of prediction (67)

third-generation human rights collective rights of groups, including the rights of ethnic or indigenous minorities and designated special groups such as women and children, and the rights to democracy and development, among others (351)

total war armed conflicts usually among multiple powerful states involving widespread destruction and major loss of life in which participants acknowledge no limits on the use of force to achieve their political aims, and in which those aims encompass an adversary's unconditional surrender (246)

track-two diplomacy unofficial overtures by private individuals or groups to try and resolve an ongoing international crisis or civil war (168)

traditional peacekeeping the use of multilateral third-party military forces to achieve several different objectives, generally to address and contain interstate conflict, including the enforcement of cease-fires and separation of forces; used during the Cold War to prevent conflict among the great powers from escalating (193)

transnational across national or traditional state boundaries; can refer to actions of various nonstate actors, such as private individuals and nongovernmental organizations (56)

transnational movements groups of people from different states who share religious, ideological, or policy beliefs and who work together to change the status quo (146)

Treaties of Westphalia treaties ending the Thirty Years War in Europe in 1648; in international relations represents the beginning of state sovereignty within a territorial space (22)

unitary actor the state as an actor that speaks with one voice and has a single national interest; realists assume states are unitary actors (71)

universal jurisdiction a legal concept that permits states to claim legal authority beyond their national territory for the purpose of punishing a particularly heinous criminal that violates the laws of all states or protecting human rights (222)

universal rights human rights believed to be basically the same at all times and in all cultures, a controversial notion (352)

war on terrorism a powerful rhetorical call to exploit a given society's total available resources (both material and non-material) in order to defeat a political tactic; a key implication of declaring "war on terrorism" is that few if any limits on the use of a society's resources either should or will be observed (62)

Warsaw Pact the military alliance formed by the states of the Soviet bloc in 1955 in response to the rearmament of West Germany and its inclusion in NATO; permitted the stationing of Soviet troops in Eastern Europe (49)

Washington Consensus the liberal belief that only through specific liberal economic policies, especially privatization, can development result (300)

weapons of mass destruction (WMD) chemical, biological, and radiological weapons distinguished by an inability to restrict their destructive effects to a single time and place; they therefore share a quality of irrationality in their contemplated use because attackers can never be entirely protected from the harm of any attacks they initiate with such weapons (62, 252)

World Bank   a global lending agency focused on financing projects in developing countries; formally known as the International Bank for Reconstruction and Development, established as one of the key Bretton Woods institutions to deal with reconstruction and development after World War II (291)

World Trade Organization (WTO)   intergovernmental organization designed to support the principles of liberal free trade; includes enforcement measures and dispute settlement mechanisms; established in 1995 to replace the General Agreement on Tariffs and Trade (296)

CREDITS

Chapter 1: p. 2: Chesnot/SIPA/AP Photo; p. 5: Steve Liss//Time Life Pictures/Getty Images; p. 12: AP Photo

Chapter 2: p. 20: Bettmann/Corbis; p. 25: Bettmann/Corbis; p. 26: Photo © Bonhams, London, UK/The Bridgeman Art Library; p. 31: Giraudon/The Bridgeman Art Library; p. 48: AFP/Getty Images; p. 59: David Turnley/Corbis

Chapter 3: p. 66: Q. Sakamaki/Redux; p. 80: Ludovic/REA/Redux; p. 89: Chris Hondros/Getty Images

Chapter 4: p. 97: Bettmann/Corbis; p. 106: Jacob Silberberg/Panos Pictures; p. 111: Pool/Getty Images

Chapter 5: p. 117: Rina Castelnuovo/The New York Times/Redux; p. 126: AP Photo; p. 145: Robert Wallis/Panos Pictures; p. 149: AP Photo

Chapter 6: p. 158: Hulton-Deutsch Collection/Corbis; p. 163: AP Photo; p. 170: AP Photo; p. 171: Mian Khursheed/Reuters/Corbis; p. 177: Abedin Taherkenareh/epa/Corbis

Chapter 7: p. 183: Joseph Sohm/Visions of America/Corbis; p. 197: MARKA /Alamy; p. 213: AP Photo; p. 217: GLEB GARANICH/Reuters/Corbis; p. 224: Jerry Lampen/epa/Corbis

Chapter 8: p. 243: AP Photo; p. 247: Thomas Grabka/laif/Redux; p. 250: AP Photo; p. 255: SIPA/Newscom; p. 258: AP Photo; p. 268: Oliver Hoslet/epa/Corbis; p. 280: ALI HAIDER/epa/Corbis

Chapter 9: p. 290: AP Photo; p. 298: Harish Tyagi/epa/Corbis; p. 310: AP Photo; p. 315: AP Photo; p. 321: J.B. Russell/Panos Pictures

Chapter 10: p. 328: AP Photo; p. 343: Edward Parker /Alamy; p. 354: YM YIK/epa/Corbis; p. 365: Julie Remy/AFP/Getty Images

INDEX

Page numbers in *italics* refer to boxes, maps, figures, and tables.

bipolar systems
    international system and, 94–95, 96,
        97–98
    nuclear weapons and, 56
Bismarck, Otto von, 128
Blackwater, 280
Blair, Tony, 159, 161
"boat people," 176
Bodin, Jean, 21–22
Bólivar, Símon, 162
Bolivia, 162
Bonaparte, Napoleon, 25–26, 253
Bono, 332
Boserup, Esther, 358
Bosnia
    human rights and, 355
    peacekeeping in, 193, 195, 269
    war crimes in, 222, 224
    women's rights and, 359
Botswana, 331
bourgeois class, 45, 123
Brazil
    economic activity in, 97
    economic globalization and, 294, 295,
        322
    environmental issues and, 346
    HIV/AIDS and, 331
    nuclear weapons and, 277
    terrorism and, 260
Bretton Woods institutions, 201, 291–93,
    302, 319
Britain, *see* Great Britain
British East India Company, 284
British Petroleum, 307
bubonic plague, 327–28
Buffett, Warren, 332
Bulgaria, 44, 270
Bull, Hedley, 103
"Bulldozer Revolution," 177
bureaucratic/organizational model of foreign
    policy decision making, 139–41
bureaucratic politics, 140
Burkina Faso, 320–21
Burma, *see* Myanmar
Burundi, 61, 152, 196, 359, 364
Bush, George H. W., 175, 241
Bush, George W., 66, 67, 68, 86, 134, 135,
    155, 255, 345
Byzantine Empire, 16, 17

Calderón, Felipe, 146
Cambodia, 51, 167, 193, 195, 354, 356
Cameroon, 31

Canada
    Afghanistan and, 90–91
    APEC and, 313
    Cold War and, 49
    comparative advantage and, 287–88
    ethnonational groups in, 152
    intangible power sources in, 128
    NAFTA and, 314, 315–16
    niche diplomacy, 132
    petroleum and, 295
    pollution and, 341
CAP (Common Agricultural Policy), 296, 313
capitalism
    liberal view of, 76, 236–37
    Marxist view of, 81, 104–5, 122, 123
    natural resources and, 339
    radical view of, 82, 83, 122
    system stratification and, 105–7
    United States and, 45
    Westphalian system and, 24
carbon dioxide emissions, 344, 345–46
Cardoso, Fernando Henrique, 83
CARE (Cooperative for Assistance and
    Relief Everywhere), 331
Caribbean, 215, 299
Caribbean Community (CARICOM), 209
CARICOM (Caribbean Communit), 209
Carr, E. H., 39
Carson, Rachel, 340
Carter, Jimmy, 161, 168–69, 172
Castro, Fidel, 162
Catholic Church
    in Northern Ireland, 170
    population issues and, 339, 346
    in pre–Westphalian world, 17–18, 21
Ceauşescu, Nicolae, 156
CEDAW (Convention on the Elimination
    of All Forms of Discrimination Against
    Women), 358, 361
CFE (Conventional Armed Forces in
    Europe) Treaty, 276
Chad, 237, 249, 310
Chamberlain, Neville, 166
Charlemagne, 17, 18
Chávez, Hugo, 162–63
cheating, neorealism on, 75
chemical weapons, 250–51, 252
Chemical Weapons Convention (CWC),
    276, 279
Cheney, Dick, 352
Chernobyl nuclear plant explosion, 170
Chiang Kai-shek, 256
Chile, 294, 354

International Republican Institute, 216
International Rescue Committee, 219
International Sanitary Conference, 328
international security, 279–81
international society
    international political economy and,
        285, 286, 288, 289
    international system and, 103, 112
international system
    China and, 109, 110–11
    constructivism on, 107–8, 112, 113
    environmental issues and, 348
    intergovernmental organizations in,
        181, 185
    levels of analysis for, 108–9, 112–13
    liberal view of, 79, 87, 102–4, 109, 112,
        113
    neoliberal institutionalism on, 79, 87,
        103, 112
    neorealism on, 74, 87, 112
    nongovernmental organizations in, 181
    radical view of, 82, 87, 104–7, 112, 113
    realist view of, 3, 70–71, 74, 87,
        94–101, 109, 112, 113, 225
    stratification of, 104–7
    war and, 238–40
international system level of analysis, 68, 70
International Trade Organization, 292
International Union for the Conservation
    of Nature (IUCN), 346
International Whaling Commission, 346
Internet, 145, 215, 259, 357
interstate wars, 245–46, 248–49
intrastate wars, 245–46
Iran
    balance of power and, 268
    economic sanctions and, 133
    ethnonational groups in, 152
    Iraq and, 241
    mass public on, 172, 177–78
    nuclear weapons and, 171, 254–55
    oil and, 163, 307–8
    terrorism and, 258, 259, 260, 261
Iranian hostage crisis, 161
Iran-Iraq War, 308
Iraq
    Cold War and, 54
    ethnonational groups in, 152
    human rights and, 354, 355, 356
    invasion of Kuwait, 60–61, 126, 134,
        191, 239, 240–41, 308
    Iran and, 241
    NATO and, 269

oil and, 307–8, 309
terrorism and, 259, 261
weapons of mass destruction and, 62,
    65–66
women's rights and, 359
Iraq War (2003)
    European Union on, 208
    Great Britain and, 161
    in historical perspective, 5, 6
    level of analysis on, 68–70
    motivating factors in, 65–67
    oil and, 309
    private security contractors and, 280–81
    public diplomacy during, 131
    theory on, 66–67, 86–89
    United Nations and, 191–92, 197, 226
Ireland, 175, 206
Irish Republican Army, 259
irredentism, 119
Islam, social identity and, 109, 112
Islamic fundamentalism
    extremist, 147
    oil and, 308
    population issues and, 339
    terrorism and, 258
Israel
    aircraft hijackings and, 257–58
    balance of power and, 268
    Cold War and, 50, 54–55
    Egypt and, 248, 274
    establishment of, 54
    freshwater issue and, 340
    globalizing issues and, 364
    history of bombings in, 4
    intangible power sources in, 128
    interstate wars, 248
    Lebanon and, 256
    nuclear weapons and, 277
    oil and, 308
    Palestinian self-determination and,
        119, 120
    Romania and, 156
    terrorism and, 260
Italy
    alliances of, 35
    European Union and, 203
    fascism and, 41
    invasion of Ethiopia, 39, 40, 226, 273
    post–World War I, 38
    in pre–Westphalian world, 19, 20
    unification of, 29, 117
IUCN (International Union for the
    Conservation of Nature), 346

Powell, Colin, 131
power
    centralization of, 17
    challenges to state, 144–53
    geographic position and, 124–26, 127
    intangible sources of, 128–29
    natural sources of, 124–27
    nongovernmental organizations and,
        211–12, 218–19
    population and, 126–27
    soft, 128
    state
        exercise of, 129–37
        nature of, 124–29
    tangible sources of, 127
    veto, 273
    see also balance of power
Power and Independence (Keohane and
    Nye), 102
power potential of states, 124
power transition theory, 239
Prebish, Raul, 83
precautionary principle, 335
preventive action principle, 335
pre–Westphalian world, 16–21
Prince, The (Machiavelli), 20, 72
principal actors, 71, 76
prisoner's dilemma, 78–79
private individuals, 168–72, 179
proletariat, 45
Protestant Church, 21, 170
Prussia
    alliances of, 29, 34
    Concert of Europe and, 27
    Napoleonic Wars and, 25, 26, 27
    Westphalian system and, 22, 23
psychological mechanisms for information
    processing, 165–68
public diplomacy, 129, 131
public health, *see* health and communicable
    disease
public opinion, impact of, 172–73, 174–76
Puerto Rico, 32
Putin, Vladimir, 157, 167, 244
Putnam, Robert, 130

Qaddafi, Muammar, 128
Qing dynasty, 31

racism, 42, 43, 355
radicalism
    definition of, 3
    on environmental issues, 348

on global governance, 368–69
on globalizing issues, 367
on health issues, 334
on human rights, 357
on individuals, 82, 87, 178, 179, 286,
    289
on intergovernmental organizations,
    226
on international law, 226–28, 229
on international organizations, 226–28,
    229
on international political economy,
    286, 289, 305–6
on international system, 82, 87, 104–7,
    112, 113
on nongovernmental organizations, 226
overview of, 81–84, 87
on population issues, 338
on sanctions, 132
on state, 3, 82, 83, 87, 122, 123, 143,
    153, 286, 289
view of Iraq War (2003), 88
on war, 233, 236–38, 239
on women's rights, 360
Rainforest Action Network, 346
rape, 359–60
rational actors, 71, 106
rational model of foreign policy decision
    making, 137–39, 167
RAWA (Revolutionary Association of the
    Women of Afghanistan), 359
Reagan, Ronald, 132
Reagan Doctrine, 51
realism
    definition of, 3, 70
    on environmental issues, 348
    foreign policy elites and, 156–57
    on global governance, 368
    on globalizing issues, 366
    on health issues, 334
    on human rights, 356, 357
    on individuals, 74, 87, 178, 179
    on intergovernmental organizations,
        225, 226, 227, 229
    on international law, 225–26, 227
    on international organizations, 225–26,
        227
    on international system, 3, 70–71, 74,
        87, 94–101, 109, 112, 113, 225
    on managing insecurity, 266–72
    on nongovernmental organizations,
        225, 226, 227, 229
    overview of, 70–76, 87